COLOURED DRAWING OF HORATIA NELSON AS A CHILD (AE. TWO) endorsed in Lady Hamilton's handwriting: '. . . it was taken by dear glorious Nelson with him to sea and was with him till the fatal 21st October which deprived her of the best of Fathers—Oh God protect her Amen—Amen'

WINIFRED GÉRIN

HORATIA NELSON

CLARENDON PRESS · OXFORD

1970

Oxford University Press, Ely House, London W.1

GLASGOW NEW YORK TORONTO MELBOURNE WELLINGTON
CAPE TOWN SALISBURY IBADAN NAIROBI DAR ES SALAAM LUSAKA ADDIS ABABA
BOMBAY CALCUTTA MADRAS KARACHI LAHORE DACCA
KUALA LUMPUR SINGAPORE HONG KONG TOKYO

PRINTED IN GREAT BRITAIN
BY WILLIAM CLOWES AND SONS, LIMITED
LONDON AND BECCLES

To the Name
of
NELSON

PREFACE

THIS is the first biography to be attempted of Horatia Nelson, though she died as long ago as 1881. The time of her death, and the feelings of her family, were, indeed, among the chief causes for the silence that has hitherto surrounded the facts of her life. The passage of the years has altered these things, and, together with the changes in moral outlook, and in her family's attitude, the increased knowledge of Nelson and Lady Hamilton that the successive and scholarly editions of their letters has allowed, Horatia can now be seen in a just perspective, without prejudice, and of interest in her own right.

The fear of damaging the image of a national hero that prompted the late Victorians to leave Nelson's daughter "uncommented and unsung", need no longer deter the modern biographer from directing the light onto a subject which is so little detrimental to his fame; Nelson is not lessened by the facts of his daughter's life. He is, surprisingly, seen to greater advantage in his role of father than ever before.

There are many people still to-day for whom the very existence of Horatia is a mystery; yet the evidence about her is abundant, and certainly repays examination. Particularly, it has seemed to me, it is important to show her in the known context of her parents' lives, so fully documented and known as they are, for the new light that her existence throws on them. Her childhood has, therefore, been examined in detail here, fully illumined as it is by Nelson's letters.

To the lasting loss of the biographer, none of Lady Hamilton's letters to Nelson remain (except the last which reached him too late, and was returned to her by Captain Hardy). Nelson scrupulously destroyed every one of his mistress's letters as and when he got them, but, despite his emphatic commands to her that she should do the same with his, she kept them all; by which means the whole course of their love affair, of the birth of Horatia, her infancy and upbringing, can be followed in his day-to-day outpourings on the subject nearest his heart. Nelson's letters to Lady Hamilton suffered a strange destiny. Stolen from her (or else accepted in payment as hush-money) by the unscrupulous Harrison, her former tool, turned blackmailer, they were published, probably by him, in an anonymous edition in 1814. Their effect was rather to arouse incredulity than scandal, and they were sold in an open saleroom, acquired by Croker in 1817, secreted by him for nearly thirty years, shown to successive reputable editors of Nelson's letters, like Sir Harris Nicolas and Dr. Pettigrew in the 1840's, though still not published in their entirety; re-sold on Croker's death and finally acquired by the antiquary Alfred Morrison, who published them only in 1894, thirteen years after Horatia's death.

Though she had the opportunity of seeing some of them, and was left in no doubt that Nelson was her father, they did not convince her that Lady Hamilton, who denied the relationship even on her death-bed, was in fact her mother. The riddle has long ago been solved for the student of history, but the gradual unrolling of the evidence of her parentage which Horatia herself pursued must appear to the biographer as an essential factor in any account of her life, and has been given here in detail.

In filling out the background to Horatia's life, the role of Nelson's family, of his sisters in particular, Mrs. Bolton and Mrs. Matcham, is of first importance, and is presented here in detail for the first time, thanks to the Morrison collection of their letters, by which their wholly beneficial influence on Horatia's fortunes can be fully judged. Criticised as Nelson's family has often been for the advantages they reaped from his glory, in their connection with Horatia their deeds speak for themselves; they gave her, what she entirely lacked at Lady Hamilton's hands, family life, a civilised background and a good education. Their letters are not only informative about Horatia, but they contribute something more to our knowledge of a period which has been preserved for us mainly in the fictions of Jane Austen.

In tracing the course of Horatia's life, from the infant at nurse in Little Titchfield Street, to the enigmatic old lady in her last Pinner home, I have visited every place and house connected with her long life, and those of her Nelson relations, in Norfolk, London, Sussex, Wiltshire and Kent. My thanks to their present owners are recorded on another page. I have also, as my acknowledgements testify, worked in close touch with Horatia's surviving descendants, who have stinted no help in supplying me with the remaining records of her life; these are transmitted at first hand, and as such are of unique value.

If Nelson's part in Horatia is all-important in quickening our interest in her, her own part in shaping her destiny is not insignificant. Her long years as the wife of Philip Ward and the mother of a large family are a record of struggle against material odds that shows us, if no other proofs remained, that she was a "very Nelson" in spirit.

Horatia lived into the era of photography, and, thanks to the excellent lenses of Victorian cameras, her features are known to us. While her distinctive photographs belie the insipid likenesses of her painted by the fashionable miniaturists of the 1820's—Ross, Cosway, Holmes—they also reveal something more than the strongly-marked features of a face: the thick eyebrows, the deep-set eyes, the mobile mouth, the spiritual power—they betray a likeness to the face of Nelson so arresting as to constitute a proof, if any were yet needed, of her identity.

London, November 1965–October 1968   WINIFRED GÉRIN

ACKNOWLEDGEMENTS

I WANT to express my very great gratitude to the Curator and Staff of the Department of Manuscripts of the *National Maritime Museum, Greenwich*,—to Mr. G. P. B. Naish and Mr. A. W. H. Pearsall in particular—without whose help and guidance this book could not even have been begun—who made available to me all the NELSON-WARD material left there by Horatia's grandson, the Rev. Hugh Nelson-Ward, together with the BRIDPORT, GIRDLESTONE and TRAFALGAR Papers which are a prerequisite to any study of Horatia's life.

From the Commanding Officer, *H.M.S. "Victory"*—Lt. Commander W. E. Pearce—and from Captain Pack, Curator of the *Victory Museum, Portsmouth Dockyard*, I received the greatest personal kindness and help in showing me their valuable exhibits, and permitting me to reproduce some of them here. I also thank the Keeper of the Department of MSS of the *British Museum* for permission to study, and quote from, the Nelson Papers there. During several days' study of the *Nelson Collection, Monmouth Museum*, I received every help and informed co-operation from Mr. Archibald Lumsdaine, the Curator in charge, for which I thank him here.

Since there has been, as yet, no published source of information about Horatia, I do not know how this book would have fared but for the interest, sympathy, and generous help given me by Horatia's descendants and relations, who have contributed in so essential a manner with the data on which to base this first biography of her. Foremost with help, as with family records, has been her great-grandson, Marshal of the R.A.F. Sir William Dickson, G.C.B., K.B.E., to whom I owe much personal kindness, hospitality, and all the information concerning Horatia's children and her life at Pinner during her last twenty years, together with the loan of unique family records and portraits. I have been equally lucky in the interest and most effective help of Miss M. H. Johnson, Horatia's great-granddaughter, who has supplied me with material relating to the Tenterden period of her life, and allowed her family relics and portraits to be copied as illustrations for this book. She has made the topography of Tenterden a reality to me in the course of visits that she enlivened by her keen memories and knowledge of the subject.

Nothing can express the kindness and interest shown me and the project of this book by Commander and Mrs. Jeffreys of Loosehanger Park, Salisbury, who supplied me with the family records and letters of their forbears, the Eyre-Matchams, by whom Horatia was adopted; entertained me most hospitably, and searched untiringly over many months through their family papers for every scrap of information relative to the subject of this book.

To Commander J. C. H. Nelson, of Landford, I owe very kind help and information relative to the family of his forbear the 2nd Earl Nelson.

I am also much indebted to the help of Mrs. Blount, a direct descendant of the Matchams, for her zeal in supplying me with data concerning the Matcham-Davies connection.

From many Norfolk sources I derived precious data, thanks to the great help and kindness of several persons who, by their topographical situation, are in unique positions to supply relevant information; I speak in particular of Mrs. Anne Shells of Trunch, whose own interest in Horatia spurred her on to collect rare information about the Ward family and its connection with Trunch, where Philip Ward's forbears preceded her own husband as incumbents; Dr. and Mrs. Marriott, and Mrs. Tuck, of Stanhoe, where Horatia started her married life, to whom I owe expert guidance in the district, and copies of local records; Group-Captain and Mrs. Barwood, of Bolton House, and Mrs. Matthews of Burnham House (both at Burnham Market), who showed me all over their fascinating homes and allowed me to see in great detail actual houses where Horatia once lived. The same is true of Mrs. Bennion, of Bircham Newton, whose home is the old rectory where Horatia lived. I wish to thank also the present owners of the Boltons' old home, the charming Manor Farm at Cranwich, for letting me visit it. To the Incumbents of the following Norfolk Churches I owe sincere thanks for their trouble in allowing me access to their Registers and Parish Records: The Rectors of Burnham Thorpe, Burnham Westgate, Brancaster, Bircham Newton, Stanhoe, Trunch and East & West Bradenham.

I wish also to thank the Chief Librarians of the Norwich County Record Library, and of Salisbury Reference Library, for their help in supplying me with local data that has bearings on the subject.

I owe a particular debt of gratitude to Mr. Edwin Ware, the Pinner "Historian", whose expert knowledge of the district and its past, of its curious buildings, and colourful residents, has given me so much background material for Horatia's last years.

Finally, I am most deeply indebted to Carola Oman (Lady Lenanton), for her generosity in lending me her verbatim notes of meetings with the Revd. Hugh Nelson-Ward in 1942-3, and the correspondence that passed between them on the subject of Horatia, which has brought the evidence of a living witness of Horatia's life into these pages.

CONTENTS

CONTENTS

LIST OF PLATES

ABBREVIATIONS

N	Nelson, in quotations from his letters
M	Morrison Collection of Autograph Letters; vol. II. *The Hamilton-Nelson Papers*, 1798–1815
NMM	National Maritime Museum, Greenwich
NWD	Nelson-Ward Documents
P	Pettigrew, T. J.: *Memoirs of the Life of Lord Viscount Nelson*, 2 vols., 1849
Naish	*Nelson's Letters to his Wife*, edited by G. P. B. Naish, 1958
Jeaffreson	*Lady Hamilton and Lord Nelson*, 2 vols., 1888
BRP	Bridport Papers, Greenwich NMM
BM	British Museum
Nicolas	Sir Nicholas Harris Nicolas, *Dispatches and Letters of Vice-Admiral Nelson*, 7 vols., 1844
Minto	*Life and Letters of Earl Minto*, in 3 vols., 1751–1806
Eyre-Matcham	M. Eyre-Matcham, *The Nelsons of Burnham Thorpe*, 1911
Eyre-Matcham Papers	The unpublished family records of the Eyre-Matcham family of Newhouse, Downton, Salisbury, Wilts. Not to be confused with the published family history by M. Eyre-Matcham, *The Nelsons of Burnham Thorpe*, 1911
GIR	Girdlestone Papers, NMM Greenwich
TRA	Trafalgar Papers, NMM Greenwich
Rose	*Diaries and Correspondence of the Rt. Hon. George Rose*, 2 vols., London 1860
Gamlin	Hilda Gamlin; *Nelson's Friendships*, 2 vols., 1899
Sichel	Sichel, Walter: *Emma, Lady Hamilton*, London 1905
Tours	Tours, Hugh: *The Life and Letters of Emma Hamilton*, London 1963
Oman	*Nelson*, 1947

PART ONE

HORATIA NELSON THOMPSON

CHAPTER I

'A DEAR PLEDGE OF LOVE...'[1]

IN THE first week of February 1801, Mrs. Gibson, who lived in Little Titchfield Street in the parish of Marylebone, received the visit of a lady under circumstances that were so unusual that she remembered them all her life. It was already dark and the lady, who was strikingly handsome, came apparently unattended and in a hackney coach, when, in all probability, she possessed a carriage of her own. These facts, rather than the object of the visit, were what impressed Mrs. Gibson at the time; though the object of the visit was itself sufficiently memorable: carefully concealed in the warm folds of her muff the lady brought her a new-born child.[2]

In Mrs. Gibson's expert judgement the child was no more, and probably less, than a week old.[3] The lady soon stated her business, which was to place the child at nurse with Mrs. Gibson, promising that she would be 'handsomely remunerated'[4] for her pains. In after years Mrs. Gibson showed no great cupidity; the offer must have been unusually tempting for her to accept it, since the unspecified conditions of her charge implied an absolute discretion on her part.

Mrs. Gibson had a child of her own, a little hunchback girl, old enough at the time to remember the incident perfectly well in later life. There would appear to be no Mr. Gibson, both from the absence of any marriage-entry in the parish registers during the nine years that Mrs. Gibson had lived in the same house, and also from the fact that she bore the same name as her mother, Jane Gibson. She was far from illiterate, as her letters show (they compare favourably with Lady Hamilton's) and not unintelligent; the need for discretion was the more apparent to her because the lady made no secret of her own identity or address: she was Lady Hamilton and lived at No. 23 Piccadilly. Mrs. Gibson was led to believe she was acting purely benevolently on behalf of the child's unknown

[1] N. to Ly. H., 1 March 1801 (M.532). See ch. II, n. 8.
[2] *Memoirs of Lady Hamilton*, 1815, p. 304.
[3] Capt. James Ward to Horatia, 18 Sept. 1828, NMM/NWD/9594/I.
[4] Ibid.

parents. Of those parents no information was given on this first visit, though subsequently Lady Hamilton gave profuse and conflicting accounts of their identity and whereabouts. For the time being, the baby was to be spoken of as 'Miss Horatia'; and as 'Miss Horatia' Lady Hamilton wrote in her very first note to Mrs. Gibson written within a day or two of leaving the child in her care.[1] The letter bears the postmark '7 O'clock 7 FE 1801' and reads: 'Dear Madam—my cold has been so bad I could not go out today but tomorrow will call on you write me by the penny post how the dear little Miss Horatia is—ever your sincere friend E. H.' Mrs. Gibson, who must obviously have been recommended to Lady Hamilton in the first place, was not herself in a position to act as wet-nurse for the little 'Miss Horatia', and had to call one in for the purpose; a circumstance which added to Lady Hamilton's cares at the time, since she proved unsatisfactory.

As her numerous notes to Mrs. Gibson show, Lady Hamilton was very attentive to the infant's welfare. On 11 February she wrote again giving Mrs. Gibson precise instructions on how to bring the child to Piccadilly:

I hope my dear Mrs. Gibson that Miss Horatia is well if it is a fine day tomorrow bring her in a coach well wrapet (sic) up to see me but let her be well covered getting in and out of the coach come at eleven o'clock.

Your Sincere friend
E. Hamilton[2]

Thirty-two of Lady Hamilton's notes to Mrs. Gibson have been preserved.[3] They vary little, either notifying her at regular weekly intervals to expect a visit, or to wait on Lady Hamilton at Piccadilly with the child. Apart from her obvious desire to keep an eye on the child, these frequent contacts with Mrs. Gibson were intended to establish the fact that Lady Hamilton was not the child's mother. How far she deceived Mrs. Gibson it is impossible to say, or how completely Mrs. Gibson was taken in by the 'heavy cold' and prolonged indisposition that followed Lady Hamilton's first, and rash, outing made within a few days of the child's birth. References soon appeared in Lady Hamilton's notes to the child's mother 'continuing very ill' and being 'still absent in the country', and soon she was spoken of as 'Mrs. Thompson' or 'Thomson', with the purpose of creating an identity for her. By so doing Lady Hamilton assumed the longest, and most difficult to sustain of her famous 'Attitudes'—that of mere 'benefactress' to her own child.

[1] Gibson Letters: NMM/NWD/9594/9.
[2] Ibid.
[3] At the NMM, Greenwich, in the Nelson/Ward Collection.

One important piece of evidence was supplied by Lady Hamilton's letter of 7 February; it confirmed the child's arrival at the house of Mrs. Gibson, from whom we know that the child was then only a week old. This disposes of Lady Hamilton's later—and false—declaration, made when the child was christened in 1803, that she was born on 29 October 1800.[1] The object of antedating the date of her birth by three months was obvious: in October 1800 Lady Hamilton was not in England.

The evidence of Mrs. Gibson, and Lady Hamilton's note of 7 February, is confirmed by Lord Nelson himself, whose series of letters to Lady Hamilton, known as the 'Thompson Letters', written from 21 January 1801 over the next four months, establish the fact that he received the news of Horatia's birth at Torbay on 1 February. His intense anxiety to have the news by the earliest courier would place the birth at 29 January, or the 30th at latest. The 29th seems the more likely in view of Lady Hamilton's choice of that date for the supposed October birth. She could not foresee that Mrs. Gibson would keep her letters for posterity to read; nor that, by disobeying Nelson's repeated injunctions to destroy *his* letters to her, she was the chief agent in betraying her own carefully guarded secret.

Another fact to emerge from Nelson's letters, though it remained unsuspected by Mrs. Gibson, was that Horatia had a twin sister of whose birth Nelson was informed, though he was led to believe it had not survived.[2] In fact the child appears to have been committed to the Foundlings and, significantly enough, to have been christened Emma Hamilton. Her existence added yet more to Lady Hamilton's considerable sum of burdens at the time, and explains her state of mind during this crisis in her relations with her lover and the almost intolerable pressure she brought to bear on him in the ensuing months.

Nelson was, it must be remembered, a married man, whose breach with his wife was still quite unofficial. To consolidate this breach, and secure Nelson for herself were the stakes for which Lady Hamilton had to play in that crucial year; that she won was mainly due to Horatia. In giving Nelson a child, Lady Hamilton bound him to her with no ordinary bonds; the strength of his paternal feelings, once roused, proved equal only to his patriotism, and dominated the rest of his short life. Before ever the child was born, he was wholly committed to its protection. It had to be born under Sir William Hamilton's roof, during Nelson's absence with the fleet, and this called for exceptional precautions; a code was

[1] Registers of St. Marylebone Church.
[2] See N.'s letter of 23 February 1801, quoted below: M.528.

arranged by which he could be kept daily informed of events. The fact that he believed the child, conceived the previous spring off the coast of Sicily, to be Emma's first—she being then thirty-six—greatly added to his anxieties on her account, and explains the intricate scheme for corresponding with her. By nature truthful and guileless, Nelson was inept at any kind of deception, and by inventing a couple with the name of 'Thompson' (sometimes spelt 'Thomson'), whose situation resembled their own—the man supposedly at sea with him and the woman in Lady Hamilton's care—he only further complicated the issue. Under the flimsy disguise of the double correspondence forced on him in the name and role of 'Thompson', Nelson wrote impassioned love letters, pouring out the feelings of a heart which he himself described as naturally 'susceptible and true', to the spurious 'Mrs. Thompson', whose 'trying situation' roused him to a poetic fervour of utterance. On 25 January he wrote to her from Plymouth, when under imminent orders to sail:

I shall write to Troubridge this day to send me your letters which I look for as constantly and with more anxiety than my dinner . . . I delivered poor Mrs. Thompson's note; her friend is truly thankful for her kindness and your goodness . . . Poor Man! he is very anxious, and begs you will, if she is not able, write a line just to comfort him. He appears to me to feel very much her situation; he is so agitated and will be so for 2 or 3 days, that he says he cannot write'.[1]

On the 26th he wrote: 'my heart somehow is sunk within me. I beg to hear you are well (keep up your spirits, all will be well) . . . Mrs. Thompson's friend . . . appears almost as miserable as myself'.[2]

The confusion of identities, the cross-sentiments, the weak invention respecting 'Thomson's' gestures in these excerpts are typical of the whole correspondence: no one, certainly not the wily old diplomat married to Lady Hamilton, would have been taken in had the letters fallen into his hands. On the 29th Nelson acknowledged letters from Lady Hamilton of the 26th and 27th—but still the longed-for news did not come. Sailing from Plymouth on the Saturday, 31 January, it was not until he anchored in Torbay on the Sunday morning, 1 February, that he received it at last. Letters taking two days in transit, the birth of the child can therefore be dated as 29 or 30 January; Nelson having scrupulously destroyed all Lady Hamilton's letters, it has never been possible to establish the date more exactly than that. 'I believe poor dear Mrs. Thomson's friend will go mad with joy', Nelson wrote on 1 February, immediately on receipt of the news.[3] 'He swears he will drink your health this day in a bumper . . . You are a dear good creature and your kindness and attention to poor

[1] M.502.   [2] M.503.   [2] M.504

Mrs. T. stamps you higher than ever in my mind. I cannot write, I am so agitated by this young man at my elbow. I believe he is foolish; he does nothing but rave about you and her.' 'Your good and dear friend does not think it proper at present to write with his own hand,' he wrote on 3 February. 'He charges me to say how dear you are to him and that you must, every opportunity, kiss and bless for him his dear little girl, which he wishes to be called Emma, out of gratitude to our dear, good Lady Hamilton'.[1] He added, forgetting in whose character he wrote: 'I have given Lord Nelson a hundred pounds this morning, for which he will give Lady Hamilton an order on his Agents; and I beg that you will distribute it amongst those who have been useful to you on the late occasion.'[2]

Lady Hamilton's situation had indeed called for 'useful services' and absolute devotion on the part of her mother, Mrs. Cadogan.[3] She had been Sir William's housekeeper ever since the early days in Naples, and it needed all her resources to organize Emma's lying-in without Sir William suffering either from domestic discomfort, or a deplorable revelation. A subsequent message of thanks from Lord Nelson to a Mrs. Jenkins names a secondary performer in the bedroom comedy. Lady Hamilton was reported indisposed with a 'very serious cold' which necessitated her staying in bed. As early as 21 January Nelson mentioned it: 'I sincerely hope that your very serious cold will soon be better. I am so much interested in your health and happiness, that pray tell me all.'[4] Knowing the resilience of her healthy nature and the strong flow of her animal spirits, and fearing a too great imprudence on her part once the child was born, he wrote on 2 February:[5]

I rejoice to hear you are better; only recollect the old nurse's advice: 'Nurse a cold, starve a fever'; therefore pray be sure and nurse yourself. If I was Sir William you should not get out of bed for a week, nor out of the house for a fortnight. You ought to follow my advice, as you know how exactly I follow yours when I am sick.[5]

The mention of Sir William in this context necessarily raises the question of how much he knew about his wife and Nelson. There is no conclusive evidence. Thirty-six years in the diplomatic service had trained him neither to reveal, nor to probe into, awkward situations. He was an

[1] M.505.   [2] Ibid.
[3] Legally, she had no right to the name. She was married to Henry Lyon (11 June 1764) who died the next year. Mrs. Cadogan went through a variety of names before settling on Cadogan when her daughter joined Sir William's household at Naples in 1786.
[4] M.500 or 501.   [5] Pettigrew, i, 421.

amiable cynic, with few ideals, and not much morality (his acquisition of
Emma in the first place was a discreditable transaction), but he was highly
intelligent and not easily duped: the chances are he knew everything that
his wife sought at such pains to conceal.[1] Neither Emma nor Nelson could
be more concerned to preserve appearances than was the injured husband.

It was fortunate for Nelson's peace of mind that he did not see the press
reports of Lady Hamilton's presence 'in full evening dress' at a 'Grand
Concert' given by the Duke of Norfolk at his house in St. James's Square
on 3 February. The need for such a gesture, at such a time, was paramount
with her, no matter at what risk to her health. To save her reputation was
her first concern; though, as her notes to Mrs. Gibson show, she paid
for her temerity by a recurrence of the 'bad cold'. But she could afford to
give her enemies no weapon to use against her.

From that February of 1801 when she had, for the first time, to enter
London society (ever since Sir William married her in 1791 they had
lived abroad) her greatest aim and objective was to be received at Court.
She was too lately returned from Naples—her only experience of high
society—to perceive the finer distinctions of protocol between the Courts
of St. James's and Caserta. Bearer of a personal letter of commendation
from Queen Maria Carolina to Queen Charlotte, she firmly believed that
it must effect her entry at Court, where Sir William made his bow on 8
November—immediately on their arrival in London. Nelson in his un-
worldliness was no better judge of these matters than Lady Hamilton,
ignoring moreover those circumstances of her past which excluded her for
ever from the Queen's Drawing-Room. He wrote angrily of Sir William's
attendance there that season: 'I would not in Sir William's case have gone
to Court without my wife, and such a wife, never to be matched.'[2]

Lady Hamilton's phenomenal success at the Court of Naples ill prepared her for the social set-back she encountered at home. She might well
have believed that nothing could be denied her when she reflected on her
rise from poor nurse-maid to Ambassador's Lady in the course of about
ten years. Her very temperament had aided her success at Naples, where
her North-country qualities of energy and drive, sound nerves and courage, were an asset in a demoralized court in the throes of revolution.
It could be said that her innate vulgarity and the violence of her nature
gave her immense prestige there. Not so in England. Ever since the
Hamilton-Nelson ménage had returned to London the previous November, the gossip-mongers had been busy with her reputation. Lady Nelson's

---

[1] For Sir William's attitude to the affair, see below, pp. 114, 153.
[2] M.522'

cold reception of her husband, his inconsiderate conduct towards her, and the many public appearances made without her in the Hamiltons' company, gave every indication of a rupture with his wife and of a liaison with Lady Hamilton. The suspicions these incidents aroused, above all the suspicion that she might be bearing Nelson's child, were epitomised in the caricatures of Gillray showing her as a mountain of fat. The *Morning Herald* of 19 November 1800, reporting the presence of the Hamiltons and Nelsons at Covent Garden in two communicating boxes, did not hesitate to describe Lady Hamilton as 'rather embonpoint...'. Mrs. St. George,[1] in her private diaries reporting on the passage of the Hamilton party through Dresden the previous October, had declared Emma's figure to be 'colossal' and that 'her waist is absolutely between her shoulders'. To such conjectures Lady Hamilton was determined to give the lie; she showed herself, therefore, at the earliest opportunity at the Duke of Norfolk's concert on 3 February, and the next day to Nelson's confidential agent and friend, Alexander Davison, when she received him at her Piccadilly house and handed him a packet of letters for Lord Nelson. To Nelson Davison reported on his kind reception by her and added that she 'had grown thinner' but 'looked handsomer than ever'.[2]

The ordeal of her confinement safely over, Lady Hamilton's first concern was how to conceal the existence of the child. It represented the main obstacle to her current ambitions, but an obstacle which she was confident could be overcome. In this optimistic state of mind she now prepared to conquer London society.

The correspondence during the next few weeks shows how different Nelson's attitude was. Apart from the obligations of his post as commander of a British fleet in action (he was on the eve of the Copenhagen campaign), all Nelson's energies, feelings, hopes, were taken up in planning for his daughter's future, and in attaching the mother indissolubly to her fortunes. It took him some little time to realize that, in the latter respect, Lady Hamilton was not with him.

Four days after receiving the news of Horatia's birth he wrote Emma from the *San Josef* still in Torbay:

It blows so very hard that I doubt if it will be possible to get a boat on shore, either to receive or send letters, but if it moderates in time for the post of course mine shall go, and I hope from my heart to hear you are better, and it has made my head ache stooping so much, as I have been making memoranda for my will,

[1] (St. George) *Remains of the late, Mrs. Richard Trench*, 1862.
[2] M.509.

and, having regularly signed it, if was (sic) to die this moment I believe it would hold good . . . I have been obliged to be more particular than I would, as a wife can have nothing . . . If you disapprove of any part say so and I will alter it . . . I shall now go to work and save a fortune.[1]

The memorandum drawn up by Nelson on 5 February was a curious document, the wording and transparent subterfuges of which not only puzzled but alarmed Emma. She thought it would betray their secret. By it he left her

the entire rental of Bronté [the Sicilian estate bestowed on him by the King of Naples] for her particular use and benefit and in case of her death, before she may come into the possession of the estate of Bronté, she is to have the full power of naming any child she may have in or out of wedlock, or any child male or female which she . . . may choose to adopt and call her child by her last Will and testament.[2]

He further specified that four portraits given him by the Emperor of Russia, the Kings of Naples and Sardinia, and the Grand Vizir, framed in diamonds, were to be sold for her use and the income

to be given to a child called —— in whom I take a particular interest, and as Emma Hamilton is the only person who knows the parents of this female child I rely with the greatest confidence on her unspotted honour and integrity that she shall consider the child as mine and be a guardian to it, shielding it from want and disgrace, and bringing it up as the child of her dear friend Nelson & Bronté, and to this female child, of which Lady Hamilton shall only be the declarer that it is the one I mean, I give and bequeath all the money I shall be worth above the sum of twenty thousand pounds, the interest of it to be received by Lady Hamilton for the maintenance and education of this female child, the principal to be paid her at the death of Lady Hamilton if she has attained the age of 21 years or that she may marry, the guardians of my adopted child to be named by Lady Hamilton in her Will.[3]

Two years later, not satisfied with these provisions, Nelson made a further bequest to Horatia of £4,000, vesting it in trustees, for as he then wrote Lady Hamilton: 'I will not put it in my own power to have her left destitute.'[4]

In view of the eventual doubts, denials and fabrications regarding Horatia's parentage, made in the first place by Lady Hamilton herself, it is of importance to note Nelson's actual wording in these earliest documents relating to the child; his concern, as the letter of 5 February 1801 shows,

[1] M.507.
[2] BM Egerton MS 1614. See Naish, p. 575.
[3] Ibid.
[4] N. to Ly. H., 14 March 1804. Harris Nicolas, vii, 382.

was not merely to provide materially for her, but 'to shield her from want and *disgrace*'—disgrace attaching only to illegitimacy; the 'parents' referred to in the same letter are thus early shown to be merely an invention.

The question of the child's name, left a blank in the memorandum, next occupied his attention. In an enclosure addressed to the fictitious 'Mrs. Thompson' he wrote in a letter to Lady Hamilton of 4 February:

Your dear and excellent friend has desired me to say that it is not usual to christen children till they are a month or six weeks old; and as Lord Nelson will probably be in town, as well as myself, before we go to the Baltic, he proposes then, if you approve, to christen the child and that myself and Lady Hamilton should be two of the sponsors. It can be christened at St. George's Hanover Square; and, I believe, the parents being at the time out of the Kingdom, if it is necessary, it can be stated born at Portsmouth, or at sea. Its name will be Horatia, daughter of Johem and Morata Etnorb. If you read the surname backwards, and take the letters of the other names it will make, very extraordinarily, the names of your real and affectionate friends, Lady Hamilton and myself.[1]

Having indulged, with schoolboy-like relish, in this piece of invention, Nelson added with some greater show of sense: 'The child, if you like it, can be named by any clergyman, without its going to church'. Lady Hamilton did not agree with either plan, and made Nelson see the perils. Writing in the fictitious role of 'Thompson', he acceded to her wishes. 'He thinks it might be better to omit Xening the child for the present, and even privately baptising it. The clergyman would naturally ask its parents' names which would put poor Mrs. T. in trouble or cause suspicion.'[2] It had been a natural reflex with him, who was the son of a parson and brother of parsons, connected by so many family ties and affections with the church, to wish his child baptised. In the event Horatia remained unchristened until she was two years old, when the death of Sir William Hamilton had removed one possibly awkward witness.

To return to 1801. On 6 February Nelson received a lock of the child's hair enclosed in a letter from Lady Hamilton. Thanking 'Mrs. Thompson' for the 'kind present', he wrote 'It is very like what I remember his [i.e. his own]. He has put it in a case with her dear mother's. . . . He is sorry for the trouble you have had about the nurse, but he says children bring their cares and pleasures with them'.[3]

While Nelson indulged in dreams of domestic bliss, his thoughts jumping the present time with its cares and dangers to that distant period

[1] M.507.   [2] M.509   [3] M.510, 650.

when he might openly make a home for his mistress and daughter, Lady
Hamilton was undoubtedly dealing with some of the less pleasant aspects
of the situation. The child was ill and the wet-nurse unsatisfactory. A
replacement not being easily found, Lady Hamilton was not so prompt
in dismissing her as the situation required. It was not till 23 March that
she wrote in some agitation to Mrs. Gibson:

My dear Mrs. Gibson—pray do send the nurse a way and change the milk for I
don't like the nurse much and her parents advise it the mother is very ill in the
Country therefore do all thats right—tomorrow I will pay see you pay her and if
you like give her five shillings over   ever   Your E. H.[1]

Apart from the day to day anxieties attending any infant's progress,
Lady Hamilton was constantly afraid of her secret being divulged. Even
Nelson's provisions for the child's maintenance—which were open to
one interpretation only and had to be confided to a legal man (in this
case his solicitor William Haslewood) filled her with dismay. Answering
her fears he wrote her further on 6 February (he sometimes wrote her as
many as four letters on the same day, if the ship's boat could not put off
and the inland post was lost):

You may rely I shall not open my mouth on poor dear Mrs. Thomson's business
to any creature on this earth. You and I should be very unworthy if we did any
such thing, as all the secret of those two people rests solely in our bosoms. He
desires to say he approves very much of the sum of money, [to be paid Mrs.
Gibson] and submits it to your discretion if a small pension should not be
promised if the secret is well kept, but desires that nothing should be given under
handwriting. He also desires you will now and then give the nurse an additional
guinea . . . He will send you more money as Mrs. T. wants it, only let him know
everything. He says, poor fellow, he would give anything to have seen the child,
especially in your charming company.[2]

The prospect of a few days' leave before sailing north, which would
give him a sight of his daughter, buoyed him up during the weeks immediately following her birth. Yet despite his joy in the child, the period
was one of intense unhappiness for him and of dissension with the woman
he loved. To understand his state of mind, the situation in the Hamilton
household must be examined.

When Sir William returned to London in November 1800 after thirty-
six years in the diplomatic service he had very little to show for his pains.
The royal favour was lost to him (lost to him for ever as he soon found)

[1] NMM/NWD/9594/9.   [2] M.509.

by his ill-advised marriage to his nephew's cast-off mistress—Emma Hart. Not even a pension was a certainty in his case (since pensions went by favour) and advancement at his age was out of the question. Sir William considered that he had earned his country's gratitude and had, over and above his years of service, a valid claim on government for losses incurred during the Neapolitan revolution, when art treasures which he valued at between £10,000 and £13,000, furniture and personal belongings, had been looted. In addition, he had suffered the misfortune of losing a great part of his collection of paintings and antique vases at sea, when the *Colossus* in which he had despatched them was wrecked. His finances were in fact at so low an ebb that he had had to borrow the money for the journey home from Lord Nelson. Arrived in London, he had been glad of the loan of the house, No. 22 Grosvenor Square, belonging to his notorious relative, William Beckford of Fonthill. Mr. Beckford, who was his second cousin, was a millionaire, which did not prevent him harbouring great ambitions: he desired above all things a peerage. The scandal of his past life, and the isolation of his existence in the fabulous Abbey at Fonthill in Wiltshire, made the satisfaction of this ambition seem all the more desirable. Accustomed to conjuring up architectural phantasmagoria in the style of the Arabian Nights, Beckford formulated a plan which was to transform not only his own but his cousin William Hamilton's position as well. He proposed that Sir William should ask for a peerage in place of the monetary compensation due to him from the government, and that it should be secured upon himself, Beckford, Sir William having no direct heir. In exchange for this he undertook to pay Sir William an annuity of £2,000 for life, and of £500 to his widow afterwards. The proposal was quite seriously entertained by Sir William, and rapturously so by his wife, who easily saw herself in the role of a peeress.[1] Lord Nelson's support in petitioning for his friend's peerage was soon obtained; elevated himself to a Barony after the victory of the Nile (1 August 1798) he took his seat in the Lords on 20 November 1800. The impracticability of the whole transaction did not seem to strike any of the parties concerned—least of all Nelson, whose only wish was to serve his friends. When the Treasury came at last to consider Sir William's claims, he was offered a pension of £1,200 a year for life, with no mention of a reversion of any part of it on his widow. To accept what he could get was the sort of good sense which, as a Scot, he understood; meanwhile, however, he did not abandon the hope of a peerage, or of satisfying his cousin by securing a further £2,000 a year for himself.

[1] See Sir William's letter to the Marquis of Douglas, 2 July 1802. M.673.

The basis of Sir William's income came from the rents of his Pembroke-shire estates (inherited from his first wife, Catherine Barlow), as did the annuity of £800 he settled on Emma at their marriage. A comfortable retirement might have been assured him on the government pension had not the mirage of a peerage arisen to dazzle him and, above all, his wife.

At the beginning of January 1801 (when Emma was expecting Horatia) the Hamiltons moved into a small but ideally situated house at No. 23 Piccadilly (situated between Down Street and Half Moon Street) at a rental of £150 per annum, and a rateable value of £33 2s. 6d. To furnish and appoint it in the style to which they were accustomed and which their coveted position required, was beyond Sir William's present means, and it was Lady Hamilton who supplied the money by selling the dia-monds given her by the Queen of Naples. In all fairness to his wife, Sir William then and there drew up a Deed of Settlement [1] which conveyed to her the furniture and contents of the house, which thus passed to her on his death some two years later. To match her devotion, Sir William sold some pictures and antique vases, salvaged from the wreck of the Colossus, at Christie's Auction Rooms (for a total of £5,085), incurring thereby the fury of Lord Nelson, for among them was Romney's portrait of Emma as St. Cecilia. This Nelson commissioned a friend to buy anonymously for him at a cost of £300. [2]

Living in Piccadilly in a house decorated with Italian paintings and genuine antiques from Herculaneum and Pompeii, and furnished with Sir William's assured good taste (he was far better known as a con-noisseur of the arts than as a diplomat) was expensive. Sir William's other interests and pursuits—attending meetings of the Royal Society and the British Museum (of which he was respectively Vice-President and a Trustee), of the Society of Antiquaries, his Clubs, and the Sale Rooms, where his expertise in objets de virtù was often in demand, necessitated separate carriages for husband and wife. The household, consisting up to then of the invaluable Mrs. Cadogan, of Fatima, Emma's Nubian maid, and of Sir William's courrier-secretary-factotum, Francis Oliver, brought over from Vienna with them, very soon expanded to meet the new requirements of the pair. But the real expenses of the establishment only began with the entertainments which Emma relied upon to crown or precipitate her social success. In Naples her musical evenings, her

[1] Dated 4 Feb. 1801. Jeaffreson, ii, 220–35.
[2] See N.'s letter of 19 March 1801: "I have bought your picture, for I could not bear it should be put up to Auction," p.i, 445.

performances of the famous 'Attitudes', had crowded the rooms of her husband's embassy; she fondly believed that a repetition of them could achieve similar triumphs in London. The singers from the Italian Opera (several of her former circle were now established in London, like the Banti, the Bianchi ménage, Mrs. Denis) were soon established favourites in Piccadilly, from where invitations to attend Lady Hamilton's 'musical parties' were profusely distributed. Sir William was related either directly, or through his first wife, with several influential noblemen; the Earl of Warwick, the Marquis of Abercorn (who had, indeed, been his best man, at Marylebone Church on the occasion of his marriage), the Marquis of Queensberry ('Old Q', who conceived an instant admiration for Emma), and the Marquis of Douglas, who was only waiting for Beckford to get his peerage to propose for his daughter. With such sponsors to launch them on London society, Lady Hamilton believed she could ignore the snubs with which the great hostesses, almost to a woman, met her advances. Upon her beauty and enterprise her husband's fortunes could be built again. All her reserves of seduction—the famous 'Attitudes', the vocal powers—were pressed into service, exploited to the full. Well might Nelson, barely recovered from his anxiety over her confinement, be bewildered by the tempo of life suddenly unleashed in the Piccadilly house. A great deal more money than the Hamiltons possessed was needed for such a style of living, and he dreaded to know its purpose. He wrote her indignantly on 10 March: [1]

What can Sir William mean by wanting you to launch out into expense and extravagance? He that used to think that a little candle-light and iced water would ruin him, to want to set off at £10,000 a year, for a less sum would not afford concerts and the style of living equal to it. Suppose you had set off in this way, what would he not have said . . . ? [1]

He blamed Sir William, but all the while dreaded to learn the extent to which Emma herself was responsible. Sir William, he did not hesitate to say, was using his beautiful wife as a bait to secure the patronage of the Prince of Wales, and through the Prince, the countenance of the great Whig families. 'You are at auction, or rather to be sold by private contract', [2] Nelson fulminated. Even before the birth of Horatia it had reached his ears that the Prince had invited himself to supper at the Hamiltons. The Prince, Nelson did not forget, had long been one of Emma's admirers; as long ago as 1791, the year of the Hamilton marriage, the Prince had commissioned Romney to paint three pictures of Miss

[1] M.542.   [2] Ibid.

Emma Hart; in the presence of Nelson's stepson, Captain Nisbet, the Prince had been heard to say that Lady Hamilton had 'hit his fancy'— which, in the case of a man of the Prince's record, was proper cause for alarm.

In telling him of the Prince's impending visit, there can be little doubt that Lady Hamilton was playing a double game. She knew the intensity of Nelson's feelings, and wrought upon them in order to get even more than he was already providing for her future security. She needed before all things to separate him permanently from his wife. Of Nelson's feelings on the subject she could not be sure; the social climate in England was very different from that of Sicily where their love-affair had been consummated. She had everything to fear from the influence of Nelson's family on his wife's behalf. Despite her hypochondria, her negative character and retiring ways, Lady Nelson had sterling qualities which bound the family to her. They were especially beholden to her for her attentive care of Nelson's old father, the Revd. Edmund Nelson, Rector of Burnham Thorpe, in Norfolk, then in his eightieth year, a frail invalid with whom she had made her home during most of Nelson's seven-year absence in the Mediterranean. Latterly also, Lady Nelson had shown herself equally useful and kind towards the rising generation of the family—the children of Nelson's sisters, and especially those of his elder brother the Revd. William Nelson, Charlotte and Horace, whom she constantly entertained in her London house during school holidays. Such obligations, Lady Hamilton rightly reckoned, laid a burden of gratitude on the Nelson family which must bind them to Lady Nelson's interests. To win them away from the legitimate wife became one of Emma's most important objectives; and through them she hoped to consolidate her hold on Nelson. Without a definitive breach between the husband and wife, her whole future was at risk. Counting upon the likelihood of her own husband's death within the next few years (he was thirty-five years older than herself and seventy-one at the time) she calculated that Nelson would then marry her. The child, whose birth fulfilled one of Nelson's fondest hopes, was her first great claim upon him; to work upon his passionate feelings for herself in order to keep him she did not hesitate now to rouse his jealousy.

In doing so she got more than she bargained for. The thought of the Prince's pursuit of Lady Hamilton almost unhinged Nelson. It moved him to expressions which, as he himself admitted, could have had him hanged for high treason. (The letters were stolen later and anonymously published in 1814, at the very time Lady Hamilton was petitioning the Prince for a pension.) Nelson wrote her on 4 February: 'I know his aim is

PORTRAIT OF LADY HAMILTON by J. Schmidt, Dresden Oct. 1800

to have you for a mistress. The thought so agitates me that I cannot write . . .'. Again, on 17 February he wrote her:

I knew it would be so, and you can't help it . . . Your character will be gone. Do not have him en famille, the more the better. Do not sit long at table. Good God! he will be next you, and telling you soft things! . . . Oh, God that I was dead! . . . Can nothing be thought of? I am gone almost mad, but you cannot help it. It will be in all the newspapers with hints. Recollect what the villain said to Mr. Nisbet, how you *hit his fancy*. I am mad, almost dead.[1]

He wrote again the next day:

I knew that he would visit you, and you could not help coming downstairs when the Prince was there, notwithstanding all your declarations never to meet him, to receive him and by his own invitation, en familly. But his words are so charming that, I am told, no person can withstand them . . . Hush, hush, my poor heart, keep in my breast, be calm. Emma is true! But no one, not even Emma, could resist the serpent's flattering tongue, and knowing that Emma suits him . . . what will they all SAY and think, that Emma is like other women, when I would have killed anybody who had said so, must *now hang* down my head and admit it. Forgive me. I know I am almost distracted.[2]

'May God blast him!' he wrote on 19 February, 'Be firm! Go and dine with Mrs. Denis on Sunday. Do not, I beseech you, risk being at home. Does Sir William want you to be a whore to the rascal?'[3]

The evidence of the letters raises the whole question of Emma's good faith. To receive the Prince of Wales to supper at the very time that she found herself excluded from the Queen's drawing-room was the kind of triumph the former Emma Hart knew how to relish; it carried risks that appealed to the 'giddy' side of her nature. It was not easy for her to forgo such an excitement—that being the element by which she lived, and one which was, with Naples behind her and in the present period of her husband's retirement, in rather short supply. She knew Nelson too superficially to realize the effects of his jealousy. From the strong undercurrent of distrust perceptible in his letters to her, it would seem that for the first time he was shaken in his faith in her. Till then he had rejected rumours about her past. The very names he chose for her—'Santa Emma', 'My Guardian Angel', showed his romantic adulation. The matter of the Prince of Wales gave him a glimpse into the other side of her nature, for even he, with all his infatuation, perceived that her protestations did not square up to her actions. She could, with a word, have allayed his sufferings by flatly declining the Prince's advances (this was precisely what, in

[1] M.518.   [2] M.520.   [3] M.521.

the end, she had to do, confronted by the violence of his jealousy) and nothing shows the moral difference between them more clearly than Nelson's extravagant offer to defect from his duty in order to withdraw from the world and to be with her. In time of war, expecting orders every day to proceed against the enemy, he could so far forget his situation as to make her that offer to 'quit the world and its greatness to live with you a domestic, quiet life'.[1] 'If it please God', he wrote on 8 February, 'that I should retire into the country, I should not want a carriage, for I can walk, and my affairs would soon arrange themselves'. 'I long to be alone with you', he wrote on 10 March, 'I hate company, it ill accords with my feelings. Damn Lord A [Abercorn] do not let him take liberties'.

To these idyllic visions the replies from Piccadilly must have brought little encouragement; there was small comfort in Lady Hamilton's letters, as his answers show.[2]

Your dear friend, my dear and truly loved Mrs. T. is almost distracted; he wishes there was peace, or that your uncle would die, he would instantly then come and marry you, for he doats on nothing but you and his child; and, as it is his godchild, I desire you will take great care of it. He has implicit faith in your fidelity, even in conversation with those he dislikes, and that you will be faithful in greater things he has no doubt.[2]

How easily Lady Hamilton could calm the storm she had raised, and dispose even of the menace of the Prince's visits, is shown by her actions on hearing that Nelson was to have three days' leave at the end of February, 'to settle his affairs' before sailing for the Baltic. From the *St. George* at Spithead, Nelson wrote to her on 22 February: 'Noon. I have received your truly comforting letters. In doing what I wish you win my heart for ever. I am all soul and sensibility; a fine thread will lead me, but with my life I would resist a cable from dragging me . . .'.[3] On the morning of the next day he wrote: 'My dear Mrs. T. poor Thompson seems to have forgot all his ill health, and all his mortifications and sorrows, in the thought that he will soon bury them all in your dear, dear bosom; he seems almost beside himself. . . . I daresay twins will again be the fruit of your and his meeting. The thought is too dear to bear . . . Kiss dear Horatia for me.'[4]

Among Lady Hamilton's papers eventually acquired by Horatia was a letter dated 20 May 1801 addressed to Lady Hamilton which read:[5] 'Mrs. Sarah Snelling takes the liberty to acquaint Lady Hamilton that the child (Emma Hamilton) what she received from the Foundling is well

[1] M.518.   [2] M.513.   [3] M.527.
[4] M.528.   [5] NMM/NWD/9594/29.

and much grown.' Nelson had evidently been told that Lady Hamilton had brought twins into the world, but though there would be obvious difficulties in hiding two illegitimate children it is uncharacteristic of him to have instructed her to abandon one of them. It is more likely he was told it was dead, while, in fact, it was committed to the Foundlings.

Though her life was full of problems at the time, Lady Hamilton was still chiefly bent on undermining Lady Nelson's influence with her husband's family. Undaunted by the anomaly of her position (they must be the last to suspect she was Nelson's mistress, and the mother of his child) she boldly took the lead in establishing relations with his brother and his wife —the Revd. William Nelson, Rector of Hilborough. She first met them at the time of Nelson's departure for the fleet in January; in February they were again in town, and from Lady Hamilton's letters to Mrs. Nelson it appears their friendship was speedily established. Before the summer was out she wrote the lady's husband that 'the Queen of Naples excepted, I never loved any female better than her.' and was calling her 'my jewell'.[1] The main object of the correspondence, as soon appeared, was to traduce the character of Lady Nelson. While achieving this, Emma's path was not devoid of thorns, as the following letters show. Convening Mrs. Gibson to Piccadilly on 18 February (during an absence of Sir William) to bring Horatia to the house the next morning, she had hurriedly to put off the final visit of Mrs. Nelson who had announced herself for the same hour. The letter to Mrs. Gibson reads: 'Dear Mrs. Gibson at eleven to-morrow morning pray bring Miss Horatia to see your sincere friend come in a Coach as the weather is bad. E. H. her Mama is better.'[2] The letter to Mrs. Nelson, the first of many read:

Piccadilly, February 19th. My dear Mrs. Nelson—I am so ill with a headaich that I cannot move, and I feil I cou'd not take leive of you and Mr. Nelson; it wou'd be too much for my heart. I will send by the coach *all* your things and caps. Write to me, and believe me, my dearest, ever dear friend, your's sincerely, Emma[3]

This was followed by another letter written the next day; dated 'Friday, Noon, February 20th 1801', it reads:

I have been ill in bed, my dearest Mrs. Nelson; I cou'd not take leave of you. My soul was torn in pieces. It is such pain to part with dear friends, and you and I liked each other from the moment we met; our souls were congenial. Not so with 'Tom Tit' [Lady Nelson] for their was an antipathy not to be described. I am laying down, writing to you, so it is not Legible, but my heart says everything

[1] NMM/BRP/9292.   [2] NMM/NWD/9594/1.   [3] BM Add. MSS 34989.

that's kind to you and good, honest Mr. Nelson. I received letters yesterday from
that great *adored being* what we all love, esteem and admire . . . I am so unwell that
We cannot have his Royal Highness to dinner on Sunday, which will *NOT vex
me*. Addio mia Cara amica. You know, as you are learning Italian, I must say a
word or so. How dull *my bedroom looks* without you. I miss our little friendly
chats, but in this world nothing is compleat Give my love to Mr. Nelson.[1]

Lady Hamilton's outspoken references to Lady Nelson here and in her
subsequent correspondence, clearly indicate that the 'little friendly chats'
held in her bedroom had already produced their desired effect in undermining the legal wife's position in the family. Ridicule was a ready weapon
with Lady Hamilton, and by pinning derogatory nicknames to her rival
she both entertained—and influenced—her hearers.

Soon even the younger generation of the Nelson family would speak of
Lady Nelson as 'Tom Tit'.

The friendship of this branch of his family with Emma was welcomed
by Nelson as a godsend; he saw in it a means for providing his mistress
with a chaperone to guard her against the advances of the Prince of
Wales and other undesirable admirers. While in London he arranged for
Mrs. William (at his expense) to make a further prolonged visit to town,
with that object in view. It was to safeguard Emma, as much as to see his
daughter, that he made his journey to London. Travelling all through the
night, he reached Piccadilly at seven o'clock in the morning and, as it was
close to the Hamiltons' house, took rooms at Lothian's Hotel, Albemarle
Street.

[1] Ibid.

CHAPTER II

LITTLE TITCHFIELD STREET

THE SUBJECT of Lady Nelson, and not that of Horatia, had first priority at the lovers' meeting, as letters from both Nelson and Lady Hamilton written on 24 February show. Lady Hamilton's was addressed to Mrs. William Nelson at Hilborough, Brandon, Norfolk, and read:

My dearest Friend—Your dear Brother arrived this morning by seven o'clock. He stays only 3 days; so by the time you wou'd be here, he will be gone. How unlucky you went so soon. I am in health *so so*, but spirits to-day excellent. Oh, what real pleasure Sir William and I have in seeing our great, good, virtuous Nelson. His eye is better. Tom tit does not come to town. She offered to go down, but was refused. She only wanted to go, to do mischief to all the great JOVE'S relations. 'Tis now shewn, all her ill-treatment and bad *heart*. JOVE has found it out. Apropos, Lady Nelson is in Brighton yet.[1]

Plainly derived from the same pernicious source, Nelson's letter to his wife was written from Piccadilly on the same day; it read:

As I am sent for to town on very particular business for a day or two I would not on any account have you come to London but rest quiet where you are. Nor would I have you come to Portsmouth for I never come on shore . . . I hope Josiah [her son Captain Nisbet] may be able to get a ship now this change of ministers has taken place. As ever your affectionate Nelson.[2]

Procuring Josiah the frigate *Thalia* was Nelson's last act of kindness towards the wife and stepson who had once possessed his heart entirely. After 4 March when he advised his wife of this appointment, he never addressed her directly again. Communication was held through his agent Davison, who paid her the quarterly allowance—a generous one of £400— settled on her by Nelson. During his stay in London Nelson saw Davison at his offices in St. James's Square to arrange this settlement, as well as those he had drawn up in favour of Lady Hamilton and Horatia. Towards his wife, as Nelson wrote Davison on 23 April 'his mind was fixed as fate'; rather than live with her again, he 'would live abroad for ever'. By these financial provisions for his wife (he left her £1,000 per annum for life in

---

[1] BM Add. MSS 34989.   [2] BM Add. MSS 28333.

his Will) Nelson believed himself freed from all obligations towards her. How he, the son, grandson, and brother of parsons could suppose he could legally replace a blameless wife, is not easy to understand. He was in Lady Hamilton's hands, and acted on her inspiration. The degree of his infatuation for her, particularly at that time when both his professional duty and the presence of her husband separated him from her, was greater than at any other time; the frustration may explain, even if it does not excuse, his conduct towards his wife.

The way he spent his time in London during these few days was faithfully recorded by Lady Hamilton in letters to her new friend, Mrs. William Nelson. To her she related everything—except his visit to his daughter. Writing at noon on 25 February she said:

I have only just time to say, how are you? Your good Brother has just left us to go to pay a visit to Mr. Nepean [Secretary to the Admiralty] but is coming back to dinner with Morice his brother whom he brings with him, and Trowbridge allso. We shall be comfortable but more so if *you had been here*. Oh, I wish you was, and how happy would Milord have been to have had that happiness. To have walked out with Mrs. Nelson. How unfortuante it was!... Our dear Nelson is very well in health. Poor fellow, he travelled allmost all night, but you that know his great, good heart will not be surprised at any act of friendship *of his*. I shall send for Charlotte to see him before he goes, and he has given a guinea for her.[1]

Charlotte, who was Mrs. Nelson's thirteen-year-old daughter, at school in Kensington at the time, would shortly become one of Lady Hamilton's most-favoured allies (as would Charlotte's brother Horace) in her campaign to win the family favour.

On 26 February she wrote further to Mrs. Nelson:

Yesterday I could not write, my dearest friend, and milord was not yet returned from the admiralty time enough to frank your letters, and sorry I was you shou'd pay for such trash that I sent you, but I thought you wou'd be uneasy. We *had* a pleasant evening and night [erased] I often thought of you, but now the subject of the King's illness gives such gloom to everything, 'tis terrable all turned upside down... Our good Lord Nelson is lodged at Lothian's. Tom tit at same place Brighton. The CUB [Josiah] is to have a frigate, the 'Thalia'... I suppose HE will be up in a day or so. I onely hope he does not come near me. If he does, *not at home* shall be the answer. I am glad he is going. I hope never to— ... We supped and talked politicks till 2. Oh, my dearest friend, our dear Lord is just come in. He goes off to-night and sails immediately. My heart is fit to *Burst* with greef. Oh, what pain, God only knows... I shall go mad with grief.

[1] BM Add. MSS 34989.

Oh, God only knows what it is to part with such a friend, *such a one*. We were truly called the 'Tria Juncta in uno' [the Hamilton motto] for Sir William, *he*, and I have but *one heart in three bodies*.[1]

The family's acceptance of the situation has, inevitably, been open to censure; it has been attributed to self-interest, for Lady Hamilton made it a part of her policy to use their brother's influence on their behalf, and to procure the Revd. William in particular favours and benefits that had not been forthcoming from Lady Nelson. The family's surmises and suspicions regarding the Hamilton connection may have been honestly put off by the very *foreignness* of the household's manners; such exuberance of language and gesture as Lady Hamilton indulged in could, to their English way of thinking, be nothing more than the effect of long residence abroad. At this stage, at any rate, the William Nelsons should be given the benefit of the doubt and exonerated from the charge of condoning an adulterous connection. They knew nothing, naturally, of the purpose of Nelson's visit to Little Titchfield Street, where his daughter was out at nurse.

A gap in Lady Hamilton's weekly notes to Mrs. Gibson at the end of February to bring 'Miss Horatia' to Piccadilly, corresponds with the date of Nelson's visit to London on the 24th or 25th when he obviously preferred to see his daughter at her nurse's than under Sir William Hamilton's roof. The child was barely a month old, but it was a beautiful and healthy child who fulfilled his fondest hopes. He had longed to know how she looked and had written Emma on 17 February: 'I fear saying too much—I admire what you say of my god-child. If it is like its mother it will be very handsome, for I think her one, aye, the most beautiful woman of the age. Now, do not be angry at my praising this dear child's mother, for I have heard people say she is very like you.'[2] On his return to the fleet he wrote, in the character of 'Thompson', to Lady Hamilton: 'I have seen and talked much to Mrs. Thomson's friend. The fellow seems to eat all my words when I talk of her and his child! He says he never can forget your goodness and affection to her and his dear, dear child. I have had, you know, the felicity of seeing it, and a finer child never was produced by any two persons. It was in truth a love-begotten child.'[3] 'I love her the more dearly,' he later wrote on 4 August 1801, 'as she is in the upper part of her face so like her dear good mother, who I love, and always shall, with the truest affection.'[4]

---

[1] Ibid.   [2] M.516.
[3] Nicolas, vii, 374. Letter of 10 March 1801.   [4] P. ii, 139.

To Emma who had given him this child, Nelson now solemnly dedi-
cated his life and love; all of him that was not at the service of his country.
Taking the first opportunity that offered after his visit to London of
sending a letter by hand, he wrote on 1 March on the eve of sailing for
the Baltic:— [1]

Now, my own dear wife, for such you are in my eyes and in the face of heaven, I
can give full scope to my feelings . . . You know my dearest Emma, that there is
nothing in this world that I would not do for us to live together, and to have
our dear little child with us. I firmly believe that this campaign will give us
peace, and then we will set off for Bronté [the Sicilian estate previously men-
tioned] . . . Nothing but an event happening to him [Sir William] could prevent
my going, and I am sure you will think so, for unless all matters accord it would
bring 100 tongues and slanderous reports if I separated from her (which I
would do with pleasure the moment we can be united; I want to see her no
more) therefore we must manage till we can quit this country or your uncle dies.
I love, I never did love anyone else, I never had a dear pledge of love till you
gave me one, and you, thank my God, never gave one to anyone else . . . You, my
beloved Emma and my Country, are the two dearest objects of my fond heart—
a heart susceptible and true . . . My longing for you, both person and conversation, you may readily imagine. I am sure my love and desires are all for you . . .
Kiss and bless *our* dear Horatia—think of that . . . You may readily believe, my
dearly beloved Mrs. T.

He wrote her further,

how dear you are to me, as much as life . . . altho' I am much worn out since we
parted, yet, I am sure, that the sight of my heaven-given wife will make me
again a happy father, and you a mother. Be assured that I love nothing but you
in this world and our dear child. Fancy what would happen, and will happen,
when we meet. I can say no more . . . When you see our dear mutual friend Ly
Ham, say every kind thing for your husband to her, and hug our dear child.

The sight of the child decided Nelson finally to abandon all other
domestic ties. Lady Nelson, who had not in fourteen years of marriage
been able to give him this one 'dear pledge of love', was more condemned
on this count than if she had been a thoroughly bad wife. Her last hold
on him was gone. For Emma too, the visit brought its revelations. From
then on she understood enough of Nelson's feelings to realize that in
Horatia she had, if not a hostage to fortune, at least the key to Nelson's
heart, should it at any time become closed to her. Noticeable in the correspondence of Nelson and Emma are his repeated expressions of gratitude
to her for whatever was done for the child; as though he realized that

[1] M.532.

LITTLE TITCHFIELD STREET

Emma's feelings for her were not comparable to his own. He took great
alarm when, after his visit to London, the child's wet-nurse went sick,
with ill-effects on Horatia: he received the news on the eve of the Battle
of Copenhagen, 1 April, and wrote Emma:

You are, my dearest Mrs. Thompson, so good, so right in all you do . . . I shall
take care that your dear friend does no wrong. He has cried on account of his
child; he begs, for heaven's sake, you will take care that the nurse had no *bad*
disorder, for he has been told of Captain Howard, before he was six weeks old,
had the *bad* disorder which has ruined his constitution to this day.[1]

Horatia escaped the infection, and on 3 April Lady Hamilton wrote to
Mrs. Gibson to bring her to Piccadilly at 11. By then the Battle of Copenhagen had been fought and won. Nelson was once again a national hero.

The news of the victory reached London on 15 April, and Sir Nathanial
Wraxall, looking in at No. 23 Piccadilly at ten o'clock that evening, found
a celebration party going on. It was the usual exclusively masculine
gathering, made up of Sir William's kinsmen for the most part, with a
sprinkling of theatre people and Italians, only too glad to be patronized by
Lady Hamilton, and, somewhat incongruously in this setting, the Revd.
William Nelson. Lady Hamilton sang, and after singing, began to dance
the Tarantella.

Sir William began it with her [recorded Sir Nathanial] and maintained the conflict for such it might well be estimated, for some minutes. When unable longer
to continue it, the Duke of Noia succeeded to his place; but he too, though
nearly forty years younger than Sir William, soon gave in. Lady Hamilton then
sent for her own servant, who being likewise exhausted, a Copt, perfectly black,
who Lord Nelson had presented her on his return from Egypt, relieved her
companion. It would be difficult to convey any idea of this dance; the Fandango
and Segudilla of the Spaniards present an image of it. We must recollect that the
two performers are supposed to be a Satyr and Nymph, or, rather a Fawn and a
Bacchante. It was certainly not of a nature to be performed except before a
select company; as the screams, attitudes, starts, and embraces, with which it was
intermingled gave it a peculiar character. I only mentioned it in order to show
Sir William Hamilton's activity and gaiety at that advanced period of life.'[2]

The rejoicings for the victory of Copenhagen cannot fail to rouse in the
biographer of Horatia Nelson reflections on what would have been her
fate if her father had been killed then instead of four years later at Trafalgar. The unacknowledged child in Little Titchfield Street would not
then have borne his name—as she later did—or been accepted by his
family. Despite the provision Nelson made for her in anticipation of such

[1] M.557.   [2] G. Street, *Ghosts of Piccadilly*, 184-5.

an eventuality, it may be doubted whether her fortunes would have taken her very far with only Lady Hamilton to guard her.

For, despite Nelson's belief, expressed in the letter quoted above ('I never had a dear pledge of love till you gave me one, and you, thank my God, never gave one to anyone else'), Lady Hamilton had previously had one, if not more than one, illegitimate child. Its paternity is generally ascribed to Sir Harry Fetherstonehaugh, of Up Park, Sussex, whose mistress she was in 1781, though the possibility is that another man of fashion, Captain, later Rear-Admiral Willet-Payne, was the father. Whoever it was, the Hon. Charles Greville, her next protector, provided for it, and even for a time allowed Emma to have it with her in his establishment at Paddington Green. In her early days Emma had strong maternal feelings, as her letters to Greville show. Time, and her extraordinary successes, changed her considerably. After her removal to Italy under the aegis of Sir William Hamilton she never sought to see the child again. Sir William accepted, like his nephew before him, to provide for its keep and schooling in Lancashire and, by a strange chance, in the very week of the national rejoicings over the victory of Copenhagen, Emma's mother, Mrs. Cadogan, visiting relatives in the north, called to see the girl—another Emma—at Mrs. Blackburn's school near Manchester. She was by then a young woman earning her living. Her unsuccessful attempts to receive recognition from her mother, and Lady Hamilton's repudiation of her some years later, ended the connection. Her ill-starred fortunes make the analogy with Horatia Nelson all the closer, when the insecurity of Horatia's situation at the time of Copenhagen is considered. Well might Nelson fear that, in the event of his death, she would suffer 'want and shame'.

News of the victory of Copenhagen brought comment of a different—and sadder—sort from Nelson's wife and father. Writing from Bath Lady Nelson said:

I cannot be silent in the general joy throughout the Kingdom. I must express my thankfulness and happiness it hath pleased God to spare your life. All greet you with every testimony of gratitude and praise. This victory is said to surpass Aboukir. What my feelings are your own good heart will tell you.[1]

His father wrote him, also from Bath: 'Yesterday I received your joyous news, but all things have their alloy, Lady [Nelson] was heavily affected with her personal feelings at not receiving a line from your own hand.' Mr. Nelson, despite his eighty years, did not flinch from saying some hard things in the hour of Nelson's triumph.

[1] Naish, 585-6.

He who created all things [he wrote] . . . has bestowed upon you great abilities and has granted you His Grace to use them to His Glory, the good of your fellow creatures and the salvation of your own soul. I have sometimes a hope of receiving you once more surrounded not with public honours alone, but . . . a return to domestic joys, the most durable and solid of all others. So be it O God.[1]

No answer to either letter was received. Mr. Nelson's part in defending his daughter-in-law was not overlooked by Lady Hamilton who ventured to denounce even him to the William Nelsons in her general attack on the family.

Lady Nelson's sorrows received bewildered sympathy from Mrs. Bolton, moreover, Nelson's elder sister, who wrote to her after Nelson's visit to town:

Will you excuse what I am going to say? I wish you had continued in town a little longer, as *I have heard* my brother regretted he had not a house he could call his own when he returned. Do, whenever you hear he is likely to return, have a house to receive him . . . I hope in God one day I shall have the pleasure of seeing you together as happy as ever, he certainly as far as I hear is not a happy man.[2]

Writing to her again after Copenhagen, Mrs. Bolton urged her: 'Keep up your spirits, my dear Madam, and all will come right again, for tho' he is warm, he has a truly affectionate mind.' Pressing her to visit them in Norfolk, Mrs. Bolton added:

Do not say you will not suffer us to take too much notice of you for fear it should injure us with Lord Nelson. I assure you I have a pride, as well as himself, in doing what is right, and that surely is to be attentive to those who have been *so to us*, and I am sure my brother would *despise* us if we acted contrary.

The comments of the family on the separation—and its cause—failed to move Nelson; and they only aroused in Lady Hamilton a concentrated enmity. She enveighed against them all to her uneasy confident, Mrs. William Nelson.'

And *your* father, Nelson's father, protects this woman and gives a mortal blow to his son. The old man could never bear her and now he *conspires against the saviour of his country* and his darling who has risen him to such a height of honour, *and for whom?* A *wicked false malicious* wretch who rendered his days wretched and his nights miserable; and the father of Nelson says, 'I will *stab* my son to the heart' . . . Oh! how cruel . . . shocking it is and I am afraid the Boltons are not without their share of *guilt* in this affair jelous of you *all* they have, with the Mashams, pushed this poor dear old gentleman to act this bad and *horrible part*,

[1] Ibid., 586.   [2] Ibid., 587.

to support a false proud bad woman, artful and with every bad quality to make wretched those she belongs to and yet command over her own cold heart and infamous soul to shew an appearance to the bad part of the world of gentleness and strugling with opression, but let her own wickedness be her punishment.[1]

It is not surprising to learn from a further letter of Lady Hamilton's that she was prostrate with headache and sickness the day after writing that diatribe.

[1] BRP/NMM/9292.

CHAPTER III

'PARADISE MERTON'

THE separation from his wife was made easier for Nelson because they had no home of their own. They had never had one, from the time he first brought her to England in 1787 after their marriage in the Antilles. They had gone to his father's rectory at Burnham Thorpe where, as the years of Nelson's unemployment were prolonged, the considerate old man had left them in occupation, going into lodgings in his neighbouring parish at Burnham Ulph. When at last Nelson was given a new command, at the reopening of hostilities with France in 1793, he left his wife in the care of his father and of his sisters; and it was only in the autumn of 1797, after the convalescence following the loss of his arm, that he bought the house near Ipswich, called Roundwood, which he intended for a happy retirement for his future, and a present residence for his wife. It was his destiny never to live in the house or even to spend one night there. On his landing at Yarmouth in November 1800 he had particularly requested his wife *not* to await him at home but to meet him in London with his father. The obligation of sleeping under his own roof in the uneasy circumstances of his return in the company of the Hamiltons, could thus be obviated. For Lady Nelson the home she had never shared with her husband held few attractions, and she left it to spend the remainder of her life in furnished houses in London, Bath, Brighton or the west country, varying her residences with the seasons.

The situation left Nelson without a home. When after the victory of Copenhagen and the pacification of the north, he returned to England on leave (1 July) he had, literally, no place to call his own. He stayed at hotels, at Lothian's in London, at the Inn at Burford Bridge, near Dorking, at 'The Bush' at Staines, following the Hamiltons wherever Sir William liked to indulge his favourite sport—fishing. Merely to be with Lady Hamilton he accepted what was, in all other respects, an intolerable situation. He had all the seaman's love of home-life and of the countryside, and this nomadic existence, following the Hamiltons about from hotel to hotel, made him resolve, if the money would run to it, to buy a house. From the first he never thought of it otherwise than as a country home; he wanted somewhere better than Little Titchfield Street for Horatia, a place where she need not be hid, and where eventually he could 'live retired' with her and his beloved Emma.

Horatia's position was brought home to him the very day following his return. Lady Hamilton, writing to Mrs. Gibson on 1 July, convened her for the next day to Piccadilly. 'I hope you are well,' she wrote, 'and Miss Thomson. I will call on you to-morrow at one a clock to carry you an airing.' The heat of London was particularly intolerable that month, and the resolution to procure Horatia more than an occasional 'airing in a carriage' became fixed in Nelson's mind. While having to take Emma's assurances that all was for the best, he needed to restore his own health during his short spell of leave. He suffered much from dysentery while on active service from the cold conditions on board ship, and came on shore after each prolonged absence a shadow of himself. So as not to appear alone in the Hamiltons' company, he surrounded himself now with those members of his family who accepted Emma—that is the Revd. William Nelson, his wife and children. Charlotte and Horace were on holiday and asked nothing better than to be with their famous uncle. 'Brave little Parker', Captain Edward Parker, one of the admiral's youthful protégés, was also invited to join the party for a fishing holiday at the 'Bush'. With them went Nelson's servant Tom Allen, and Emma's black maid 'Fatima'. They found the 'Bush' had a pleasant garden by the Thames good for picnicking and eating up Sir William's catch of the day. The idyllic pursuits included, for Nelson and Emma, escapes to Laleham with the ostensible purpose of calling on 'poor blind' Mrs. Nelson (his brother Maurice's widow). When it was over, and Nelson back with the channel fleet, Parker wrote to assure Lady Hamilton of his redoubled care of his commander; he it was who sat by him at table and cut up his meat. In his letter of thanks of 30 July from Deal, occurred a surprising sentence:

We got down to Sheerness very quick and well, and were received by the acclamations of the people, who looked with wild but most affectionate amazement at him, who was once more going to step forward in defence of his country. He is the cleverest and quickest man . . . In the short time we were at Sheerness, he regulated and gave orders for thirty of the ships under his command, made everyone pleased . . . and set them all on the qui vive . . . We arrived at Deal last night, and this morning the flag was hoisted on board the Leyden . . . [Nelson had been put in command of a task-force to block the enemy massing in the channel ports] . . . Not a word of little Horatia. You don't mean to mention her for sixteen years I suppose—Pray send him cream cheese and whatever you can get you think he likes, and *I will cut it up*. . . . Remembrances to Mrs. Nelson and Charlotte.[1]

The reference to Horatia was too teasing, too ingenuous, to hide any secret implications. Parker had been to Piccadilly on various occasions to carry letters for his chief, and at such times he must have had some such sight of the child as Captain Hardy recorded having many years later. That Parker had no inkling Horatia was more than a protégée of Lady Hamilton's who, for her beauty, she would be supposed to envy, and hence keep hidden, is all too evident. Lady Hamilton had so frank a manner that she disarmed suspicion; it was far more effective than secretiveness. Hardy related how,[2] calling on her after the action of Copenhagen, she soon left the room and presently returned with a child in her arms: 'Look what a pretty baby I have got' she said to him, but offered no further explanation. Hardy believed he knew all about the baby then, Nelson having told him the tale about Thompson, the ship's sail-maker in the *Elephant*, who lost his wife in childbirth; Lady Hamilton was befriending the little orphan; he therefore made no comment at the time. Parker was no more embarrassed than Hardy had been; he was simply more curious and asked the baby's name, and learnt that she was Nelson's god-child and under the protection of Lady Hamilton.

Nelson's new command kept him from home from 27 July to 23 October. Much of the time, spent in patrolling the coast, he was inactive and intensely dissatisfied.

At the end of August he invited his brother the Revd. William to bring his family down to Deal, so that the Hamiltons might stay there also, without arousing comment. The frequency of Nelson's contacts with the Revd. William at this time should not be taken as proof of his preference for this brother (Maurice had always been his favourite), but William was nearest him in age, had shared his schooldays, even served as chaplain in one of his ships. They were quite unlike each other; despite their different callings, it was the divine who had rough manners, the seaman who was ultra sensitive. A mutual need, rather, brought the brothers together at this time; Nelson needing the countenance of William's wife for Lady Hamilton, and William looking to Nelson's glory to serve his social ambitions. Nelson took lodgings for the whole party at the 'Three Kings', which allowed him to breakfast with them most days. It permitted the ladies also to bring comfort to the wounded after the action off Boulogne on 15 August. In this engagement Captain Parker was severely

---

[1] P. ii, 135.   [2] Nicolas, vii, 386.

wounded and, together with a fellow officer, Captain Langford from Norfolk, was taken ashore into lodgings at Nelson's expense. Parker's sufferings and death on 29 September cut Nelson to the heart: 'He was my child for I found him in distress', he later wrote of him. He paid for a headstone to his grave in Deal churchyard, and instantly set about procuring a pension for the father who was without means.

The whole period of this command was an unhappy one for Nelson, and turned his thoughts more than ever towards the return of peace, and the acquisition of a home of his own. Before leaving London he had charged Lady Hamilton to house-hunt for him. Sending '10,000 kisses to my dear Horatia', and thanking Emma for her 'tender care of my dear little charge Horatia', he wrote: 'I am very anxious to have a home'. He did not mind where the house was, so long as it was in a 'dry situation— and quickly found.' 'From my heart,' he wrote to Emma from off Boulogne on 15 August, the very day of the raid, 'I wish you could find me out a comfortable house . . . At this moment I can command £3,000.' A suggestion that he borrow what further sum he needed from Sir William, he firmly rejected: 'as to asking Sir William' he wrote her, 'I could not do it, I would sooner beg.'

A possible house at Turnham Green fell through, a further house at Chiswick was found unsuitable; Nelson returned to the charge: 'I am very anxious for a house, and I have nobody to do any business for me, but you, my dear friend . . . as to a house, you are an excellent judge, only do not have it too large, for the establishment of a large household would be ruinous.' On 20 August Nelson heard that Emma had found a house at Merton, and he wrote to her by return: 'I approve of the house at Merton and must beg and entreat of you to work hard for me. Messrs Booth & Haslewood will manage all the law business. I have £3,000 ready to pay tomorrow . . . therefore, my dear Emma, look to it for me.'

There was never any hesitation over buying the house at Merton; he heard enough without seeing it to know at once that it was just what he wanted. Mrs. William Nelson, chaperoning Emma for a further spell, wrote to her husband from Piccadilly: 'I received your letter just as we were going to Merton, it is in Surrey, seven miles from Town, I think your Brother will like it, and I hope we shall all spend very happy days there.' [1]

Mrs. William, who was above all, a good mother, had every reason to approve of Merton; its closeness to town would benefit her children in the holidays, and 'mylady' as she wrote her husband, promised 'often to

[1] BRP/NMM/9292.

PORTRAIT OF LORD NELSON, 1805 by Sir William Beechey
(study for the completed portrait)

fetch Charlotte of a Sunday'. Moreover, one room of the house was to be 'called ours, and we and the children must be there for the Christmas holidays.' The family character of the house was thus early established, and the good-will of Nelson's relations secured by Lady Hamilton.

Meanwhile, Nelson pressed for the purchase to be completed. The price was £9,000, and Davison, his loyal friend, offered to advance the extra sum required. 'Can your offer be real?' Nelson wrote him in amazed delight; 'Can Davison be uncorrupted by the depravity of the world? I almost doubt what I read; I will answer, my dear friend, you are the only person living who could make such an offer.'

Though the house was called Merton Place Nelson spoke of it always as 'the farm'. 'Love my Horatia,' he wrote to Emma, 'and prepare for me the farm'[1] (2 September). He left the entire arrangement of the interior and gardens to Lady Hamilton, ordering his agent to send down what furniture, plate, and glass he possessed and had left in store with him. 'Would to God I was on shore at the farm,' he wrote on 21 September. 'I have sent to Mr. Dodds (Davison's partner) to carry you a list of my things at his house, and to receive your orders what is to go to the farm.' 'I trust the farm will make you more happy than a dull London life,' he wrote Emma on 23 September, knowing full well that it was not dull to her. 'Make what use you please of it.' These were not empty words, for no sooner was the purchase completed than Nelson settled Merton on Emma in the event of his death, as a sure future home for Horatia. 'You may rely on one thing,' he wrote on 26 September, 'that I shall like Merton, therefore do not be uneasy on that account. I have that opinion of your taste and judgement that I do not believe it can fail in pleasing me. We must only consider our means and for the rest, I am sure, you will soon make it the prettiest place in the world. . . .'[2]

Having stipulated only two things—that the house be in a dry situation and that it be not too large—Nelson now insisted in almost every letter that no possession of the Hamiltons, neither sheets, towels, books, nor pictures—nor even their proffered cook—be admitted to Merton; everything must be his, and they and those other friends, his fellow officers, and relations he wished to invite, must be his guests alone. 'Respecting the farm and all the frugality necessary for the present to be attached to it, I know your good sense will do precisely what is right. I only entreat again that everything, even a book and a cook at Merton, may be mine.'[3]

He had inside information that a peace with France was being negotiated, and he could indulge his dream of a country-life with some

[1] M.162. [2] Naish, 590-1. [3] Nelson to Ly. H., Sept. 30 1801.

confidence that it might be fulfilled. How he visualized that life, with scrupulous regard to his limited means and yet with every generous intention of sharing its pleasures, he confided in a letter to Emma of 26 September:

If I can afford to buy the Duck Close and the field adjoining it would be pleasant but I fear it is not in my power, but I shall know when my accounts are settled at New Year's year.

To be sure we shall employ the tradespeople of our village in preference to any others in what we want for common use, and give them every encouragement to be kind and attentive to us. From my heart do I wish that I was with you and it cannot be long, for to-day I am far from well, violent headache and very cold, but it may be agitation. Whatever my dear Emma you do for my little charge I must be pleased with. Probably she will be lodged at Merton at least in the spring when she can have the benefit of our walks. It will make the poor mother happy I am sure. I do not write to her to-day as this goes through the Admiralty . . . I shall have the child christened when I come up. Have we a nice church at Merton? We will set an example of good ness to the whole parish.[1]

There is no reason at all to doubt Nelson's sincerity; he remained so much the country parson's son, believing in the virtue of others and his own good faith. He saw no more difficulties in 'fixing' Horatia at Merton than in having her christened. Emma, who saw more clearly than he did on such issues, did not reveal her misgivings until his arrival, promising him meanwhile a picture of Horatia. 'I shall long to have the picture of the little one,' he wrote on 3 October, 'you will send it to me; but very soon I shall see the original and then I shall be happy.'

To prepare for that event Emma wrote to Mrs. Gibson on 9 October to have 'Miss Thompson' measured for a complete new outfit.

My dearest Mrs. Gibson, I have sent a person to you to take orders for Miss Thompson pray tell her what you want I am going out of town but come back on Tewsday I shall have the pleasure of seeing you I recommend Miss T. to your care write to me at Merton Place near Merton Surry and tell me how you all are milord will be in town soon Kiss my goddaughter from your affectionate friend—E. Hamilton.[2]

Appointed by Nelson 'whole and sole commander of Merton', Emma was in her element, playing several roles at once: house-decorator, land-surveyor, 'farmer's wife'—setting all in order for her Lord. 'You are to be, recollect, Lady Paramount of all the territories and waters of Merton and we are all to be your guests,' Nelson wrote on 6 October. With the in-valuable Mrs. Cadogan to help her, she worked unsparingly, creating out of the abundance of her energy the right rural setting for the tired hero whose haven it was to be. Despite the unfortunate end of Marie Antoinette the fashion was still for the mock shepherdess life, and none knew better than Lady Hamilton how to indulge it.

The possession of Merton was so dear a wish fulfilled that Nelson lost no time, on the purchase being concluded, in settling it on Emma in trust for Horatia. On 1 October he wrote

At this moment I fancy you setting forth to take possession of your little estate, for this very day I shall make a codicil to my will, leaving it in trust for your use, and to be at your disposal until you wish me to leave it to *my nearest and dearest relation*. We die not one moment the sooner by doing those acts, and if I die, my property may as well go to those I tenderly regard, as to those who hate me [his step-son].[1]

By then Emma was prostrate with overwork and anger at the lawyers' delays in getting possession of the house, and on 6 October wrote her 'jewell', Mrs. Nelson, some plain truths on the matter:

I have got such a pain in my head my jewell my dear friend that I am in bed . . . Tuesday a bed   I shall not get to Merton till Saturday [10th] if then—that false mother Greaves she never intended with her cant to let us she would be a good match for tom tit [Lady Nelson] what does she think that Nelson will cheat her . . . I am in a passion the lawyers are a lot of villons and it might have been finished ten days past yesterday I sent Dods [Nelson's agent] to beg her to give it up as milord was expected and could not sleep in town she had the impudence to say well let milord come down with one servant and stay with us till the thing is finished we will make it comfortable for him What do you think my dearest friend of her impudence . . . my patience is gone and my head not the better for it.[2]

'Impudent Mother Greaves' indeed!

For Nelson to arrive at Merton unheralded by his Emma was not at all in her plan; happily the point was conceded, and all was in order in time to receive the new owner of Merton.

A complete *mise-en-scène* had been arranged, even to fetching young Charlotte from school to be there when he came so that, family man that he was, he should not be allowed to feel he had none of his own to come home to. 'Sir William is gone to fetch Carlotte,' Emma wrote in a hurry to her 'jewell' on the Saturday of the move. 'She shall be early at school on Monday morning and as milord is to arrive on Friday for dinner she shall be here to receive him and go back to school on Monday early . . . Sir

---

[1] M.628.   [2] BRP/NMM/4.

William is quite charmed with her" [1] the fond mother in Norfolk was told. Sir William, barely settled in, and expecting the master of Merton any day, wrote his congratulations on 16 October:

you might get a thousand pounds to-morrow for your bargain. The proximity to the capital, and the perfect retirement of this place, are for your Lordship, two points beyond estimation; but the house is so comfortable, the furniture clean & good, & I never saw so many conveniences united in so small a compass. You have nothing but to come and enjoy immediately; you have a good mile of pleasant dry walk around your own farm. It would make you laugh to see Emma & her mother fitting up pig-sties and hen-coops, & already the Canal is enlivened with ducks & the cock is strutting with his hens about the walks. Your Lordship's plan as to stocking the Canal with fish is exactly mine. I will answer for it, that in a few months you may command a good dish of fish at a moment's warning ... This neighbourhood is anxiously expecting your Ldp's arrival, and you cannot be off of some particular attention that will be shewn you, of which all the world know that you have merited above all others. [2]

Anything like a planned invasion of his privacy was distasteful to Nelson; the Merton preparations sounded ominous to him, and he wrote to Emma by return of post: '... You may rely that I shall be with you by dinner on Friday, at half-past three or four at farthest. I pray that I may not be annoyed on my arrival; it is retirement with my friends that I wish for. Thank Sir William for his letter.' [3]

Warned by Sir William, he drove all through the night, arriving at the gates of Merton before the October sun had risen on the morning of the 23rd. Though a triumphal arch was in place in the village street, and rows of candles were set on the window-sills of the house-fronts, he managed to elude the 'particular attentions' planned by his new neighbours, and to enter in possession of his property unobserved.

For that first encounter he had what he wanted, silence and solitude. The fallen leaves on the gravelled drive muffled the sound of his wheels; the lawns and bow-windows of the house, reflected in the little piece of ornamental water in the ghostly light, seemed a pure enchantment; it was all even better than he had dreamed. When the sleepers were wakened, and he was hurried into the house, he clasped not only his friends to his heart; in that hour the feeling for Merton, for 'dear, dear Merton', was born. From thenceforth, it was 'Paradise Merton', to him.

[1] Ibid.   [2] M.638.   [3] P. ii, 222–3.

CHAPTER IV

THE FAMILY CIRCLE

IN 1815 when Merton was once again for sale, it was fully described in a 'Times' advertisement of 22 March as

very desirably situate . . . 7 miles from London, containing five spacious bedrooms, with dressing-rooms (and water-closets) and eight servants' rooms; two large drawing-rooms, a dining-room, library, and gentleman's dressing-room; convenient servants' offices of every description, excellent cellars for wine and beer, detached dairy and ice-house, a spacious lawn and pleasure-ground, intersected with gravel walks and a sheet of water, a large kitchen-garden and orchard, with greenhouse, a paddock of rich pasture-land skirted by extensive shrubbery; the whole contains upwards of 22 acres enclosed with lofty park palings; also 2 contiguous enclosures of arable land containing 17 acres.

The earliest part of the house, the north front built in palladian style, with central pediment and wings, was at least one hundred years old when Nelson moved in, as it was owned by a Mr. William Hubbard, an accountant in the Navy Office who died in 1709. It was then bought by Sir William Phippard on whose death in 1723 the property was divided among his children and from them passed through many hands until it came into the possession of the Mr. Greaves from whom Nelson bought it in 1801. The main entrance and most pleasing aspect of Merton Place was on the double-fronted east side where the bow-windows of the drawing- and dining-rooms looked out on the tree-studded lawns. Access to the interior could be had direct from the garden up a flight of steps and by way of twin verandahs (called 'Miradores' by Emma) whose pillars supported a trellised framework in the rustic style of the later eighteenth century. Here on future summer days, Horatia rode her rocking horse, and the ladies of the party reclined in chaise-longues, reading or embroidering as they took the air, while sheltering their complexions from the sun. Behind the dining-room, on the south side, were the kitchen, pantries and servants' offices; behind the drawing-room was a Breakfast parlour, and behind that again, facing west, was the library.

The most distinctive feature of the interior of Merton was the abundance of wall mirrors and glass doors in the continental style, which were long remembered by one of Nelson's servants, a man called Saker, a general factotem and carpenter. 'Plenty of glass and light seemed to be the predominant taste,' he recorded. 'Glass doors in front, and a long passage with glass doors opening onto the lawn behind and even plate glass doors to some of the principal rooms threw an abundance of light about the interior.'[1]

The brightness was continued out of doors in the little stream of ornamental water threading the grounds, a feed from the Wandle which bounded Nelson's property and supplied the power to the neighbouring printing-mills, fuller's works, copper and iron mills which, since the early eighteenth century, had been the main occupations of the village beside husbandry.

It did not take Nelson's party long to dub their tiny stream the 'Nile'. Well stocked with fish, it became in due course Sir William's favourite haunt. Spanning the 'Nile' was a graceful little bridge in the Italian style, which allowed him to pass from one bank to another. The elements, indeed, were not wanting to make Merton—for Sir William as for Nelson—the Paradise Emma soon called it.

The pattern of family life to be led at Merton was laid down by Nelson during the very first week-end of his arrival. Charlotte had been fetched from school to greet him when he arrived, and on the Sunday morning the whole party attended morning service at Merton Church.

Nothing could be more domestic than the scene presented to the curious gaze of the parishioners than the group in the Admiral's pew, the second pew from the pulpit under the north wall. Emma lost no time in describing the scene to her friend Mrs. William, and in making plain how well disposed the Merton neighbours were, and how indeed, if she and Nelson desired it (which she declared they did *not*), they could have plenty of visiting among the best society. This was true; Merton was not disposed, then or later, to be censorious; seeing only in the new proprietor of the Place England's most illustrious hero, who had come among them to take his well-earned rest. Nelson's Merton neighbours, with whom he soon made lasting friendships—including the Vicar, the Revd. Thomas Lancaster—added not a little to his happiness there; offering hospitality when it was acceptable, but refraining from indiscreet intrusion. The proximity of Merton to London made it an ideal residence for busy city men, as well as for retired people like Rear-Admiral Smith. Nelson's nearest neighbour, at Wandlebank House, was the editor of the *Morning Chronicle*, James Perry; at 'Morden Hall' lived one of the wealthy Goldsmid brothers (Abraham) and at 'The Grove' lived another, Benjamin.

[1] Bartlett, *History of Wimbledon*, 1865.

They were bullion brokers with offices in Fenchurch Street and after the week-ends, in company with James Perry and other city-bound residents, they would take the London road on Monday mornings. On his first Monday home, Nelson drove up early with the Hamiltons for an appointment at the Admiralty. Emma was soon at her desk writing to her 'jewell': Dated 'London, Monday morning, ten o'clock' her letter read:

We are arrived here early, stoped at Whitelands, and Lord Nelson, Sir William and self went out with dear Charlotte, and Milord beg'd a Holoday to-morrow, and Miss Nelson, permitted to give tea. She, Miss V [Voiller, the headmistress], with a good grace gave permission. I saw Miss Fuss [Furse] more stupid than ever I think, but all girls pall when near Charlotte. She Loses no lessons by coming on Monday morning, for she is their by a little after nine.

I am sorry to tell you I do not think our Dear Lord well. He has frequent sickness, and [is] Low, and he throws himself on the sofa *tired and says, I am worn out*, but yet he is better, and I hope we shall get him up. He *has* been *very*, *very* happy since he arrived, and Charlotte has been *very* attentive to him. Indeed we *all* make it our constant business to make him *happy*. Sir William is fonder than ever, and we manage very well in regard to our establishment, pay share and share alike, so it comes easy to booth partys. When will you come? Pray do as soon as possible.

We were all at church, and Charlotte turned over the prayers for her uncle. As to Sir William, they are the greatest friends in the world; and our next neighbour, Mr. Halfhide and his family, they wou'd give us half of all they have; very pleasant people.

And I like Mr. and Mrs. Newton also, but like Mrs. Halfhide very much indeed, and she sent Charlotte grapes, etc., etc. We *cou'd* have plenty of visiting in the neighbourhood, but we none of us like it. Sir William and Charlotte caught 3 large pike. She helps him and milord with their great *coats on*; so now I have nothing to do. Lord Nelson says he never saw such a difference, such an improvement as in Charlotte. He is quite proud of her, and as to you, he Loves you better than his own sisters. He has wrote you a few Lines, but in a day or two he will write his brother a Long Letter. Dear Horace, he shall soon come. Sir William and Milord are gone into town to do their business, and at 2 o'clock we go down to dinner to Merton. All the town of Merton was illumined for him.[1]

Before the return to Merton. Nelson had an appointment to keep at Piccadilly at one o'clock, which Lady Hamilton had arranged the previous Saturday. On that day she had written to Mrs. Gibson:

Dear Mrs. Gibson, Will you come to picadilly with Miss Thomson on Monday at one o'clock not later I hope my dear god child is well—

ever Yours

E. Hamilton,[2]

[1] BM Add. MSS 34989.   [2] NMM/NWD/9594/9.

The healthy ten-month old child presented to its god-papa—decked out in her new clothes—undoubtedly did credit to her nurse. The occasion, as Mrs. Gibson noted to her surprise, was kept as a first-birthday celebration, and was unquestionably marked by a guinea tip. Having made a very shrewd guess at the child's right age, she never 'made out', as she afterwards said, why its birthday was kept on 29 October; but so it was, and she was paid to be silent.

Nelson, who only wanted to take Horatia 'home to Merton' as soon as Lady Hamilton could be persuaded to do so, had not only her welfare to fret him at the time: he wanted to establish his old father at Merton as well. The decision on all domestic matters, as he well knew, lay with Emma, and before striking his flag on 22 October, he had written her on the subject from the Downs:

I think of writing my poor old father to this effect—that I shall live at Merton with Sir William and Lady Hamilton—that a warm room for him and a cheerful society will always be there happy to receive him—that *nothing* in *my conduct* could ever cause a separation of a moment between me and him, and that I had all the respect and love which a son could bear towards a good father ... and that I should ever conduct myself towards him as his dutiful son—Tell me, my friend, do you approve? If he remains at Burnham he will die, and I am sure he will not stay in Somerset Street [with Lady Nelson] Pray let him come to your care at Merton. Your kindness will keep him alive, for you have a kind soul. [1]

For Emma, Nelson's invitation to his father posed a challenge which she met with her usual courage. She could not doubt what were the views of a clergyman on domestic fidelity and the sacred permanence of marriage, nor on her own position as mistress of Merton; yet she would triumph over them, and turn them to her own advantage, going even so far as to convert old Mr. Nelson into her advocate and ally. Realizing how deep-rooted was Nelson's affection for his family, Emma had only one course open to her; a course quite consonant with a woman of her temperament: to make herself liked, to dispel suspicions, gain their confidence, and indeed to emerge so far removed from their original conception of her as an adventuress as to appear in their eyes as a disinterested, devoted friend to whom not only Nelson but his entire family should be and were deeply beholden. By her beauty and vivacity she would create an ambiance of gracious living around the Admiral, of cheerful lively society made equally attractive to old and young alike, so that by comparison the image of the legitimate Lady Nelson would shrink and fade. Needless to say, if Emma

[1] P. ii, 211.

were to succeed the first thing was to convince one and all of the perfect innocence of the relationship existing between herself and the Hero. In a family of such moral rectitude, reared in country simplicity and the unquestioning acceptance of an age-old religion, it was not difficult to gain credence. Nelson himself, the least hypocritical of men, lent every appearance of decency to his conduct. While Sir William lived, indeed, 'appearances', as then socially understood, were preserved. Nobody was more determined than Emma to maintain them, and it was precisely because the existence of Horatia must at all costs remain unknown to Nelson's family that their invitation inevitably meant that Horatia should be excluded from Merton. This certainly was how the argument was presented to Nelson, and he, who had arrived home determined to establish Horatia under his roof and have her christened with his name, had for the time being to accept it.

For old Mr. Nelson the situation was peculiarly distressing. He had reached the age of eighty after a life of chronic ill-health, a feeble old man no longer able to perform his duties as incumbent of Burnham Thorpe, and dependent on the services of a locum for the greater part of the year. His survival owed much to the care and kindness of his daughter-in-law, and when not staying with her, he lived in Bath to be near his favourite younger daughter, Catherine Matcham. Now the famous son who had been the source of his pride was become the cause of his secret sorrow and shame. Mr. Nelson could not countenance his son's desertion of his wife; Lady Nelson's plight demanded his chivalrous support even though his enfeebled spirits might be unequal to the task. What he most wanted was domestic peace for the short remainder of his life, but through no fault of his own he found himself at the centre of a violent family storm. 'Upon the return of peace', he wrote to his son from Burnham on 8 October 1801,

I may, with a little variation, address you in the words of an apostle and say, You have fought a good fight, you have finished your military career, with glory, and honour, henceforth, there is laid up for you, much happiness, subject indeed in this present time, to uncertainty, but in a future state, immutable and incorruptible. As a public character I could be acquainted only with what was made public respecting you. Now in a private station possibly you may tell me where it is likely your general place of residence will be, so that sometimes we may have mutual happiness in each other, notwithstanding the severe reproaches I feel from an anonymous letter for my conduct to you, which is such, it seems, as will totally separate us. This is unexpected indeed.

Most likely the winter may be too cold for me to continue here, and I mean to spend it between Bath and London. If Lady Nelson is in a hired house by herself, gratitude requires that I should sometimes be with her, if it is likely to be of any comfort to her.[1]

Nelson, who had no idea in what terms Lady Hamilton habitually spoke of his father to her confidant Mrs. William, accusing him of 'conspiring against the saviour of his country' and acting 'a bad and horrible part', had little patience with reports of anonymous letters; they were not in his line, nor in that of his family. Neither he nor his father were to be moved by underhand manoeuvres; their affection was life-long and based on mutual respect. Among the few instructions for furnishing Merton that Nelson had given to Emma was one written on 19 October:[2]

'Why not have the pictures from Davison's [his agent] and those from Dodds, especially my father's and Davison's.' The portrait of Mr. Nelson by William Beechey, had been painted during the winter of 1799–1800, as a gift for his son. Beechey, when approached by Lady Nelson respecting his fees and whether he painted his subjects at their homes, had snapped: 'Only Royalty'; but on hearing the identity of his prospective sitter, he had declared 'My God! I would go to York to do it!'[3]

For Lady Nelson, the parting of the ways with Nelson's family had been reached. She realized that to insist on her father-in-law continuing to live with her would be to cut him off from his children. After visiting him a last time at Burnham, she wrote at the end of October:

The impression your situation has left on my mind is so strong that I cannot delay any longer offering my opinion on the subject of your living with me . . . the deprivation of seeing your children is so cruel. I told Mrs. M. [Matcham] at Bath that Lord Nelson would not like your living with me. 'Oh! my dear Lady Nelson, my brother will thank you in his heart for he knows no one can attend to my father as you do.' I had seen the wonderful change pass belief. She had not.'[4]

Of all the family, Lady Nelson alone had no illusions about the nature of the relationship between her husband and Lady Hamilton. Shrink from it as they might, she saw it for what it was. 'Even supposing his lordship resided in Italy, the offence would be just the same and in my opinion greater', she declared in the same letter to her father-in-law.

To Mr. Nelson, who had once declared to his son that he wanted words to express the kindness of his daughter in-law 'as a friend, a nurse, a daughter', the alternative was exquisitely painful. 'Be assured I still hold fast my integrity,' he wrote to her on 17 October, 'and am ready to

[1] Naish, 591.   [2] P. ii, 227.
[3] Oman, 350.   [4] Naish, 593–4.

join you whenever you have your servants in the London house . . . In respect of this business, the opinion of others must rest with themselves, and not make any alteration with us.' [1]

The visit to Merton between 19 and 29 November, was an unexpected success; Nelson even urged his father to make his permanent home there. Emma's experience of country clergymen was understandably limited, but her fears of finding a foe in the Reverend gentleman were completely dispelled; she found Mr. Nelson disarmingly sweet and gentle.

On his arrival at Bath where the Matchams had found lodgings for him and his old servant, Mr. Nelson wrote his son a letter showing his judgement was not impaired. 'What you possess, my good son, take care of,' he wrote, 'what you may still want, consult your own good sense in what way it can be attained. Strive for honours and riches that will not fade, but will profit in time of need. Excuse my anxiety for what I esteem your real good.' [2]

Reunited with his favourite daughter and her children, Mr. Nelson was now Emma's best advocate with the rest of the family. He had met the syren, tasted the charms of her hospitality, and witnessed the domestic happiness of his son. Inevitably a change must affect the family's relations with Merton.

Redoubling her efforts to please one and all, Emma set about organizing Nelson's Christmas for him. In addition to Charlotte, young Horace was brought from Eton, and from Piccadilly he wrote to his mother:

My dear Mama—I came to London this morning and my uncle has given me a new pair of boots . . . Pray tell Papa that I shall be much obliged to him for Hume's History of England and I will certainly read it. We are going to Merton presently . . . You can't think how much Charlotte studies and how much she is improved. My Lady takes a great deal of pains with her and we are to dance a figure dance at Christmas. [3]

While the ladies of Nelson's family, his sisters Mrs. Bolton and Mrs. Matcham, hesitated to commit themselves by actually visiting Merton (Mrs. Matcham had the excellent and invariable excuse of being in 'the family way') they yet permitted their children to accept their uncle's invitation; the little Boltons, Eliza and Anne, aged twelve and ten at the time, who were at school at Edmonton were authorized to go, as eventually was their brother Tom. Their enthusiastic reports of Lady Hamilton's 'kindness and attention' elicited their mother's grateful, though somewhat belated thanks in May, when the inevitability of accepting Lady

[1] Ibid., 595.   [2] P. ii, 235-6.   [3] NMM/BRP/4.

Hamilton as a member of the family circle had become apparent. Here at least Nelson and Emma shared the same tastes: they both delighted in the company of children, and under their ownership Merton became the regular holiday home for the younger generation.

Before the official Christmas party, another visitor was brought to Merton for the first time. Writing to Mrs. Gibson on 14 December, Emma instructed her:

If you will take a post Chaise tomorrow *Tewsday* and set off at half past ten a clock and bring my god daughter and your little girl with you I shall be glad to see you tell them to drive you to Merton the best way you can come is over Clapham Common hire a Chaise for the day you can be back at 3 oclock do not fail, ever yours sincerely E. Hamilton.[1]

The order not to 'fail' was dictated no doubt by the convenient absence of Sir William that day, on his own 'particular business' in town. As he wrote to Charles Greville on 5 December, there was little chance of being 'much in town until after Christmas', adding however: 'I shall go to attend my particular business at the Museum or Royal Society occasionally.'

Nelson's pleasure in seeing his own daughter at Merton for the first time must have been alloyed by the shortness of the visit. It was only for the day. But otherwise his first Christmas at home was a happy one. That he made it so for others, and not only those of his house-party, the daughter of his vicar, the Revd. Thomas Lancaster, later attested: 'In revered affection for the memory of that dear man,' she wrote Sir Harris Nicolas,

I cannot refrain from informing you of his unlimited charity and goodness at Merton. His frequently expressed desire was that none in that place should want, or suffer affliction that he could alleviate; and this I know he did with a most liberal hand, always desiring that it should not be known from whence it came.'[2]

From Bath Mr. Nelson sent his son the season's greetings. 'My dear Horatio,' he wrote on 21 December, 'From an old man you will accept the old fashioned language at the approaching happy season which is, I wish you a merry Christmas and a happy new year. For multiplied favours Lady Hamilton has my respectful thanks.'[3] To Lady Hamilton herself he wrote with all the charity of his nature:

[1] NMM/NWD/9594/9.   [2] Nicolas, 228 et seq.   [3] P. ii, 236.

Even the severity of the season, which makes many a poor creature such as myself, to shake, gives much pleasure to the skating parties, so that I hope all in their turns have their hours of enjoyment at a season when all the Christian world do celebrate with songs of praise the return of Christmas. Long may you all feel the happy influence of such an event *here*, and the inestimable benefit of it hereafter.[1]

The wish, coming from such a man, and intended without a doubt as a blessing, must have seemed to Emma like the justification of all her ways. The year that had begun with such tribulation for her, was ending on something like a note of triumph.

For Sir William, however, life at Merton was not altogether coming up to expectations. He found it alarmingly expensive: 'If we had given up the house in Piccadilly', he wrote to his nephew Greville 'the living here would indeed be a great saving; but, as it is, we spend neither more nor less than we did . . . Nothing at present disturbs me but my debt,' he wrote further on 24 January 1802,

and the nonsense I am obliged to submit to here to avoid coming to an explosion, which wou'd be attended with many disagreeable effects, and would totally destroy the comfort of the best man and the best friend I have in the world. However, I am determined that my quiet shall not be disturbed, let the nonsensical world go on as it will. I have now fully opened my mind to you my dr Chs.[2]

Emma's love of ostentation and display, held in check for a time by Nelson's decided preference for the simple life, was quickly taking the upper hand at Merton. Sir William, fretting over household bills to Greville told him 'I have a bill for wine only, since we came home, of near £400'. Invitations were extended far and wide, and included hangers-on of every sort from the Naples days, and from operatic and musical circles in London, so that the guests seated round the admiral's table sometimes bore little resemblance to the society his admirers might have expected to find assembled there.

Lord Minto, the former Sir Gilbert Elliot, viceroy of Corsica since 1797, who had known Nelson in the Mediterranean since 1794, was disgusted at the whole tone of the establishment when he stayed at Merton for the week-end in March. Writing to his wife on 22 March 1802 he said:

The whole establishment and way of life is such as to make me angry, as well as melancholy; but I cannot alter it, and I do not think myself obliged or at liberty to quarrel with him for his weakness, though nothing shall ever induce me to give

[1] P. ii, 237.   [2] M.651.

the smallest countenance to Lady Hamilton. She looks ultimately to the chance of marriage, as Sir W. will not be long in her way, and she probably indulges a hope that she may survive Lady Nelson; in the meanwhile she and Sir William and the whole set of them are living with him at his expense. She is in high looks, but more immense than ever. She goes on cramming Nelson with trowelfuls of flattery, which he goes on taking as quietly as a child does pap. The love she makes to him is not only ridiculous, but disgusting; not only the rooms, but the whole house, staircase and all, are covered with nothing but pictures of her and him, of all sizes and sorts, and representations of his naval actions, coats of arms, pieces of plate in his honour, the flagstaff of 'L'Orient', etc.—an excess of vanity which counteracts its own purpose. If it was Lady H's house there might be a pretence for it; to make his own a mere looking-glass to view himself all day is bad taste. Braham, the celebrated Jew singer, performed with Lady H. She is horrid, but he entertained me in spite of her. Lord Nelson explained to me a little the sort of blame which had been imputed to Sir Hyde Parker for Copenhagen.[1]

Emma's letter of 21 March referring to the same occasion fairly confirms Lord Minto's assessment of her ambitions. Writing to Mrs. William she naturally reported those details most likely to flatter her wifely and maternal pride.

When Lord Nelson said 'I only wanted a Canonship or Deanery for my only Brother' Lord Minto answered . . . he ought not to accept that . . . ministers ought to have thrown a Bishopric at you saying give it to your Brother you are our Saviour . . . You would like him of all things . . . he doats and worships Nelson he is a great friend of ours. My head is not yet well these winds kill me but we have a deal of company to-day and a great dinner we shall be 19 at dinner. Lord Minto is charmed with Charlotte he says she will be a beautiful woman he likes her manner. Miss Furse is not grown a Bitt but she holds herself remarkably well so does Charlotte much better Miss Furse eat so much that in the evening she vomited before us all Charlotte covered her retreat and got her out she came in again & played cards I tipt them both . . . Charlotte is now practising as we do not go to church the day being bad and Lord Minto not having ordered his coach. Ten past 12 I am writing and they are talking Politics . . . the Cub is in town and has called at Tysons . . . tom tit is despised and hated and even those that pretend to protect her *fall off*. She is now *bursting* and abuses him you and us openly and all our friends. I wish she would *burst* but their is no such good luck does she ever write to the Boltons? Charlotte and Miss Furse slept in your room in Horrace's bed.[2]

The ambiance created all too soon at Merton by Emma did not, despite the enchantment, reflect Nelson's true nature; he hankered after simplicity and homeliness and wanted to be among his own people. He had a

---

[1] Minto, iii, 252.   [2] BRP/NMM/4.

strong sense of obligation towards them, for none were rich, and this made him resentful of squandering money on strangers while they might need his help. On hearing of the death of his favourite brother Maurice in April 1801, he at once settled a pension on the widow ('poor blindie', Mrs. Sarah Ford) whose illegal position did not entitle her to an official pension, and wrote immediately on landing after Copenhagen:

I beg you will stay at Laleham [Maurice's home two miles from Staines], with horse, wiskey, and keep every convenience there to make your stay comfortable, and by Michaelmas you can determine as to the mode and manner of your future residence. Nothing, be assured, shall be wanting on my part to make your life as comfortable and cheerful as possible, for believe me, with every respect and regard, your affectionate friend. I send hundred pounds which you will accept from me.[1]

He made provision also for his brother's old black servant: 'there is an old black servant, James Price,' he wrote to Emma from the Baltic, with instructions to do everything 'to comfort poor blind Mrs. Nelson', who 'is as good a man as ever lived, he shall be taken care of and have a corner in my house as long as he lives'.[2]

It is untrue, as has often been said, that Nelson's relatives were self-interested in their conduct towards him: though the Boltons, who depended on farming for a livelihood were admittedly never prosperous, the Matchams had an assured income of £3,000 a year, and led the life of country gentlefolk. Both sisters genuinely loved Nelson, for his intrinsic qualities and not for his position; as to his ascetic old father, his only comment on hearing of the title conferred on his son after the victory of Copenhagen was that 'he liked him as well *plain Horace* as with all these high-sounding titles'.[3]

This was not the case, however, with Nelson's brother, the Revd. William, who did not suffer the same qualms of modesty when soliciting his brother's patronage. Success was in his eyes a family affair, the fruits of it to be shared by all. As incumbent of Hilborough he did not consider his position worthy of the brother of a viscount, and plainly told him so. He coveted a deanery, or at least a prebendal stall. Meagrely and slowly small crumbs of advancement came his way; in the previous October his old university, Cambridge, conferred a doctorate of divinity on him. 'What can Reverend Sir want to be made a Doctor for?' Nelson irreverently asked Emma (his brother's warmest advocate). 'He will be laughed

---

[1] M.605.   [2] M.589.   [3] BM Add. MSS 34989.

at for his pains.'[1] However, knowing his brother's susceptibilities he submitted to the conduct required of him, though not without humour. 'His
being a Doctor is nonsense; but I must write to-morrow and congratulate
him, or else the fat will be in the fire.'[2] Reverend Doctor took his new
honours most seriously, and even took Lady Hamilton—his best ally—to
task for not addressing him correctly as Revd. Dr. 'He is as big as if he
was a bishop,' Nelson commented on hearing the report. To satisfy his
brother's extraordinary expectations, Nelson had the patent of Viscountcy so worded as to extend the title of the original Barony—Baron
Nelson of the Nile—to 'Viscount Nelson of the Nile and of Hilborough in
Norfolk'.

'I hope Revd. Sir will be satisfied with the new patent,' Nelson had
written Emma on 7 August, 'as it is taken from Hilborough on purpose to
please him, and if I leave none, he must breed stock from his own place.'[3]
In the event the Revd. Doctor was not satisfied; though the title
passed to him and his heirs male on his brother's death, after them it
passed to the heirs male of Nelson's two sisters. He eagerly took up Lady
Hamilton's regrets that the title had not been extended to Charlotte's
heirs male rather than to the Boltons and Matchams as specified by
Nelson.

In the days of Horatia's infancy Lady Hamilton and the 'Revd. Dr.'
were very close allies, and this has some bearing on Emma's future and
that of Horatia, when her expectations of gratitude from the William
Nelsons for services rendered were so signally disappointed.

As the spring of 1802 advanced, Nelson renewed his invitation to his
father to make his home at Merton. On 23 March 1802 Mr. Nelson
answered him:

My dear Hor,—Your 2 last kind letters I esteem as fresh marks of your affectionate attention. When the expected stranger is arrived at Kensington Place [Mrs.
Matcham's baby] and I can see your sister in a way of recovering, I shall then
begin to think of leaving Bath. When I am deprived of Kitty's daily visits to
dine with me, my comforts here will be much curtailed. My strength returns
very slow, yet still have hopes I shall with the assistance of the May sunshine
get able to travel, and smell a Merton rose in June.[4]

On 20 April Mr. Nelson wrote to Lady Nelson to announce the baby's
arrival: 'My good Madam,—I am truly glad to have it in my power to
acquaint you that my dear daughter was yesterday safely delivered of a

[1] Ibid.   [2] Ibid.
[3] P. ii, 144.   [4] Naish, 597.

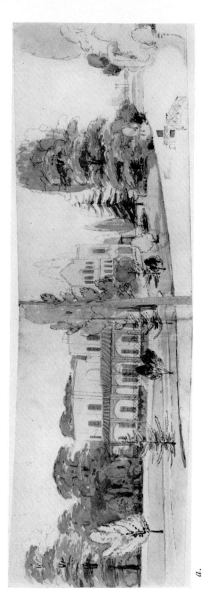

a.

b.

MERTON PLACE, SURREY. Water colour sketches by Thomas Baxter, 1802. Front and side views

girl [Susanna Matcham born 19 April 1802], both in a prosperous way.'[1] The pleasure, the small effort required to communicate the news, were apparently too much for the strength that was so slow to return; for Mr. Nelson there were to be no roses at Merton that June. On 24 April George Matcham sent a hurried note to Nelson to tell him that his father was fatally ill, and on the 26th he died.

It was Emma's birthday. To the surprise of the Matchams and the annoyance of the 'Revd. Dr.', Nelson made no attempt to go to Bath; he acted out of character so far as to plead ill-health, though he was indeed suffering from chronic dysentery and there was even a question of an operation. But there were other reasons. Accustomed to scenes of carnage as he was, he had a strange horror of witnessing a death-bed. When Parker had died the previous September, after visiting him twice a day for a month for as long as there was hope, he shirked the final scene, using almost the same words he now used about his father: 'unless he expresses a desire to see me'; he wrote George Matcham by return, 'unwell as I am, I should have flown to Bath, but I believe it would be too late; however, should it be otherwise, and he wishes to see me, no consideration shall detain me for a moment'.[2] The 'consideration' which effectually detained him was the fact of its being Emma's birthday, which they were accustomed to celebrate in an almost theatrical fashion. The total unexpectedness of Mr. Nelson's illness and death had allowed a domestic festivity to be planned for that day, the christening at Merton Church of Emma's black maid, Fatima, brought for her by Nelson from Egypt after the Nile. Under the sponsorship of Lady Hamilton and Nelson, and with the whole party from Merton Place driving to church in three carriages, she was given the names 'Fatima, Emma Charlotte Nelson Hamilton', the fact being entered in the register for baptisms for 26 April 1802 with the comment: 'from Egypt, a Negress, about 20 years of age, under the protection of the Right Honourable Lady Hamilton.'[3] The occasion was too attractive for Emma to forgo; she was to appear as benefactress and missionary, but without Nelson's presence the ceremony would lose its lustre. Emma had her way, and Nelson did not go to Bath.

The death of Mr. Nelson provided Emma with the occasion for a frontal attack on the remaining members of the family, whose connections with Lady Nelson had hitherto ranged them on the side of her enemy. Writing letters of condolence all round, she now established direct contacts first with Mrs. Bolton and then with Mrs. Matcham, inviting both very

---

[1] Ibid., 598.   [2] Eyre-Matcham, 194.   [3] Registers of Merton Church.

cordially to Merton. The disarming gesture, and the fondness of the sisters for Nelson, made acceptance a foregone conclusion; but it was not without some awkwardness that Mrs. Bolton acquainted Lady Nelson with the fact.

'I am going to Merton in about a fortnight,' she told her on 15 May, 'but my dear Lady N. we cannot meet as I wished, for every body is known who visits you. Indeed I do not think I shall be permitted even to go to town.' [1] Though she signed herself as having always been and 'shall always be your sincere friend', the connection was brought virtually to an end. Lady Nelson preferred to efface herself, and the Boltons were inevitably drawn in to the Merton sphere of influence. Nelson's affection was not only for his sister Susanna, but also for his brother-in-law Bolton with whom he had always had cordial relations ever since his Norfolk days. As an aspirant farmer Nelson had now more in common with his brother-in-law than ever, seeking his advice on livestock and crops.

Mrs. Bolton made her first visit to Merton in June 1802, and was accompanied for part of the time by her sister Mrs. Matcham. It was not an easy gesture to make, acknowledging Lady Hamilton as their brother's hostess; but the happiness of the occasion is sufficiently vouched for by two letters of Nelson's at the visit's end. To Mr. Bolton, who had not been able to accompany his wife at haymaking, he wrote:

Merton June 10th 1802

My dear Bolton,

These rains may give me a little hay. I shall not allow it being cut too soon, nor in too great a hurry to sell, but I mean to sell it in the cock or standing— this weather suits Cranwich [the Boltons' home in Norfolk] it will give you good turnips and I am farmer enough to know that gives everything. We only regret that we have not the means of doing all the kindness for my Sister which my heart wishes. Mrs. M. [Matcham] goes off Saturday, Mrs. B [Bolton] on Monday when we shall be quite alone. Lady Hamilton desires her kind regards. [2]

The satisfaction of Lady Hamilton was conveyed in a postscript written by herself at the foot of Nelson's letter: 'I am glad my dear Sir you have got the wine. Mrs. Bolton has made me very happy by her company and we are truly sorry to lose her we had yesterday a magnificent fête at Mr. Goldsmids in haste yours sincerely E. H.' (The lavish entertainments given by Nelson's neighbours, the Goldsmids of Morden Hall, were frequently mentioned in Emma's letters; in due course she would be beholden to them almost for the necessities of life.)

¹ Naish, 599–600.   ² GIR/1/9590/NMM.

To Mrs. Bolton on leaving Merton on 11 June, Nelson wrote a characteristic note:

My dear Sister, here is £100 which I shall pay you on the 11th June for three years towards the education of your children by that time other things may turn up, and there is a trifle in case you may [want] any little things going through London. All I desire is that you would not say or write me a syllable on the subject for I am sorry I cannot do more being truly your most affectionate Brother.[1]

Thus began the first of those family visits to Merton which eventually brought Horatia within the circle of her relatives' influence and affection; it was from them, by a reversal of all foreseeable circumstances at the time, that her future happiness derived.

The Boltons had a family of four girls and a boy in 1802, the eldest being twin sisters, Susanna and Kate (born at Wells on 20 November 1781), marriageable young ladies of twenty. Their little sisters, Eliza and Anne respectively twelve and ten years old (who had spent the previous Christmas at Merton) were only just gone to boarding school at Edmonton; Tom, the future 2nd Earl Nelson, born 7 July, 1786, was at Norwich Grammar school; he went in due course, thanks to his uncle's financial help, to Cambridge.

Mrs. Bolton (Susanna Nelson born 12 June 1755) was three years older than her famous brother. Her father, who had kept a detailed 'Family History',[2] noted of her that he had given her a good education but that he 'could not give her a fortune equal to independence', and therefore apprenticed her at eighteen to 'Messrs Walters reputable milliners at Bath', where at the end of her term she went as assistant into a shop. Two legacies, one from her rich uncle Maurice Suckling, brought her £2,000; with part of which she appears to have allowed herself a season at Wells (Norfolk) like other young ladies of the time in pursuit of husbands. There she met, and married in 1780, Thomas Bolton, member of a Suffolk family from Woodbridge which had been granted a patent of Arms in 1615.

He was the second son of Samuel Bolton of Coddenham, Suffolk, and was born there on 11 December 1752. He had two brothers, the elder, Samuel, settling nearby at Akenham, and the younger, William, born in 1754, who took Holy Orders and eventually migrated to Norfolk with Thomas; they remained closely linked with his family fortunes, and with those of his children.

[1] Ibid.   [2] NMM/NWD/9594.

Thomas was 'in a prosperous line of business in the corn, malt and coal trade' at Wells, when Susanna Nelson married him.

Nelson's readiness to serve his family did not always have happy results. In 1799 the Bolton's eldest boy George, aged twelve, was sent out to the Mediterranean to join his uncle's command as a midshipman, but was at once stricken with 'the flux' and after an illness of thirteen days died on board *The Bulldog* in the passage from Gibraltar to Minorca. Sailing under Sir Edward Berry, one of Nelson's 'Band of Brothers', no auspices could have been happier than his. Lady Berry, writing to console Mrs. Bolton, assured her that 'everything was done that was possible. He was loved and regretted by all.' [1] The grief that Mrs. Bolton carried with her for the rest of her life, decided the family to leave Norwich, and the same year they settled at Cranwich, five miles from Hilborough. There they stayed until 1811. It was considered a large farm when they bought it at the height of the war when food was scarce, but, as Lady Nelson told her husband at the time, with a rare touch of humour, the purchase was considered 'a glaring impropriety by the Revd. Dr. who considered his pride wounded at the situation of the Boltons'. [2]

From Mr. Bolton's land regular tributes of game and poultry found their way by carrier to Merton. Mr. Bolton it was who chose and sent by road the first cows for Nelson's 'farm'. On 30 December 1802 he wrote:

I have sent you by Josiah Griggs two cows which I hope you will approve. They will be at the 'Pied Bull' at Islington on Sunday next at 10 o'clock. You'll be so good as to order some body there to take care of them . . . I hope Lady Hamilton will like the cow, its an extravagant price, I am well assured she is a good one. [3]

The extravagant price, according to whether the cow's calf which accompanied it was ten days or six weeks old, was £16 or £10, and the charge for driving them to Islington was one guinea.

With Mrs. Matcham, who had made a brief appearance at Merton in June, Emma was able to establish closer contacts in the course of a tour undertaken in July by Sir William, with Nelson and herself, to visit his Milford Haven estate in Wales. They set out from Merton on 21 July in the company of the Revd. Dr. and Mrs. Nelson, Charlotte and Horace, and stopped at Oxford overnight, where Nelson had arranged for Mr. and Mrs. Matcham and their son George, then aged twelve, to join them. Instructing his brother-in-law with almost naval brevity to arrange

[1] GIR/1/NMM/9590.   [2] Naish, 529.   [3] GIR/1/NMM/9590.

accommodation for them, Nelson had written Mr. Matcham in advance: 'The Star Inn, Oxford, Wednesday the 21st July. Dinner for 8. Be so good as to order it. Need not say for who' [1]—a precaution to avoid publicity which was hardly necessary as Nelson was to be given an official reception by the city and have an honorary degree conferred on him the next day.

There had always existed a close affection between Nelson and his sister Catherine (Kitty); and family portraits show that there was a strong physical likeness. The youngest of the family, born 19 March 1767, she was nine and a half years younger than her brother (twelve years younger than their sister Mrs. Bolton) and Nelson always had a strong protective feeling for her. Her mother had died when Kitty was only nine months old, and her father's feeble health whilst she was yet in her teens often threatened to deprive her of both parents and a home. It was Nelson, as yet unmarried, who undertook to provide for her. Writing from overseas to his brother William he said: 'My small income shall always be at her service, and she shall never want a protector and a sincere friend while I exist.' [2] She was, he wrote in a further letter of the time, 'a charming young woman, and possesses a great share of sense'. The charm, happily for Kitty, worked on others besides her brother, and during one short season with cousins at Bath in the winter of 1786–87 she met and became engaged to George Matcham within the space of two months. George, after a spell in India, had settled finally in England, although a love of travel, even of exploration, left him always with a longing for wider horizons.

The Hamiltons' tour of Wales lasted six weeks. During their absence, work on the house and grounds at Merton planned by Nelson to improve the property was begun; he never lived to see it completed. To the lasting misfortune of Horatia and of Lady Hamilton the improvements which began on a modest scale captured her imagination and exhausted her resources in the years to come, and were in due course the chief factor in her eventual ruin.

'We are so busy getting our house in order,' she wrote Mrs. Matcham on 13 September, 'that I have not had time to write . . .'.[3] So busy had she been that some days had also elapsed before Mrs. Gibson was summoned to Piccadilly with Horatia, to receive Lord Nelson's instructions to take the child to the seaside. Her instructions were unequivocal; she was not to take any risks: 'Mrs. Gibson may go to Margate or Ramsgate with

[1] Eyre-Matcham, 201.
[2] Ibid., 25.
[3] Ibid., 202.

Miss Thompson,' she was told, 'but not to go with the Hoy as it is danger-ous and to let Lord N. know were they are and how Miss Thompson is in her health and spirits if Bathing is necessary to let her Bathe.'[1]

Horatia so far resembled her mother as to respond satisfactorily to sea bathing. All her life Emma suffered from skin infections which were treated successfully by sea baths, and from certain letters exchanged between Sir William and herself at this time it would seem that she made the necessity of sea-baths for herself the excuse for going to Ramsgate now with Lord Nelson to be near Horatia. No summer passed without her going for some time to the sea. Sir William, only just returned from the fatiguing tour of Wales, and anxious for a few quiet days fishing on the Thames, was apparently provoked into a rare expression of discontent, to which Emma, with fine dramatic emphasis replied:

As I see it is a pain to you to remain here, let me beg you to fix your time for going. Weather I dye in Picadilly or any other spot in England, 'tis the same to me; but I remember the time when you wish'd for tranquility, but now all visit-ing and bustle is your liking. However I will do what you please, being your affectionate and obedient.[2]

The habit of exchanging notes on debatable questions was an old one in the Hamilton household, and Sir William replied on the back:

I neither love bustle nor great company, but I like some employment and diversion. I have but a very short time to live, and every moment is precious to me. I am in no hurry, and am exceedingly glad to give every satisfaction to our best friend, our dear Lord Nelson. The question, then, is what we can best do that all may be perfectly satisfied. Sea bathing is usefull to your health; I see it is, and wish you to continue it a little longer; but I must confess that I regret, whilst the season is favourable that I cannot enjoy my favourite amusement of quiet fishing. I care not a pin for the great world, and am attached to no one so much as you.[3]

'I go when you tell me the coach is ready,' Emma wrote him back; to which Sir William yet again replied: 'This is not a fair answer to a fair confession of mine.'

Sir William's impatience to be gone was not Emma's only problem during the stay at Ramsgate. Having received Mrs. Gibson's 'direction' at Margate, she lost it, and in some agitation, occasioned no doubt by Lord Nelson's queries, hurried there in search of the nurse and child. 'I was yesterday at Margate,' she wrote Mrs. Gibson, 'and had lost your

---

[1] NMM/NWD/9594/1.   [2] M.679.   [3] M.680.

direction and sent the servant all over the town to Church Square or Church Place but could not hear from you write me a note directly and send me your proper Direction my love to H. and believe me ever yours E. H.'[1] Having re-established contacts and visited her godchild, Emma wrote again: 'Dear Mrs. Gibson, I am glad to find you and Miss Thompson well let me know how you all go on and believe it is a real pleasure to find you are so comfortable believe me ever your sincere friend E.H.'[2]

By 29 September Mrs. Gibson and her charge were returned to London and Lady Hamilton was appraised of the fact. 'This with my duty to you,' Mrs. Gibson wrote, 'to inform you of our safe arrival on Wednesday night, Miss Thomson is verry well and Self—from Your Hum^b Ser^t M. Gibson.'[3]

For poor Sir William who so acutely felt the passage of time, the sense of valediction in all about him acted rather as a spur to last-minute activity. The uncharacteristic outbursts of irritability that marked his decline are evidence of the growing frustration that not only his age and infirmities caused him, but also of his awareness of the domestic situation at Merton. The philosophic cast of mind that had once earned him the affectionate nickname of 'Pliny the Elder' was no longer proof against the encroachments of age, loss of fortune, and a harassing wife. In a further letter of complaints, he once more made his unhappy position clear to Emma.

. . . I am arrived at the age when some repose is really necessary, & I promised myself a quiet home, & altho' I was sensible, & said so when I married, that I shou'd be superannuated when my wife wou'd be in her full beauty and vigour of youth. That time is arrived, and we must make the best of it for the comfort of both parties. Unfortunately our tastes as to the manner of living are very different. I by no means wish to live in solitary retreat, but to have seldom less than 12 or 14 at table, & those varying continually, is coming back to what was become so irksome to me in Italy during the latter years of my residence in that country. I have no connections out of my own family. I have no complaint to make, but I feel that the whole attention of my wife is given to Ld.N. and his interest at Merton. I well know the purity of Ld N's friendship for Emma and me, and I know how very uncomfortable it would make his Lp, our best friend, if a separation shou'd take place, & am therefore determined to do all in my power to prevent such an extremity, which wou'd be *essentially detrimental* to all parties, but would be more sensibly felt by our dear friend than by us. I cannot expect to live many years, every moment to me is precious, & I hope I may be allowed sometimes to be my own master, & pass my time according to my own

[1] NMM/NWD/9594/9.　　[2] Ibid.　　[3] Ibid.

inclination, either by going my fishing parties on the Thames or by going to London to attend the Museum, R. Society, the Tuesday Club, & Auctions of pictures. I mean to have a light chariot or post chaise by the month, etc. . . . This is my plan, & we might go on very well, but I am fully determined not to have more of the very silly altercations that happen but too often between us and embitter the present moments exceedingly. If really one cannot live comfortably together, a *wise* and well *concerted separation* is preferable. I have fairly stated what I have on my mind. There is no time for nonsense or trifling. I know & admire your talents & many excellent qualities, but I am not blind to your defects, & confess having many myself; therefore let us bear and forbear, for God's sake. [1]

Sir William's conditions for continuing the status quo meant inevitably that he was more often away from home. This may well have been the reason why, at this precise moment, Charlotte Nelson was brought to Merton to stay permanently. The overt reason was the advantage she would get from Lady Hamilton's instructions in music and foreign languages; the unspecified reason was the value her mere presence— barely turned fifteen as she was—would have in silencing the censure of society, only too ready to comment upon the peculiarities of Lord Nelson's ménage. Charlotte's presence at Merton was made widely known by Emma; her kindness in giving a social polish to the school-girl education received at Whitelands was duly appreciated by the loyal friends of Nelson; Captain Ball, appointed Governor of Malta, wrote to Lady Hamilton: 'Miss Charlotte Nelson, I dare say, is fully sensible of the great and rare advantages she has in the tuition of so accomplished a patroness . . .', and humble Thomas Bowen,[2] who had had no schooling after the age of eleven and marvelled at Lady Hamilton's accomplishments wrote to her on 22 October: 'Miss Nelson is truly fortunate; she is a good girl, and have not a doubt but what she is sensible and will be more so every day of her good fortune, in having so good an instructress.' Charlotte's own mother, self-effacing where her children were concerned, could but comply and tell her daughter to be 'a comfort to all your Friends and to those that take pains to instruct you—I am sure you will ever love and be grateful too—Although you are a fine girl, without accomplishments, you would be nothing.'[3]

Christmas brought a houseful of visitors to Merton. Horace came from Eton and Tom Bolton accompanied his sisters Eliza and Anne upon their second Christmas visit there. 'Our house is tolerably filled,' Nelson wrote Mrs. Matcham in evident satisfaction; 'Tom is still little Tom

[1] M.684. [2] M.689. [3] NMM/BRP/1.

but seems a meek; well disposed lad.' 'Here we are as happy as Kings,' Emma wrote in postscript to Nelson's letter; 'and much more so. We have 3 Boltons, 2 Nelsons and only want 2 or 3 Little Matchams to be quite en famille, happy and comfortable, for the greatest of all joys to our most Excellent Nelson is when he has his Sisters or their Children with him; for sure no brother was ever so much attached as he is.' [1] It was barely a year since she had written to Mrs. William Nelson: '. . . as to you, he Loves you better than his own sisters.' But in the interval the unhoped-for conquest of Nelson's sisters had been achieved.

The New Year was brought in with a children's ball at Merton. Writing to Mr. Matcham on 4 January, Nelson told him: 'Lady Hamilton gave a little Ball last night to the children; they danced till 3 this morning and are not yet up . . .'; and from Lady Hamilton herself further echoes of the festive occasion reached Bath in a postscript to his letter: 'We have had a delightfull Ball. Charlott outdid herself. Like an angel she *was that* night. The little Boltons were Charmed. Tom Bolton is a good boy & is well behaved & we like him much. Sir W. is better & gets his appetite. We are all very comfortable and happy.' [2]

Sir William's 'improvement' was understandably not sustained. Almost on the eve of Christmas he received a further shock to trouble the domestic truce recently entered into with his wife: Emma left open for him to see a statement from her bank—Coutt's Bank of Piccadilly—dated 21 December, which begged to inform her Ladyship 'that the present balance of your money in our hands is twelve shillings & eleven pence'—a discovery which necessarily invited enquiry on Sir William's part, from which he learnt that his wife was in debt to the sum of £700. Dying before his financial position was re-established, he did the best he could by his wife in adding a last-minute proviso to his Will by which his executors were empowered to discharge Emma's debts. By doing so, he reckoned on leaving her in an unencumbered position and in possession of an annuity of £800.

In February 1803 the whole household at Merton was ill, Nelson suffering so greatly from eye-strain in his one good eye that he either employed Lady Hamilton or her Italian factotem, Oliver, to write his letters. To his family the possibility of renewed hostilities with the end of the Peace of Amiens brought special fears. 'What is the rumour of war that our papers are full of?' Mrs. Bolton enquired of Emma in February. 'I hope the storm will blow over. God forbid my Lord should be called for again', adding the hope in the same letter that 'Sir William is daily

[1] Eyre-Matcham, 204.   [2] Ibid., 206.

getting strength'.[1] During a debate in the Lords upon defence on 9 March, Nelson though taking no part himself, scribbled a hurried note to Addington, the Prime Minister, which simply said: 'Whenever it is necessary, I am your Admiral.'

By 21 March the inevitability of renewed hostilities was recognized in the country. From Norfolk Mrs. Bolton wrote to Emma: 'I am afraid all hopes of keeping my dear brother with us is now over . . . God preserve and restore him again to us in safety, then what a happy party we shall all meet at Merton, may it be soon is my prayer.' Realizing that for one inmate of Merton such a reunion was unlikely, Mrs. Bolton added: 'I find by a letter from Capt. Bolton Sir William has taken a medicine which has made him better; this mild weather must be greatly in his favour. I sincerely hope he will be restored to you.'[2]

At no time, either then or later, was the sincerity of such a wish, addressed to Sir William's wife, called in doubt by members of the Nelson–Hamilton circle. The event, so realistically discussed in the 'Thomson letters' of two years before, where the death of Mrs. Thomson's 'Uncle' was not only anticipated but desired, was now at hand, and found the principal actors in the drama strangely moved. Sir William's death which liberated Emma, found her lover not only still a married man but bound by stronger ties to a higher duty than his love—the duty towards his country which called him away from England at the very time when the first step towards his union with Emma could have been made.

Sir William, in a last diplomatic gesture of propriety, left Merton at the end of March to die in his own house. During six nights and days Nelson shared Emma's vigil at her husband's bedside; he was there when Sir William died on the morning of 6 April. It would be to misunderstand Nelson's spontaneous and emotional nature to doubt his sincerity when writing to his sister two days later: 'Lady Hamilton suffers very much.' For Lady Hamilton the loss of such a husband could not be measured at once. The mixture of cynicism and tolerance which he had brought to their union—accepting the claims of her youth and beauty upon his age—were rare indeed. Without choosing to appear complacent, Sir William was forbearing, and carried his sense of style and good taste in living to the ultimate limit. He did not see what he did not wish to see. The wording of the Codicil to his Will by which he bequeathed Emma's portrait by Vigée Le Brun to Nelson, remains a masterpiece of eighteenth-century wit:

[1] M.700.   [2] M.706.

"The copy of Madam le Brun's picture of Emma, in enamel, by Bone, I give to my dearest friend, Lord Nelson, Duke of Bronté; a very small token of the great regard I have for his Lordship, the most virtuous, loyal and truly brave character I ever met with. God bless him, and shame fall on those who do not say 'Amen'.[1]

No evidence except one cryptic statement of Nelson's in a letter of 13 August 1804[2] remains to show that Sir William ever knew of Horatia's existence, though the circumstances of her birth at 23 Piccadilly make it highly probable. In any event he showed absolute discretion in the matter.

Both at Merton and over the door of 23 Piccadilly, the hatchment bearing the Hamilton coat of arms was displayed, signifying to the world that had known him that Sir William Hamilton had now passed from its midst. 'All London is interested in the fate of such a character',[3] Nelson wrote Mrs. Bolton during the last days, in words that pay tribute to the essential originality of his friend. Pending the departure of the funeral cortège from Piccadilly for the Pembrokeshire mausoleum where Sir William had asked to be buried with his first wife, Mrs. Gibson received written instructions from Emma to the effect that 'Horatia nor any body can go out till after the funeral as we are very close and sincere mourners.'[4] The note contained a money enclosure which Mrs. Gibson was begged to accept and believe that 'you will ever find a sincere friend in your affectionate E. H.'

The proprieties were observed on every count: Nelson moved out from his late friend's house and took lodgings a few doors away at No. 19 Piccadilly; Mrs. William Nelson was convened from Canterbury to chaperone the widow.

[1] Oman, 449.   [2] See below: M.779, N.'s letter of 13 Aug. 1804.
[3] Naish, 603.   [4] NMM/NWD/9594/9.

CHAPTER V

'WIDOW DIDO'—

FOR the widow of Sir William Hamilton the weeks immediately following his death were fraught with nothing but problems and vexations which Nelson's imminent return to active service left her to face alone. The house in Piccadilly, belonging to the Hamilton estate, had to be vacated (Greville gave her until the end of the month) and though the furniture and appointments were hers, estimated to be worth £5,000, her circumstances were greatly reduced. Sir William left her a life-annuity of £800, an immediate legacy of £800, and the payment of her outstanding debts. As a first gesture of economy she ordered mourning for her household and herself for the sum of £185, and jewellery for £167 11s. 7d.—which had, in due course, to be paid by the executors of Sir William's will. She addressed a memorial to the Prime Minister, the first of many, setting out her husband's claim on Treasury for losses incurred in the government service, and set out her *own* claims to a pension for 'services rendered' to the state. With the passing of the years these claims were magnified in proportion as they were ignored. That she had by her own exertions and influence on the Queen of Naples 'got the fleet into Sicily . . . on which depended the refitting of the fleet . . . and with that, all which followed so gloriously at the Nile', became the leitmotif of all her subsequent appeals. Neither now nor later were her claims regarded with any benevolence by the governments in office, despite the support of a few loyal friends. Nelson, who gave her £100 a month for the upkeep of Merton, and an annuity of £500 on his Bronté estates, urged her not to look to government for help. 'If Addington gives you a pension it is well; but do not let it fret you. Have you not Merton? . . . and I hope one of these days you will be my own Duchess of Bronté, and then, a fig for them all.' (19 October 1803). But Nelson never knew the truth about her financial position. And Emma would not accept the economies he urged upon her: his ardent wish was that she should make Merton her permanent home and Horatia's during his absence, but she preferred to take a house in Clarges Street, Piccadilly (No. 11), which only plunged her further into debt.

Sir William's death, so impatiently awaited the previous year, left her not better, but worse off than before; his 'protection' was gone, and in Nelson's absence she was without guidance. Gillray's cruel cartoon of an earlier season—'Dido in despair'—was not far from telling the actual truth: the sleeping figure in the alcove of the complacent husband was now a corpse: her Aeneas had sailed, and she was once again a mountain of fat, expecting Nelson's second child. Madame Vigée Le Brun, who had painted Emma in Naples in 1790, and was now an emigrée in London, recorded seeing her during the first weeks of her widowhood:

I left a card on her and she soon came to see me, wearing deep mourning, with a dense black veil surrounding her, and she had had her splendid hair cut off to follow the new 'Titus' fashion. I found this Andromache enormous, for she had become terribly fat. She said that she was very much to be pitied, that in her husband she had lost a friend and father, and that she would never be consoled. I confess that her grief made little impression on me, since it seemed to me that she was playing a part. I was evidently not mistaken, because a few minutes later, having noticed some music lying on my piano, she took up a lively tune and began to sing it.[1]

In her search after the correct 'Attitude' to adopt in her present circumstances, Emma appears to have wavered between Terpsichore and Melpomene. Within six weeks of Sir William's death she was indeed sufficiently recovered to give a family party in her new Clarges Street home for the wedding reception of Nelson's eldest niece, Kitty Bolton, to her first cousin, Captain William Bolton R.N.—son of the Revd. William Bolton, Rector of Brancaster. It was 18 May 1803; war had been declared that morning on France, and Nelson had to drive away at 4 a.m. The Bolton family had come up from Norfolk in strength; Dr. and Mrs. Nelson were there with Charlotte and Horace; only the Matchams were missing. Poor Mrs. Matcham with a family of eight children had written to say she had no hope of coming as 'George is now ill with the measles and I expect to have all the children with the same disorder'.[2]

The occasion which was to have marked a double family festivity was sadly marred by Nelson's absence. On the very next day, at an investiture of the Knights of the Bath at Westminster Abbey, he was to have been invested with the insignia of his order, and had chosen two of his nephews to be his esquires: Tom Bolton and Horace Nelson.

In his absence, Captain William Bolton was accepted to stand in as his proxy, and since a knighthood was required for such a role, he was then

[1] Le Brun Memoirs [trans. Lionel Strachey].
[2] NMM/NWD/9594/1.

and there given one. Thus, thanks to their famous uncle, the young couple, married from Lady Hamilton's, began life with a title. 'You will say all that is proper from me to the Young Bride, My dear Sister and Sir William Bolton,' Nelson instructed Emma from Portsmouth the next day; 'who, I hope will make her a good Husband.'[1] Born in 1777, William Bolton had sailed with Nelson on the *Agamemnon* in 1793 as a midshipman, and was due to join him again shortly with the Mediterranean fleet. To Emma was given the credit by the bride's mother for having 'made the match'; when their first child, a little girl, was born in March 1804, Emma and Nelson stood sponsors, giving her the names Emma Horatia.

In his own hurried departure, the only one of Nelson's plans for Horatia that he was able to carry out was to have her christened. Even so, it was not as he intended, at his own church at Merton, but furtively at St. Marylebone's (in which parish Mrs. Gibson lived), and the ceremony was attended only by Mrs. Gibson. The fact is recorded in the old parish registers which show that she was one of eight children baptized that day —Friday 13 May 1803. St. Marylebone, reputed to be 'the smallest place of worship attached to the church of England in the Metropolis', had also the largest parish in London, consisting at the time of 70,000 souls, a circumstance that necessitated baptisms and burials alike being conducted en masse. Sometimes as many as eight coffins were piled up 'in the most indecent manner on the pews' awaiting burial.[2] The church had no font, so that the infants brought for baptism received the sign of the cross from a basin of water placed on the communion table for the occasion. It has been said that Lord Nelson and Lady Hamilton were present at Horatia's christening, but the evidence points to the contrary: Lady Hamilton gave Mrs. Gibson written instructions 'to give the Clergyman a double fee, and the same to the Clark the Register of the Baptism to be taken out'. In obedience to which, Mrs. Gibson brought away a copy of the entry.[3] This read:—

Parish of St. Marylebone in the County of Middlesex
Baptisms 1803
May 13   HORATIA NELSON THOMPSON   B 29 Octr 1800
The above is a true copy of the Entry in the Register of Baptisms in the Parish of St. Marylebone—as witness my hand, etc, etc.

In striking contrast to the seven other infants baptized the same day, all born within the last weeks, or months, Horatia Nelson Thompson,

[1] Eyre-Matcham, 208.   [2] *Gentleman's Magazine*, July 1807.
[3] NMM/NWD/9594/9.

who was two and a half years old, was the only one to have no parent mentioned.

In his first letter from Portsmouth, Nelson charged Emma: 'When you see my elève which you will when you receive this letter, give her a kiss from me, and tell her that I never shall forget either her or her dear good mother, and do you believe me.' [1] After eighteen months at Merton, the sense of separation was too bitter to be easily borne. 'What a change,' he wrote, 'it will not bear thinking of, except in the sweet hope of again returning to the society of those we so sincerely love.' Sailing from Portsmouth two days later the pain of parting drew from him the cry:

the being afloat makes me now feel that we do not tread the same element. I feel from my soul that God is good, and in His due wisdom will unite us, only when you look upon our dear child call to your remembrance all you think that I would say was I present, and be assured that I am thinking of you every moment. My heart is full to bursting! [2]

From off Ushant on 22 May he wrote again of his intense homesickness:

I look at your and my God Child's picture; but, till I am sure of remaining here [i.e. in that ship] I cannot bring myself to hang them up. Be assured that my attachment and affectionate regard, is unalterable; nothing can shake it. And pray say so to my dear Mrs. T. when you see her. Tell her, that my love is unbounded, to her and her dear sweet child; and if she should have more it will extend to all of them' [3] . . .

The message shows he already knew Emma was expecting another child.

A week later he was 'in the middle of the Bay of Biscay', 'with a foul wind' and 'not a vessel to be seen on the face of the waters'. The isolation made his few mementos the more precious: 'Your dear picture and Horatia's are hung up,' he wrote Emma, 'it revives me even to look upon them.' [4]

Madame Le Brun's observant eye had noted, among other things, that at a reception of the French emigré princes, to which Lady Hamilton was invited to give a performance of her 'Attitudes', she was drinking vast quantities of porter. Emma herself always explained her addiction to porter on the score of her voice; the reason, as Nelson's letter betrayed, was that she was pregnant again, and expecting a child at the year's end. Though Nelson believed the war would soon be over and he would be back in time to 'support' Lady Hamilton, her situation was really worse

[1] P. ii, 299. [2] M.713.
[3] 1814 ed. *The Letters of Lord Nelson and Lady Hamilton*.
[4] P. ii, 302.

than it was before Horatia's birth; she had now no husband to countenance her and her lover was at sea. It is not surprising that her spirits sank on more than one occasion and that her courage was not always equal to facing the ordeal alone. She twice acted so far out of character as to urge Nelson to let her join him in the Mediterranean, even suggesting bringing Charlotte and Horatia with her—an irrational impulse that he obviously could not indulge.[1]

He urged her to accept an invitation from Mrs. Bolton to visit the family at Cranwich, which he usually referred to as Hilborough, which was close by. On 10 June writing 'twenty leagues east of Algiers' he said 'This letter will probably find you returning from Hilborough, where my fancy tells me you are thinking of setting out, for it will amuse you by change of scene.'[2] On 12 July he wrote again: 'I long to hear of your Norfolk excursion, and everything you have been about, for I am ever most warmly interested in all your actions.'[3]

Emma went to Cranwich, as arranged, and wrote to Nelson from there on 26 June. Mr. Bolton's farm was an active place at that time of the year; when school holidays were made to coincide with the hay harvest and other rural pursuits, June was the month that brought the children home, Tom, Eliza, and Anne Bolton among them. Emma found the family at Cranwich at full strength (even the recently wed Lady Bolton had returned home during her husband's absence in the Mediterranean), and soon established a great hold over old and young alike. In their eyes she was a 'Lady Bountiful', a prodigy of elegance and knowledge, bestowing on them not only the gift of her vital presence, but the effects of her good taste and worldly wisdom. Thereafter she was consulted in all matters relating to the girls' education and appearance, was appealed to in the matter of their ball-dresses and hats. Mrs. Bolton had a lively nature, was quick to enjoy simple pleasures, and had something of the outspoken manner of Emma herself, which she took for a candour equal to her own. But there the resemblance ended. Mrs. Bolton was a real countrywoman, advocating the open-air life and healthy exercise, constantly urging Emma to quit the overheated drawing rooms of London, the late hours and exhausting social obligations with which she increasingly engrossed herself. A kind and indulgent mother, Mrs. Bolton had limited resources; she was therefore only too glad to accept for her girls the social 'advantages' that Lady Hamilton was profuse in offering them. Mrs. Bolton longed for them to have as many 'accomplishments' as Charlotte Nelson, their cousin; to hold themselves as well, to dance as gracefully,

[1] P. ii, 305-6.   [2] P. ii, 305.   [3] Ibid., 320.

to be as much admired; and since these miracles had been performed for
Charlotte, as she understood, by the intervention of Lady Hamilton, she
soon regarded her as her children's benefactress. It was a role that Emma
liked playing above all, and one that she swiftly assumed towards the
Bolton family. Her prestige with the family derived, it must be remembered, not so much from her 'friendship' with Nelson, as from her status
as ambassador's wife, and favourite at the Neapolitan court.

As an earnest of her interest in Nelson's nieces, Lady Hamilton now
introduced to Cranwich a young relative of her own, one of her Connor
cousins, who since the previous year had gravitated into the Merton
entourage. There were several Connor girls, daughters of her mother's
sister, Mrs. Sarah Connor, named respectively Sarah, Mary, Cecilia;
young women who were sufficiently well educated to aspire to earn their
livings as governesses.

Sir William Hamilton had not relished the Connor connection and, if
we can believe his wife, had refused to admit them to his Piccadilly house.
At the time Merton was bought, Emma brought up the forlorn state of
her cousins and elicited from Nelson the permission to introduce at least
one of them into his house. 'Sir William', he wrote, 'can have no objection
to your taking your relation to the farm; the pride of the Hamiltons
surely cannot be hurt by settling down with any of your relations. You
have surely as much a right for your relations to come into the house as
his could have.' [1]

In Emma's widowed state the Connor girls proved themselves useful
additions to her household, acting in various capacities in the Clarges
Street house whilst Mrs. Cadogan, who always preferred country to
town, remained in charge at Merton. In due course, the Miss Connors
acted in turn as governesses to Horatia, a position of trust which, however well sustained, did not exempt them from Emma's eventual enmity.

After her first visit to Cranwich, Emma made herself as busy on the
Boltons' behalf as she had formerly been on that of the Revd. Dr. Nelson
and his family, and roused even Nelson's incredulous surprise at her
reported prodigalities. 'I admire your kindness to my dear Sister Bolton,'
he wrote her on 26 August 1803 on hearing that she had given Mrs.
Bolton £100 out of her own pocket, 'how could you afford to send Mrs.
Bolton a hundred pounds? It is impossible out of your income'.[2]

It pleased him extremely to think of Emma being on good terms with
his family, but he always dreaded committing himself—or being committed by Emma—to an extravagant way of life that his means were not

[1] M.628.   [2] Nicolas, vii, 379.

equal to. He never promised more than he could perform; though he wrote now to his sister that he would 'assist Tom Bolton at College', he never lost an occasion for urging Emma to settle quietly at Merton, and make a home for Horatia; it runs through all his letters. 'This letter will find you at Merton,' he wrote on her return from Norfolk.

I do not think it will be a long war, and I believe it will be much shorter than people expect; and I hope to find the new room built; the grounds laid out, neatly but not expensively; new Piccadilly gates; kitchen garden, etc . . . It will be a great source of amusement to you; and Horatia shall plant a tree. I dare say she will be very busy. Mrs. Nelson or Mrs. Bolton, etc, will be with you; and the time will pass away till I have the happiness of arriving at Merton. I feel all your good mother's kindness; and, I trust that we shall turn rich by being economists. Spending money to please a pack of people is folly, and without thanks. I desire that you will say every kind thing from me to her, and make her a present of something in my name.[1]

Emma was restless and not well, but instead of returning to Merton after her visit to Norfolk, she went on to Canterbury to stay with the Revd. Dr. and his family. Her visit coincided with the house-warming party in celebration of the family's removal to Canterbury where the Revd. Dr. had been presented to a stall by the King in the previous May. Conviviality on an unprecedented scale in the frugal Doctor's household marked the occasion. Canon Gilbert, a scholar from Canterbury, recalled in after years the dinner at the house in Brick Walk within the Precincts, which was henceforth the family home:

It was not easy to get ladies to visit Lady Hamilton; however, Mrs Bridges [mother of Sir Egerton] had no scruples. The doctor procured two or three bottles of champagne, then a rare and expensive wine for a dinner party during Lady Hamilton's visit. These were used during dinner quickly, but when her Ladyship challenged some gentlemen in a glass of wine, there was none forthcoming . . . an untoward incident.[2]

With Dr. and Mrs. Nelson, Charlotte and Horace, Emma went on to Southend for a spell of sea-bathing. She sought to enlarge the party still further by inviting the Abbé Campbell, an acquaintance from Neapolitan days, to join them there. Her pregnancy, despite her splendid constitution, was proving difficult. She was moody, restless, and constantly seeking change.

It is evident that Horatia was not sent to Southend, nor to Ramsgate as in the previous year; nor, as presently appeared, was any attempt made

[1] P. ii, 337.   [2] *Reminiscences of the Revd. George Gilbert.*

to establish her at Merton. From Nelson's continued references to Horatia's presence at Merton, it is clear that Emma avoided for as long as she could an open avowal of the fact that she was not establishing the child there. The contrary indeed is shown by a letter from Emma to Mrs Gibson posted at Romford on 31 August, indicating not only that Horatia had been ill but that Emma had not seen much of her recently. The letter read:

Dear Mrs. Gibson I am sorry Miss Thompson has been ill pray write and say she continues better tell Her I shall bring her many pretty things and she must love Her God Mother write to me and tell me what she says I hope to see you more often this winter in Town ever believe me yours sincerely Kiss Horatia often for me   E.H.[1]

To provide for Horatia remained Nelson's great concern; at this very time, on 6 September 1803, he added a Codicil to his Will the provisions of which were intended to complete those made at the time of her birth. The Codicil, endorsed for Haslewood: 'Private for yourself—and most secret' and beginning 'I send you home a Codicil to my Will which you will not communicate to any person breathing' was a sufficient confession of the true facts not to deceive any lawyer about Nelson's relationship towards the beneficiary; but like all his subsequent statements concerning Horatia, it scrupulously avoided implicating Lady Hamilton. To her was attributed the role of Guardian to Nelson's child which, from this first document onwards, became her official, and definitive role, even in the eyes of his family. Nelson's unrealistic plan to leave Horatia his name was to marry her off to his nephew and heir, young Horace Nelson, and he made a further clause to that end in the Codicil. Leaving the child to the guardianship of Lady Hamilton he added: 'Knowing that she will educate my adopted child in the paths of religion and virtue, and give her those accomplishments which so much adorn herself, and I hope make her a fit wife for my dear nephew, Horace Nelson, who I wish to marry her, if he should prove worthy in Lady Hamilton's estimation, of such a treasure as I am sure she will be.'[2] Using almost identical words, Nelson wrote from off Toulon to tell Emma of the Codicil.

I have, my dearest Emma, done what I thank God I have had the power of doing —left £4000 to my dear Horatia, and desire that she may be acknowledged as my adopted daughter, and I have made you her sole guardian; the interest of the money to be paid you until she is eighteen years of age. I trust, my dearest friend, that you will (if it should please God to take me out of this world) execute

---

[1] NMM/NWD/9594/1.   [2] Nicolas, vii, 380.

this great charge for me and the dear little innocent, for it would add comforts to my last moments to think that she would be educated in the paths of religion and virtue, and receive as far as she is capable, some of those brilliant accomplishments which so much adorn you. You must not allow your good heart to think that although I have left you this important charge I fancy myself nearer being knocked off by the French Admiral. I believe it will be quite the contrary, that God Almighty will again and again bless our just cause with victory.[1]

To give his bequest to his adopted daughter a yet more personal appearance he now wrote her a letter in confirmation of the fact. Dated 21 October 1803 from 'Victory Off Toulon' it read:

My dear Child,

Receive the first letter from your most affectionate Father. If I live it will be my pride to see you virtuously brought up, but if it pleases God to call me I trust to himself in that case I have left Dear Lady Hamilton your Guardian I therefore charge you my child on the value of a Father's Blessing to be obedient and attentive to all her kind admonitions and instructions, at this moment I have left you a codocil dated the sixth of September. The sum of four thousand Pounds Sterling the interest of which is to be paid to Lady Emma Hamilton your Guardian for your Maintenance and education. I shall only say my Dear Child may God Almighty Bless you and make you an ornament to your sex which I am sure will be if you attend to all Dear Lady Hamilton's kind instructions and be assured that I am my dear Horatia your most affectionate Father

Nelson & Bronte.[2]

From Emma he had evidently received an assurance that she was taking Horatia to Merton for the winter, for he wrote on 19 October; 'I am glad to find, my dear Emma, that you mean to take Horatia home. *Aye*! She is like her mother; will have her own way, or kick up a devil of a dust. But you will cure her. I am afraid I should spoil her, for I am sure I would shoot any one who would hurt her.'[3] In reply to a reminder that he had promised Horatia a watch (which caused him some considerable trouble to procure) he further added: 'She was always fond of my watch; and very probably I might have promised her one; indeed, I gave her one, which cost sixpence! But I go no where to get anything pretty; therefore do not think me neglectful.'[4] It was not until January that he was able to get hold of a watch and by then Nelson little knew of the troubles accumulating round Emma and Horatia when he wrote the latter:

My dear Horatia—

I feel very much pleased by your kind letter and for your present of a lock of your beautiful hair. I am very glad to hear that you are so good and mind every-

[1] Ibid. [2] NMM/NWD/9594/1 (P. ii, 352).
[3] M.734. [4] M.734.

thing which your governess [Miss Connor] and dear Lady Hamilton tell you, I send you a lock of my hair and a one pound note to buy a locket to put it in and I give you leave to wear it when you are dressed and behave well, and I send you another to buy some little thing for Mary and your governess.

As I am sure that for the world you would not tell a story, it must have slipt my memory that I promised you a Watch therefore I have sent to Naples to get one and I will send it home as soon as it arrives—the Dog I never could have promised as we have no Dogs on board ship, Only I beg my dear Horatia be obedient and you will ever be sure of the affection of   NELSON & BRONTE [1]

To Emma, Nelson added 'You have sent me, in that lock of beautiful hair, a far richer present than any monarch in Europe could if he were so inclined. Your description of the dear angel makes me happy. I have sent to Mr. Falconet to buy me a watch, and told him if it does but tick, and the chain *full* of trinkets, that is all that is wanted.' [2]

Forwarding the watch a week later he wrote to Lady Hamilton: 'I send a very neat watch for our god-child, and you will see it is by a good maker, that is, I suppose, it will *tick* for a year instead of a month or two. You will impress her that it is only to be worn when she behaves well and is obedient.' [3]

The improvements to Merton occupied much of Nelson's thoughts during the two years and four months of his absence. On 12 July he wrote to Emma:

It is my intention the first money I get, to pay off Mr. Greaves £2000 mortgage which is due 1st October next, and after that Mr. Davison; then I shall have Mr. Matcham's mortgage money lodged, after which I shall send you some to begin next spring our alterations; but first I will if I can, get out of debt.

I would not have you lay out more than is necessary at Merton. The rooms, and the new entrances, will take a good deal of money. The entrance by the corner I would have certainly done; a common white gate will do for the present; and one of the cottages, which is in the barn, can be put up, as a temporary lodge. The road can be made to a temporary bridge; for that part of the Nile, one day, shall be filled up . . . For the winter the carriage can be put into the barn. The footpath should be turned. I did shew Mr Haslewood the way I wished it done . . . and, I also beg, as my dear Horatia is to be at Merton, that a strong netting, about three feet high, may be placed round the Nile, that the little thing may not tumble in; and then, you may have ducks again in it. I forget at what place we saw the netting; and either Mr. Perry or Mr. Goldsmid told us where it was to be bought. I shall be very anxious till I know this is done . . . The expenses of the alterations at Merton *you are* not to pay from the income. Let it all be put to a separate account, and I will provide a fund for the payment. [4]

[1] NMM/NWD/9594/16.   [2] Ibid.
[3] M.742.   [4] P. ii, 319.

Despite Nelson's repeatedly expressed wish that Horatia be 'fixed' at
Merton, Lady Hamilton did not take her to live there during his absence.
The house in Clarges Street was the real centre of her existence. The
proximity of Clarges Street to 'Old Q's' house at 138 Piccadilly proved, in
the event, to be one of the reasons for her residing in town; she quite
unashamedly angled for a legacy from the immensely wealthy old man
who was, she could justly claim, a relative of her late husband.

Something of the pattern of her life during the autumn and winter of
1803–4 can be gleaned from the letters of Charlotte Nelson who was
permanently living with her then. All things considered, the education
provided Charlotte Nelson by Lady Hamilton, though it afforded her the
entrée into shady circles where her aunt Lady Nelson would certainly
not have penetrated, was instructive as well as bohemian; it left her an
unquestioning admirer of her benefactress's ways. 'My dear Mama,' she
wrote from Clarges Street on 11 November 1803,

we spent a very pleasant day at Mrs. Voillers My Lady and myself sung Hear
my Prayer. On Tuesday we drank tea at Mrs. Bianchi's . . . My instrument was
thought one of the best that Broadwood ever made . . . Mrs. Billington dined
with us yesterday she sung in the evening. Yesterday I had a letter from Horace
he was quite well . . . We were to have dined at Merton to-day if My Lady had
not been ill . . . My Aunt Bolton thinks I am improved in my shape . . . I hope
you like Canterbury. My Lady is so kind as to Promise to buy me a gold watch
and she is so kind as to have some more short dresses made for me . . .
P.S. The letters from my Uncle make us very happy as he writes in very good
spirits. He has sent My Lady two of the most beautiful Gold chains that were
ever seen. My Lord also mentions his having sent some Shawls for my Lady.[1]

Four days later, when Charlotte again wrote to her mother, Emma
was still too ill to be present at dinner when Mr. and Mrs. Bianchi
were the guests. The usefulness of the Bianchis to Emma is sufficiently
apparent from the rest of Charlotte's letter.

My cousins Eliza and Ann came from Edmonton yesterday to stay two or three
days—they are both grown very much. My cousins Miss Moore and myself are
to go this Evening to Mrs. Bianchi's. I had a lesson from Mr. Bianchi yesterday
. . . My Lady Begs me to say she has been confined to her Bed since Wednesday
and is not able to write.

There can be little doubt that 'my lady's' frequent indispositions in the
late autumn of 1803 were connected with her pregnancy, and the birth
of the child, another girl, whom Nelson, when he at last had news of it,
called 'dear little Emma'. The child did not live, and Lady Hamilton

[1] BRP/NMM/9292/4.

herself was very ill. The event, which occurred at Clarges Street, appears to have taken place at the very end of December or early January 1804. On 5 January Emma herself wrote to Mrs. William:

I have been ill my dearest friend these 8 days a bed with soor throat cold cough but I am better now thank God and the sight of Horrace has done me good the Boltons went yesterday morning Horrace dear boy arrived safe at eleven yesterday morning He sleeps next room to us and His dog allso We were all a bed by ten last night I am a bed yet but all the children in my room as it is snowing hard Charlotte is taking her dancing lesson I have one of the best mistress's for her I ever saw Mademoiselle du Croix she takes great pains and comes every day.[1]

With her usual intrepidity Lady Hamilton filled her house with children at a time when seclusion would seem to have been called for. The *mise-en-scène*, organized for the Christmas holidays was calculated to deflect suspicion, if any were aroused by her prolonged indisposition. For once her phenomenal constitution failed her, and she was in bed three weeks, during which time the young people were kept fully occupied rehearsing their parts for a play, Charlotte wrote to her mother on 17 January: 'Miss Connor my Cousins [Boltons] and myself have been making ourselves a short dress trimmed with blue Ribbons. The Petticoats also trimmed with the same. We are to wear them on Tuesday to a dance at Dr. Moseley's. Miss Connor and myself are learning a figure dance to dance on Tuesday. Horatia went to the Play on Friday with Mr., Mrs. and Master Davison.'[2] Emma herself wrote to Mrs. Nelson at the beginning of February: 'I have not been out these three weeks so very ill I have been yesterday I got them a box at the Opera and sent them our Charlotte went with them and they brought her home to me the 2 Miss Boltons are in town and dine with me also so we have a good family party.'[3]

To mark her recovery, Lady Hamilton gave the young people a ball. Charlotte told her mother on 1 February,

My Lady was so kind as to give us a very pleasant dance yesterday as it was Miss Moseley's Birthday . . . The party consisted of all the Linds [Mrs. Denis etc.] Mr. & Miss Yonge Mr. & Mrs. Bianchi and a few others We sat down to a very elegant supper at twelve o'clock & did not break up till 4 in the morning. I danced the Scotch Minuet with Lucy Moseley . . . My Cousins go to school to-morrow.[4]

News of the expected birth was not received by Nelson till 2 April. The delay caused him a month's agitation; throughout February and March he

[1] Ibid.   [2] BRP/NMM/9292.
[3] Ibid.   [4] Ibid.

waited for assurances regarding her health, asking to be told she was 'happily past all danger'. When the news came, it gave him 'a raging fever all night'. On 2 April 1804 he wrote:

I have, my dearest beloved Emma, been so uneasy for this last month, desiring most ardently to hear of your well being. Captain Capel brought me your letters sent by the Thisbe from Gibraltar. I opened—opened—found none but December, or early in January. I was in such an agitation. At last I found one without a date—which, thank God, told my poor heart that you was recovering; but that dear little Emma was no more.[1]

The undated letter may well have been from Mrs. Cadogan for upon her Nelson was relying to keep him informed '. . . Our dear, excellent Mrs. Cadogan is the only one who knows anything of the matter', he had written earlier; 'and she has promised me when you are well again to take every possible care of you.'[2] Her illness and the child's death were made even worse for Nelson by the further news that Horatia had been gravely ill. The probability that this illness was smallpox will be examined below. 'It quite upset me,' he wrote.

But it was just at bed-time, and I had time to reflect, and be thankful to God for sparing you and our dear Horatia. I am sure the loss of one—much more of both—would have drove me mad. I was so agitated as it was, that I was glad it was night, and that I could be by myself. Kiss dear Horatia for me, and tell her to be a dutiful and good child, and if she is, that we shall always love her. You may, if you like, tell Mrs. G[ibson] that I shall certainly settle a small pension on her.[3]

Horatia's illness, occurring just before Emma's confinement and lasting during her convalescence, had laid the entire responsibility for nursing her on Mrs. Gibson. An undated letter of Nelson's, found among Lady Hamilton's effects enclosed in one dated 13 August 1804, and therefore wrongly assumed as belonging to that date, refers to Horatia's smallpox. From the text it is evident that the news of it reached Nelson before the news of Emma's lying-in. 'My beloved,' he wrote to Emma,

how I feel for your situation and that of our dear Horatia, our dear child . . . I wish I had all the smallpox for her, but I know the fever is the natural consequence. I dreamt last night I heard her call papa, and point to her arm just as you described. Give Mrs. Gibson a guinea for me, and I will repay you. Dear wife, good, adorable friend, how I love you, and what would I not give to be with you this moment, for I am for ever yours.[4]

[1] Nicolas, vii, 382.   [2] 1814 ed. *Nelson Letters*, vol. I, 26.
[3] Nicolas, vii, 382.   [4] M.778.

The fact that Horatia took the smallpox—and as she herself told Sir Harris Nicolas in later life, took it 'very severely and was not expected to live' was a proof that Nelson's repeated injunctions to Emma to have the child vaccinated were not complied with. He had written her from the Baltic long ago on this debatable subject: '. . . Poor T[homson] is gone to Petersburg with Capt Fremantle but I can answer that his wife may have the child inoculated and for his sake I hope it will do well, for his life is wrapt up in the mother and child.' On 31 July 1801 he wrote again, still further confirmed in his views by the report of a gentleman he had met.

Yesterday the subject turned on the cow-pox. A gentleman declared that his child was inoculated with the cow-pox and afterwards remained in the house where the child had the small-pox in the natural way, and did *not* catch it. Therefore, here was a full trial with a cow-pox. The child is only feverish for two days, and only a slight inflammation of the arm takes place, instead of being all over scabs. But do that you please.[1]

The strangest feature of the story is Lady Hamilton's contribution to it related by Horatia in after years: she told Sir Harris Nicolas: 'I always heard Lady Hamilton say that it was at the express desire of Lord Nelson that I was not vaccinated as he would not hear of the cow-pox.'[2]

Happily for Lord Nelson's peace of mind, the news of Horatia's illness, and recovery, reached him together, so that his alarm was retrospective only. By 10 April he could write 'I rejoice that dear Horatia is got well' and still more he rejoiced at the news Lady Hamilton sent him of taking Horatia home and beginning her education: 'I rejoice that dear Horatia is got well; and, also, that you, my dearest Emma, are recovered of your severe indisposition . . . I am glad to hear that you are going to take my dear Horatia to educate her. She must turn out an angel, if she minds what you say.'[3]

On 13 April Nelson wrote to Horatia herself:

My dear Horatia—I send you twelve books of Spanish dresses, which you will let your Guardian Angel, Lady Hamilton, keep for you, when you are tired of looking at them. I am very glad to hear you are perfectly recovered and that you are a very good girl. I beg, my dear Horatia, that you will always continue so; which will be a great comfort to your most affectionate NELSON & BRONTE.[4]

The 'education' of Horatia, aged three, held small place in the battle for position in London society that Lady Hamilton still waged, undaunted

[1] Nicolas, vii, 374–5.   [2] NMM/NWD/9594/13–14.
[3] NMM/NWD/9594/1.   [4] Ibid. (NMM/NWD/9594/16).

by her many reverses. In this campaign, the innocent presence of Charlotte Nelson at her side was her strongest weapon. While vaunting her
services to Charlotte to Charlotte's parents, Lady Hamilton never admitted to the reciprocal obligations under which she lay to the unsuspecting Charlotte. The great ladies who welcomed the debut in society of
Lord Nelson's niece, had to accept her chaperone, whatever their mental
reservations. She wrote to the gratified parents:

We are to be at the Goldsmid's grand fete on the 10th [April 1804] on the 11th
we rest, the 12th be with you—as to the Grand Routes, I hate them but I thought
it right to shew myself in some respectable houses as Tom Tit said she would
shut me out I have been invited to every party about Town so has Charlotte we
went to the Ladies Concert and to the most Chosen Places to shew we *could do so.*
and your good sense will approve I am sure Charlotte is so much admired and
justly so I think—the Duchess of Devonshire was so civil to Charlotte and told
her she wou'd invite her to all her Balls the Walpoles were there every body
came up and spoke to me and made so much of us the most fashionable Ball
next week is Mrs. Orby Hunter all the girls of fashion are to be there also one on
Friday at Mrs. Broadheads and one at Mrs. Wolfs on Wednesday were we are
invited—also to Lady Louisa Manners tom tit is in town bursting with rage and
envy—but more of all when we have the pleasure to meet.[1]

'. . . I never quit her for a moment,' the mother was told; 'My whole
time is given up with pleasure to this lovely girl. I told you I took her to
dine with Lady Stafford who is in love with her. She is to dine there
soon again with me she is immensely admired.' Among Charlotte's
'admirers' was 'Old Q', as Emma reported:[2]

The poor old Duke I think is going fast He calls but sometimes and is very low
indeed. He admires Charlotte but is more like a father He recommended me to
have Madlle du Croix who is old and ugly but very very clever. Charlotte has
never had a word with Her she does all I wish Her and Mr & Mrs Bianchi are
very good and attentive to her.[3]

Horace Nelson came in also for his share of praise and, during his
holidays from Eton, was taught how to make himself agreeable and useful.
'He is all our darlings,' Emma told them after the Christmas holidays
spent in Clarges Street.

He has been out with different people at the play and opera and Madame
Grafini is quite in love with him . . . Charlotte makes great improvement is
admired much—She will be the most accomplished girl of the age. Her dancing
mistress is excellent Charlotte and I have been to see Lady Mansfield Lady
Stafford is also fond of Charlotte so she has got good friends.

[1] BRP/NMM/9292/4.   [2] Ibid.   [3] Ibid.

A first attempt was now made to introduce the dutiful and pliant Charlotte to Horatia, with as plausible an explanation of her presence as Lady Hamilton could devise. The story varied in its details, but remained constant in essentials: Horatia was an orphan in whom Lord Nelson took a great interest and to oblige him Lady Hamilton had undertaken her 'protection'. The onus for the child, if onus there were, was firmly placed on Lord Nelson; Lady Hamilton's role was entirely philanthropic. As the child's origins must never be suspected by Lord Nelson's family (though his own relationship was barely disguised) the increasingly frequent appearances of Horatia in Clarges Street and at Merton, under pressure from Lord Nelson, could only be explained by yet another of Lady Hamilton's deeds of benevolence. To please Lord Nelson Charlotte was cajoled into writing him of her affection for the 'little orphan'. Written in January, after Horatia's illness, the letter reached Lord Nelson in mid-April, and he did not delay in sending his thanks.

Galling as it was to have to solicit kindness for his daughter, he took a high tone in making it plain from the outset that she was not without means. In a society where the financial position of women was all-important in securing them consideration, Nelson was quick to insure his daughter against the slights to which financial insecurity would have exposed her. She might be without a family, but she was not destitute of a fortune. He wrote to Charlotte,

I thank you very much for your kind letters of January 3rd and 4th, and I feel truly sensible of your kind regard for that dear little orphan, Horatia. Although her parents are lost, yet she is not without a fortune; and I shall cherish her to the last moment of my life; and *curse* them who *curse* her, and Heaven *bless* them to who *bless* her! Dear Innocent! she can have injured no one. I am glad to hear she is attached to you; and, if she takes after her parents, so she will to those who are kind to her. I am ever, dear Charlotte, Your affectionate uncle Nelson & Bronte.[1]

To Emma he wrote on the same occasion: 'I am pleased with Charlotte's letter; and as she loves my dear Horatia, I shall always like her. What hearts those must have who do not! But, thank God, she shall not be dependent on them.'[2]

The prolongation of the war, contrary to all Nelson's calculations, and his own indefinite absence, were only one of the reasons prompting him now to urge a change in Horatia's situation. The destruction of Lady Hamilton's letters deprives the biographer of essential evidence of her

[1] Ibid.   [2] P. ii, 384.

conduct in the affair, but some of her arguments, griefs, and fears can be guessed from Nelson's answers to her letters. It would seem that Charlotte's presence in her house was used as an excuse for not establishing Horatia there, and that it was to propitiate his displeasure that Charlotte was prompted to write to him of her fondness for the 'little orphan'. One thing is clear: Lady Hamilton persisted in not 'taking Horatia home'. The death of her second child removed the chief excuse for not doing so as 1804 advanced. A suggestion apparently emanating from Mrs. Gibson that she accompany Horatia to Merton was vetoed by Lady Hamilton, who said she 'spoilt the child too much'. This argument was well remembered by Horatia herself who related it to Sir Harris Nicolas in later years. That Mrs. Gibson 'spoilt the child' in Little Titchfield Street did not seem to weigh with Lady Hamilton as an argument against leaving her there; what she could not and would not do was to burden herself with the child's constant presence in her house. To the child's father, who had provided her with a suitable home, she had to find sufficient reasons for not taking her there, and among the chief of these was the impossibility of explaining the child's identity to her own entourage, young Charlotte Nelson and Nelson's other relatives in particular. The clever three-year-old child, whose upbringing called for something better now than a nurse's care, posed a problem that Lady Hamilton was unwilling to shoulder on her own; its solution lay with Nelson—so she gave him unequivocally to understand. The tangled story he thereupon invented to explain Horatia's origin, like the 'Thompson' story of two years before, was replete with improbabilities and, while serving no immediately useful purpose, confused the issue of Horatia's parentage, to her lasting disadvantage.

THE 'EXTRAORDINARY CIRCUMSTANCE'

THE origin for Nelson's story of Horatia's parentage can be found in the almost parallel case that came to his notice in the autumn and winter of 1803-4. The former British Consul at Palermo, Mr. Abraham Gibbs, well known to Nelson and the Hamiltons during their residence there, asked Nelson to convey his daughter Mary to England in the autumn of 1803 so that she might be educated there. It being wartime, any civilian's passage by sea was dangerous, and Gibbs looked to Nelson's old friendship to oblige him in the matter. He could the more readily do this as he was rendering Nelson frequent services with his Bronté estate, investigating into arrears of rents, reporting on necessary repairs, etc. Forwarding Gibb's letter to Emma on 18 October [1803], Nelson made the further comment:

I have just had a letter from Gibbs of which I send you a copy. You will see what interest he is taking about Bronté . . . You will see Gibbs, at last, has fixed on sending his daughter home; and I shall be glad of so good an opportunity of obliging him, as it will naturally tie him to my interest. He was a great fool, not to have sent the child with you, as you wished.[1]

In the same letter he referred to Horatia and it is clear that there was already at the back of his mind the idea that Horatia, like Mary Gibbs, could be supposed to have been committed to his and Lady Hamilton's care. The quite unnecessary publicity Lady Hamilton gave to Mary's arrival in England and her own active role in placing her at school and in inviting her to Clarges Street, suggests that some such motive as this prompted her conduct. It is otherwise difficult to understand why she went to considerable lengths to interest the William Nelsons in the totally unknown Mary Gibbs, if it were not to explain the equally sudden appearance of Horatia at Clarges Street. Certainly Nelson acted on the suggestion when he wrote to Lady Hamilton the statement regarding Horatia's origins which they concerted together later in the year.

On 25 January 1804, recovered from her lying-in, Emma wrote to the William Nelsons:

[1] 1814 ed. Nelson Letters, vol. 1.

Little Mary Gibbs is arrived from Palermo Lord Nelson sent the Niger Frigate for her I am one of her guardians I am going to place her at a school in Cumberland Street. She will be a great fortune 2 or 3 thousand a year and I have written to Mr. Gibbs and milord I entend her for Horace. He likes her and they consider themselves as affianced so you see the thing as well begun when shall we meet to talk over all this.[1]

Considering that Emma knew by then of Nelson's hopes of an eventual marriage between Horatia and her cousin Horace—hopes that he had even inserted into the codicil to his Will dated 6 September 1803—her reference to the supposed flirtation between the children is the more inexplicable. The idyll, however, continued; there are frequent mentions of the little girl in Charlotte's letters of the time and of her supposed partiality for Horace. The child moved to and fro between Clarges Street and Merton on every school holiday (she was placed by Lady Hamilton at a boarding-school on Clapham Common), acting unconsciously all the time as a kind of lightning conductor to divert attention from the parallel figure of Horatia who, as Charlotte's letters show, was also being introduced to the inner circle of Clarges Street and Merton.

To justify his daughter's permanent residence with Emma either in London or the country, Nelson wrote the following explanation of her existence for Lady Hamilton to show to all and sundry—presumably under the impression that others were as naïve as himself in crediting this 'extraordinary circumstance'.

> Victory 13th August 1804,
>
> I am now going to state a thing to you and to request your kind assistance, which, from my dear Emma's kindness of heart, I am sure of her acquiescence in. Before we left Italy I told you of the extraordinary circumstance of a child being left to my care and protection. On your first coming to England I presented you the child, dear Horatia. You became, to my comfort, attached to it, so did Sir William, thinking her the finest child he had ever seen. She is become of that age when it is necessary to remove her from a mere nurse and to think of educating her. Horatia is by no means destitute of a fortune. My earnest wish is that you would take her to Merton, and if Miss Connor will become her tutoress under your eye, I shall be made truly happy. I will allow Miss Connor any salary you may think proper. I know Charlotte loves the child, and therefore at Merton she will imbibe nothing but virtue, goodness, and elegance of manners, with a good education, to fit her to move in that sphere of life she is destined to move in.
>
> I shall tell you, my dear Emma, more of this matter when I come to England, but I am now anxious for the child's being placed under your protecting wing. Perhaps I ought to have done this before, but I must not, in justice to my charge,

[1] BRP/NMM/9292/4.

defer it for any consideration longer. May God bless you, my dear Emma, and reward you tenfold for all the godness you have already shewn Horatia, and ever be assured that I am, etc, etc.[1]

The elaborate precautions taken to account for Horatia may, on certain occasions, have served Lady Hamilton when showing her off to her visitors; but they did not advance Nelson's intentions for establishing her at Merton: she remained, as hitherto, in the care of her nurse in Little Titchfield Street.

The main reason for this was the unexpected turn in the conduct of the war, the entry of Spain as an ally of France, and the threat from the combined enemy fleets which sent Nelson half across the world in pursuit of them. Instead of being at home for Christmas 1804 as he had expected he was away until August 1805.

One fact is certain: Horatia was not introduced to either of Nelson's sisters when they visited Lady Hamilton during the course of the year—an omission which reflects on Lady Hamilton's want of judgement, for the child was instantly taken to their hearts when they finally met her during Nelson's last days on shore. While never doubting she was Nelson's child, Mrs. Matcham and Mrs. Bolton obligingly accepted Lady Hamilton's version of her own purely benevolent role in relation to the 'little orphan'. But this is to anticipate.

In April 1804 the Matchams stayed with Lady Hamilton in Clarges Street. The visit, which began as a business trip, Mr. Matcham bringing his wife and George junior with him and asking Lady Hamilton to engage 'two bedrooms and a sitting-room' for them near her, ended in a round of pleasure for all. On 5 April Charlotte wrote to her mother of her cousins Eliza and Anne Bolton being come from Edmonton to join the party, and urging Horace to 'come soon' as George Matcham wanted him very much. 'My Aunt Matcham will leave us very soon which I shall regret much,' added Charlotte, detailing the flow of visitors and engagements that had filled the week: 'General Dumouriez and the Countess St. Martin dined with us yesterday and Mr. & Mrs. Denis came in the evening . . . The Duke ["Q"] goes on just the same comes every night when we are at home. My Aunt Matcham begs her kind love, All my cousins beg to be remembered to Horace—also Miss Gibbs.' Lady Hamilton herself, Charlotte reported 'very low spirited to-day as to-morrow is the anniversary of poor Sir William's death otherwise she would write to you'.[2] The date being 5 April, decorum required nothing less.

[1] M.779.   [2] BRP/NMM/9292/4.

7

Lady Hamilton charmed the Matchams with her kindness. 'How many thanks [are] due to you,' Mrs. Matcham wrote on her return to Bath, 'for the happy time we spent under your hospitable roof; God grant we may some future time all meet in happier days, when peace and fresh laurels will . . . restore to us our dear loved friend. May God almighty protect him.' Sending her 'most affectionate love to my ever dear Charlotte',[1] Mrs. Matcham, it is noteworthy, made no mention of Horatia. Lady Hamilton celebrated her birthday on 26 April by giving the young people a dance at Clarges Street. Reporting on the event to her mother, Charlotte wrote: 'We sat down about eighty to supper and danced till six in the morning.'[2] By that time Mrs. Bolton had joined the party and all of them, with young Horace in attendance, went to the Play. Nelson did not forget the date, nor the improvidence of his beloved. He wrote on 18 March: 'I send you, my beloved Emma, a note, in order that you may, upon your birthday, make some little presents, and if you do not give it all away it will look in bank notes very pretty in your pocket-book.'[3]

The fine weather allowed Nelson's plans for the improvement of Merton to be put in hand. He pictured Emma as constantly there supervising the work, and commented on her reports: 'With respect to the improvements at Merton, I never meant that they should be paid out of the £1,200 a year, and I send you an order that Davison will pay the bills, as I wish to know exactly what the alterations cost.'[4] Picturing Horatia at Merton, he wrote:

Every thing you tell me about my dear Horatia charms me. I think I see her, hear her, and admire her, but she is like her dear, dear mother. I wish I could but be at dear Merton, to assist in making the alterations. I think I should have persuaded you to have kept the pike and a clear stream, and to have put all the carp tench, and fish who muddy the water into the pond. But as you like, I am content. Only take care that my darling does not fall in and get drowned, I begged you to get the little netting along the edge; and particularly on the bridges.[5]

He concluded his letter by charging Emma to 'Kiss my dearest Horatia for me' and added, 'I shall hope to see her at Merton on my arrival.'

While the main work was in progress, Emma planned to visit the William Nelsons at Canterbury, and with them make a prolonged stay at Ramsgate for the sea-bathing. By the time Nelson heard of her intention on 9 July it was too late to prevent it; she was already there. He was horrified, believing in the imminence of a French invasion, and foreseeing

[1] M.756. [2] BRP/NMM/9292/4. [3] M.750.
[4] P. ii, 392. [5] P. ii, 393.

the impossibility of her getting away. 'Your trip to Canterbury I should suppose the very worst you could take,' he wrote, 'for, on any alarm, there you must stay, and in a town filled with soldiers; but if you like it, I am content.' When he heard of her being actually on the coast and supposed Horatia with her, he wrote more forcefully still: 'I am very uneasy at your and Horatia being on the coast, for you cannot move, if the French make the attempt; which I am told they have done and been repulsed. Pray God it may be true! I shall rejoice to hear you and Horatia are safe at Merton; and happy shall I be the day I join you there.'[1]

Emma had promised to visit the Boltons for the christening of the infant daughter of Sir William and Lady Bolton, born on 18 March. Sir William was with Nelson in the Mediterranean 'and is got a very fine young man and good officer,' Nelson told Emma. They were the child's sponsors and he reminded her of their obligations: 'Apropos! I believe you should buy a piece of plate value fifty pounds, for our god-daughter of Lady Bolton.'[2] Emma sent a coral, inscribed with the infant's name—'Emma Horatia'—and all were in delighted anticipation of her coming to Cranwich. But Emma was still sea-bathing at Ramsgate with the William Nelsons and disappointed her hosts by postponing her visit for a month.

There can be no doubt that Lady Hamilton was very attractive to young people; when she wished to please, she was all-conquering; and it must be remembered that the friendship of Nelson's relatives was essential to her overthrow of his legal wife's claim on their affections. The sympathy Emma displayed, the small attentions paid to unspoilt girls like the Boltons, had immense effect. They spent their holidays increasingly under her roof (to them Clarges Street was 'a Fairy Palace') and she assumed in their eyes the stature of a beneficent goddess. She took their social education in hand, and poor Mrs. Bolton regarded the possibility of Anne's 'carriage' becoming in any way comparable to her cousin Charlotte's under Lady Hamilton's care as an unattainable happiness. Anne was delicate, subject to nervous attacks and to melancholy; the little attentions of Lady Hamilton transported her with delight. From school she wrote to her benefactress. 'I live in the pleasing hope of seeing you once more before we begin our journey, which will not be till the 22nd August, but possibly as you are so well and happy, you may prolong your stay at Ramsgate ... Pray write to me; if it is but such a little scrap as I have hitherto had from you, I shall be content.'[3]

She wrote further on 6 August: 'How very good you are to think of me and write to me so often. All I can do in return is to tell you how truly

[1] P. ii, 422.   [2] N to Ly H 6 June 1804.   [3] NMM/NWD/9594/7.

grateful I am, and with all the affection of which my heart is capable do I love you . . . thank you for the little darling pin-cushion, which is treasured up and only taken out occasionally to be kissed.'[1]

Emma's visit to Cranwich for the christening of Emma Horatia Bolton was delayed till October. Echoes of its success are found in Mrs. Bolton's letter of the 21st, to Emma, which feelingly laments her departure:

. . . poor Mrs. Pierson with her palpitations [Mary Ann Pierson was sister to Sir William Bolton] and Lady Bolton with her nervous complaint, Susanna drowned in tears, & Mr. Bolton and myself not the best of the party; we never went to church or ever even changed our dress, but set talking of the travellers . . . We have seen none of our pleasant neighbours since you left us. The Mayor's ball is put in grand style in the Norwich papers. It says, after supper Lady Hamilton rose and drank the Mayor's health in *three times three*.[2]

Lady Bolton (Kate) wrote on 25 October:

I was so much affected at parting with you, that I could not express my thanks for all your kindness to me during your stay at Cranwich, and indeed at every other time since I have had the pleasure of knowing you. I hope you will believe that it was not feeling your great kindness *too little*, but *too much*, that made me unable to express it as I ought and wished, but *felt* it the more.[3]

From Norfolk, parcels of provisions followed Emma to Merton: 'a brace of hares' by one coach, 'a basket of dryed apples' by another, and to help furnish the plantations there, Mr. Bolton's brother, the Revd. William, Rector of Brancaster, was called in to 'make a choice collection of shrubs' to forward by the coach to Merton. 'Not a soul have I seen or heard of since you left us', wrote Mrs. Bolton on 28 October. 'I wish I was your neighbour. Susanna and I amuse ourselves by thinking if we were within a ride or walk of Merton, how pleasant it would be to us; next to reality, you know, visions are the happiest.'[4]

The coach from London brought gifts in return for Cranwich, the extravagance of which drew from Mrs. Bolton a protest—(the terms of her letter might serve to answer those critics who accuse Nelson's kindred of interested motives for 'countenancing' Emma). Thanking Lady Hamilton for a tippet, she wrote on 31 October:

you say you think I shall like the tippet. Can I do otherwise? But indeed I do not like to receive so many presents. Nothing can make me love you better, but so many handsome things as you do for me and mine makes me feel uncomfortable. Be assured I have now everything I want, and do not send me more . . . I shall be afraid you think me a mercenary wretch who has a price, but surely you have a poor opinion of yourself and me.[5]

   [1] Ibid.   [2] Ibid.   [3] Ibid.
   [4] Ibid.   [5] Ibid.

Mrs. Bolton did not know that the beautiful gifts lavished on her and her daughters were unpaid for. The extent of Emma's debt that autumn can be judged from the bill presented her by Mrs. Gibson on 7 November for arrears in the payments for Horatia; if Mrs. Gibson remained unpaid, for whose account Nelson constantly sent money, the rest of Lady Hamilton's liabilities can be guessed. Mrs. Gibson's bill shows something else as well: Horatia's continued presence in Little Titchfield Street at a time when Nelson was urging her establishment at Merton. He expected shortly to get home on sick leave; his cough was 'very, very bad' and aggravated his old wound in the groin received at the battle of Cape St. Vincent. He applied to the Admiralty for leave in October, and the reports of his ill-health in the press alarmed his sisters. Writing to Emma in anticipation of his arrival, he said: 'I would wish you, my Emma, to remain at Merton. If all our house is not finished it can be done next summer, and we shall get through the winter very comfortable, I have no doubt . . . I hope you have fixed Horatia at Merton.' [1] On his birthday, 29 September, he wrote again: 'I well know that you will keep it, and have my dear Horatia to drink my health . . . Kiss my dear Horatia. I hope she is at Merton *fixed*.' [2]

Mrs. Gibson's bill conclusively disproves the fact, and indicates by an endorsement written on the envelope, that she was not always kept informed of her employer's whereabouts. This could argue carelessness on Emma's part; it could also argue the need to elude her creditors. The envelope addressed 'Lady Hamilton, No. 11 Clarges Street, Piccadilly', and delivered by hand, was endorsed: 'Called twice and Nobody at home.' The letter contained a receipt for 'lodging and attendance on Miss Thompson for £30', and an enclosed slip, dated Tuesday 7 November 1804 which stated: 'there now remains due up to Nov 5th 24 pounds two shillings'. An accompanying letter reads:

Mrs. Gibson's duty to Lady Hamilton and am happy to inform her Ladyship that Miss Thompson is very well and desires her love and a kiss to her Ladyship and to her Godpapa I have sent the receipt and there now remains due up to Nov[er] 24 pounds two shillings.

Your most Hum[b] serva[nt]
Mary Gibson[3]

Nelson was not granted leave, and Emma, despite injunctions, left Horatia with the nurse. On occasions she sent for her to Merton, as when she gave a party for her—on the supposed anniversary of her birth, 29

---

[1] M.783.   [2] Nicolas, vii, 384.   [3] NMM/NWD/9594/6.

October, which happened to coincide with Anne Bolton's birthday. It became an annual event sumptuously celebrated with cakes from Cranwich and a children's ball. To the younger generation of the Nelson family Horatia was gradually introduced: first to Charlotte Nelson, and then to the little Boltons, to whom her presence was no more surprising than that of little Mary Gibbs. Anticipating a house full of young visitors at Merton, Lady Hamilton wrote to Mrs. Gibson from Clarges Street that winter: 'Dear Mrs. Gibson,—Will you and Horatia be with me by eleven o'clock to go to Merton. We must defer Mary's visit till next week, as the house is full of company. Come by half-past eleven in the morning. Ever yours.—E. Hamilton.' (The Mary referred to here was of course Mrs. Gibson's little girl.) [1]

December came and Nelson, anxious to be relieved of his post, was outraged at Sir John Orde's discourtesy in not communicating with him for fully ten days after reaching the Mediterranean; his letter when it came dashed Nelson's hopes of a speedy deliverance. Sir John was not superseding him, only taking over the Cadiz Command (rich in prospective prize-money) and leaving Nelson still in expectation of orders from the Admiralty. They reached him on Christmas day, irretrievably too late for him to reach England before the winter gales. That and the declaration of war by Spain on 12 December necessarily altered his plans. He wrote sadly to Emma on 30 December: 'I received by the Swiftsure your letters of 29 October on your return from your long expedition into Norfolk, on Christmas-day, the day I had devoted to spend most happily with you and our dear adopted Horatia at dear Merton' [2] (he was careful how he wrote for, he said, he guessed the letter would be 'smoked' before it reached her).

Nelson was intensely unhappy. As the new year advanced, and he saw no prospect of relief from his vigil over the enemy fleets bottled up in Toulon, he wrote bitterly home:

What a time! I could not have thought it possible that I should have been so long absent; unwell, and uncomfortable, in many respects... I send you a trifle for a birth-day's gift. I would to God, I could give you more; but I have it not. I get no Prize-Money worth naming; but, if I have the good fortune to meet the French Fleet I hope they will make me amends for all my anxiety; which has been, and is, indescribable. [3]

He fretted about Horatia; he obviously felt she was neglected and spoke of the need to begin her education. He was placated by a letter from Horatia herself, and commented in reply: 'I admire dear Horatia's writing.

[1] Ibid.   [2] Nicolas, vi, 207.   [3] P. ii, 463.

I think her hand will soon be like her dear mother's, and if she is but as clever, I shall be content'.[1] Seeing no end to the war, he sought—though always in vain—for the assurance that his daughter was safely established at Merton. In his letter of 9 March he asked: 'How is my dear Horatia? I hope you have her under your guardian wing, at Merton? May God bless her!' His concern for her future should he be killed became obsessive as 1805 advanced; he doubted whether he would even be able to protect her in the years ahead. On 4 April he wrote to Emma:

I dare not send a little letter [i.e. a *personal* one enclosed] for what with sneaking and cutting, all would be read. But let them read this, that I love you beyond any woman in this world, and next our dear Horatia. How I long to settle what I intend upon her, and not leave her to the mercy of any one, or even to any foolish thing I may do in my old age.[2]

A still further doubt—considering his infatuation for Lady Hamilton—had been expressed in a previous letter—dated 17 August 1804—in which he told her his latest testimentary dispositions:

In case of any accident happening to me . . . I have given you £500 sterling a year out of the [Bronté] estate, but I hope we shall live many years. The moment I get home, I shall put it out of your power to spend dear Horatia's money; I shall settle it in trustees' hands, and leave nothing to chance. If Horace behaves well he shall marry her.[3]

This further Codicil to his Will, vesting his legacy to Horatia in trustees' hands, and bequeathing £500 a year pension to Lady Hamilton, was sent home to Haslewood on 9 May 1805 for safety: 'for if I kept them on board ship,' Nelson told Emma, 'they might be lost, and then you and my Horatia would not get what I intend, which would embitter my last moments.' To be doubly sure, he sent copies of the documents by another ship.

The great pursuit of the French fleet, which escaped from Toulon in the foulest weather possible for the watching Nelson, began on 11 May. Convinced that the West Indies was its destination, Nelson and the ships under his command set sail after them. He had settled his wordly affairs and thought to give his mind undividedly to the duty before him. But an important document relating to Horatia was written while in full pursuit of the French, which suggests that further news had come from home to prompt some afterthoughts. On 16 May he wrote to his solicitor William Haslewood and also to Lady Hamilton to ensure finally that Horatia was taken to live at Merton. It would seem that Lady Hamilton

[1] M.813.   [2] M.814.   [3] P. ii, 421.

had brought up Mrs. Gibson's unwillingness to part from Horatia as a further argument for not taking her there. To put an end to this, Nelson settled a pension on Mrs. Gibson on condition she gave up the child to Lady Hamilton for good. To Emma he wrote in terms that might be seen by all:

> Victory, at sea,
> May 16th 1805
>
> My dearest Lady Hamilton,
>
> As it is my desire to take my adopted daughter, Horatia Nelson Thompson, from under the care of Mrs. Gibson, and to place her under your guardianship, in order that she may be properly educated and brought up, I have, therefore, most earnestly to entreat that you will undertake this charge: and as it is my intention to allow Mrs. Gibson as a free-will offering from myself, (she having no claim upon me, having been regularly paid for her care of the child) the sum of twenty pounds a-year, for the term of her natural life; and I mean it should commence when the child is delivered to you. But should Mrs. Gibson endeavour, under any pretence, to keep my adopted daughter any longer in her care, then I do not hold myself bound to give her one farthing; and I shall, most probably, take other measures.
>
> I shall write to Mr. Haslewood, upon your telling him that you have received the child, to settle the annuity upon Mrs. Gibson; and if you think Miss Connor disposed to be the governess of Horatia, I will make her any allowance for her trouble you may think proper. I, again and again, my dearest friend, request your care of my adopted daughter, whom I pray God to bless. I am ever, for ever, my dear Lady Hamilton, your most faithful and affectionate,
>
> NELSON & BRONTE.[1]

The letter to Haslewood, dated the same day, read:

> Victory May 16th 1805
>
> It is my desire that Mrs. Gibson is given an Annuity of Twenty Pounds a year when she gives up my adopted daughter Horatia Nelson Thompson to the Guardianship of My Dear Friend Lady Emma Hamilton and promises not to have anything more to do with the Child either directly or indirectly, and I leave my estate chargeable with this Annuity.
>
> NELSON & BRONTE [2]
>
> William Haslewood, Esq

It is doubtful whether Nelson's wishes for Horatia's settlement would have been carried out had he been killed there and then. In the event, she was not removed from Mrs. Gibson's care until his return to England in August.

---

[1] Nicolas, vi, 444 (TRA/14/NMM/9421).   [2] NMM/TRA/9421.

CHAPTER VII

FATHER AND DAUGHTER

NELSON'S instructions to Haslewood would have taken two months to reach England. By then, having chased the enemy fleets to the West Indies and back (covering 3,458 miles), Nelson was patrolling the Spanish coast again and preparing to hand over his command. He was dazed with fatigue and the frustration of his quest, as far as ever from enticing the enemy ships within range of his guns, and desperately in need of rest. He had not heard from England since April and was sick for news of home. The unusual ill-success of his mission darkened even his anticipations of leave: 'I have brought home no honour for my Country,' he wrote, when finally within sight of his goal, 'nor any riches . . . God send us a happy meeting as our parting was sorrowful.'[1]

Nothing was changed in the circumstances of those he loved. How Lady Hamilton spent her time during the spring and summer of 1805 is known in detail from the letters of Charlotte Nelson to her mother; the social round did not vary, nor did the constant pressure of Emma's debts —except that both increased. 'We had a very pleasant day at Lady Mansfield's', wrote Charlotte in June: 'Mrs. Bianchi went with us Lady H. and Mrs. Bianchi sang a great many duets I also sung a trio with them . . . We stopped at the Duke's ['Q'] as we came home. We are going this morning to Merton.'[2] 'We went yesterday to a House in Palace Yard,' she wrote again, 'to see the King go to the House of Lords. Mrs. Bianchi is sent for to sing at the Queen's House on Friday Evening and the King has chosen what songs she is to sing . . . Horatio is gone out this morning with Mr. Coppindale. Mary Gibbs is with us she leaves us tomorrow.'[3] On 6 June Lady Hamilton with her young protégées (Eliza Bolton began to stay regularly with her this summer) went to Eton for Montem and Charlotte wrote to her mother from Windsor: 'We all went in the Evening to see the Boats—Horatio's was the first. He was in a beautiful Gold and White dress. His pullers were Gallic Slaves. We were all quite delighted with the sight . . . We are going to see the Castle & afterwards we are

---

[1] N. to Ly H., 18 Aug. 1805. See below, Note 1, p. 89.
[2] BRP/NMM/9292/1.   [3] Ibid.

going to Langly Park to see Mrs. Lutwidge.'[1] During their absence at
Windsor and the ensuing visits, Lady Hamilton had her house in Clarges
Street redecorated. From Merton on their return, Charlotte reported:
'You cannot think how well the house in Clarges Street looks it does not
smell much of paint.' The season was beginning to tell on Lady Hamilton
who, Charlotte reported, was 'very ill with Nettle Rash' and ordered by
her doctor 'to take a hot bath every day'. She was overdue at Southend
for her annual sea-bathing, where she had told the Boltons she was
going on 10 July, but still the pressure of engagements kept her in town.
Charlotte wrote to her mother on 20 July that they were 'going to a party
at Mr. Braham's this evening . . . and to a Masquerade to-morrow . . .
Lady Hamilton and I are going in Neapolitan dresses.'[2] 'Miss Gibbs' was
the subject of frequent mention in Charlotte's letters, joining in many of
the social engagements for which she was expressly fetched from school;
but no mention of Horatia 'Thompson' ever appears in the same letters.
The omission, viewed in the light of Charlotte's reputed 'fondness for the
child', is the more surprising, unless she was under clear instructions
from Lady Hamilton not to mention the child in her letters home.
The William Nelsons' total change of front towards Lady Hamilton
after Nelson's death, learning of his provisions for Horatia, would
suggest that they, at least, were not left in any doubt of the child's
parentage and were not prepared to countenance either her or her
mother. One of Lady Hamilton's chief reasons for keeping Horatia
hidden may well have been a clear perception of these disagreeable consequences.

No one in Lady Hamilton's social circle dreamt that the nervous fatigue
and the 'nettle-rash' were caused by anything else than exhaustion. The
fact was that her financial position was extremely grave and causing her
mother untold anxieties. Mrs. Cadogan, left in charge at Merton, urged
her on 18 July to leave town not only for her health but for economy's
sake. On that date, she wrote to her daughter,

My dear Emma, I shall be very glad to see you to-morrow and I think you quite
right to keep yourself quiet for a while. My dear Emma, Cribb [the Merton
gardener and general factotum much considered by Nelson] is quite distrest for
money, would be glad if you could bring him the £13 he paid, for the taxes, to
pay the mowers. My dear Emma, I have got the baker's and butcher's bills cast
up; they come to 1 hundred pounds, seventeen shillings. God Almighty bless
you, my dear Emma, and grant us good news of our dear Lord. My dear Emma,
bring me a bottle of ink and a box of wafers.[3]

[1] Ibid.   [2] Ibid.   [3] M.821.

Lady Hamilton was deeply in debt and there was no way out of it, for even when Nelson came home she could never confide to him its extent. Before he had bought Merton he had written to her in all good faith: 'I trust, my dear friend, to your economy, for I have need of it. . . . You are right, my dear Emma, to pay your debts—to be in debt is to be in misery, and poor tradespeople cannot afford to lay out their money.' The 'poor tradespeople' of Merton who had given credit for over two years, and would still continue to 'lay out their money' for the mistress of Merton, would in the event, never get it back: a contingency that would have been unthinkable to Nelson. Providing £100 a month for the expenses of his house, he did not imagine that the bills for the barest necessities remained unpaid. Emma went to Southend and Mrs. Cadogan remained to face the creditors alone.

Nelson's return in mid-August was sudden and dramatic. News of his approach reached Lady Hamilton on the 18th while she was still on the coast and little expecting his arrival, and she had barely time to hurry back to Merton to receive him there. His breathless impatience can be sensed in a hurried note he sent her from Spithead where he was held up by quarantine regulations:

Victory, Spithead, 18th
August 1805

I am, my dearest Emma, this moment anchored and as the post will not go out till eight o'clock, and you not get the letter till eleven or twelve o'clock to-morrow, I have ordered a Post-office express to tell you of my arrival. I hope we shall be out of quarantine to-morrow, when I shall fly to dear Merton. You must believe all I would say, and fancy what I think; but I suppose this letter will be cut open, smoked, and perhaps read. I have not heard from you since April by Abbé Campbell. The boat is waiting, and I must finish. This day two years and three months I left you [18 May 1803, i.e. two years and four months]. God send us a happy meeting as our parting was sorrowful.[1]

The next day, on receiving her answer, his anticipations seemed fulfilled: 'I have this moment got yours of last night from Merton. I shall rejoice to see dear Horatia, Charlotte, and Ann (sic) and Eliza, and I would not have my Emma's relative [Sarah Connor] go without my seeing her.' Rarely had Emma had to move more quickly than in the twenty-four hours preceding Nelson's arrival; Horatia had to be brought from Mrs. Gibson's, and the family convened; the world must not find matter for censure, and Nelson must be pleased.

'Thanks, my dear Lady,' Mrs. Bolton wrote from Cranwich, 'for your

[1] P. ii, 486.

scrap. It was, indeed, short and *sweet*, for *sweet* was the intelligence that my dearest brother was arrived in England. What a Paradise he must think Merton, to say nothing of the Eve it contains. I need not give you joy, for I am *sure* you have it.'[1]

Driving through the night, Nelson reached Merton at 6 a.m. on Tuesday, 20 August. From Clarges Street the next day Lady Hamilton wrote to Mrs. Matcham:

Our Nelson begs his love to you and Mr. Matcham, and shall be most happy to see you at Merton and I need not say how glad I shall be to see you in Clarges Street. I shall meet you at Merton. Nelson when he is in town goes to an Hotel [Gordon's Hotel, Albemarle Street] . . . The town is wild to see him. What a day of rejoicing was yesterday at Merton. How happy he is to see us all I have not time to say more than God bless you.'[2]

The hero's return had rekindled not only the fires of love, but all Lady Hamilton's zest for living; once more she was at the centre of public events, one of the most observed actors in a national drama. Nelson could not appear in the London streets without being recognized by the crowds and cheered.

On his first day in town he had appointments at the Admiralty, at the Navy Office, at his Agents, with Pitt; he made time to go to his sword-cutler in the Strand, Mr. Salter, to order a knife, fork and spoon to be engraved with the name 'Horatia', and a silver-gilt cup which was to be engraved: 'To my much loved Horatia'. His daughter was no longer to eat and drink out of common wares, but to have her name blazoned for all to see. She was to take her place at his table and to be accepted by his kin. Whatever the explanations offered by the proud man to his brother and sisters now gathered round his board, Horatia was to be imposed by his will. There is an eye-witness's account preserved in Harrison's *Life of Lord Nelson* (the first in the field, published in 1806) describing how, with the family at full strength during those days at Merton, a second dining-table was necessary to accommodate the children of the party—Charlotte and Horace Nelson; Tom, Eliza and Anne Bolton; and George Matcham junior: 'Among this amiable and interesting group', wrote Harrison, 'was Miss Horatia Nelson Thompson, Lord Nelson's adopted daughter, an infant about five years of age.' Harrison added: 'the sight of these young persons associated under his roof constituted the chief bliss of his life.'[3]

Horatia was put under the care of Fatima, Lady Hamilton's black maid,

[1] NMM/NWD/9594/7.   [2] Eyre-Matcham, 226.
[3] Harrison, ii, 460 et seq.

who took the place of Mrs. Gibson. Cribb's son-in-law, Thomas Hudson, a boy of twelve when Lord Nelson drove away from Merton to Trafalgar, and who lived until 1889, recalled seeing the child playing in the grounds of Merton closely followed by her black attendant.[1]

Portraits of Horatia as Nelson knew her show her in accordance with the fashion of the day with her hair cropped like a boy's and wearing long pantellettes. A sketch dating presumably from this time, in which she is holding Nelson's silver cup in her hand, emphasizes the resemblance to Lady Hamilton in the upper part of the face, as Nelson had noted when she was much younger. Another portrait shows her with her rocking-horse on the terrace at Merton, equipped with riding-crop and top hat—a very enterprising little Amazon. Nelson's prodigious love for her could not find outlet enough in the short time during which he had her for his own. His pride in her would not tolerate any secrecy; she was taken to church. When the whole party from Merton attended the service on the first Sunday after Nelson's return (25 August) she took her place for the first time among the other residents' children at the Revd. Thomas Lancaster's afternoon service, at which they were taught their Catechism and hymns. Her age was given as five some time before she had reached it, and it was learned that she had been christened at Marylebone Church. Among her classmates she was soon found to be 'a very clever child.'[2]

Harrison, who when he wrote his *Life* was Lady Hamilton's mouth-piece, loyally kept her secret at the time—however much he betrayed her later. The wording of his introduction of Horatia is significant:

What real affinity, if any, that charming child may bear to his lordship, is a secret at present known by few; and, as it should seem, by none who feel at liberty to divulge it. She was certainly an object of his constant and most tender regard; and, though the family in general appear disinclined to believe her his daughter, it seems highly probable that she is so ... With respect to the mys-terious child, whose unfortunate mother may, most probably, now be no more, it is only certain that Lady Hamilton was induced to receive her at a very tender age, as his Lordship's adopted daughter ... and her ladyship, at Lord Nelson's request, kindly undertook the care of Miss Horatia's education, as she has al-ready done, for some years, that of the present highly accomplished Lady Charlotte Nelson; and since, of the amiable Miss Ann (sic) Bolton.[3]

The successful upbringing by Lady Hamilton of the other two girls was thus used to explain, and excuse if need be, the parallel position of Horatia in her house.

[1] Chamberlain: *Reminiscences of Old Merton.*
[2] Note by Canon Plunkett of Waddington, NMM/NWD/9594.   [3] Harrison, op cit.

Certainly during these last days at Merton Horatia's presence cast no suspicion on Lady Hamilton. Among Nelson's victories this was, admittedly, a minor one, yet from Lady Hamilton's point of view it was of capital and lasting importance. The part allotted to her of benevolent patroness was never openly contested; in future Nelson's adopted daughter was regarded as a sacred trust that none but corrupt hearts could betray. From then on the little girl so openly cherished by Lord Nelson at Merton became an accepted accessory to Lady Hamilton's public image—one that, whatever liabilities her childhood might entail, lived to pay handsome dividends to her patroness. It may be questioned, indeed, whether Nelson's family would ultimately have maintained such good relations with Lady Hamilton but for the continued presence at her side of Nelson's child.

If Nelson's Vicar, Mr. Lancaster, had any suspicions about the little girl introduced to Merton, Nelson's countless virtues outweighed everything else in his eyes. It must have been hard for him to believe that Nelson could do any wrong; he knew the admiral's unobtrusive charities better than any. In after years, his daughter, then Mrs. Ullock, attested to the deep devotion in which his memory was held by their family. When Sir Harris Nicolas was preparing his edition of Nelson's letters (1844–6) she wrote to him:

In revered affection for the memory of that dear man, I cannot refrain from informing you of his unlimited charity and goodness during his residence at Merton. His frequently expressed desire was that none in that place should want or suffer affliction that he could alleviate, and this I know he did with a most liberal hand: always desiring that it should not be known from whence it came. His residence at Merton was a continued course of charity and goodness, setting such an example of propriety and regularity that there are few would not be benefited by following it.[1]

How complete was Mr. Lancaster's trust in Nelson is shown by his confiding his twelve-year-old son to his care at his last departure. The boy sailed with Nelson as a '1st Class Volunteer' in the *Victory*, and Nelson lost no time in writing home to tell the anxious parents that the boy 'would do well'. Mr. Lancaster, who doubled his duties as incumbent of Merton with those of schoolmaster, prevailed on Nelson during those last crowded days to visit his 'Academy' at Eagle House with Lady Hamilton to hear his senior boys recite. This Nelson did, and obtained a half-holiday for them in return! A cult grew up at Eagle House for the national hero that resulted in the school's name being changed after Trafalgar to 'Nelson House'.[2]

[1] Nicolas, vii, 228.   [2] J. K. Laughton, *Nelson's House at Merton*.

The record of these last domestic days at Merton is supplied by numbers of witnesses and varies according to the eye of the beholder, but all were agreed on one thing—Nelson's great affection for his family and old friends. Mrs. Bolton, writing to her sister to urge her to come to Merton despite her recent loss of a little boy, told her 'you will find him such a kind and affectionate Relation and Friend as seldom is to be met with. Seeing and hearing him will soothe your Griefs.'[1] Lord Minto, who was with him often, has left a picture of a man at peace with himself and with his fellow men. 'Nelson is kinder and more confidential with me than ever,' he wrote to his wife on 29 August. Not waiting for an invitation Minto hurried down to Merton on the first Saturday after Nelson's return. On 26 August he noted:

I went to Merton on Saturday and found Nelson just sitting down to dinner, surrounded by a family party, of his brother the Dean, Mrs. Nelson, their children, and the children of a sister. Lady Hamilton was at the head of the table, and Mother Cadogan at the bottom. I had a hearty welcome. He looks remarkably well and in spirits. His conversation is a cordial in these low times . . . Lady Hamilton has improved and added to the house and the place extremely well without his knowing she was about it. He found it all ready done. She is a clever being after all; the passion is as hot as ever.[2]

On 28 August Minto dined with Nelson at Lady Hamilton's in Clarges Street, where again 'it was a family party of brothers and sisters with their husbands, and Mr. Greville (Charles)'. It was for such emergencies that Lady Hamilton kept her town house open, to preserve an appearance of complete independence from Lord Nelson, by returning hospitality for hospitality—always under the aegis of his family's presence. To help his sister's family, Nelson so far departed from his invariable rule never to ask favours for himself of the government, as to write to Mr. Rose, Secretary of the Cabinet, to solicit Pitt for a place in the Customs and Excise for Mr. Bolton. Writing on 29 August from his hotel in town, he said:

Although I certainly want nothing for my individual self, yet you, and every one, must be sensible that I have many and dear relatives who I am anxious to get something for, and such a place as they will do credit to as Servants of the State . . . Although I have seen Mr. Pitt, yet at a time when he is pleased to think that my services may be wanted, I could not bring my mouth to ask a favour, therefore I beg it may pass *through you*.[3]

By the end of August the Matchams had arrived from Bath. Already ten days of Nelson's 'uncertain stay' at home had passed and in official

[1] NMM/NWD/9594/6.   [2] Minto, iii, 363 et seq.   [3] GIR/NMM/1.

circles, where he spent much of every day, returning to Merton only in time for dinner at 3.30 p.m., no secret was made of the fact that he would shortly be called out again. The family's sense of his impending departure decided the Matchams to send for their son George—'to see Lord N. my Uncle before his departure', as George headed this section of his journal.[1] He set out from Bath at 4.30 in the morning of 3 September and reached the White Horse Cellars in Piccadilly, where the coaches stopped, at 10 p.m. His journey was not yet over, having still to cover the eight miles to Merton. 'On alighting,' recorded George,

was accosted by a man who offer'd to take my Trunk. Refused thinking him some thief. Told me he was Ld. N's Gardener [Cribb] waiting with an open Chaise to take me to Merton . . . It rain'd . . . On arriving at M. found them all in bed. Lady H. came out en chemise, & directed me to my cousin T's [Tom Bolton] room where I was to sleep. Had not seen him for ten years, soon made acquaintance.[2]

From the time of George Matcham's arrival, the daily incidents at Merton were faithfully recorded, sometimes in great detail. His interests were centred mostly on the comings and goings of the celebrities who thronged the house during Nelson's last days in England. George had a critical and inquisitive mind and an observant eye for the attitudes and opinions of the visitors, recording his likings and antipathies with perfect frankness. Few came by invitation—apart from Royalty who imposed themselves. Nelson indeed confined his dinner engagements to two at home (Lord Minto, and his neighbour at Wandle Bank, the journalist James Perry) and two outside—his neighbour at Morden Hall, Mr. Goldsmid, and the Duke of Queensberry in town. But callers were numerous and not always timely. A Danish historian arrived on the very day of Nelson's return, 20 August, wishing to discuss details of Copenhagen with the victor of the battle; he was received with great patience and courtesy and without the least show of 'pride of rank' before Nelson had fairly taken off his uniform.

A trace of 'ennui' shows in George's reports of the organized entertainments offered his boy cousins and himself; on the morning after his arrival—having duly paid his respects to his host and the assembled uncles and aunts—he went out shooting with his cousin Horace: 'After a tedious morning he shot a brace'. There was 'a Large Company at dinner' and cards afterwards, at which he lost 11s. 6d., a disaster that was made good by a tip of two guineas from Lord Nelson presented by Lady Hamilton. Fishing in the 'Pond' after breakfast on his second morning at Merton,

[1] Eyre-Matcham, 228 et seq.   [2] Ibid.

HORATIA STANDING ON A CHAIR, holding Nelson's cup, original drawing

HORATIA WITH HER ROCKING-HORSE at Merton, Water colour by Baxter

young George was less favoured than Sir William Hamilton, and 'caught nothing'; a desultory afternoon 'Sauntering about ye Grounds' was terminated by the arrival of the Duke of Clarence to dinner. To the Duke Nelson presented his nephews as his 'three props': George observed that the Duke 'Talked much', that he showed 'deference to Ld. N's opinion', that he was 'Violent against Mr. Pitt', seemed 'estranged from ye K—g' and altogether that the evening in his company and that of his equerry Lord Errol was 'Heavy'.[1]

On Sunday, after church, Sydney Smith arrived. George found him 'Handsome' and listened to his talk about the Siege of Acre. But Mr. Goldsmid's dinner, to which all the young people from Merton Place were invited on Monday, 9 September, whilst Nelson and Lady Hamilton dined in town in company with the Duke of Devonshire and Lady Elizabeth Foster, George frankly did not like, because it was 'jewish'. Mr. Beckford's singing and 'extempore performance on the Harpsichord' when he called next day to express his disappointment at Nelson's declining an invitation to Fonthill, George pronounced 'a horrible noise'.

The evidence of this hypercritical young man, when it touches Lord Nelson himself, is the more valuable therefore to the biographer; it shows Nelson in his rare moments of privacy, not dressed for the parade of history, nor speaking to the crowds of his admirers, but at his own dining-table, with only his family about him, at home at Merton. Lord Minto had caught him in a different setting, 'in a mob in Piccadilly' on 26 August, and left posterity the description of the scene that has been so often quoted: 'I . . . got hold of his arm, so that I was mobbed too. It is really quite affecting to see the wonder and admiration, and love and respect, of the whole world; and the genuine expression of all these sentiments at once, from gentle and simple, the moment he is seen. It is beyond anything represented in a play or a poem of fame.'[2] Charles Lamb, glimpsing him in Pall Mall shortly before his departure, remarked that he was 'looking just as a Hero should', and could not get his image out of his mind. Lady Elizabeth Foster, a devotee of Nelson's, wrote in her Journal: 'Wherever he appears he electrifies the cold English character, and rapture and applause follow all his steps. Sometimes a poor woman asks to touch his coat. The very children learn to bless him as he passes, and doors and windows are crowded.'[3]

But George Matcham remembered something different, the family man whose liking was for sober clothes and whose voice was the least

[1] Ibid.   [2] Minto, iii, 363.
[3] D. M. Stuart, Dearest Bess.

heard at his own table. When the *Remains of the late Mrs. Richard Trench*
(formerly Mrs. St. Denis) were published in 1861 George Matcham
wrote to *The Times* (6 November) to refute the passages relating to Lord
Nelson—the passages concerning his meeting with the author in Dresden
in 1800.

I visited my Uncle twice during the short periods he was on shore, once in 1802
during his journey to Wales, . . . and the second time at his house at Merton
in 1805 . . . and I can assert with truth that a more complete contrast between
this lady's portrait and my thorough recollection of him could not be forced on
my mind. Lord Nelson in private life was remarkable for a demeanour quiet,
sedate and unobtrusive, anxious to give pleasure to everyone about him,
distinguishing each in turn by some act of kindness, and chiefly those who
seemed to require it most. During his few intervals of leisure, in a little knot
of relations and friends, he delighted in quiet conversation, through which ran
an undercurrent of pleasantry not unmixed with caustic wit. At his table he was
the least heard among the company, and so far from being the hero of his own
tale, I never heard him voluntarily refer to any of the great actions of his life . . .
he seemed to me to waive homage with as little attention as was consistent with
civility . . . It would have formed an amusement to the circle at Merton if
intemperence were set down to the master of the house, who always so prematurely cut short the sitting of the gentlemen after dinner. A man of more
temperate habits could not . . . have been found . . . in his plain suit of black,
in which he alone recurs to my memory, he always looked what he was—a
gentleman . . . his disposition was truly noble . . . it revolted against all wrong
and oppression. His heart, indeed, was as tender as it was courageous. Many
like myself could bear witness to his gentleness, kindness, good breeding and
courtesy.

Whilst the ladies sat on the verandah at Merton, or were rowed by the
gentlemen on the 'Nile', and Horace and George and Tom went fishing in
the pond and caught nothing for their pains, rumours of the coming
events were gathering momentum. George Matcham's father later revealed to his son what had been happening a day or two before George's
own arrival. On the evening of 31 August Nelson had been deeply pre-
occupied throughout dinner. The next day, Sunday, instead of going to
church, he hurried to town to see Pitt and to lay his views on the enemy's
movements before him; he differed from Pitt, who reckoned the French
were bent for the West Indies, and eventually persuaded him that the
French and Spanish, with great augmentation of sails, were bound for
Cadiz or Toulon. To meet them, the English must send out more ships
than the cabinet had agreed on. Having discussed the number of ships to
send, Pitt said 'Now who is to take command?' 'You cannot have a

better man than the present one, Collingwood,' Nelson answered.
Whereupon Pitt insisted: 'No, that won't do, *you* must take command.'
He asked Nelson if he could be ready to sail in three days, and Nelson
answered, 'I am ready now.' [1]

Having first confided this to his brother-in-law alone Nelson was not
able to keep it from the rest of the household for very long. At 5 a.m. the
next morning Captain Blackwood called at Merton on his way to Whitehall
with the news that the enemy fleet had been sighted exactly where Nelson
had predicted, off Cadiz. Nelson followed Blackwood up to town where
he had an appointment with Lord Minto, from whom he hid nothing.
Lord Minto reported categorically: 'He is going to resume the command
of the Mediterranean as soon as the "Victory" is ready, which will be
within a week.' [2]

Subsequently Lady Hamilton insisted that he had declined the command and was resolved to retire into private life, and had only on her
instance been persuaded to go. The theatrical incident, related by her to
Harrison as having taken place in the garden at Merton, gave her the
decisive, heroic, self-sacrificing role. The story tells how, on her insistence
that it was his duty to go, he had exclaimed: 'Good Emma! Brave Emma!
If there were more Emmas there would be more Nelsons.' [3] Time and
repetition so convinced her of its truth, that within a couple of years she
could proudly reproach herself for being responsible for Nelson's death.
It was not until after the glory of Trafalgar had crowned Nelson's career,
however, that Lady Hamilton made any such claim; she accepted the
inevitable necessity of his going, and wrote to Lady Bolton (who was not
with the party at Merton) on 4 September 1805 with the grief natural to
her situation: 'My dear Friend, I am again broken hearted, as our dear
Nelson is immediately going. It seems as though I have had a fortnight's
dream, and am awoke to all the misery of this cruel separation. But
what can I do? His powerful arm is of so much consequences to his
Country.' [4]

No one, least of all the ministers meeting at Downing Street on 6
September to deliberate upon the scale and direction operations were to
take, suspected that the man they were sending out to 'annihilate' the
enemy fleet (that was the word he insistently used in urging adequate
supplies) was going against his will; his fire and energy impressed them
quite otherwise. On that day the news of Nelson's appointment appeared
in the press.

[1] Eyre-Matcham, 234.   [2] Minto, iii, 369.
[3] Harrison, op. cit.   [4] Nicolas, vii, 28.

'I hope my absence will not be long', [he wrote to his old friend Alexander Davison] 'and that I shall soon meet the Combined Fleets, with a force sufficient to do the job well; for half a Victory would but half content me . . . But I will do my best; and I hope God Almighty will go with me. I have much to lose, but little to gain; and I go because it's right.' [1]

The next day he wrote to Collingwood, who was still in the Mediterranean: 'My dear Coll, I shall be with you in a very few days, and I hope you will remain Second in Command.' [2]

Despite the official appointments, the naval despatches, recommendations, and requisitions that had kept him at his desk, he found time to see his Merton neighbours. He stood sponsor for his friend Colonel Suckling's child, brought on purpose to Merton Church on 6 September to be christened; called on the Goldsmid brothers, both on Abraham Goldsmid at Morden Hall and on Benjamin at Roehampton—whose eight-year-old son Lionel clamoured to go to sea, like Mr. Lancaster's son. Nelson, pacing the Goldsmid's library with the boy's mother, declared he was too small, and that he must grow before he would take him. The recommendation was not lost on Lionel; every day he did exercises to make himself taller, measuring the result by standing on tiptoe and trying to get his nose onto the edge of the library round table. He never forgot being in that library one November day with his mother and sisters when the servant came in with a letter. When his mother opened it she shrieked: 'Children! Lord Nelson is kill'd!' [3]

Nelson talked with Cribb, his gardener, during those last days, examining every part of the grounds, concluding with him what was to be done, and deciding on next year's planting. Thomas and Anne Cribb were parents of three children and were shortly expecting a fourth; hearing this on his last morning at Merton, Nelson told Cribb 'If it's a boy call him Horatio, if a girl, Emma,' and gave him money for a christening robe. [4]

Nelson himself paid the contractor, Chawner, for the work done so far at Merton, and settled with Davison to pay 'what is ordered to be done— the kitchen, anteroom, and alterations to the dining-room', writing detailed instructions to that effect even after rejoining the fleet on 16 September. On leaving home he fully believed that not a penny would be owed for the work at Merton. He could not have imagined that before

---

[1] Nicolas, vii, 30.   [2] Ibid., 32.
[3] *Transactions of the Jewish Historical Society*, xiv, 225–45.
[4] Jagger, *Nelson's Home and Life at Merton*.

long Lady Hamilton would blame the 'crippling expenses for Merton' for her bankruptcy.

By 10 September Nelson knew that he would be leaving on the 13th. As he and Lady Hamilton had had so little time alone together most of the family discreetly decided to leave on the day before: the Revd. Dr. and his wife took the young people with them and only Nelson's sisters Mrs. Bolton and the Matchams (the last to arrive) remained to the end. A summons to Carlton House, sent late on the evening of the 11th by the Prince of Wales's equerry, laid the disagreeable obligation on Nelson to go to town and pay his respects early on the morning of the 12th. Lady Hamilton drove with him so as not to lose a moment of his company, but did not accompany him to Carlton House. The incident gave her the excuse in later years to claim the Prince's protection on the grounds of his 'great devotion to Lord Nelson'; for the Prince's equerry had said in his letter to Nelson that His Royal Highness 'would feel miserable if his lordship were to take his departure without giving H. R. H. the happiness to see him'.[1]

A quiet family dinner had been planned for that day; Lord Minto and Nelson's Merton neighbours, the Perrys, were the only guests expected. Lord Minto wrote to his wife an account of it the next day:

I went yesterday to Merton in a great hurry, as he, Lord Nelson, said he was to be at home all day, and he dines at half-past three. But I found he had been sent for to Carlton House, and he and Lady Hamilton did not return till half-past five. I stayed till ten at night, and took a final leave of him. He is to have fifty sail of the line, and a proportioned number of frigates, sloops, and small vessels. This is the largest command that any admiral has had for a long time. He goes to Portsmouth to-night . . . Lady Hamilton was in tears all yesterday; could not eat, and hardly drink, and near swooning, and all at table. It is a strange picture. She tells me nothing can be more pure and ardent than this flame. He is in many points a really great man, in others a baby. His friendship and mine is little short of the other attachment, and is quite sincere.[2]

The reason for Nelson's delay was only known later when Sir Arthur Wellesley related their fortuitous meeting in the waiting room of the Colonial Office, where Lord Castlereagh's pressure of work kept them waiting long enough for them to become known to each other for the first time.

Young Tom Hudson and the other Merton boys were on the alert to see Lord Nelson drive to London on the morning of the 13th to get his final orders from the Admiralty. He was back to dinner for half-past

[1] P. ii, 492.   [2] Minto, iii, 370.

three and spent the evening closeted with his family. The chaise to drive him through the night to Portsmouth had been ordered from the King's Head for half-past ten. Nelson was concerned at not having been able to repay Mr. Matcham his loan towards the purchase of Axe's field, fearing that with such a large family to rear he might find himself short, and discussed the situation with him after dinner. Mr. Matcham had no thought of pressing for a payment and soothed him with the words: 'My dear Lord, I have no other wish than to see you return home in safety. As to myself, I am not in want of anything.' The excuse to talk business in those last tense hours may have been welcome; it helped defer the dreaded moment of parting from Emma. She told Lady Elizabeth Foster afterwards how, when the supreme moment came, 'he had come back four different times, and the last time he kneeled down and holding up his hand prayed God to bless her'.[1] Emma did not confide to Lady Elizabeth another scene which had preceded this, but which she later reported to Harrison:[2] how Nelson had gone up to the sleeping Horatia and prayed by her cot. For the unconscious child there was no moment of parting, no need for tears. For the rest of her life she would remember her father as he had been to her during these twenty-five days at Merton, a vital presence filling every room and the sunny garden walks with his enfolding love.

Mr. Matcham accompanied him to the door when the chaise drew up. Mr. Matcham proved himself a good friend to Horatia in the years to come, and it is not improbable that in these last moments he was asked to protect her if her natural protector were killed. Mr. Lancaster, bound for Portsmouth with his boy, also drove from Merton that night. The travellers changed horses at Liphook, and there, at the 'Anchor Inn' where they served Nelson with tea, he wrote in his private journal:

Friday Night, 13th September. At half-past ten drove from dear dear Merton, where I left all I hold dear in this world, to go to serve my King and Country. May the Great God whom I adore enable me to fulfil the expectations of my Country; and if it is His good pleasure that I should return, my thanks will never cease being offered up to the Throne of His Mercy. If it is His good providence to cut short my days upon earth, I bow with the greatest submission, relying that He will protect those so dear to me, that I may leave behind.—His will be done: Amen, Amen, Amen.[3]

This prayer, copied by his chaplain after his death, was given to Lady Hamilton.

---

[1] Journals of Elizabeth Foster: D. M. Stuart, *The Two Duchesses*, 127–8.
[2] Harrison, ii, 460 et seq.   [3] Nicolas, vii, 33–5.

He reached Portsmouth at 6 a.m. and as always alighted at the 'George Inn'. He lost no time in writing to Emma, benefiting by the return of Mr. Lancaster to Merton to send her a note by hand.

My dearest Emma, I arrived this moment, and Mr. Lancaster takes this. His coach is at the door, and only waits for my line. Victory is at St Helens, and, if possible, shall be at sea this day. God protect you and my dear Horatia, prays, Yours ever Nelson & Bronte.
6 o'clock, George Inn,
Sept 14th 1805 [1]

Nelson's embarkation from the beach at the point where the bathing machines were drawn up to avoid the great crowds pressing to see him go has been immortalized by Southey; Nelson himself recorded it in few words in his private journal; 'At six o'clock arrived at Portsmouth and having arranged all my business, embarked at the Bathing Machines with Mr. Rose and Mr. Canning at two; got on board the Victory at St. Helen's who dined with me; preparing for sea'. Mr. Rose, staying at his Hampshire house, Cuffnells, had come at Nelson's special request to see him off, for he wished to impress on him the need to help Lady Hamilton get a pension from Pitt in case of his death. Rose never forgot the injunction and acted on it loyally, though unavailingly, in the ensuing years.[2]

Nelson wrote to Lady Hamilton whenever he could, exhorting her on 17 September: 'I entreat, my dear Emma, that you will cheer up; and we will look forward to many, many happy years, and be surrounded by our children's children . . . My heart and soul is with you and Horatia. I get this line ready in case a Boat should get alongside.' [3]

In their common anxiety the members of Nelson's family clung together pending the events for which all waited—the battle against the combined enemy fleets, the expected victory, and Nelson's safe return. Mrs. Bolton went with the Matchams to Bath and remained there until 23 October.

Eliza and Tom Bolton returned home to Cranwich, Anne accompanied the William Nelsons to Canterbury to keep Charlotte company, and Emma soon joined them. Writing to her on 26 October Eliza Bolton made the first reference to Horatia in the family correspondence. Supposing Horatia to be with her, she sent the family's united love to 'Anne, Horatia, and all the party'.[4] Horatia was in fact left at Merton in the care of Mrs. Cadogan and her new governess, Cecilia Connor. Cecilia wrote daily

[1] P. ii, 497. [2] Rose's *Diaries*, i, 264–5.
[3] Nicolas, vii, 40. [4] M.840.

reports about her little charge which, in due course, were forwarded to
Nelson. To judge by one written to Charlotte Nelson on 4 October,
Horatia was lucky in having so kind, judicious and sensible a guardian:
'I am excessively obliged to you for your kind letter,' Cecilia wrote:

> You see I take advantage of your request to write soon by answering it as quickly
> as possible . . . Little Horatia sends a kiss to you & Lady H. & her love to all
> your party. She is looking very well indeed, & is to me a most delightful com-
> panion. We read about twenty times a day, as I do not wish to confine her long
> at a time, & she is now learning the names of the keys on the pianoforte. I am
> quite busy dressing her doll. I've just completed a mattress & pillow for the
> bed; it is a continual source of amusement . . . Mr. Bolton left us yesterday
> morning & set out for Cranwich the same evening. We went to town on Wednes-
> day about Tom's clothes, & meant to have dined in Clarges Street. We had
> forgot they were busy papering, so we dined at Mrs. Roberts. Horatia liked it
> amazingly, & we bought some shoes & stockings & a hat for the doll. (She is now
> very busy making her doll's bed) She is uncommonly quick, and I dare say will
> read tolerably by the time you see her again. I told her she was invited to see a
> ship launched; every morning she asks if it is to be *to-day* & wanted to know
> if there will be any *firing of guns*. . . . Horatia has written & indited the whole of
> what is written at the end. She wants to guide my hand as I did hers, while I
> write this. My love to my lady.[1]

Horatia wrote: 'My dear my Lady I thank you for the books. I drink
out of my Lord's cup every day give my love to him every day when you
write, and a kiss. Miss Connor gave me some kisses when I read my book
well. O here three kisses my love to Miss Nelson my dear my Lady I
love you very much. Horatia.'[2]

From Canterbury Emma forwarded the letter to Nelson the same day.

> I send you a letter of Miss Connor's, for there is much in it about our dear girl,
> you will like it. I also had one from my mother who doats on her, she says she
> could not live without her. What a blessing for her parents to have such a child,
> so sweet, altho' so young, so amiable? God spare her to them, and be assured,
> my life, my soul, of your own Emma's fondest affections. You are my all of
> good. Heavens bless you.[3]

Four days later, 8 October, Emma wrote again: 'My dearest life, we
are just come from church, and I am so fond of the Church Service and
the Cannons are so civil; we have every day a fine anthem for me . . .'[4]

A glimpse of the civilities exchanged between Lady Hamilton and the
'Cannons' of Canterbury is afforded by the Revd. George Gilbert who

---

[1] NMM/NWD/9594. See also M.842.   [2] Ibid.
[3] Ibid.   [4] Ibid. See also M.845.

recollected an occasion when 'Lady Hamilton and Madame Bianchi sang an Anthem in the choir one day after service a few persons being present. The anthem was Kent's "My Song shall be of Mercy & Judgement". The singing was very fine, for the compass of Lady Hamilton's voice was surprising. Dean Powis was present near the entrance of the presbytery. "Shall I sing an anthem for the benefit of the County Hospital, Mr. Dean?" shouted her ladyship. The Dean, affecting deafness, returned no answer, and her Ladyship understood him.'[1]

From Canterbury, Emma continued to supply Nelson with news of Merton: 'I was obliged to send for Marianna down' she wrote on 8 October, referring to one of the Merton servants,

she gives me such an amiable account of our dearest Horatia. She now reads very well, & is learning her notes, & French, & Italian, & my mother doats on her. The other day she said at table, 'Mrs. Candogging, I wonder Julia did not run out of the church when she went to be married, for I should, seeing my squinting husband come in, for, my God! how ugly he is, and how he looks cross-eyed; why, as my lady says, he looks 2 ways for Sunday.' Now Julia's husband is the ugliest man you ever saw, but how that little thing cou'd observe him; but she is clever, is she not, Nelson? . . . To-day we dine alone, to eat up the scraps, & drink tea with old Mrs. Percy. Charlotte hates Canterbury, it is *so dull*; so it is. My dear girl writes every day in Miss Connor's letter & I am so pleased with her. My heart is broke away from her, but I have now had her so long at Merton that my heart cannot bear to be without her. You will be even fonder of her when you return. She says, 'I love my dear, dear, godpapa, but Mrs. Gibson told me he kill'd all the people, and I was afraid.' Dearest angel that she is! Oh, Nelson! how I love her, but how I do idolize you—the dearest husband of my heart, you are all in this world to your Emma.[2]

By mid-October Emma was back at Merton and wrote to invite Mrs. Bolton to join her there on her return from Bath. Mrs. Bolton replied that she should 'obey yr commands, or rather, I may say, wishes . . .', and urged Lady Hamilton to keep up her spirits, else 'What in the world will my Lord think if he comes back & finds you grown thin and looking ill?'[3] By the time Mrs. Bolton reached Merton on 22 October the battle, for news of which the country was waiting, had been fought and won. But no one in England heard of it until 6 November.

Nelson, shot soon after noon at the height of the action, died at 4.30 p.m. on Monday 21 October. Two letters for Lady Hamilton and for Horatia written within the last hours before the engagement lay on his cabin desk, undelivered, till Captain Hardy brought them himself to England.

[1] Gilbert, op. cit.   [2] NMM/NWD/9594.   [3] Ibid.

The letter to Horatia read:

> Victory, October 19th 1805
>
> My dearest Angel,—I was made happy by the pleasure of receiving your letter of September 19th, and I rejoice to hear that you are so very good a girl, and love my dear Lady Hamilton, who most dearly loves you. Give her a kiss for me. The Combined Fleets of the Enemy are now reported to be coming out of Cadiz; and therefore I answer your letter, my dearest Horatia, to mark to you that you are ever uppermost in my thoughts. I shall be sure of your prayers for my safety, conquest, and speedy return to dear Merton, and our dearest good Lady Hamilton. Be a good girl, mind what Miss Connor says to you. Receive, my dearest Horatia, the affectionate Parental Blessing of your Father,
>
> NELSON & BRONTE.[1]

In a last Codicil to his Will, written in his pocket-book on the morning of the day he died, when in sight of the Combined Enemy Fleets, Nelson wrote a statement, setting forth Lady Hamilton's services to the Mediterranean Fleet before the Battle of the Nile, which in his opinion entitled her to a government pension, and concluded with these words:

> Could I have rewarded those services, I would not now call upon my country; but as that has not been in my power, I leave Emma, Lady Hamilton, therefore, a legacy to my King and Country, that they will give her an ample provision to maintain her rank in life. I also leave to the beneficence of my country my adopted daughter, Horatia Nelson Thompson; and I desire she will use in future, the name of Nelson only. These are the only favours I ask of my King and country, at this moment, when I am going to fight their battle.
>
> NELSON & BRONTE.[2]

This document he called in Captains Hardy and Blackwood to witness.

By the time the letters and the Codicil reached their destination, they had taken on the tone and nature of a testament—a testament that in the event would not go undisputed. While there were some, even in government circles, who considered that Lady Hamilton had a claim to a pension as the widow of a former ambassador who had rendered services in wartime, Horatia's claim was not considered by anyone. It was, indeed, a characteristic gesture on Nelson's part, showing his simple and trusting nature, that he left his natural daughter as a legacy to the state.

---

[1] Ibid.   [2] Nicolas, vii. Preface X.

CHAPTER VIII

THE LAST CODICIL

LADY Elizabeth Foster was reading Herodotus with her daughter Caroline St. Jules at Chiswick House when the Duchess of Devonshire entered the gallery where they sat to tell them of the victory of Trafalgar and the death of Nelson. It was 6 November, and the news had been brought to the Admiralty at 1 a.m. that morning by Lieutenant Lapenotière of the *Pickle* Schooner. An edition 'extraordinary' of the London Gazette was instantly set up, the Park and Tower guns fired salvos, and by 7 a.m. the King was informed at Windsor. The guns were heard, so Lady Hamilton later told Lady Elizabeth, as far out as Merton. Lady Elizabeth called on her on 13 November at 'her little house in Clarges Street', and has left a first-hand report of the interview.

I found her in bed. She had the appearance of person stunned and scarcely as yet able to comprehend the certainty of her loss. What shall I do? and How can I exist? were her first words. She then showed me some of the letters which were lying on the bed—they were from Lord Nelson of the 1st and 7th—and I think the 13th day of October. The greater part of them had appeared in the 'Morning Chronicle' of to-day . . . Lady H. said she had heard nothing, knew no particulars. I asked her if she knew when the 'Victory' came. She said, 'Oh, no— I know nothing.' . . . I asked her if she thought he had any presentiment of his fate. She said No, not till their parting. That he had come back four different times, and the last time he had kneeled down and holding up his hand had prayed God to bless her. She also told me he had requested her to take the sacrament with him at Merton, 'for', said he, 'we both stand before our God with pure hearts and affection'. I asked her how she had heard the dreadful news. 'I had come to Merton,' she said, 'my house not being ready, and feeling rather unwell I said I would stay in bed, on account of a rash. Mrs. Bolton was sitting by my bedside when all of a sudden I said, I think I hear the Tower guns. Some victory perhaps in Germany to retrieve the credit lost by Mack. "Perhaps," said Mrs. Bolton, "It may be news from my brother." "Impossible, surely. There is not time." In five minutes a carriage drove up to the door. I sent to enquire who had arrived. They brought me word, Mr. Whitby, from the Admiralty. "Show him in directly," I said. He came in, and with a pale countenance and faint voice said, "We have gained a great Victory."—"Never mind your victory," I said, "My letters—give me my letters"—Capt. Whitby was unable to speak—tears in his eyes and a deathly paleness over his face made me comprehend him, I believe I gave a scream and fell back, and for ten hours after I could neither speak nor shed a tear—days have passed on, and I know not how they end or begin—nor how I am to bear my future existence.' [1]

Captain Whitby was the bearer of an official letter for Lady Hamilton from the Comptroller of the Navy, Sir Andrew Snape Hammond, who wrote to each individual member of Nelson's family that morning to announce his death. To Lady Nelson only was the communication made by the First Lord himself, Lord Barham. Mrs. Bolton was already at Merton, as has been seen. The letter addressed to her read:

Admiralty, 6th November 1805

Madam,

I am sorry and grieved to the heart, that it should ever have come to my lot to announce to you, that after gaining the most compleat Naval Victory that ever happened, my dearest Friend has fallen in the conflict—a loss the Nation will for ever deplore; altho' it was the death Ld Nelson wished most for.

He died by a Musket Ball in the Shoulder received from the Spanish Admiral's Ship.

I can say no more. My heart is too full to attempt to give comfort to others.

God bless you and all his Relations

Ever your sincere Friend,
A. S. Hammond. [2]

Despite his many foibles the 'Revd. Dr.', as Nelson himself had said, was not without heart. The Revd. George Gilbert witnessed the emotion with which he received the news, and his evidence is worth quoting; it is contained in his *Reminiscences*

Dr. Nelson of course took deep interest in his brother, the Admiral's proceedings. For some days before the battle of Trafalgar he went regularly about 8 o'clock to Bristow's Reading Room on the Parade to gain the earliest information. At last the news of the Victory over the French and Spanish Fleets arrived, and also of Lord Nelson's death. Mr. Bristow (who was I think then Mayor of Canterbury) with great tact came to the Church Yard (part of the Precincts, on the South side of the Cathedral—opposite the Canons' houses) to meet Dr. Nelson and prevent his discovering the intelligence in a public news-room. They met on the Church pavement. I was present. Mr. Bristow gave the news. The Dr. seemed much affected and shed tears, and turned back to his house, applying his white handkerchief to his eyes. In a few hours came the news directly from Government. [3]

[1] D. M. Stuart, Life & Times of Ly Eliz.-Foster, 1955, 127–8.
[2] GIR/NMM/1.   [3] Gilbert, *Reminiscences*.

With his family the Revd. Dr. hurried up to town, as did Mr. and Mrs. Matcham. Sensing the role he would be called upon to play in the following weeks, Dr. Nelson took rooms first at No. 34 Fitzroy Square, and later rented a whole house in Berkeley Square. The Matchams went direct to Merton. Recording the mournful events of that week, young George wrote in his journal for 7 November: 'All the ill news confirmed. Admiral Collingwood's letter received. Mama very ill. Received a letter from the Admiralty. Lady Hamilton very ill.' On the 8th, 'Papa and Mama resolved to go to Town. Set off about 2.'[1] Left at home in charge of his younger brothers and sisters, George forwarded the letters of condolence that streamed into the Matchams' home, and received injunctions from his mother how his sisters were to demean themselves in the public eye. Mrs. Matcham wrote from Merton on 17 November

My dear George,

Let us have a letter either from you or Kate every day ... I shall expect to see your Sisters very much improved in every respect, as it would not be proper for them to be walking about the streets, they will have time to attend to every part of their education [they had a governess]. You may always direct to Merton as we are only a day or two each week in London and the letters are always sent on to us. We are anxious to wait here for the last sad scene, when that will happen God only knows, there is no intelligence when the frigate is likely to arrive. [It was expected Nelson's body would be sent home by frigate.] If we hear nothing in a few days we shall think of returning home, for here we feel our Loss more every day, but it really is cruel to mention our going to my Lady at present. Merton is very dull; quite the reverse to what you knew it ... I do not mean your sisters should not walk out, but I don't wish them to be seen much in the streets till all is over.[2]

When it became apparent that the funeral would be delayed for a considerable time, the Matchams returned home on 23 November. They brought the particulars of Nelson's Will, deposited with his solicitor Mr. Haslewood, which had been carried, together with its seven Codicils, to Doctors' Commons for registration at the first news of Nelson's death. The Matchams brought the further news of the first honours paid the family, the King's grant of an Earldom for the Revd. Dr. and a Viscountcy for the seventeen year old Horace. In his capacity as joint executor of his brother's Will, the new Earl was the first of the family to know the terms of the Second Codicil (dated 6 September 1803) under which Nelson acknowledged and made provision for his 'adopted daughter Horatia Nelson Thompson'.[3]

[1] Eyre-Matcham, 238, et seq.   [2] Ibid., 241-2.
[3] Nicolas, vii, Addenda 236.

It was the Codicil by which he settled £4,000 on her and placed her under the guardianship of Lady Hamilton. If the acknowledgement, and the settlement of £4,000 upon Horatia, came as something of a shock to the reverend gentleman, despite what he saw and may have surmised during the last days at Merton, the proviso affecting his son whom Nelson wished Horatia to marry, 'if he proves himself worthy', appears to have been wholly unwelcome. Horace's parents were nothing if not ambitious for him and it is obvious that from the outset they regarded such a connection as unacceptable. For that reason, if not for the many others shortly to accumulate, the close former intimacy existing between their children and Lady Hamilton was discontinued. By early January excuses were made for withdrawing Charlotte permanently from under her care, and as Horace was going to Cambridge at the same time, intercourse between the two houses lapsed. By then, moreover, Lady Hamilton considered herself a cruelly injured party, and directed the whole force of her animus against the Earl. The reason for this lies in the Earl's conduct regarding Nelson's last Cocidil, and belongs to the long and complicated course of events following the arrival of that document in England.

Not until the *Victory* anchored at St. Helen's on 4 December was the existence of such a Codicil even suspected, and then the delicate character of its bequest placed Nelson's executors, family and friends, in no ordinary dilemma, as will be shown.

Every item of news attaching to the national hero was avidly reported in the press in the weeks following Nelson's death and preceding his funeral, a fact that called for special circumspection on the part of his friends. As Lady Elizabeth Foster had remarked on seeing Nelson's October letters spread out on Lady Hamilton's bed, 'the greater part of them had appeared in the "Morning Chronicle" of that day,' a circumstance that did not escape the notice of Mr. Rose. He was profoundly shocked at such a want of reticence on Emma's part, and wrote at once to Lady Hamilton, supposing that she had allowed the editor (Mr. Perry, her Merton neighbour) a sight of them. Mr. Rose could not know that the excerpts quoted represented only a small part, and not the confidential parts, of the original letters. Lady Hamilton's answer to him of 29 November, while more than usually specious in its avoidance of the truth, gives a first indication of her growing hostility towards the new Earl.

Clarges Street, Nov 29th, 1805

I write from my bed, where I have been ever since the fatal sixth of this month, and only rose to be removed from Merton here. I could not write to you, my dear sir, before, but your note requires that I should justify myself.

Believe me, then, when I assure you I do not see any one but the family of my dear Nelson. His letters are in the bed with me; and only to the *present Earl* did I ever read one, and then only a part. It is true he is leaky, but I believe would not willingly tell anything; but I have been told something like some of my letters have been printed in some paper. I never now read a paper, and my health and spirits are so bad I cannot enter into a war with vile editors. Of this be assured, no one shall ever see a letter of my glorious and dear departed Nelson . . . My dear Sir, my heart is broken. Life to me now is not worth having; I lived but for him. His glory I gloried in; it was my pride that he should go forth; and this fatal and last time he went I persuaded him to it. But I cannot go on;—my heart and head are gone;—only, believe me, what you write to me shall ever be attended to. Could you know me you would not think I had such bad policy as to publish any thing at this moment. My mind is not a common one; and having lived as a *confidante* and friend with such men as Sir William Hamilton, and dearest, glorious Nelson, I feel myself superior to vain tattling woman. Excuse me, but I am ill and nervous, and *hurt* that those I value should think meanly of me.

When you come to town, pray call on me. I do not know if I shall live in England, as I promised the Queen of Naples to go back to her in case of accidents. You will not be able to read this scrawl, but I am very, very ill. Mr. Bolton feels all your kindness to him, and firmly relies on you. All the family are with me, and very kind. *The Earl you know*; but a man must have great courage to *accept* the honour of—calling himself by *that* name.

Write me a line to say you have got this, and that you believe

Your grateful
Emma Hamilton

You shall see what pictures I have got, and have any copied.[1]

The reference to the Queen of Naples, it may be observed, was rather disingenuous. Nelson had written to the Queen more than once since Sir William's death and during the last Mediterranean campaign, and the Queen had clearly shown that she had no further use for her former favourite: she must expect no help from her. This he had fully reported to Emma in his letters home.

Emma's sense of insecurity was, naturally enough, an alarming addition to her private griefs; Nelson's death put the whole of her position in jeopardy. She was not his widow; she knew that her rights ended with his life, that she was financially crippled, that her enemies could easily succeed in ruining her now that she had no legitimate defender. In the crumbling of her world, she expected to find more enemies than friends about her. In point of fact, Nelson's friends rallied loyally, though she was

---

[1] Rose's *Diaries*, i, 245.

perceptive enough to recognize that it was for love of him, rather than for respect of her, that they acted. This was particularly the case with Hardy.

In the past he had not shown himself one of her devotees, but no sooner was he arrived at Spithead with the *Victory* on 4 December than he wrote her a reassuring letter. It was as though he realized her fear that he might slight her in the discharge of his delicate duty. Nelson had urgently, vehemently, committed 'dear Lady Hamilton, poor Lady Hamilton' and Horatia, to Hardy's kindness and care, and Hardy was too much a man of his word not to interpret that dying bequest quite literally. He was also a man of feeling, and the scene in the cockpit of the *Victory* was too recent for him not to be still deeply under its spell. Nelson had charged him in a dying whisper to let Lady Hamilton have his hair 'and all other things belonging to me'; and Hardy intended to discharge that trust. He wrote her immediately on anchoring:

> Victory, St. Helen's
> Wednesday night (December 4, 1805)
>
> My dear Lady Hamilton, —I lose not a moment to acquaint you with our arrival and inclose you by Chevalier [Nelson's servant] the last letters written by our most dear and ever to be lamented friend. Be assured my dear Lady Hamilton, that I will do everything that lays in my power to serve you and I trust you will believe that I am your sincere friend, T. M. Hardy.[1]

Sensing her anxiety on the attitude Hardy would take towards her, the wife of Captain Blackwood (so recent a witness at Merton of Nelson's domestic happiness) wrote to Emma from Portsmouth on 6 December:

> Captain Blackwood is anxious to communicate to your mind the relief which, allow me to say, *we* trust the purport of this letter may afford you, in informing your Ladyship that he saw Captain Hardy this morning, who has in his possession papers of the *last* will of this ever-to-be-regretted Commander, which will prove highly gratifying to you; that it is Captain Hardy's determination not to deliver any of them up to *any* person until he has seen you.[2]

To which Captain Blackwood himself added the lines:

> Dear Lady Hamilton, Hardy may have spoken his mind on former occasions more freely than you would have wished; but depend upon it that the last words of our lamented friend will influence his conduct. He desires me, in the most unequivocal manner, to assure you of his good intentions towards you. This I hope will ease your mind.[3]

These letters were followed by another one from Hardy himself on 8 December.

[1] D. M. Stuart, op. cit.   [2] M.853.   [3] M.854.

Every thing shall be preserved for you that you can wish; and it shall be my constant study to meet your wishes, as it was our ever dear Lord's last request to be kind to you, which, I trust, I never shall forget . . . I have his hair, lockets, rings, breast-pin, and all your Ladyship's pictures in a box by themselves, and they shall be delivered to no one but yourself . . . I beg of you, my dear Lady Hamilton, to keep up your spirits under this most melancholy and trying occasion; and you may be sure of always meeting a most sincere friend in

T. M. Hardy.[1]

Nelson's personal relics, delivered to Lady Hamilton by Captain Blackwood, were seen by a young eye-witness who left a description of the manner of their display when friends called to condole with Emma. Lionel Goldsmid, who had so ardently wished to go to sea with Nelson, was allowed to accompany his family when they called on the bereaved lady. She was still in bed in Clarges Street when she received them. He recorded in his journal:

I was eight years old and was allowed to accompany my mother and those of the family who made up the party from our House. I was a great favourite of Lady Hamilton's and bathed in tears at times as she talked over his virtues and ex-hibited the various gifts he had made her on different occasions. I was on the bed to aid in passing the rings, shawls, bracelets, etc shewn to the company of about 15 persons seated in a semi-circle at the foot of the bed—and as she thought perhaps at moments of her truly lamented Hero and friend, I came in for numer-ous kisses and her usual remark—thank you my funny boy—or child you must come every day. The very coat in which the dear old Admiral was dressed in the fatal battle and received his death wound was on the outside of the bed—the hole where the bullet passed through stiffened with congealed blood. There was most certainly a very serio-comic performance throughout the visit.[2]

However kindly disposed Hardy was to the bereaved Emma in the emotional atmosphere preceding Nelson's funeral, the legal representa-tive of the dead Admiral was his brother, and to the Earl Hardy was bound to remit all the documents found in the Admiral's cabin, other than those specifically addressed to Lady Hamilton. Chevalier was therefore des-patched to the Earl in town with an inventory of the Admiral's effects on the same occasion as he called at Lady Hamilton's. In acknowledging this courtesy, the Earl wrote Hardy on 6 December:

I am very much obliged by your kindness in sending Mr. Chevalier to me with the inventory of my poor Brother's effects now on board the Victory.

He has my orders to take charge of the whole of them & have them conveyed to London by water, where he will receive further directions from Mr. Davison

[1] D. M. Stuart, op. cit.
[2] *Transactions of the Jewish Historical Society*, xiv, 225-45.

how he is to proceed. If there is any Will or Codicil or any paper of that sort intrusted to your care, I will esteem it a favor, if you will send a confidential person without loss of time, to bring it to me, with orders to deliver it to no other person . . . Please to give orders that whoever is sent to me that they come to my House at No 18, Charles Street, Berkeley Square, where all letters and parcels must be directed. ¹

Already on 25 November, writing to Dr. Fisher, Bishop of Exeter, Earl Nelson had made it clear that he and his family were not staying with Lady Hamilton but had taken quarters of their own. 'I have not been at Merton lately except for a few hours now and then on particular business. I have taken a small house at No. 18 Charles St. Berkeley Sq, where I shall remove with my family in a day or two.' ² While working in close touch with his dead brother's solicitors and agents, the Earl tactfully indicated that he was not necessarily in close contact with his dead brother's mistress.

As the Earl's letter shows, he supposed there might be a later Will or Codicil in Hardy's keeping superseding the earlier ones lodged with Haslewood. That he felt some anxiety on this score is understandable; his brother's infatuation for a lady not his wife and for a child not his legitimate offspring, might prompt him to an unconsidered act in the moment of death that would be detrimental to the family. The sooner the Earl received reassurance on this subject, the better for his peace of mind: hence the careful instructions to Hardy.

Nelson's last Codicil proved, in effect, to be far less damaging to the family's interests than the Earl must have feared; in material terms the family had nothing to lose by it, since it left Lady Hamilton and Horatia to the nation's care. This should be borne in mind when considering the likelihood of his suppressing it, as Lady Hamilton later accused him of doing.

As one of the witnesses of Nelson's last Codicil, Hardy knew its contents and its importance; more than anyone alive Hardy knew his friend's wishes, whispered repeatedly during his agony, that a government pension might be procured for Lady Hamilton and adequate provision for Horatia. He had, moreover, Nelson's instructions to contact his friend George Rose, who as Secretary to the Treasury and Vice-President of the Board of Trade, was well-placed to advise. Rose, already in Nelson's confidence on the question of a pension for Lady Hamilton, genuinely believed that Pitt would be sympathetic. Hardy's first act, therefore, after despatching Chevalier to London, was to have himself rowed by the ship's boat to

¹ BM Add MSS 34992.   ² Ibid.

Lymington, to drive the ten miles from there to Rose's Hampshire home, and to show him the Codicil, clearly regarding it as a state paper to be dealt with at Cabinet level. Rose's advice confirmed him in this view: he considered that the Codicil must be brought to the Prime Minister's notice, and undertook to do so himself. Among Nelson's familiars it was known that Pitt was 'kindly intended towards Lady Hamilton'. Rose wrote to Lady Hamilton himself to tell her what had been done in the matter and what he further planned to do: dated Cuffnells December 9th 1805, his letter read:

Captain Hardy had the goodness to take the trouble at much inconvenience to himself, to come over here soon after the Victory anchored at Spithead, to tell me what passed in the last moments of my late most invaluable friend . . . when he manifested a confidence I would do all in my power to make effectual his last wishes, I shall consider it a sacred duty . . . You will learn from the Captain that Lord Nelson . . . made an entry in his Pocket Book strongly recommending a remuneration to you for your services to the country . . . on which subject he had spoken to me with great earnestness more than once. I cannot therefore delay assuring you I will take the earliest opportunity of a personal communication with Mr. Pitt, to enforce that solemn request upon him. . . . My application must be to Mr. Pitt, but the reward . . . must, I conceive, be from the Foreign Secretary of State, on account of the nature of the service. I can promise nothing but zeal; you shall know within a few days at latest after I shall see Mr. Pitt either at Bath or in London.[1]

Having put the matter in Rose's hands in full confidence of a successful issue, Hardy despatched Captain Blackwood to London with the original of the Codicil with the trunk containing Nelson's personal effects. Though these were undoubtedly the concern of the executors it would appear that the Earl was agreeable to their being opened at Lady Hamilton's house in the presence of the family. At the same time Alexander Davison made a 'true copy' of Nelson's last Codicil 'from the original'. The Codicil which he signed and dated thus became known to Nelson's best friends and business advisers as well as to the Earl and his fellow executor, William Haslewood. Before another day passed, it was brought to the attention of yet another influential person, the Prince of Wales, to whom Davison wrote on the 17th. By return of post the Prince wrote from Brighton:

I am extremely obliged to you, my dear Sir, for your confidential letter, which I received this morning. You may be well assured that did it depend on me, there would not be a wish or desire of our ever to be lamented and much loved

[1] Rose's *Diaries*, i, 255.

friend, as well as adored Hero, that I would not consider as a solemn obligation upon his Friends and Country to fulfil. It is a duty they owe his memory and his matchless and unrivalled excellence.[1]

Far from 'suppressing' the Codicil, Earl Nelson took it between 16 and 21 December to Doctors' Commons and showed it confidentially to Sir William Scott at the Registry of Wills, to ask his advice upon it. As it was not in a legal sense a Will, its value depended entirely on how far the government could be made to feel beholden to a public servant who had died in the country's cause. After reflecting on the matter, Sir William Scott wrote to the Earl from his country house on 21 December.

Earley Court, nr Reading

My Lord,

Before I left Town, I saw the Chancellor with whom I communicated upon the subject of the Entry in the Book. He was clearly of opinion that the first and fittest thing, and indeed the *only* thing, to be done respecting it, was to communicate it to Mr. Pitt, for that Mr. Pitt was the only person who could give any proper direction on it which it would be discreet for your Lordship to act, and that the withholding of it for any time from his knowledge might eventually be injurious to your Lordship's interests. I confess that this is strongly my own impression of what is proper to be done. If your Lordship. . . should concur in the same opinion and will authorize me to make the communication, I will make it. No time should be lost about it, if it is to be done.[2]

Sir William's advice thus coincided with Mr. Rose's: the matter was one for the Prime Minister. The newly created Earl, intensely enjoying his elevation to the peerage, was little likely to incur the kind of censure hinted at in Sir William's letter, by withholding the document; he could but concur with the Chancellor's views, and leave the Codicil in Sir William's hands. Sir William himself took the further step of calling on Lady Hamilton (at her request) and securing her agreement. He wrote to Earl Nelson:

I found her in a good deal of Agitation which gradually subsided in conversation. I informed Her of two things in which she appeared to acquiesce, that the Book belonged to your Lordship and that I had the custody of it but without the power of communicating it to any Person without your Lordship's Authority and Consent.[3]

No one, least of all Mr. Rose who had an appointment to see the Prime Minister, realized how near Pitt himself was to his end. His sudden and quite unexpected death on 23 January was the reason why the matter of

---

[1] Nicolas, vii, 310.   [2] BM Add. MSS 34992.   [3] Ibid.

the Codicil had to be shelved: it had nothing to do with Earl Nelson's machinations.

Pitt was succeeded as Prime Minister by Lord Grenville. He had previously been in office, and Nelson had long ago told Lady Hamilton that nothing was to be hoped from him. She knew this well enough, and had already estimated her poor chances of help from him. Allowing for a decent interval of time to elapse after the death of one Prime Minister and the confirmation in office of another, Earl Nelson fetched the Codicil from Sir William Scott and went himself with it to Lord Grenville on 15 February 1806. In a memorandum which he drew up on the subject later, the Earl recorded that:

Before Mr. Pitt's death it was determined that the memorandum book should be given or sent to him: after that took place, as soon as conveniently could be, after Lord Grenville was fixed in his office of Prime Minister, it was the opinion of many persons of consequence, that as the said memorial contained secret matters relative to the part the Queen of Naples privately took in assisting our fleet, etc. etc., that no other person ought to have it but the Minister, accordingly Lord Nelson took it from Sir William Scott and gave it to Lord Grenville on the 15th February last, and at the same time he read it to his Lordship, and strongly pointed out to him the part relative to Lady Hamilton and the child, and in doing this Ld. Nelson observed to Lord Grenville that he thought he was most effectively promoting the interest of Lady Hamilton, and doing his duty, in which Ld. Grenville acquiesced.[1]

Lord Grenville kept the Codicil till 30 May (a delay of two and a half months); he then returned it to Earl Nelson's fellow executor William Haslewood, with a letter ignoring Lady Hamilton's interest in the matter entirely as though it were no concern of hers at all.

The timing of Lord Grenville's return of the Codicil, even more than its slight to Lady Hamilton, put 'an end' to the affair, for he had waited for Parliament to make its munificent grants to the Nelson family first, as an effectual silencer of all further application. On 12 May, indeed, on a message from the King, a Motion of Lord Henry Petty was laid before the House to grant a pension to the Nelson family; debated throughout the following day, a vote to make unprecedented grants to Nelson's widow, his brother and heir, and his two sisters was taken. An annuity of £5,000 was granted to Earl Nelson and his descendants, and 'likewise a sum £120,000 as a further Provision for the Family', which Resolution was 'unanimously voted'. Mr. Rose, asking 'in what manner the sum was to be disposed of', achieved nothing for Lady Hamilton of course, whose

[1] P. ii, 626.

very existence was anathema to the King. Rose did succeed, however, in apportioning the grant so as to benefit Nelson's sisters, who each received £10,000 apiece.

The magnitude of the grant—which bestowed £90,000 on Earl Nelson for the purchase of an estate to be called 'Trafalgar'—did of course by contrast make Lady Hamilton's plight appear more painful still, and in the bitterness of her own disappointment she did not hesitate to hold the fortunate Earl responsible for her loss. He certainly showed a want of delicacy, even of common feeling when, according to Lady Hamilton, he chose the day Parliament voted the grants in his and the family's favour to throw Nelson's pocket-book back at her with the comment that she must do what she could with it now. The poor woman who had invited the family to a dinner in celebration of their good fortune, and was disposed to rejoice with them on the event, was unprepared for the news of her own failure. Her account of the scene which accuses the Earl of throwing the book at her with an oath across her own dinner table is, as usual with her statements, incorrect in detail: Parliament voted the grants on 13 May, and Nelson's pocket book, as Lord Grenville's letter shows, was not returned to the Earl until the 30th. Lady Hamilton's subsequent allegation that he kept it back until the grants were voted with the malign purpose of preventing her from sharing in the government's liberality, is disproved by all the foregoing correspondence. Mr. Rose, Sir William Scott, Mr. Davison, the Prince of Wales, Mr. Haslewood, all had knowledge of Nelson's Codicil; it was not the fault of any of them that Lord Grenville, unlike Mr. Pitt, was *not* 'kindly intended' towards Lady Hamilton.

The grants, moreover, were the direct decision of the King's; it was upon a message to the House from him that they were voted. She stood no chance of sharing in a benefaction originating with him. The King's animus against Lady Hamilton was well known and long established. The King had no love for Nelson either; if he honoured his memory now, it was in compliance with the whole country's feelings, but even the new Earl was much offended with the King's behaviour when he went formally to restore to him Nelson's ribbon of the Bath. Lady Elizabeth Foster, to whom the Countess related the incident, recorded it in her Diary:

At first the King looked at it, fumbled with it a little, and was walking away without a word when the Earl stopped him, expressed his gratitude for the honours heaped on him and his family owing to his 'loved and honoured brother'. He then proceeded to speak of his brother's religion—'the true religion that

teaches to sacrifice one's life for one's King and country', to which the King
merely replied: 'He died the death he wished.'[1]

Once in possession of Nelson's pocket-book, Lady Hamilton lost no
time in going to Doctors' Commons to have the document registered. The
gesture availed her no more than the previous ones; it was not in the legal
sense a Codicil, and could only be implemented by a special measure
taken at government level. As time passed, and her fortunes became more
desperate, her pretensions became more extravagant; every Prime
Minister for the next ten years was petitioned with her 'just claims' to a
recognition of her 'services'. She had the misfortune to turn even well-
wishers like Rose against her by the violence of her accusations, the
inaccuracy of her statements, and the exaggerations of her claims. There
can be no doubt that in course of time the subject became an 'idée fixe'
and was exploited on every occasion to excuse her rising debts. In a
bragging mood, to hide the deep discomfiture of her first rebuff, she told
Lady Elizabeth Foster how Nelson had bequeathed her to the Nation,
adding: 'ought I not to be proud? Let them refuse me all reward. I will
go with this paper fixed to my breast and beg through the streets of
London, and every barrow-woman shall say, "Nelson bequeathed her to
us." '[2]

The fact remains that, despite the heart-break and the theatrical
gestures indulged in by Lady Hamilton, nothing was done for her by the
state, nor, more notable still, did any member of Nelson's family come
forward to give any part of their grants to Nelson's daughter. She remained unprovided-for despite his last passionate appeal to government
on her behalf. Such an omission was certainly not from want of heart in
Nelson's sisters (they were very good to Horatia later) but from a wholly
mistaken view of Lady Hamilton's financial circumstances. They judged
these from her style of living, the extravagance of her establishments at
Clarges Street and Merton, and from the conviction that, as an ambassador's widow, she was not left in any embarrassment by her late husband.
Lady Hamilton's ill-luck proceeded from the very truth of these sup-
positions; her husband had provided decently for her, and so had Nelson;
no one could believe how incapable she was of living within her means and
the deeper she fell into debt, the less able she was to avow it.

Upon what terms Lady Hamilton and the new Earl and Countess came
to live after the great intimacy of the preceding years, is shown in the
early exchanges between them following Nelson's funeral. Emma's claim

[1] D. M. Stuart, op. cit.   [2] Ibid., 130.

to consideration as chief mourner within the family circle was peculiarly irksome to the official inheritor of the name and fortune, and she was made to feel that it was merely from kindness that they allowed her to keep some of the relics. On the question of the coat worn by Nelson when he was killed, the Countess, Emma's former 'dearest friend and jewell', wrote to her on 13 February 1806:

In point of *right* there can be no doubt to whom this precious relic belongs, and it certainly is my Lord's most ardent wish as well as my son's who spoke very feelingly on the subject before he left us, to have retain'd it in his possession to be kept as a memorial in Trafalgar House as long as it can hold together. But notwithstanding all these feelings My Lord is willing, tho' done with a bleeding heart, to part with it to you provided my dear friend you will give us assurances it shall at some future time be restored to the Heir to the Title.[1]

The Countess concluded by wisely recommending Lady Hamilton to have the coat placed in a glass case hermetically sealed, 'the same as Miss Andreas will do hers in Westminster Abbey'. Right or no right, the coat was in due course sold by Lady Hamilton to Alderman Smith for ready money and only by the intervention of the Prince Consort eventually retrieved for the nation for the sum of £150. From their correspondence it would appear that the Earl and his wife maintained courteous relations with Lady Hamilton; they invited her to join them at the sea when they went on holiday; they did not fail to enquire after her health and to send polite messages; the violent language and the accusations were all on Lady Hamilton's side. More difficult was the position of Charlotte who had lived with her for over three years and whom Lady Hamilton claimed to have educated. During the time Sir William Scott was in possession of Nelson's last Codicil, Charlotte wrote to Lady Hamilton from Canterbury: 'Sir William Scott came on Friday and left us on Monday. He slept at our house. He talked a great deal about you, and says that you have great claims on government, and we all sincerely wish they would do what they ought.'[2] Still, it could be argued with some justice that instead of wishing that government would do 'what they ought' by Lady Hamilton, the Earl, for whom Parliament voted a grant of £90,000, might have made a gesture in her favour.

What still further strained the relations between the former friends were the Earl's investigations into the affairs of Merton. The house, with its contents and the pleasure grounds were left to Lady Hamilton; but the arable and agricultural land acquired in addition by Nelson as an investment, had now to be sold to pay the legacies and dues provided for under

[1] BM Add. MSS 34992.   [2] P. ii, 631.

the Will. Upon the Earl as executor this disagreeable task now devolved. Three significant letters from Mrs. Cadogan to her daughter dated respectively 13 February, 29 March, and 26 April 1806, betray the degree of suspicion and deceit existing between Lady Hamilton and the executors of Nelson's Will in the first months after his death; they also betray the extent of her financial straits only six months after he had left England.

Explaining that she had had 'a very canting letter from Haslewood . . . saying the Earl and him was coming down to-day,' Mrs. Cadogan wrote:

I will not show them one bill or receipt; I will tell them you have them locked up. Some were as Cribbe (sic) has sumed it up. I have receipts for thirteen hundred pounds, besides the last forty-two. Mrs. Cribbe advises me not to show them till you have seen them. On Saturday I shall send Sarah [Connor or Reynolds as she was indiscriminately called] with them.[1]

In her next letter she wrote,

I have enclosed to you Cribb's account he brought me from Haslewood the other day. Let me know whether you have a copy of the will or not, as I understand the executors are to pay every expence for six months after his death . . . I am well informed of the measure of the land your house stands upon, and will not allow the pleasure ground that is taken in, that you have a right to take in what part you like of Linton's farm, and leave out what you like of the Wimbledon estate. Write me every particular that I may not be taken unawares. Don't you think if you was to write to Mr. Goldsmid and let me know very particularly who I am to apply to. I was in hopes Mr. Bolton would have been here at the time. Pray, my dear Emma, let me know whether you have answered Mr. Roberts's bill or not, as I shall write to Mr. Roberts and Mrs. Burt.[2]

Upon Emma's birthday, 26 April, her mother wrote her again from Merton:

I pray God send you many happy returns of this day. I have sent you a gown of Sarah Reynolds's making. If I had ten thousand pounds to send you this day, I should have been very happy. I have sent Mariann [one of the maids] as I thought she might be of use to you to-day. I am all over with bricks and dust and stinking paint, being no-body but our own family. On Saturday you shall have a 'menestra verde' [one of Emma's favourite Italian dishes] and one thing roast. Mariann will tell you how miserable I have been this week.

My dear Emma, I owe Mariann 4 months' wages which is two guineas. I had it not to give her, and she wants shoes and stockings. If you can, give Sarah Connor thirty shillings to pay her washer-woman, as she is indebted to her for three months' washing; I have got her washing down here. You must send Mariann as soon as you can in the morning. God bless you, my ever dear Emma.

Sarah added a postscript: 'I wish you many happy returns of the day. I should have been happy had it been in my power to have made you a small present on this day, but not having anything but what my dear aunt and you have been so good as to give me.' [1]

Poor Mrs. Cadogan who often saw the folly of her daughter's ways, and pleaded for a more reasonable way of life for them all, could not prevent the extravagance still proceeding in Clarges Street, even at that time of mourning. The constant threat of Lady Hamilton's growing embarrassments and eventual ruin was all-important in shaping the course of Horatia's next ten years. It dictated her frequent changes of home, and the shifting character of her mother's circle of acquaintances. Insecurity and instability became the only constant factors in the upbringing that Nelson had fondly imagined he had ensured to her once and for all within 'the paths of religion and virtue', by leaving her under the guardianship of Lady Hamilton.

[1] M.874.

PART TWO

HORATIA NELSON NELSON

CHAPTER IX

'THIS INTERESTING LITTLE CREATURE'[1]

IN ONLY one respect were Nelson's last wishes honoured, and one clause of his last Codicil legalized. On 14 May the Earl took the Codicil to the College of Arms to enter application for a Licence 'on behalf of Horatia Nelson Thompson an Infant, that she may assume and use the surname of Nelson only', a licence which was granted 'to a Warrant from the Most Noble Charles Duke of Norfolk Earl Marshal' on the 14 October following. Thus Nelson's Horatia received his name, if little else.[2]

The fact of her existence, however, became generally known before that date. The publication of Nelson's Will in the press on 24 and 26 December 1805, in particular the terms of the second Codicil concerning her settlement, aroused the keenest interest in her. Who 'this interesting little creature' might be became a matter of widespread and lively speculation among the dead hero's friends, and a new source of consideration for Lady Hamilton. The role of Guardian, devolving on her by Nelson's Will, lent her a lustre, an aura of sublimity in the existing climate of opinion, which no cynical interpretation of the facts was allowed to sully. Lady Hamilton's latest 'Attitude' in accepting the charge of bringing up the dead hero's orphan, was her most successful to date, deluding, as it did among others, even the hero's sisters. However much she may have dreaded the discovery being made in the past, the existence of Horatia now, revealed in the darkest hour following Nelson's death, when the nation was so sensitive to the pathos of the situation, proved wholly beneficial to her interests.

In the *Morning Chronicle* of 24 December under the heading 'Lord Nelson's Will', the following paragraph appeared:

The testamentary papers of the lamented Lord Nelson were yesterday proved in Doctors' Commons by Earl Nelson & Mr. Haslewood, the executors. The Will is dated 10th May 1803 and there are seven codicils ... The only legacies to persons not of Lord Nelson's family are to Lady Hamilton, to Mr. Davison, to Mr. Haslewood, Captain Hardy, to Miss Horatia Nelson Thompson, to Mr.

[1] Nelson's Chaplain, Revd. A. J. Scott: See Stuart, op. cit. 132–3.
[2] NMM/NWD/9594.

John Scott, his Lordship's secretary [killed at Trafalgar], to the Rev. A. J. Scott. The house and furniture at Merton, and seventy acres of adjoining land, are given to Lady Hamilton, etc.'

On Boxing day the full text of the codicil, dated 6 September 1803, which related to Horatia, was published in the *Morning Chronicle*.

I give and bequeath to Miss Horatia Nelson Thompson, who was baptized on the thirteenth day of May last, in the parish of St. Marylebone, in the County of Middlesex, by Benjamin Lawrence, Curate, and John Willock, Assistant Clerk, and whom I acknowledge as my adopted daughter, the sum of four thousand pounds sterling of Great Britain, to be paid at the expiration of six months after my decease, or sooner if possible; and I leave my dearest friend Emma, Lady Hamilton, sole guardian of the said Horatia Nelson Thompson, until she shall have arrived at the age of eighteen years and the interest of the said four thousand pounds to be paid to Lady Hamilton for her education and maintenance. This request of guardianship I earnestly make of Lady Hamilton, knowing that she will educate my adopted child in the paths of religion and virtue and give her those accomplishments which so much adorn herself, and I hope make her a fit wife for my dear nephew, Horatio Nelson who I wish to marry her if he proves worthy, in Lady Hamilton's estimation, of such a treasure as I am sure she will be.

The public curiosity aroused by this was perhaps lulled by the more immediate excitement over the great pageant being arranged for the arrival of Nelson's body; its passage up the Thames in a yacht of the Commissioner of the Navy, its lying in state for three days in the Painted Hall at Greenwich, its passage by river from there to Whitehall Steps and along the Mall to the Admiralty where it remained for the last night, and the state funeral at St. Paul's on 9 January. Daily notices issuing from the College of Arms gave directions regulating every item of the procession; on 1 January it was 'recommended that Servants attending the carriages of the Nobility, Clergy and Gentry in the procession, will be put in mourning'; and on 4 January it was announced: 'On the day of the funeral the carriages of those attending, must be in the park before 9 a.m. Admittance to Hyde Park on show of tickets only.' All London was in the streets; on the day of the funeral from 20,000 to 30,000 persons were admitted to St. Paul's, and though the 'interment concluded at 6 p.m. the church was not vacated till 9 p.m.'. The Duchess of Devonshire, Lady Elizabeth Foster and the ladies of their family, like the rest of society, flocked to Greenwich to see the lying-in-state, watched the arrival of the body at the Admiralty, filled the balconies of Kemshed's Dublin Hotel at Charing Cross to see the funeral cortège on the 9th and were under-

MARBLE BUST OF HORATIA AS A GIRL

standably exhausted and in need of a quiet week-end, as Lady Elizabeth
wrote to her son in America, when the excitements were over:

the procession and the funeral pomp at Greenwich and to town and from the
Admiralty to St. Paul's was affecting beyond measure . . . In short, what with
that and seeing people connected with Lord Nelson and collecting a variety of
anecdotes about him, you cannot conceive how knocked-up I feel. We are
going . . . to Brocket to-morrow for a couple of days.' [1]

'Seeing people connected with Lord Nelson' included for Lady
Elizabeth, Nelson's chaplain, the Rev. A. J. Scott who, it happened, had
been at college with her brother Lord Bristol. The introduction being
thus assured, Lady Elizabeth dined at her brother's to meet one of the
close witnesses of Nelson's death. She could not wait, she later confessed,
for her brother to introduce them. Mr. Scott told her of the last moments,
how, when Nelson asked him 'I have not been a great sinner, have I' he
could not say 'No' but bent and kissed his forehead. How the talk had
naturally turned to Horatia, and how Mr. Scott had said: 'Little Horatia is
a lovely child.' 'Is she his?' Lady Elizabeth asked. 'For I should love her
more.' 'I don't know,' answered Mr. Scott. 'But she is a most interesting
little creature.' 'I cannot help thinking that she is and that motives of
prudence for the mother made him call her his adopted daughter in his
Will. He must have had good motives for what he did.' [2]

Kind Mrs. Lutwidge (the wife of Nelson's first Captain in 1773), of
whose long and genuine affection for him and Emma there can be no
doubt, only waited for the funeral day to be past to take up her pen to
ease the curiosity that was consuming her.

> Holm Rock, Whitehaven,
> January 10th 1806

I have long wished to write to you, my dearest and beloved Emma, but had
not the courage to take up my pen; but there has not a day passed in which my
Admiral and self have not thought of you. Our hearts bleed for your sufferings,
and, had it been possible to have alleviated your sorrow, dearest, Emma, we
should not thus long have remained silent; but we could only add our tears to
yours for the loss of the greatest hero and best man that ever existed. From the
bottom of our hearts do we most truly feel for and compassionate your situation,
and beg to assure you of our tenderest sympathy.

'The last, sad duty, has been paid ere this. My Admiral was most anxious to
attend this awful ceremony, but was really unable—indeed he never has been
well since the fatal news reached us . . . His eyes are in so weak a state he is

---

[1] Lady Elizabeth Foster to Augustus Foster: Vere Foster, *The Two Duchesses*, 17
January 1806, 265.
[2] Stuart, op. cit., 132–3.

unable to write, else, my dearest Emma, he would have added a few lines to this letter . . .

'Tell me, my beloved Emma, that you will take care of yourself for the sake of the interesting little being consigned to your care, and with such a public testimony of *his* high sense of all those great and good qualities you eminently possess. I own, my dear Emma, I shall have no small curiosity to know who this dear little being is, who is so distinguished. . .'.[1]

The veil being partially lifted, curiosity was not soon satisfied. At Devonshire House, where Lady Elizabeth Foster received the bereaved Emma, together with Countess Nelson and Lady Charlotte Nelson in her private apartments on 17 January, Emma made her hostess a promise to show her Horatia. Scarcely a week was allowed to pass before she was reminded of her promise. 'Lady Elizabeth F. enquires after you earnestly,' Mr. Scott wrote, 'and Horatia whom you promised to shew her.' Poor Mr. Scott, who had vowed and kept his promise not to leave the dead body of his lord all the long journey home and throughout the vigil at Greenwich and the Admiralty, had become Emma's favourite, often at Clarges Street and constantly dining there. He wrote frequent, touching notes to Lady Hamilton accounting for his movements lest she should doubt his concern for her; even from Cambridge where he went in February about an honorary D.D. in consideration for his services to Nelson, he wrote to her: 'I write chiefly to give some account of myself & to tell you that I constantly remember you, and that no selfish consideration can supersede the regard and attachment which I bear you. Pray kiss Horatia for me, and let her not forget the sound of my name.'[2]

Horatia was now as much an inmate of the Clarges Street house as of Merton, receiving her first regular lessons there from Cecilia Connor. In March 1806 she accompanied Lady Hamilton on her first visit to the Boltons' home at Cranwich, where she was admitted into the family circle as a cherished member, never again to be omitted from any reunion in which they were concerned.

Of Horatia's success in Norfolk there is no doubt. After her departure, Mrs. Bolton wrote to Lady Hamilton, accepting without question the child's paternity: 'My dear Horatia! The more *I think* the dearer she is to me'[3] (29 May 1806). She quoted the elder ladies of the family, her aunt Rolfe, widow of the Revd. Robert Rolfe sometime rector of Hilborough, and her cousin Mrs. Taylor, living in genteel retirement at Swaffham, as saying that they had wished so much to see Horatia, and giving it as their opinion that 'every one ought to adore that child' (13 May 1806). The

---

[1] P. ii, 559.   [2] M.866.   [3] M.881.

generations of the Nelsons, from jovial old Mrs. Rolfe—sister of the late Revd. Edmund—and reported in her seventy-eighth year to look 'as well and as cheerful as she did ten years back', were agreed on opening their arms and their hearts to the child of whose very existence they had only just been made aware. In their eyes she was something sacred, a relic of the dead man who had been their pride and darling. Her coming into Norfolk could not be hidden; after her first visit to Cranwich she was invited everywhere.

Cranwich, unlike Merton, was a real country home, almost isolated in fields, except for two or three houses—one of them the rectory. Mr. Bolton's land lay astride the road from Mundford to Methwold, five miles south of Hilborough, the parish which could with justice be called the cradle of the Nelson family. Here three generations of Nelsons had served as rectors since 1734, and almost from the beginning of the century in the two parishes of East and West Bradenham, some six miles further to the North East. The background of the Nelson family, despite its Walpole connections, remained predominantly rural and clerical; and the families into which it married retained essentially the same character.

The Boltons were no exception to this. Although Thomas, Nelson's brother-in-law, entered trade, he was the only member of his family to do so. His grandfather, the Revd. Thomas Bolton, was Rector of Hollesley, on the Suffolk coast, within the family's native Woodbridge area, where Samuel, the eldest son, remained. The move to Norfolk of Thomas himself, the Revd. William his younger brother, and their only sister Anne, may have been the result of her marriage to Dr. Henry Girdlestone of Wells-next-the-Sea. The Survey of Wells of 1793 shows Dr. Girdlestone to have had considerable property there. By 1777, when his eldest son was born, the Revd. William was settled in Wells, and in 1780 Thomas, who was 'in a prosperous line of business in the grain, corn and coal trade', brought there his bride, Nelson's sister Susanna. Their eldest (twin) daughters Susanna and Catherine, were born there on 20 November 1781. As has already been seen, Kitty Bolton married her cousin, Captain Sir William Bolton, son of the Revd. William, in 1803; only the first of many intermarriages between the Bolton–Girdlestone cousins who were brought up in close intimacy.

In 1804 the Revd. William became Rector of nearby Brancaster and remained in office there till 1829. At his hospitable rectory, some eight miles further west along the coast from Wells, as at the Girdlestones' home in Wells, Lady Hamilton and Horatia became regular visitors upon their annual trips into Norfolk.

The farmhouse at Cranwich, an original Tudor building, had eighteenth century additions, like the square stone portico borne on two sturdy pillars, and the french windows opening onto the lawns at the front and side of the house. It was an irregular roomy place, with high chimney-stacks and straggling red-brick out-buildings. There were three large parlours on the ground floor of which the 'drawing-room' ran the whole length of the house, its french windows opening on the side lawns and orchard beyond. Seven bedrooms upstairs were reached by three stair-cases, the incidence of so many passages and floor-levels creating an impression of unlimited space and easy living, which perfectly mirrored the character of the open-hearted family whose home it was. The Boltons were truly hospitable people, living without pretentions, but with much good humour and genuine harmony. 'You know my accomodations here,' Mrs. Bolton wrote to Lady Hamilton in June 1806 when expecting her second visit that year, 'they are the same as you left. I wish they were better but a cheerful heart and a hearty welcome you will be sure to find.' As a hostess, Mrs. Bolton was not exacting, asking only for a couple of days' notice so as to 'have something in the Pot' with which to greet her visitors.[1]

Across the road from the farm, flat fields of turnips, barley, and rye stretched to the horizon. Nelson had written to his brother-in-law in his own first year at Merton: 'These rains may give me a little hay. I shall not allow its being cut too soon . . . this weather suits Cranwich it will give you good turnips and I am farmer enough to know that gives everything.'[2] Good turnip country though it was, Mr. Bolton did not find that his land yielded everything he needed for the support of a large family: he had not altogether prospered since buying the farm in 1798. It was a perennial problem, dependent on the state of the weather, as poor Mrs. Bolton had all-too-often to note. In April 1807 she wrote to Lady Hamilton: 'How is the weather with you? Here nothing grows; the sheep and lambs, I fear, will be all starved . . . We are all ill with colds.' The wish to put his sister and her family beyond the caprices of the weather prompted one of Nelson's last actions before leaving England, when he wrote to Mr. Rose soliciting a place for Mr. Bolton in the Customs.

In March 1806 when Lady Hamilton and Horatia visited Cranwich, the family was at full strength. Besides Eliza and Anne, whom they al-ready knew, there were Susannah (her mother's right-hand) and her twin, Lady Bolton, with her little girl Emma Horatia, just two years old. Between her and Horatia there sprang up one of those fond attachments

[1] M. 884.   [2] GIR/NMM/9590.

that exist between a tiny girl and a slightly older one. After the visit, which lasted from 20 March to mid-April, the Norfolk party was left disconsolate. Mrs. Bolton wrote to Lady Hamilton on 22 April: 'What a blank you have made in our party. I went to bed far from well, and when we all met at dinner we were all in tears to see the *vacant places*, where so lately they had been filled with those so dear to us. Even poor Emma is constantly calling for you *all*; tell Horatia she wants to go to her bed in a morning.'[1] In a further letter of 13 May Mrs. Bolton sent messages to tell Horatia that 'Emma tries to imitate her attitudes every day'. Lady Hamilton's 'accomplishments' were being transmitted to the second generation.

Other members of the family to welcome Horatia at Cranwich were Mary Ann Peirson, the young widow of one of Nelson's Captains of Marines (Charles Peirson, who had died of yellow fever during the West Indian campaign of 1799); and her daughter Caroline, aged seven; born a Bolton, she was daughter of the Rector of Brancaster and sister of Sir William Bolton. Mrs. Peirson and Caroline returned with Lady Hamilton and Horatia to Merton. Hearing of all the family doings afterwards, Mrs. Matcham wrote to Lady Hamilton on 15 May from Bath a commentary which sufficiently shows that she also fully recognized Horatia's paternity.

What a winter, my dear Lady Hamilton have I spent and I am sorry to own even now I cannot bring myself to look forward with pleasure to anything that can happen. God knows, nothing can ever make up to me and mine for our loss. I can only say, God's will be done; but I feel quite heart-broken. Pray remember me to Mrs. Peirson. I suppose her little girl is grown quite out of my knowledge. She must be a nice companion for Horatia, who, I am glad to find, is so quick at her studies. Pray tell her not to forget *her aunt Matcham*.[2]

With the Boltons Lady Hamilton maintained the closest relations. Tom Bolton was a special favourite at Merton, and Anne, who was delicate, and had not finished her schooling at Edmonton, was frequently there (just as Charlotte Nelson had been), nursed with care and kindness by Mrs. Cadogan when Lady Hamilton was in town. It was Mrs. Cadogan who made Merton a home for them all.

By mid-July 1806, Lady Hamilton and Horatia were again expected in Norfolk, urged by Mrs. Bolton to bring 'all the party down with you we had in the spring, and Tom added to them. Kiss dear Horatia, and tell her how happy her aunt Bolton will be to see her. When will good Mrs. Cadogan perform her promise of visiting me? I hope I shall see you in the

[1] M.873.   [2] M.877.

course of next week. Give me two days' notice, that I may have something in the pot for dinner.'[1]

During this, Horatia's second visit to Norfolk, she was introduced to more members of her father's family. In that rural area the centre of entertainment was the market town of Swaffham, situated six miles from Hilborough and about eleven from Cranwich. Only at Swaffham, with its old Inns, stately houses, Assembly Rooms, and Theatre surrounding the wide oblong of the market place, could the young Boltons hope to find balls and parties, and their elders the pleasures of cards and conversation organized on anything like a grand scale. In 1798 a 'Grand Ball' had been given at Swaffham when the news of Nelson's victory of the Nile had been received, and ever since, on the anniversary of the battle, the members of Nelson's family living in the neighbourhood were expected to attend the ball organized in honour of the county hero; and there were many grumbles from the younger generation if the occasion was inadequately marked. In Swaffham, the family of the new Countess Nelson was paramount. Her brother, Chancellor Yonge (the last clerical chancellor of the diocese of Norfolk), was vicar of Swaffham for the exceptional period of sixty-five years (1779–1844). He was the grandson of Sir Joshua Reynolds' sister Eliza, and a man of great energy and character. He and his family lived in the Old Vicarage at the west end of the churchyard, demolished in 1846. Here he frequently entertained his sister and her husband the Revd. Dr.—now Earl—Nelson.

Besides the Yonges, the Rolfes, the Taylors—all connections of the Nelsons—Swaffham society was made up of such families as the Langfords, the Dashwoods, the Days, all of whom were in due course introduced to Lady Hamilton and contributed to the entertainment during her Norfolk holidays. The presence of Captain Johnson with his Company of Militia in the town also contributed to the local gaiety, as well as to Mr. Fisher's 'New' theatre.

In July 1806 Swaffham society marked the presence in their midst of the late Lord Nelson's family and their guests by a succession of social occasions which were duly recorded in the local press. The *Norwich Mercury* for 2 August reported:

Lord and Lady Nelson with their daughter Lady Charlotte Nelson, Lady Bolton, Lady Hamilton, Miss Horatia Nelson Thompson, her Ward, with Miss Pearson [sic] (the two latter between three and four years old) have been passing some time at the farmhouse of Thomas Bolton, Esq, of Cranwich, in this County,

[1] M. 884.

who married the sister of the gallant deceased Admiral, and last week, accompanied by the charming daughters of Mr. Bolton, they proceeded to Swaffham where the noble Lord and his party bespoke the play 'She Stoops to Conquer' on Friday night last when the house was very genteely filled. On the previous day, Lady Hamilton entertained at dinner some of the most considerable families at that town at the Crown Inn, where herself and most of the other ladies of the party took up their a bode. Lord and Lady Nelson were domesticated with Captain Johnson of that town. On Saturday morning 26th July Lady Hamilton with the two children, Lady Bolton, Miss Boltons, left Swaffham for Brancaster, to visit the Revd. William Bolton of that place, for a few days, but are expected back at Swaffham to rejoin the Earl and his family.'

On the occasion of the family party at Swaffham Lady Hamilton made Caroline Peirson the present of a book which, in her role of educational adviser to the young ladies of the family, she inscribed:

Swaffham, July 15th 1806

My dear Caroline

I hope to hear you articulate and pronounce well every word of this Book & may you every year month week & day improve & be a comfort to your good Mother & to

Your friend
Emma Hamilton [1]

The book was *A Continuation of the Comic Adventures of Old Mother Hubbard and Her Dog.*

Lady Hamilton intended going on to Hilborough after her visit to Swaffham and Wells, with a particular purpose in view. Earl Nelson was giving up the living of Hilborough which had been held in the family (by his father and grandfather before him) since 1734 and she was sanguine of obtaining the reversion of the living for the Revd. A. J. Scott, Nelson's chaplain. She had, unfortunately, encouraged him to share in her unfounded expectations, and was the more deeply chagrined when she found that the Earl had given the place to his wife's nephew, the Revd. William Yonge. Lady Hamilton had some excuse for her wrath, since the Earl might be reckoned to have equal obligations to his late brother's chaplain and to have known Nelson's wishes respecting him quite as much as she. The Revd. A. J. Scott was still unplaced and the Earl had the living in his gift: instead he chose to benefit his wife's family. His ambitions for his family were still uppermost in his mind, and the family itself, knowing his foible, watched his plots and contrivances for the advancement of his children with amused speculation. With Horace's

[1] TRA/NMM/43.

entry at Cambridge (he went to his father's old college, Christ's, in March 1806) Charlotte was reckoned—by her aunt Bolton at least—to be certain of making a good match. 'The Earl will look sharp after his daughter,' wrote Mrs. Bolton to Lady Hamilton, 'none but men of fashion must have her.'[4] The Earl had secured as private tutor for his son the Public Orator, Mr. Outram, and recounted to his wife all the foreseeable benefits that could accrue to young Horace from the arrangement.

Horace's holidays were further planned by the proud father to secure him invitations to country-house parties where he would be sure to make only advantageous contacts, and be most certain not to meet Lady Hamilton or his Bolton relatives. The future of Viscount Merton, as his father invariably referred to him, promised to be everything ambition could prompt. It was made as plain as possible that the hope expressed by Nelson for the marriage of Horace to his little 'adopted' cousin formed no part in the plans laid down for him by his parents. Despite the parental manoeuvring, and the ceaseless social climbing, Horace appears however to have retained a fresh and lovable character.

Thwarted in her projects for Dr. Scott, and further disappointed on her own count by a government reshuffle that brought her no satisfaction, Lady Hamilton wrote to Dr. Scott on 7 September 1806 from Cranwich:

My dear Friend—I did not get your letter till the other day, for I have been with Mrs. Bolton to visit an old respectable aunt of my dear Nelson's [Mrs. Rolfe].

I shall be in town, that is, at Merton, the end of the week, and I hope you will come there on Saturday and pass Sunday with me. I want much to see you; consult with you about my affairs. How hard it is, how cruel their treatment to me and Horatia. That angel's last wishes all neglected, but to speak of the fraud that was acted to keep back the Codicil; but enough! when we meet we will speak about it. God bless you for all your attentions and love you showed to our virtuous Nelson, and his remains, but it seems those that truly loved him are to be victims to hatred, jealousy, and spite. I know well how he valued you, and what he would have done for you had he lived. You know the great and virtuous affection he had for me, the love he bore my husband, and, if I had any influence over him, I used it for the good of my country. Did I ever keep him at home? Did I not share in his glory? Even this last fatal victory, it was I bid him go forth. Did he not pat me on the back, call me brave Emma, and said 'if there were more Emmas, there would be more Nelsons.' Did he not in his last moments do me justice, and request at the moment of his glorious death, that the King and Nation will do me justice? And I have got all his letters, and near eight hundred of the Queen of Naples's letters to show what I did for my King and Country, and prettily I am rewarded. Psha! I am above them, I despise them—

[1] M.835.

for, thank God, I feel that having lived with honour and glory, glory they cannot take from me. I despise them, my soul is above them, and I can yet make some of them tremble, by showing them how he despised them; for in his letters to me he thought aloud . . . Look at Alexander Davison courting the man he despised, and neglecting now those whose feet he used to lick. Dirty, vile groveler! But enough till we meet . . . Write to me at Merton, and ever believe me etc Horatia is charming. She begs her love to you. She improves daily. She sends you 100,000,000 kisses.[1]

Alexander Davidson incurred her Ladyship's special animus at the time for acting on behalf of Earl Nelson in the matter of his government grant, £10,000 of which he invested for him at the beginning of September in 3 per cent Consols. The grants voted by the government for the Nelson family were paid out on 2 August. The presence of Mr. Bolton and Mr. Matcham had been required in town and it may be noticed that on the occasion of the family gathering at Swaffham reported by the *Norwich Mercury*, Mr. Bolton's name had not been mentioned. He had gone up to London, where he was joined by Mr. Matcham and young George, thanks to whose journal it is learned that on 5 August the Matchams devoted the day to 'settling the government concerns and the prize money with Mr. Bolton. From the Strand we went to Change to invest £10,000 of it.'[2] Government would appear to have decided that with this grant Mr. Bolton must be content to receive no further favours from them. No place was found for him, despite Mr. Rose's continued exertions on his behalf.

While in London Mr. Bolton had been witness of the investment of Mrs. Matcham's government grant, a part of which was spent on buying an estate for the family. Young George reported in his journal how with his father and uncle Bolton they had gone down to Sussex on 6 August to view a property which so delighted Mr. Matcham that they concluded the bargain on the spot. It was six miles from Horsham and belonged to a Dr. Lawrence; Mr. Bolton's judgement was appealed to as a man knowledgeable in land-values and he gave it as his view that the place was cheap at the money. In course of time the Matchams spoke of 'Ashfold' with as deep an affection as Nelson had once done of Merton. It became a dearly-loved home where, in after years, Horatia was taken to live. For years the Matchams had been undecided where to settle, Mr. Matcham having even invested in property in Schleswig which he had believed would be a profitable concern when peace was restored. But the continuation of the war necessarily altered his plans, and he had to look at home. Mrs.

---

[1] Nicolas, vii, 394–5. [2] Eyre-Matcham, 254.

Matcham greatly desired to settle nearer London and, though the move was not intended to take place before the following spring, she already counted among the pleasures in prospect being able to invite Lady Hamilton and Horatia to 'our little farm', adding in a letter of 10 November 1806 that

all we can promise is homely fare and a hearty welcome, for, be assured my dear Lady Hamilton, I never can forget the many happy days we have spent together. We shall be in Sussex, I hope, early in the summer, as we intend to dispose of our house [in Bath] as soon as possible . . . Pray give my love to Horatia and tell her not to forget her aunt Matcham, and that I hope to present all her cousins to her in the summer.[1]

The importance to Lady Hamilton of Mrs. Matcham's acceptance of Horatia as Nelson's child cannot be over-estimated. It was only equalled by the importance of the fact that they did not assume that Horatia was her child. As her letter to Mr. Scott shows, she was none too careful in the vindication of her own character, to preserve Nelson's good name; the story implying his unwillingness to fight his last battle but for her exhortations was now fairly launched and fast becoming, as she intended, a part of history. Similarly, in her declarations regarding Horatia, whom she did not scruple to call Nelson's child, she always implied that the mother was some other person than herself. Despite Nelson's known infatuation for her, reputable biographers like Southey and Harris Nicolas accepted that there must have been another woman in his life. Lady Hamilton's success in establishing this moral alibi appears to have been complete; at no time did the family appear to doubt her word. (Earl Nelson alone remained aloof where Horatia was concerned, referring to her only as 'the child'.) As guardian of Nelson's daughter, in pursuit of an official recognition of her past services that would place her both financially and morally beyond ruin, the countenance of Nelson's family was a first requisite to Lady Hamilton's position in society. A year after the death of Nelson she might, excusably, have thought this achieved.

[1] M.898.

CHAPTER X

LIVING ON CREDIT

LADY HAMILTON was the more unprepared for the sudden threat to her reputation that occurred in the autumn of 1806. Her reaction to the event shows how relatively secure she believed her position in the Nelson family to be. The anomaly of that position lay in its dependence on Horatia. The family's feeling for Nelson's daughter was so deep and so genuine that Lady Hamilton was emboldened to call on it to defend her character. Called upon now to disprove the existence of the child born to her in 1782, she particularly emphasized her role as the chosen guardian of the child she was not suspected of having borne in 1801.

The existence of Emma Carew (the presumed daughter of Captain Willett-Payne) whose upbringing had been entrusted to her grandmother at Hawarden, was of course known to Charles Greville and Sir William Hamilton. The fees for the girl's education at Manchester—£100 a year— were paid first by one and then by the other; she was trained to earn her living, as a governess or as a lady's companion. Her existence was at no time revealed to Lord Nelson. This is sufficiently proved by his rapturous declaration when Horatia was born: 'I never had a dear pledge of love till you gave me one, and you, thank my God, never gave one to anyone else.' [1]

Whereas Sarah and Cecilia Connor were introduced to Merton and salaries secured for them, nothing was done for the girl whom Emma had declared was their elder sister. The emergence of 'Anne Connor' as she called her, laying claims to recognition in the autumn of 1806, was most untimely for Lady Hamilton, bent as she was on securing a government pension for herself. Whatever affection she may once have felt for her daughter she had long ago suppressed. Her daughter's claims now were met with denials and counter-charges of wickedness and lunacy. Lady Hamilton took a bold step to preserve the good opinion of those on whom she depended for her security: she chose to reveal the allegations herself rather than to conceal them. The alarm in which she wrote to the Boltons and Matchams can be judged by their replies. It is unlikely that either family would in fact have heard the scandal if it had not been for her

[1] Letter of 1 March 1801.

revelations, being far from the centres of London gossip. But their incredulity at the communication was proof enough how little they suspected her of being the mother of Horatia, and in order to secure this it may have seemed to Lady Hamilton worth taking the risk of reporting Emma Carew's allegations.

Mrs. Bolton wrote on 11 October 1806:

How shocked and surprized I was, my dear friend at the contents of your last letter. Poor wretched girl, what will become of her? What could possess her to circulate such things? It is no kindness to set you fretting, for after all Miss C. would not even have hinted a word but to your friends, who of course would not have believed anything to your prejudice; and that she well knew, for no one would have been warmer in your cause, had she heard any person living even *surmised* anything against you. Now, my dear Lady, pardon me if I have said anything to offend you. I am sure I would say and do everything to please and nothing to fret.[1]

Mr. Matcham replied on 10 November:

You guard us against malevolent tongues, but, be assured, we hear nothing of you but what is good. Knowing our attachment, even your enemies would not, in our presence, infringe the rules of civility by speaking anything derogatory of you—our associates are your admirers. You need not tell me that you will ever continue a friend and well-wisher to the family; your natural disposition sufficiently guarantees it, we therefore never doubt it . . .

At Ashfold Lodge we shall have a hope of seeing you, as the distance from London is nothing.'[2]

Lady Hamilton did not leave the matter there. In a Will dated Merton 7 October 1806 whose terms would suggest that she wrote it without legal advice, she denied her daughter's charges, and left her unprovided for. Making provision for her cousins Sarah Reynolds (£100 annuity) and Cecilia Connor (£50 annuity) she went on to say 'I do not leave anything to Ann or Mary Ann Connor, the daughter of Michael and Sarah Connor, as she has been a wicked storytelling young woman, and tried to defame her best friends and relations.' In her further Will of 16 October 1808 the charges against 'Ann Connor' were far more precise, and included a general allegation of lunacy in the Connor family. Charles Connor, the brother of Sarah and Cecilia, whom Nelson had taken to sea with him and placed under a kind Captain (Captain Capel), had on several occasions behaved with such violence as to be treated for madness, and finally discharged from the Navy. Emma stated in her Will:

[1] M.896.   [2] M.898.

I declare before God, and as I hope to see Nelson in Heaven, that Ann Connor, who goes by the name of Carew, and tells many falsehoods that she is my daughter, but from what motive I know not, I declare that she is the eldest daughter of my mother's sister, Sarah Connor, and that I have the mother and six children to keep, all of them, except two, having turned out bad; I therefore beg of my mother to be kind to the two good ones, Sarah and Cecilia. This family having, by their extravagance, almost ruined me, I have nothing to leave them; and I pray to God to turn Ann Connor's alias Carew's heart. I forgive her, but as there is a madness in the Connor family, I hope it is only the effect of this disorder that may have induced this bad young woman to have persecuted me by her slander and falsehoods.[1]

The time came when by failing to pay Cecilia's salary as Horatia's governess, Lady Hamilton set yet another member of the family against her. The Connors, whether responsible for her ruin or not, were undoubtedly in a position to cause her considerable embarrassment, if nothing worse. And her behaviour towards their reputed eldest daughter was likely to make matters worse.

The plight of Emma Carew was never relieved. In a farewell letter to Lady Hamilton, written in 1810, which showed that after the attempt at reconciliation in 1806 she went abroad, she made one final plea for recognition before leaving England for good. The text of the letter is given here, where, by its context, it belongs, rather than to the actual date of writing.

Mrs. Denis's mention of your name and the conversation she had with you, have revived ideas in my mind which an absence of four years has not been able to efface. It might have been happy for me to have forgotten the past, and to have begun a new life with new ideas; but for my misfortune, my memory traces back circumstances which have taught me too much, yet not quite all I could have wished to have known—with you that resides, and ample reasons, no doubt, you have for not imparting them to me. Had you felt yourself at liberty so to have done, I might have become reconciled to my former situation and have been relieved from the painful employment I now pursue. It was necessary as I then stood, for I had nothing to support me but the affection I bore you; on the other hand, doubts and fears by turns oppressed me, and I determined to rely on my own efforts rather than submit to abject dependence, without a permanent name or acknowledged parents. That I should have taken such a step shows, at least, that I have a mind misfortune has not subdued. That I should persevere in it is what I owe to myself and to you, for it shall never be said that I avail myself of your partiality or my own inclination, unless I learn my claim on you is greater than you have hitherto acknowledged. But the time may come when the same reasons may cease to operate, and then, with a heart

[1] Nicolas, vii, 387-8.

filled with tenderness and affection, will I shew you both my duty and attachment. In the meantime, should Mrs. Denis' zeal and kindness not have over-
rated your expressions respecting me, and that you should really wish to see me,
I may be believed in saying that such a meeting would be one of the happiest
moments of my life, but for the reflection that it may also be the last, as I leave
England in a few days, and may, perhaps never return to it again, I remain,
etc, etc.[1]

The incident of Emma Carew certainly increased Lady Hamilton's
sense of persecution which, at times, had the full force of paranoia. A
future cause for persecution had already been set in motion by her ad-
vocacy of the writer James Harrison, editor of the 'British Classics', whom
she helped with his *Life of Lord Nelson*, both financially and by supplying
information. Published towards the end of 1806 his book had the solitary
distinction of being the first in the field. Throughout it sought to exalt
Lady Hamilton and defame Lady Nelson and her son and it was not
unjustly described as 'one of the most nauseous of known books'.[2] Lady
Nelson's comment on its publication was: 'I think without exception Mr.
Harris's (sic) 'Life of Lord Nelson' is the basest production that ever was
offered to the public. It is replete with untruths.'[3] Harrison could never
have written certain pages, those specifically dealing with Nelson's
domestic and private affairs without the help of Lady Hamilton. The
misery of Nelson's marriage, the 'coldness' of his wife, who cast 'a
petrifying chill' on the 'warmth of his affectionate heart', with incidents
illustrative of his despair, could be the knowledge—or invention—of
no one outside his home, and no one but Lady Hamilton had an interest in
defaming his wife. None but she, moreover, had an interest in envenoming
the relations between Lady Nelson and her husband's family. Contrary to
the evidence of Lady Nelson's letters, and particularly those of the
Earl's family, Harrison asserted that Lady Nelson never liked her
husband's nephews and nieces and 'regarded all his Lordship's relations
as the natural enemies of her son; whom she seems unaccountably to have
considered as the rightful heir to her husband's honours'. The facts
concerning Nelson's separation from his wife (known to none but
Haslewood) were reported by Harrison, who laid the blame boldly on
Lady Nelson, alleging that she refused to live with her husband, and left
his house without notice, adding the further contradictory detail that they
separated by mutual consent, and signed a formal deed of separation. For

---

[1] M.1003.
[2] David Hannay quoted by Oman, iv.
[3] Lady Nelson to Dr. J. M. McArthur, Nelson Collection, Monmouth Museum.

Lady Hamilton the question was one of great importance and she had an understandable interest in getting her version of the facts published first. Financing Harrison therefore was no charitable deed but a sound investment—or so she reckoned. Her part in the affair is clearly established by a letter from her former factotem, Oliver, who both then and later played a leading part in sponsoring Harrison's activities and in supplying him not only with supplementary information, but undoubtedly with documentary evidence. While Lady Hamilton was still staying at Cranwich Oliver wrote to her on 16 August 1806:

Mr. Harrison is greatly beholden to your Ladyship for yr kind offer of assistance that he stands so much in need of. His affairs are quite desperate. Mr. Capel has stopped the weekly allowance. No one but Yr. Ladyship can enable him to finish his work, and without some small assistance now, the whole must be spoiled. He wished to do honour to the work and justice to those who take it, all which, and saving him from ruin, depends on a few kind remarks from your Ladyship in his extremity, for which favour he will be thankful as long as he lives. Yr Ladyship has it in Yr. power thus to alleviate his numerous suffering family, for, when once *his work* is done, he can demand his money, and not before.[1]

Oliver's timely intervention on Harrison's behalf was acknowledged by many flattering allusions to him in the course of the book. He was described as 'an English linguist residing in Vienna' whom Sir William engaged as 'confidential secretary courier and interpreter' to accompany his party home through Germany. (In fact, Oliver had been in Sir William's household in a humble capacity since his boyhood.) The collaboration with Harrison, once established, may have led to other and even less savoury joint enterprises, such as the theft of Lord Nelson's letters, resulting in their anonymous publication in 1814, of which Lady Hamilton accused them; and the even more scurrilous *Memoirs of Lady Hamilton* published in 1815 after her death, which contain evidence that only they could have known or have supplied. Oliver remained in the Hamilton household from their return to England in 1800 to the death of Sir William in 1803; and very significant it is that the anonymous author of the *Memoirs of Lady Hamilton* states that Oliver accompanied her to Mrs. Gibson's on the occasion of Horatia's birth.[2] There are many details that only Oliver or someone informed by him could have known, and he may have had blackmail in mind. Certainly Oliver became one of her bitterest enemies, and was dismissed in 1808. Mr. Matcham, to whom

[1] M.890. [2] *Memoirs of Lady Hamilton*, 304.

Oliver turned in his plight, not only helped him financially—for he considered he was shabbily treated—but recommended a patent medecine of his composition to his friend Dr. Lawrence. In gratitude for Mr. Matcham's charity, Oliver undertook not to write to Mr. Rose and the Lord Chancellor on the subject of Lady Hamilton. 'You, dear Sir', he wrote, 'have repaired the ruin She has brought me to, by her false, illusive, wicked duplicity'.[1] We cannot be sure whether Oliver actually blackmailed his former patroness, but he had plenty of material for doing so. So too did Harrison, whom she did not hesitate to accuse later of stealing her letters.

Lady Hamilton put all the blame for her failure to get a government pension on Earl Nelson. What Lord Grenville and his successors, Mr. Canning, Lord Abercorn, and the Duke of Portland, really thought of her —and possibly knew about her—must be prevented from reaching the Boltons and Matchams; hence, the blame for an otherwise inexplicable situation must be placed elsewhere. The Earl's arrogant bearing towards his sisters and their families after Nelson's death, and his absorption in his own, and his son's worldly advancement—did not endear him to the households at Cranwich and in Bath. Mystified as they might be by his conduct as reported by Lady Hamilton, they accepted her version of the facts. '. . . What use is the Codicil to him?' Mrs. Bolton squarely asked in June 1806. 'He cannot fear it should be any detriment to him *now*?'.[2]

Waiting for the pension that did not come, but in which she believed with perennial optimism, Lady Hamilton made some readjustments in her mode of living during that autumn. She left the Clarges Street house and went to live in furnished apartments at 136 New Bond Street. The furniture was left in Clarges Street (the house may indeed have been let furnished by her as she returned to it from time to time), and was only finally sold 'by virtue of an execution' in her last London home, 150 New Bond Street in July 1813. How uncomfortable she was and how limited her accommodation can be judged by Mrs. Bolton's reactions when she wrote her:

I am glad the Duke ['Q'] has said he does not approve of No. 136 for you, it looks as though he really meant to leave you something to keep up a better establishment. Shall I say the truth, I was very much hurt to see you were obliged whether you liked it or not, to mix with their society [the landlady's] indeed, if they had given you up the front drawing-room entirely and two bed-chambers you would have been more comfortable.[3]

---

[1] Eyre-Matcham, 268.   [2] M.883.   [3] M.911.

Speculation about what 'Old Q' might yet do for her was one of Lady Hamilton's reasons for staying in the region of Piccadilly, though the obvious recourse of giving up London altogether and making Merton her only home was still open to her. She resisted this until it was too late to save even Merton. So long as Merton was hers it still presumably served as a home for Horatia, whose presence in the 'uncomfortable' Bond Street lodgings cannot have been desired. By the terms of the Will drawn up on 7 October 1806, Merton with its seventy acres of ground was still Emma's to leave (a situation which no longer obtained two years later when she made a further Will, instructing her Executors to pay her debts by the sale of Merton); and she left it first to her mother 'Mary Kidd, then Lions, and after Mary Doggen, or Cadogan . . . for her natural life', and afterwards to Horatia, with the proviso that should she die intestate, the property was left to 'the heirs of Susannah Bolton, wife of Thomas Bolton, Esq of Cranwich, Norfolk, on condition that they pay Sarah Reynolds [Connor] my cousin, one hundred a-year for her life, and fifty pounds a-year to Cecilia Connor, my cousin'. There followed the clause relative to 'Ann Connor', excluding her from any benefit under the Will. Horatia was left a 'Ward in Chancery' after Mrs. Cadogan's death and the Matchams were appealed to 'to see after her education and that she is properly brought up . . . if they will do this, Nelson and Emma's spirits will look down on them and bless them'.[1] Horatia's £4,000 left her by Nelson was administered by trustees on her behalf (Haslewood and Mr. Matcham) and the income only paid to Lady Hamilton; she could not therefore dispose of it in her Will. The nomination of the Matchams rather than the Boltons as Horatia's guardians was therefore the obvious choice, although at that time Emma was on a far more intimate footing with the Boltons than with the Matchams.

Closer contacts with the Matchams were established, however, when their long-expected move from Bath took place in June 1807. Of Mr. Matcham Lady Nelson had once said 'he is the most unsettled man I ever met'; his passion for travelling, freely indulged in his adventurous youth when he explored the East, still found an outlet in his zest for moving house. Since he had swept Kitty Nelson literally off her feet at a Christmas Ball in Bath twenty years before, he had bought, built, exchanged, or rented, a number of houses in Norfolk, Hampshire and, in the last years, in Bath. He was a charming man, handsome, cultured, sufficiently well-to-do, with energy and an inventive mind. Whatever the home of the moment he threw himself into embellishing and exploiting it to the full, and while

[1] Nicolas, vii, 387.

he infatuation lasted there seemed no better place to live. 'Ashfold Lodge', to which he brought his family in three postchaises in June 1807, promised well to kindle and sustain all his great enthusiasm. Life there proved very different from life at Bath: it was situated in real country, Handcross being the nearest market town some three miles away. The picturesque village of Slaugham adjoined the Matcham's estate and not far away was Slaugham Park. In Slaugham Park were the picturesque ruins of a fourteenth-century mansion left lying side by side with the fine Jacobean house built by Sir Walter Covert in the early seventeenth century. By the time the Matchams came into the region, the property had passed to the Sergison family who lived at Cuckfield Place and with whom a great friendship was struck up. The mansion at Slaugham Park being to let, the Matchams had the unexpected good fortune of securing Mr. Haslewood within a couple of years as their neighbour. The two properties were adjoining, their parks forming one continuous wood only broken by the Ashfold pond, and Haslewood became a regular visitor. With Dr. Lawrence, former owner of Ashfold and now a near neighbour, another close friendship was established.

The family that came to Ashfold in the summer of 1807 consisted of Mr. and Mrs. Matcham and nine children, four boys and five girls: George (18), Kitty (15), Elizabeth (12), Francis (11), Harriet (8), Susanna (5), Horace (4), and baby Charles born after Nelson's death, in 1806. Mrs. Matcham had lost four other children, and was still to lose two sons. (Francis died only a year after the family's arrival at Ashfold.) By August 1807 they were sufficiently settled into their new home to receive the visit of Lady Hamilton and a large party consisting of Mrs. Cadogan, Horatia, Lady Bolton and her sister Anne, one of the Connor girls, and Mme. Bianchi, whom Lady Hamilton invited most summers on her seaside holidays. The stay at Ashfold was not for many days, the main objective of Lady Hamilton's trip being Worthing, just twenty miles away, where she planned to stay a month. George recorded how in the evening at Ashfold, 'her ladyship accompanied by Mme Bianchi, favoured us with some favourite airs'.[1] George was deputed to escort Mme. Bianchi to Worthing the next morning in search of lodgings, and they 'were fortunate in finding a good house'. Lady Bolton remained some days with her uncle and aunt, and having heard nothing from Worthing, she wrote to Lady Hamilton on 24 August:

We are very much surprised at not hearing from you to say how you like your residence at Worthing. As you promised so positively to write directly, the only

[1] Eyre-Matcham, 258.

thing we can imagine is some mistake in the direction. We are anxious to know
how you are, and whether Horatia has derived benefit from bathing . . . The
proper direction is: Ashfold Lodge near Horsham.[1]

Two days later the Matchams joined Lady Hamilton's party at
Worthing. Something more than an insight into their manner of passing
the time at the sea is afforded by Lady Hamilton's long letter to the
Countess Nelson, dated 27 August; it affords a deeper insight still into
her own evolving attitude towards Horatia.

While the Boltons and the Matchams were making so much of Horatia,
no equal sign of interest was manifested by the Earl and Countess; there is
no indication, indeed, that Nelson's daughter was ever invited to Canterbury. Nelson's expressed wish regarding her marriage with young Horace
may have been sufficient reason on their part for keeping the cousins apart.
It was sufficient reason, also, for Lady Hamilton to flourish Horatia, as it
were, maddeningly before their eyes, as a social asset they might altogether
lose if they did not alter their policy. To be able to boast of Horatia, as
Lady Hamilton now unashamedly did, must have been doubly agreeable
to her when she thought of the time when she needed to hide the child's
very existence; and agreeable too now that her own and the Countess
Nelsons' positions had so radically changed. Whereas once 'the little
woman', then plain Mrs. Nelson, had been beholden to her patronage, the
Earl and Countess were very 'grand folks' now and could afford to slight
Emma in her fallen fortune. One senses that no other motive dictated her
letter to her former 'dearest friend and jewell'. Dated Worthing 27
August, it reads:

Here we are in this delightful place and my dearest Horatia is got well and
strong She Bathes and now Eats and drinks and sleeps well and *creates universal
enterest alltho'* Princess Charlotte is here. She is left and all come to look at
Nelson's angel She improves in languages musick and accomplishments but my
Heart Bleeds to think how proud wou'd her glorious Father have been He that
lived only for Her Whose last words & thoughts were to her She that would have
been everything tis dreadfull to me however She is my Comfort and solace and I
act as alltho' he cou'd look down and approve and bless Emma for following up
His every wish We have been at Mr. Matchams a week with Lady Bolton their
place is Beautiful and their family most delightful so well brought up George
is a very fine young man Mr. & Mrs. Matcham, George, Kate, and Lady Bolton
came here yesterday and stay till Saturday. He is like a Father to poor Horatia we
stay here a month longer we live very retired we visit the Cholmondeleys, Lady
Abdy, Mrs. Douglas, Lady Dudley, and Mr & Mrs Dorott and on one else. I do

not go to the Library nor suffer my young ones except once in the morning we go to bed at Eleven and are up at seven. the sands are beautiful Ann [Bolton] drives Horatia out in a donkey Cart where all the young ladies drive princess Charlotte is a charming girl and very kind and civil to Horatia and me Mrs. Addy and Lady de Clifford are with her Give my love to Lady Charlotte and to the Earl and Lord Merton when you write to them—You see my letters are not so gay as they used to be but my dearest friend every day my affliction encreases for the loss of my dearest Nelson Mrs. Matcham and I sit and walk for Hours talking and weeping for Him at this time two years how happy we were every day we think of what we were doing with that Angel who appeared amongst us for those happy 25 days this only adds to my grief and now as the time approaches towards the fatal 13th of September I am wretched for I was the Cause of his going out unfortunately but I must not dwell on this most melancholy subject. My mother who is with [us] begs her compliments. Ever dear Lady Nelson the miserable Emma Hamilton.[1]

George Matcham, aged eighteen and, as Lady Hamilton noted, 'a very fine young man', was not allowed to absent himself very much from the family party, called upon constantly to act in the role, as she would have called it, of 'cavaliere servante' to the ladies. In his journal he recorded some of his new experiences in Lady Hamilton's train. He gave some further pictures of the donkey rides which he condescended to watch as a fit sport for little girls, while himself riding out with Mme Bianchi who

poor thing became so much alarmed as made the ride none of the pleasantest. She had however courage to meet our friends on the shore where the younger half i.e. Miss Anne Bolton, Miss Horatia Nelson, Miss Connor and Miss Matcham were driving themselves in little vehicles drawn by asses. In the evening we were favoured by some duets by Lady H. and Mrs. B.[2]

Young Viscount Merton (or Lord Trafalgar as he was more generally styled by that time) might be kept at a distance by his diplomatic parents, but Lady Hamilton (and Horatia) did not lack for allies among the young men of the family. Tom Bolton had some grouse of his own shooting to send her Ladyship, and wrote to Worthing full of curiosity about the doings there. He was on good terms with his Matcham relations and hoped that George would join him at Cambridge where he himself was going in the Michaelmas Term. Writing to Lady Hamilton from his crammer's the Revd. Mr. Haggett at Byefleet on 23 August he said:

Pray give me all the news you can to write to Sir William, as I am purposely delaying his letter till I hear from you . . . I am very happy to hear that Lady Bolton is with you, as I think the sea air will be of service to her. You have seen

[1] NMM/BRP/4.   [2] Eyre-Matcham, 259.

Mr. & Mrs. Matcham; pray how do you like their house and grounds, and what do you think of my cousins? Which do you think sings, plays, or is the prettiest, and what is the name of the place they are living [in] as I have entirely forgot, and wish to write Sir William everything and should like to be correct? Does George go to Cambridge this year as usual? Have the great folks [Earl and Countess Nelson] left town for Canterbury yet, as they were only talking about it the last time I heard from them? Pray do you like Worthing as much as you did Southend? I suppose Mrs. Cadogan is improving now very fast as to her health. Do you not find that the bathing is very beneficial both to you and Horatia? Give my kind love to her, Mrs. Cadogan Kate, Anne, and all the rest of your party. I am afraid you find my letters very insipid for want of news, which it is impossible for me to get here. I am fully engaged in business during all the week so that I am not sorry when Sunday comes that I may rest myself a little and write to a few of my friends and take a little ride, as I shall do this afternoon in order to put this into the Post Office, which is about three miles from here.[1]

Tom Bolton was still, as Nelson said of him six years before, 'little Tom —a meek, well-disposed lad', warm hearted and unpretentious, whose mother's chief hope when he left home for Cambridge was that he would remain 'what he is *now*—*good*, and then he will be comparatively *happy*'. He had little expectation then of the complete reversal of his fortunes that a very few months would bring. Of Nelson's 'three props' he was certainly the least dashing, harbouring no resentment at the airs Horace assumed, and happy enough to shelter behind his country cousin, Henry Girdle-stone, at Cambridge, or the accomplished George Matcham, with whom he got on uncommonly well.

George, making himself very agreeable to Lady Hamilton's party at Worthing, recorded how, on 23 September, he was again summoned from Ashfold through a storm of rain, to 'stay over their last day at the sea because my heels might be required to make up one at a farewell ball to be given on Thursday evening.'[2] Mme Bianchi having returned to town, he was offered her room for the night and had to avow that 'after combatting steadily against the hospitable arguments of her Ladyship, I was at length obliged to yield.' After escorting the ladies 'on the beach' for their last morning, he dined with them 'en famille and in ye evening went to ye ball, where we danced till ½ past 3 a.m. As the party resolved to dine at Ashfold next day, I rose at 7 and mounting my horse arrived home wet to the skin. After remaining with us till Tuesday, the Hamilton party set out for Merton'.[3]

Much had happened to Horatia since her hurried move to Merton in the August of 1805. Despite the scenes and the weeping fits of 'My Lady', as

[1] M.922   [2] Eyre-Matcham, 260.   [3] Ibid.

she never ceased to call her, life appeared to have many of the elements of a good fairy story (of which she had quite a collection), punctuated as it was by visits from one house to another, and delightful trips into the country and to the sea, where kind aunts and cousins made much of her. It was better than Little Titchfield Street and the kind Mrs. Gibson; so long as one danced and sang well and made smart replies that were repeated to every caller, there was nothing difficult or unpleasant to do, and things happened as by miracle when one wanted them most. After the seaside and the donkeys, there was a birthday to look forward to. George Matcham recorded how, before leaving Ashfold, Lady Hamilton engaged him to come to Merton on 'ye 28th October, that being Anne's and Horatia's birthday', and went on to describe the occasion:

24th October: I set off for Merton, where I arrived about 4 p.m. and found Tom B. had been there since Friday. We all went in the evening to Mr. Perry's [the editor of the *Morning Chronicle*] who was extremely polite to me ... 25th. Sunday morning we went to church and dined at Merton ... on Tuesday Mr. Harrison was there, he is editor of the British Classics. On Wednesday went to town with her Ladyship, Mrs. Graeffa, the widow of the superintendent of Bronté, and Tom. Lady H. gave us a curious account of Mad. du Barri whom she visited in 1792 ... on our return ... great preparations were made for the celebration of the little Horatia's birthday. 28th: A large party assembled at dinner ... There was a dance in the evening, which I had the honour of opening with the little Horatia. There were only country dances ... After supper Mr. Lancaster with solemn deportment ... favoured us with a song, which I mistook for a funeral oration.[1]

The presence of the reliable Merton friends at Horatia's birthday-party, especially of the Vicar, Mr. Lancaster (despite George's stricture), was of the greatest importance to Lady Hamilton in establishing the alibi of Horatia's birth, the myth of her identity, and her own equally mythical position as the child's Guardian. By dint of repetition, the fiction of Horatia's October birthday became an established fact, marked by more and more resounding celebrations as the years went by.

Lady Hamilton's present to Horatia on the occasion was a silver hot-water plate with cover, engraved with an elegant design of amoretti supporting a ribboned scroll on which were inscribed her name and the date: HORATIA 29th Octr 1807.[2]

Mrs. Bolton, having received a copy of Lady Hamilton's birthday 'Compliment' to Horatia, wrote in reply: 'I admire your address to dear Horatia; let me hear her answer and all about your fête. I wrote to her and

---

[1] Ibid., 261.   [2] Now preserved in the family of her descendants.

Anne to be received on their birthday' (30 October was in reality Anne's birthday).

Horatia's appearance apparently lent itself to the deception; the drawings of her as a child show her to have been big and blooming; easily to be taken for a child four months older than her real age. Her attack of chickenpox, however, in the spring of 1807, made her grow fast and so thin that, even after the holidays at Worthing, Lady Bolton wrote in some anxiety to Lady Hamilton on 18 October: 'I hope Horatia is quite recovered from her illness, children of her age are always thin growing so much. Caroline [Peirson] is quite as thin as Horatia was when I saw her last.' Tall for her age, and rapidly losing her childish resemblance to her mother, Horatia could convincingly appear in October 1807 as a seven-year-old child.

On 1 November her cousins, George and Tom, left Merton for London. Tom's prospects at the time were hardly brilliant. His parents did not wish him to be pushed into the church. The only interest the family had there lay with the Earl and his son, and Mrs. Bolton judged that they, as before, would sooner think of the countess's nephew, William Yonge, than of Tom. She was anxious about Tom, and said as much to Lady Hamilton (who promised to interest Mr. Rose on his behalf). 'He is coming into the world, and we are going out,' she wrote 'and was it not for the sake of my daughters we might as well live in the country.' Tom's own endowments —apart from his good heart and honesty—were not likely to get him very far. He was entered at Peterhouse, from where he wrote to Lady Hamilton of his first impressions of college life on 22 November:

I am afraid you will think me very neglectful in not writing before, but I flatter myself you will excuse me when I say that it has really not been in my power to write to anybody yet, for I am so unsettled even now that I scarcely know what I am about; in fact, I have not an hour that I can call my own, for I am so engaged in preparing for lectures. I am going this evening to take my supper with my friend Hodgson. Lord T [Trafalgar] did me the honour to call upon me once, and I returned the visit very soon after, but he was not home, and I have not seen anything of him since. My cousin Henery (sic) Girdlestone being here makes it very pleasant for me; indeed I hardly know what I should have done if he had not been here. He lives at Catherine Hall, which is very near to our college, so that we constantly see one another every day. If you should ever come to Cambridge whilst I am here, I am afraid you would not be able to come into my rooms to see me, for I live in a garret, and there is a terrible bad staircase to lead up to them, and the entrance into the room is so low that it would very near break your back to stoop to get in; but, after you had overcome all these difficulties, I think you would say my rooms were pleasant for garrets ... My dear Lady, I must now conclude, with my kind love to Mrs. Cadogam, Horatia, Anne and the rest of the party. Pray favour me with a letter soon.[1]

Tom's mother, commenting on Norfolk gaieties in a previous letter to Lady Hamilton, made a special mention of young Lord Trafalgar's inaccessibility to his relations: 'Our young peer, I find,' she wrote on 19 October, 'is flying about the country; he has been staying with Mr. Wilson (I mean Dick Wilson) he has been to Bury Fair, to the Sessions Ball at Norwich, and is now staying with Mr. Berny at Lord Baynings. He talks of being at the Swaffham Coursing Meeting Ball, where, if I am there, I shall see him, but not else, I am *sure*'.[2]

For Christmas 1807 Lady Hamilton stayed at Merton rather than in town for the first time since Nelson's death. Her need to economize was more pressing than ever, but a surprising feature in her plan of economy was her entertaining the royal dukes for several days at Merton. Her friends among them were principally the Duke of Sussex, who had stayed in Naples in 1792 while studying music (singing in particular), and had been partnered by Mrs. Billington at many a reception at the ambassador's. Whether the attraction at Merton for the Duke was Mrs. Billington or Lady Hamilton, he made frequent appearances there that winter, as well as in Clarges Street, and was seen there more than once by George Matcham, on his visits to and from Cambridge, who described him as 'a Gentleman of enormous stature, in his Highland dress'.

The Prince of Wales and the Duke of Clarence joined him on a prolonged visit to Merton at the end of November 1807. Their presence and her own familiarity with and ease in entertaining royalty, was duly communicated by Lady Hamilton to Mrs. Bolton, who was immensely impressed. Still more was she impressed by the notice Horatia received from the royal visitors. Lady Hamilton had not lost, as might be supposed, the opportunity of presenting Nelson's child to the future ruler of England, though what Nelson's views on the occasion would have been she perfectly well knew. Now a great welcome was accorded the royal dukes. Not only Emma, but Horatia as well, was subjected to the admiring stare at close range of three pairs of bulging Hanoverian eyes; Horatia was taught to make appropriate compliments and exhibit her prettiest 'Attitudes'. What she saw with her young eyes was still the fairy story unfolding, even though the fairy princes were gentlemen of such incredible corpulence as to resemble rather the comic figures in the Drury Lane farces and pantomimes to which she had already been taken. An assurance of paternal interest by the Prince, and promise of protection

[1] M.928.   [2] KMM/NWD/10-11.

when he should be in a 'position to act', was evidently obtained on the occasion, as in her Will of 16 October 1808 Lady Hamilton did not hesitate to leave Horatia to the Prince's protection. Committing her mother and Horatia to the care of Mr. Rose, and in the event of his death to the care of his son, she added: 'and also I beg His Royal Highness the Prince of Wales, as he dearly loved Nelson, that his Royal Highness will protect his child, and be kind to her; for this I beg of him, for there is no one I so highly regard as His Royal Highness'.[1]

Mrs. Bolton, more blinded than edified by the report of these splendours, wrote to Lady Hamilton on 29 November: 'You delight me by saying Horatia has so much notice taken of her I hope when she is Introduced at Windsor George our King will fall in Love with her and give her a good Pension out of his Privy Purse'.[2] The continued sojourn of the royal dukes at Merton made her write again on 8 December: 'How favoured you have been by their Royal Highnesses passing so many Days with you. I do not wonder their liking Merton and *your* Society. Did the Prince of Wales spend more than one Day with you?' Poor blind Mrs. Nelson was at Merton and Mrs. Bolton considered how, in her place, 'I would have kept my room the time they were there—at least the Prince'.[3]

A present of tobacco for Mr. Bolton from one of the royal dukes (most probably Clarence) was received with awe at Cranwich, and an inability to express suitable thanks. Lady Hamilton was commissioned to do so in their place: 'we are not in the habit of sending and speaking to such great personnages,' Mrs. Bolton told her.[4]

As 1807 closed, despite the shortage of money, Lady Hamilton thought the great gamble was coming off and better times were ahead. The Prince of Wales had promised his protection, Mr. Rose was approaching the new administration once again with the enumeration of her 'just claims' on government, Horatia was proving herself an asset rather than a liability. Mrs. Bolton, writing to her on 16 December perfectly expressed the family's support of her pretensions: 'when does your business come on?' she wrote; 'I am impatient till something is done for *you*. Do not delay it a moment longer than is absolutely necessary. With or without the child, if you are well provided for, she can never *want*, and depend on it she will marry *well*'.[5]

Lady Hamilton might indeed see in these words the conclusion of her

---

[1] Nicolas, vii, 388.   [2] M.931.
[3] M.932.   [4] Ibid.
[5] NMM/NWD/9594/10-11.

two years' intensive cultivation of Nelson's family, for they summed up the unquestioning trust placed in her by Mrs. Bolton. In her view Lady Hamilton was inclined to neglect her own interests in favour of the child; as the sister of the dead hero, Mrs. Bolton felt the obligation from time to time to exhort Lady Hamilton not to be too forgetful of her own needs in furthering those of Nelson's motherless daughter.

CHAPTER XI

MERTON LOST

WHILE the Boltons and the Matchams were rallying round Emma, drawn to her cause by their love for Nelson's child—the family of the new earl lived increasingly withdrawn from their kindred, in the isolation they believed appropriate to their state. They did not court popularity among their relatives, and still less, in view of her wild accusations against them, did they seek to serve Lady Hamilton. Time would show that Earl Nelson was not guilty of any of the malicious charges brought against him by her; his ungracious exterior, though hardly hiding a heart of gold, was not that of a dishonest man; his famous brother, often calling him 'a bore' and laughing at his pursuit of advancement, had nevertheless said of him years before 'My brother has a bluntness and a want of fine feeling, which we are not used to, *but he means nothing*',[1] and later Mr. Matcham observed that there were 'many men more courteous, but few of more sterling worth'. Impervious to opinion, as seen in his indifference to Lady Hamilton's charges which he could with very little trouble have disproved, the Earl's lifelong ambitions might be said to be fulfilled when he was raised to the peerage and voted a grant by Parliament for £120,000 of public money. He was, however, at heart, a family and not a public man, and his affections ruled his life. First came his love for his son, a love very similar in degree and kind to Nelson's love for Horatia. In this his wife exactly resembled him (Charlotte took second place in both parents' affection). Nothing was ever good enough for Horace. Lady Nelson had taken exception to Horace's privileged treatment even as a boy; '... I never saw a child stand a fairer chance of being spoiled than he does, his ideas will be great indeed',[2] she had written to her husband. Horace's letters from Eton were those of a young person accustomed to having his wishes met, or even surpassed by fond and co-operative parents. 'I hope my Rabbits are well,' he wrote to his mother on arriving at school in January 1800, 'send me word pray write to me the day you receive this letter'. 'I hope you have not killed any of my rabbits,' he wrote a couple of months later, 'Pray don't as I shall like to see a good many of them when I

[1] P. i, 426.　　[2] Naish, 529.

come home.'[1] Reassurances on the subject of his rabbits had evidently been coupled with news from home of the immolation of his cocks and hens, which drew from him a chagrined comment; consolation, however, was at hand in the news that his rabbits 'have got young ones'. So with the preoccupation for his livestock, and concern over pocket-money, his schooldays passed, and he was admitted a pensioner of Christ's College, Cambridge, on 3 June 1805. Handsome, upright, lively, he promised to fulfil his parents' fondest hopes.

Their anguish was all the greater when, in early January 1808 he contracted an unspecified illness with alarming symptoms which was only later diagnosed to be typhoid fever. Dissatisfied with their local doctor's management of the case, the parents decided to take him to London, and left Canterbury on 13 January. Changing horses at Rochester, the Countess wrote a hurried reassuring note home to their friends the Brydges, who answered by return to say how greatly the better news had cheered the family breakfast-table that day. Writing on behalf of his wife and daughters, Mr. Brydges said: 'How ever much we miss you all, I am not so selfish as not to rejoice that you are gone to London where you will have the advantage of the best advice.'[2]

Horace at nineteen still showed the same anxious care for his pets; Mr. Brydges reassured him now: 'Pray tell my friend Lord Trafalgar with my kind regards and best wishes that I have seen his Eagle, Horses and Dogs this morning all of which are quite well and that as long as they remain here, I shall not fail to pay attention to them.'[3]

The Nelsons put up at Warne's Hotel off Hanover Square. On hearing of their arrival and of its cause, Mr. Davison hurried to call, and followed the progress of the illness with all the old affection he had shown the dead admiral. On 15 January he sent round a note by hand to Countess Nelson which said:

I am more than anxious to know how Horace is—send me verbal word by the Bearer. I send the Chicken Broth, which I trust is what you would wish—also two bottles of Madeira lest you should want it. I shall be with you before 10 o'clock when I shall please myself with the hope of finding your Beloved Son better than he was at 2 o'clock.—Friday 5 o'clock. Should anything be wanted that this house can supply I desire you will command it.[4]

Nothing that anyone could supply could save Horace; despite the love of his family and friends, he died on the Sunday (17 January) and was buried at St. Paul's on the 25th. The Annual Register for the year recorded how

[1] NMM/BRP/9292.   [2] Ibid.
[3] Ibid.   [4] Ibid.

'his remains were . . . attended by Mr. Bolton his Uncle as Chief mourner, Mr. Alex. Davison and Mr. Haslewood who were in the first coach . . . the carriages of Earl Nelson Mr. Davison and Mr. Haslewood followed . . . The body was deposited in the vault, near the remains of his uncle.'

High as their hopes for him had been, his parents had never thought of St. Paul's, but they were beyond consolation. Their grief was made worse by their absence from home and the necessity of staying in London where, suddenly, they realized their dearth of friends, and the absolute loneliness of their situation. The Countess Nelson's letters to her Canterbury friends give some indication of the break with Lady Hamilton. In former years her home would have been their refuge, and her friendship some palliative to their pain.

'I am almost blinded with my tears,' the Countess wrote Mrs. Hamson, some weeks after the event.

Dr. Outram [Horace's tutor] gave my dear Horace such a character, he said he was one of the very first young men he would have done honour to the Name. Indeed, my dear Friend, it is heart breaking to think of it . . . I am sorry to add that my lord and I make each other worse, he looks I think Very ill, Charlotte thank God is better her cousin Eliza Yonge is with her, so that I can now sit by myself and indulge my sorrows. I sometimes think I wish I was with you, my kind Friend, I should feel better, but then our house [at Canterbury] is so Gloomy that would not do for my dear Charlotte and she is now my only comfort. In this great Town we have no Friends, or at least not such a Friend.[1]

To the irreparable loss of so beloved a son was added the bitterness, unavoidable in a nature like Earl Nelson's, of seeing the name and title pass to the Boltons. As the Annual Register worded it: 'By his death, the national honours & estate of Nelson will, on the decease of the present Earl, pass from the male to the female line through Mrs. Bolton, the gallant conqueror's sister . . . whose son Thomas is the next in remainder.'

Tom Bolton was the last person to rejoice in another's sorrow, and young George Matcham recorded his own shock at his cousin's death in the pages of his journal: 'Poor fellow,' he wrote, 'I am truly sorry for him and his loss is irretrievable to his family . . . Poor Ld. T. had been for some time indisposed, but was not supposed in a dangerous state, until a few days before his death.'[2]

Mr. Matcham and Mr. Bolton, who hurried to town to attend the funeral, were rather less sensitive than their sons to the tragedy that had stricken the arrogant head of the house; they pressed for the Licence to be

[1] Ibid.   [2] Eyre-Matcham, 262.

taken out conferring on Tom the name of Nelson. It could be, as Horatia's case had shown, a lengthy business, and they wanted to set the law in motion without delay. Fond mother as she was, Mrs. Bolton was shocked at their haste: writing to Lady Hamilton on 17 February, a bare month after Horace's death she said: 'I think Mr. Matcham and my spouse are in too great a hurry about changing the name; the poor young man is scarcely cold in his coffin, and do not think they have shewn much feeling for his parents. Some months hence very well—at least that is my idea therein . . . I act as my heart dictates.'[1]

It may have been this unseemly haste that hardened the Earl's resolution as time went on to cheat them, if he could, of the prized inheritance. With a tenacity almost equal to his great brother's courage, he hung on to life, hoping against hope for another heir, and when his wife died, marrying again in old age with the same futile hope. Time brought appeasement eventually, however, and before the end of his long life he was treating his nephews not only as his rightful heirs, but as his sons; remembering perhaps that, with Horace, they had all been young together, thrilled to be presented to the Duke of Clarence by their famous uncle as his 'three props'.

George Matcham noted in his journal a meeting with the Earl and Countess at Brighton in the March after Horace's death. Mrs. Bolton and Eliza were staying at Ashfold, and with their hosts set off for a few days at the sea. 'Mrs. Bolton and my Father and Mother in the first carriage. Mrs. Peirson, Eliza Bolton, Kate and myself in the last . . . walked over the town till dinner . . . after which Mrs. Peirson and Parents renewed their ambulations. On their return we learnt with some surprise that they had met the E–l and C–t–ss N–l–n and their daughter. By all accounts the meeting was uncommonly cordial, as the N–blem–n received his sisters after an absence of two years with (Oh! excess of fraternal affection) a–Grunt–Lady C. with Dr. Outram, the tutor of ye late Lord T., called about 10 minutes after.'[2]

Ungracious, indeed, in encountering the ladies of his family with 'a grunt', the Earl nursed his sorrows in grim humour, further envenomed against them by the ceaseless mischief being made between the camps by Lady Hamilton. The Boltons and the Matchams accepted without query her version of the Earl's conduct towards herself, and towards them as well. Instigating both families to make application to assume the name of Nelson, she blamed the Earl for their failure to obtain the desired Licence. Mrs. Matcham wished her children to bear the famous name, provided her

[1] M.936.   [2] Eyre-Matcham, 264.

husband were also authorized to do so—'for I will never take one that my good husband is not allowed to have'. Though Mr. Matcham's credulity was strained by Lady Hamilton's reports on the Earl's opposition to their case, he does not appear to have probed the matter for himself; the Earl's conduct was made to appear to him as purely gratuitous spite.

On receipt of Lady Hamilton's report he wrote to her on 8 May 1808: 'What you have written us in respect of the Earl has quite astonished me. I could never have conceiv'd he could have so betrayed Tom Bolton, but it is evident that he is as great an enemy to us as our dear lost friend was our patron. The extinction of the whole family would be a matter of the greatest exultation to him, with the exception of his own dear self and Lady Charlotte. God only knows what his shocking rancour will lead to.' [1] In the event, neither the Boltons nor the Matchams made application for the change of name; Tom Bolton himself only took it on the death of the old Earl in 1835.

Added to the old cause of resentment against the Earl, Lady Hamilton was now motivated by a new one: the need to sell Merton, and the difficulty of explaining this to the family. Their own feelings for the place were conditioned by Nelson's great sentimental attachment to it. How was she to explain her need to be rid of the place only two and a half years after his death? Her liabilities were for over £8,000 at the time. Her recourse to shady moneylenders—even more the fact that she was being blackmailed (as the bills drawn by the Neapolitan singer, Carlo Rovedino would suggest)—could never be revealed to the family. The blame must therefore be laid elsewhere, and she broadcast it far and wide that her ruin was caused by Earl Nelson's refusal to pay the building costs and alterations to Merton. She wrote to Greville in November 1808 of the 'Destruction brought on by Earl Nelson's having thrown on me the Bills for furnishing Merton by his having secreted the Codicil of Dying Nelson who attested, in his Dying moments, that I had well served my country'. [2] By a characteristic confusion of cause and effect Emma sought to hide the truth.

The valuation of the property, drawn up by J. Willock of Golden Square, was dated 4 April 1808. It was then estimated, including the 'furniture and effects in the House, Offices, Gardens and grounds', to be worth £12,930. A prospective buyer, found by Mr. Rose in July, who was prepared to pay £13,000 for it, exclusive of the furniture, wines, etc., withdrew at the last minute. It is open to question, indeed, whether in view of Lady Hamilton's financial position declared that November she was in fact free to sell the place. Only by the intervention of a group of

[1] NMM/NWD/9594/7/A.   [2] Sichel, 511.

friends who formed themselves into a Trust to administer her resources
was she then able to escape arrest.

Strange to say, in view of her declared ruin by the year's end, she
abandoned none of her London engagements that season, showing herself
more than ever in society and explaining her policy so well as to draw
from Mrs. Matcham the unsuspecting comment in March 1808:

I had a letter from my sister last week, she talks of coming soon, and I reckon
very much of seeing her, and I hope when she has left us You will give us the
happiness of your company for a few days, which is *all* I can ask you to spare from
the gay world. I am delighted to hear of your going to all these great parties;
London is certainly the place for your constant residence, where you can enjoy
the society of your friends, without the immense expense of entertaining their
servants, which you are obliged to do in the country.' [1]

So the choice between London and Merton was explained on the score of
economy, and Lady Hamilton's obligation to show herself in society
recognized as a duty by the unworldly ladies of the Nelson family. Mrs.
Bolton wrote wonderingly from Norfolk in May of her friend's stamina:

We arrived here on Friday evening a little fatigued, for I do not yet feel quite
strong, but the country and fine weather will, I hope, restore me my usual health.
I find home the only place for a weak old woman. How I wish you were with us;
it would do you so much good to what (sic) hot rooms and large parties. At this
time of the year, it seems to me the strangest things in the world that people
should prefer crowded rooms to the delightful air of the country. You have been
very kind in taking Eliza out with you so much; I hope she has left town, as I
fear her aunt will think she neglects her if she stays any longer ... Mrs. Cadogan
is, I hope, enjoying country air; I know she does not love town.[2]

Ten days later, not having heard from her friend she wrote again: 'I was
fearfull you were unwell, it was such a time, as I thought it, before I heard
from you. I know you fret a great deal; do come into the country and lay
aside your cares a few weeks (they expect you at Brancaster) it will do you
good'. Tom showed equal solicitude, writing to Lady Hamilton from his
crammer's in Surrey:

I am now addressing myself to you on my birthday ... I hope by this time Mr.
Rose has settled everything you wish'd for, and that you will be able to go into
Norfolk with a mind free from troubles ... as I am sure you, who cannot bear
the least heat, must be running a great risk of your life by remaining in town
this time of the year.[3]

Richmond had already by then been settled on as her next place of
residence. She expected to go there in the autumn. The sale of Merton,
and Mr. Rose's success with his latest application on her behalf (to Lord

Abercorn), were reckoned by the family to be sufficient for her needs; they knew little of the true position and of her danger of arrest. On 9 April Mr. Rose laid before Lord Abercorn the whole history of her claim to a government pension, relating in detail his last conversation with Nelson on board the *Victory*, how with each fresh administration, Mr. Rose had repeated his application on her behalf; how the matter had been left with Mr. Canning then Foreign Secretary, who was still considering the question of appropriating £6,000 to £7,000 of Secret Service money to compensate Lady Hamilton for her services abroad; and how Rose had urged a moderate pension 'to be procured for the child who lives with her, and who was recommended also by Lord Nelson in his last moments'.[1] Despite the successive rebuffs Mr. Rose had received, he still closed his latest application to Lord Abercorn with the words: 'My anxiety to contribute to fulfilling the dying wish of Lord Nelson is unabated.' Mr. Canning's eventual finding on the subject supplied, incidentally, the answer to Lady Hamilton's accusations against Earl Nelson, for in Canning's view, Nelson's Codicil had been all-too-much publicized for her to be able to benefit by Secret Service money. 'The Secret Service Fund', he wrote to Mr. Rose in July 1809, 'is for services that cannot be explained or avowed. Now *here* is a service published not only in Lady Hamilton's memorials, but printed in extracts of a will registered in Doctors' Commons and accessible to all mankind'.[2]

Not waiting for the result of Rose's application to Lord Abercorn, Lady Hamilton herself made a direct application to Lord St. Vincent, Nelson's former commander and friend, in July 1808.

You, my Lord, cannot be insensible of the value of my public services . . . As the widow of Sir William Hamilton, more than thirty years Ambassador at the Courts of Naples and Palermo, had I never seized the opportunity . . . to perform one act of public service, I might still have expected a reasonable pension would be granted, if duly applied for, by the benevolent Monarch whom my husband had so long, so ably and so faithfully served. Even the widow of Mr. Lock, only about two years Consul at Palermo, a man not remarkable either for great loyalty or the most correct attention to his official duties, had a pension assigned to her almost immediately on his death of £800 a year; while I, who have been seven years the widow of such a man as Sir William Hamilton . . . and have constantly done all in my power to benefit my country, continue to be totally neglected. The widow of Mr. Fox, whose *services* to his country are at best very *problematical*, had instantly a grant of £1200 per annum; and even his natural daughter Miss Willoughby, obtained a pension of £300 a year. Yet this *man of the people* did not shed his blood for his King and country; and neither

[1] Rose's *Diaries*, i, 264–5.   [2] Ibid.

asked, nor could have expected from them, when dying, like the noble and confiding Nelson, any such posthumous national support, as has humanely been
extended to those who had thus lost their only protector. Surely the daughter of
Lord Nelson, now Miss Nelson, is not less an object worthy the attention of her
King and country, than Miss Willoughby, the daughter of Mr. Fox . . . I shall
in a few days transmit you a printed copy of Lord Nelson's dying request, pre-
faced by his admirable prayer for his King and country, and accompanied by
the Rev. Dr. Scott's attestation, as registered with this remarkable codicil, in
Doctors' Commons; and relying, with the most unbounded confidence, on your
Lordship's judgement, as to what measures may be most advisable to be pursued,
for the attainment of the objects so important to Miss Nelson, as well as to myself, and so dear to the heart of Britain's greatest naval hero.[1]

The memorial addressed to Lord St. Vincent explained, indeed, Mr.
Canning's reference to the 'printed extracts of a will registered in
Doctors' Commons and accessible to all mankind'. Belittling Miss
Willoughby's claims to a government pension did not, as might be
expected, advance Miss Nelson's prospects of obtaining one.

Miss Nelson's prospects as 1808 advanced were altogether less pleasant
than in the immediate preceding years. The delightful visits to her
aunts, though repeated once again, were for shorter periods, and there
were no seaside holidays. The Matcham's move to Ashfold allowed Mrs.
Bolton and her sister to meet more frequently than before, and in March
and April Mrs. Bolton with Eliza stayed some weeks in Sussex, during
part of which time Lady Hamilton and Horatia stayed with them. After
they had gone Mrs. Bolton wrote to Lady Hamilton:

We were very dull and stupid after you left us, and such miserable weather, not
seen the sight of the sun till this day . . . We read and work and talk in the day, in
the evening a party of cards, but not me, I read, I never play cards, that is Whist,
but with you. Tell Horatia she has left many lovers behind her, her cousins all
love her, but none more than her aunt . . . The man is waiting for my letter to
set forth for Horsham. The best love of this party attend you.[2]

Merton was still as yet Horatia's home, with Mrs. Cadogan, Cecilia
Connor, and frequently Anne Bolton for companions. An attempt to
auction the house was made in June. George Matcham, passing through
London on his way from Cambridge (he had gone to St. John's in March),
heard of the ill-success of this attempt from Lady Hamilton herself:
recording his journey home he wrote: 'Saturday went of in ye landau &
four; going over Westminster Bridge I met Lady Hamilton who was low
on account of ye house at Merton not being sold when put up to auction
the day before.'[3]

[1] P. ii, 628-9.   [2] NMM/NWD/9594/7/A (M.939).   [3] Eyre-Matcham, 266.

MINIATURE OF MRS. CADOGAN, mother of Lady Hamilton

The visit to Cranwich took place at last in August. Mrs. Bolton papered and whitewashed the house for her guests' reception, telling her daughter Anne who was expected with Lady Hamilton and Horatia:

I hope my Lady will come as early in August as she can. To say the truth I am rather glad she does not come before, as I shall now have a clean room for her . . . We have now got painters, white-washers, etc, full of stinks & cleanliness. You will likewise like it better, as your sisters & your niece [little Emma] will all be at home.[1]

The visit was neither so long nor so gay as those of the preceding summers; there were no rounds of visits to the Brancaster relations, nor to Swaffham for the gaieties it could offer. In September, after their departure, Anne wrote Lady Hamilton:

All the people at Swaffham were very much disappointed at not seeing you particularly Miss Langford . . . We went to the play on Thursday . . . We were very much entertained . . . The delicate Mrs. Edwards and all her family were there; all the soldgers were there. God save the King was sung, and after it the men got up and gave three cheers—quite grand for a Barn. I can assure you I think poor Horatia would have been very much delighted pray give my love and tell her not to forget her cousin Anne. Tom would not go to the play with *us* the reason I can't tell perhaps *she* may.[2]

Though Merton was still unsold, Lady Hamilton and Horatia went straight to Richmond on their return from Norfolk. At first they were in furnished rooms in Bridge Street, where both the Boltons and Matchams wrote anxiously to inquire how Lady Hamilton 'liked her residence' and what benefit 'she felt from the good air'. Her resolve was to live in retirement 'on what I have', with two maids and a foot-boy for all her household. But within a few weeks she had launched out again, 'Old Q' having rented her Heron Court, a splendid mansion he owned just below Richmond bridge, where she resumed her habitual mode of living. When young George Matcham called on her in October on his way to Cambridge, he found her surrounded as before by a circle of sycophants prepared to help her to empty her wine-cellars.

There were some citizens at dinner, but alas! how different was that table now to what I had before been accustomed; where formerly elegance presided, vulgarity and grossièreté was now introduced. I could have almost wept at the change. A plan of economy has been most laudably laid down by her Ladyship, but I could have wished that the crowd of obsequious attendance had been entirely dismissed, instead of being partially diminished.[3]

[1] NMM/NWD/9594/7/A.   [2] M.952.   [3] Eyre-Matcham, 266.

Heron Court lay in a cul-de-sac backing onto the river, just below the site of the ferry which, in 1774, was replaced by the beautiful stone bridge, and had been rendered vacant in 1808 by the death of its only other tenant, Sir John Day, Judge Advocate for Bengal. 'Old Q' himself appears to have used it as an agreeable summer retreat. It was, however, at Heron Court that Lady Hamilton had first met him when, just before her marriage to Sir William in the summer of 1791, they were invited to a reception there at which the 'celebrated Miss Harte' performed her 'attitudes'. The impression she then made on her host had endured, and she seldom hesitated to put his admiration to the test. She was hardly settled at Richmond when she wrote to implore him to buy Merton. Her sanguine anticipations of what he was prepared to do for her, regularly transmitted to Mrs. Bolton, were high and ill-judged. 'Old Q' may have had a vast fortune and been a noted 'Rip', but he had no intention of being taken for granted, and cynic that he was, cynical reasoning would never keep pace with his reckoning. Lady Hamilton appealed to him in vain. Her letter reads:

My dear Lord & Friend, may I hope that you will read this, for you are the only hope I have in this world, to assist and protect me, in this moment of unhappiness and distress. To you, therefore, I appeal. I do not wish to have more than what I have. I can live on that at Richmond, only that I may live free from fear—that every debt may be paid. I think, and hope, £15,000 will do for everything. For my sake, for Nelson's sake, for the good I have done my country, purchase it [Merton]; take it, only giving me the portraits of Sir William Nelson and the Queen. All the rest shall go. I shall be free and at liberty. I can live at Richmond on what I have; you will be doing a deed that will make me happy, for lawyers will only involve me every day more and more—debts will increase new debts. You will save me by this act of kindness. The title deeds are all good and ready to deliver up, and I wish not for more than what will pay my debts. I beseech you, my dear Duke, to imagine that I only wish for you to do this, not to lose by it; but I see that I am lost, and most miserable, if *you* do not help me. My mind is made up to live on what I have. If I could but be free from Merton—all paid, and only one hundred pounds in my pocket, you will live to see me blessing you, my mother blessing you, Horatia blessing you. If you would not wish to keep Merton, perhaps it will sell in the spring better—only let me pass my winter without the idea of a prison. 'Tis true my imprudence has brought it on me, and villany and ingratitude has helped to involve me, but the sin be on them. Do not let my enemies trample on me; for God's sake then, dear Duke, good friend, think 'tis Nelson who asks you to befriend, etc, etc.[1]

[1] M.951.

It would look as though the move to Richmond had given the alarm to her creditors and that they threatened immediate action; her only asset was Merton, and to sell it—as she must now sell it without profit—(with just a hundred pounds in her pocket as she told the Duke) was her last chance to escape arrest. From her creditors' point of view also it was their only hope of seeing their money back. To this consideration no doubt was due her continued immunity that autumn, while the prospective sale hung in the balance.

An extant letter to her surgeon, Mr. Heaviside, dated 3 June of that year written in very dejected spirits, shows that her physical resistance was lowered by her growing financial fears and the unslackened tempo of her life; at all times a gross feeder she suffered from a chronic liver complaint and its attendant rash; her increasing recourse to drink may already by then have aggravated her condition; she was obviously frightened about her health and though telling her surgeon that her life was no longer happy, was anxious to 'make the old-age of my good mother comfortable, and educate Horatia as the great and glorious Nelson . . . begg'd me to do'.[1] These concerns prompted her to make a further Will, which she drew up on 16 October of that year. Whereas Merton was left in the preceding Will (7 October 1806) to Horatia, by the terms of the present Will Merton was 'to be sold and all debts paid' and 'whatever money shall be left after all debts are paid, I give to my dear mother, and after her death, to my dear Horatia Nelson'. She now empowered Mr. Rose, and not her mother, to be executor of her Will, and left Horatia no longer in the care of Mr. Matcham and his wife, but to a mixed assortment of guardians ranging from the Prince of Wales and the Duke of Queensberry to Mr. Rose's son. The wording of this part of the Will regarding Horatia left no doubt of her being Nelson's daughter.

I beg His Royal Highness the Prince of Wales as he dearly loved Nelson, that his Royal Highness will protect his child, and be kind to her, for this I beg of him, for there is no one that I so highly regard as His Royal Highness. Also my good friend the Duke of Queensbury, I beg of him, as Nelson beseeched him to be kind to me, so I recommend my dear mother and Horatia to his kind heart. I have done my King and Country some service, but, as they were ungrateful enough to neglect the request of the virtuous Nelson in providing for me, I do not expect they will do anything for his child; but if there should be any Administration in at my death who have hearts and feelings, I beg they will provide for Horatia Nelson, the child who would have had a father if he had not gone forth to fight his Country's Battles; therefore she has a claim on them.[2]

[1] Sichel, 510.   [2] M.959.

Her appeal to the Duke to buy Merton having failed, she had to take other and prompt action to avoid 'Destruction' as she termed it when reporting on her state of affairs that November to Greville. She had still some solid friends among those faithful to Nelson's memory, Mr. Rose and Alexander Davison, and her Merton neighbour Mr. Goldsmid in particular, and on their advice a concerted joint action to put her affairs in order was decided upon. Through Mr. Rose, the solicitor Mr. Dawson was engaged to act on her behalf in calling in the list of her creditors, and in laying their claims before a group of bankers and businessmen brought together with a view to constituting a trust to administer her affairs. The formation of this trust was a boon beyond her wildest hopes, relieving her as it did of the immediate danger of arrest.

The gentlemen concerned each advanced a sum, on the eventual sale of Merton, with which to pay her debts and ensure her the use of her income, and also undertook to press her claims with government for a pension.

After the meeting of her self-constituted trustees, held under the chairmanship and at the house of Alderman Sir John Perring, on 25 November 1808, the following statement was issued:

At a meeting of the friends of Lady Hamilton, held at the house of Sir John Perring, Bart, the 25th Novr 1808. Present Sir John Perring/Mr Davison/Mr. Moore/Mr. Gooch/Mr. McClure/Mr. Goldsmid/Sir Robert Barclay/Mr Nichol/Mr. Wilson/Mr. Lavie. Mr Dawson attending as Sol^r to Lady Hamilton

Read. A letter from Lady Hamilton addressed to the gentlemen attending the Meeting.

Read. A list of debts delivered in by Mr. Dawson as obtained by advertisement, also a list of additional debts delivered in by Lady Hamilton herself, the whole debt estimated at 8000 l. exclusive of 10,000 l. required to pay off annuities.

Upon consideration of the property possessed by Lady Hamilton the same was ascertained as follows:

Books	£1,500
Wine	2,000
Statues, Vases, China, Pictures etc	1,500
Furniture and Fixtures	1,500
House and 32 Acres	7,500
40 Acres	3,500
	£17,500

Taken at a low rate.

The above property being independent of her annuities under the wills of Sir William Hamilton and Lord Nelson, and her claim on Government.

Resolved. That an assignment of the whole of Lady Hamilton's property be taken, and that the same be made to:

Sir John Perring, Bart./Alexander Davison, Esq/Abraham Goldsmid Esq/ Richard Wilson, Esq/and Germain Lavie, Esq as Trustees for Sale etc.

That in order to afford an immediate relief the following sums be advanced by

Alexander Davison, Esq	One thousand pounds
Abm. Goldsmid	One thousand pounds
John Gooch	Five hundred pounds
Richd Wilson	Five hundred pounds
Sir Robert Barclay	Five hundred pounds
John Perring	Two hundred pounds

to be secured by the said Trust with interest.

That the money collected by the above advances be applied in payment of all incumbrances absolutely necessary to be immediately discharged.

That all the creditors be applied to to execute the Debt of Trust, and to agree to accept a payment out of the Trust Estate.

That pending the Trust Lady Hamilton be allowed to receive her annuities, but in case of deficiency the same shall be applied in liquidating the balance.

That the Trustees be a Committee to follow up the claim on Government, in which all the friends of Lady Hamilton be requested to co-operate.

That the Trustees do go to market in the most advantageous mode possible, so as not to injure the property by a premature sale. Etc, etc.[1]

Without doubt the chief agent in this timely intervention was Mr. Abraham Goldsmid, Nelson's wealthy neighbour at Morden Hall, where the Merton party had so often been lavishly entertained. Mr. Goldsmid was one of four brothers, sons of a Dutch banker, Aaron Goldsmid, who had settled in England in 1742. All of them had a singular genius for making money. They dealt in foreign exchanges and in the issue of loans; Pitt's administration was chiefly financed by them; their immense wealth and credit enabled him to float the 1795 War Loan. Nelson knew two of the brothers well; his immediate neighbour Abraham, and Benjamin (whose little boy Lionel had wanted to go to sea with Nelson) who was a bullion broker, and had built himself a mansion at Roehampton (a district in the making then, but shortly to be called by Thackeray 'a banking colony'), where he gave splendid fêtes that were reported in the social columns of the press. Benjamin was the more socially ambitious of the two, but the whole family were noted for their benevolence and gave large sums to charity.[2] Their patriotism, also, was ardent and before they ever knew Nelson Benjamin gave a fête after the victory of the Nile the equal of which,

---

[1] M.961.   [2] *Transactions of the Jewish Historical Society*, 225–45.

it was reported in the press, had never been seen in England. To help Lady Hamilton was both a matter of sentiment and of patriotism in their eyes, and the £18,000 needed to extricate her from the threat of arrest was no great matter to them. Abraham Goldsmid had already shown himself extremely obliging in raising and investing for the Boltons and Matchams the sums voted them by government; and it was undoubtedly his credit and introductions in the city that gave Lady Hamilton now the backing that established the trust in her favour. Together with Alexander Davison he gave the largest sum (£1,000) towards the setting up of the trust. Lady Hamilton was profuse in her acknowledgements: 'Goldsmid has been and is an angel to me and his bounty shall never be abused',[1] she declared to Greville that November.

The Goldsmid family was in other respects ill-fated however. In April 1808 Benjamin committed suicide, hanging himself from a tester of his bed. Both Benjamin and Abraham were subject to fits of melancholia, and Abraham took his own life in September 1810. In the event it was their elder brother, Ascher, who bought Merton in April 1809, when as Lady Hamilton put it 'he behaved like an angel about it'. To Mrs. Bolton, who needed to be consoled for the loss of Merton, the fact that the purchaser was a Goldsmid brought some alleviation: she wrote Lady Hamilton on 23 April 1809: 'I am glad to hear a *Goldsmid* has purchased Merton rather than any stranger. You, I hope, will feel easier now it is gone. Perhaps you and I may one day have *a melancholy pleasure* in tracing former times in those walks.' [2] Neither Mrs. Bolton nor Lady Hamilton lived to enjoy that pleasure. Merton did not remain long in the hands of Ascher Goldsmid; he put it on the market again in March 1815, so that the probabilities are that Horatia never saw it again. No attempt was made to acquire Merton for the nation; the house was pulled down in 1846, and not even the garden Nelson so much loved, with its miniature 'Nile' and duckpond, was preserved by the town planners who carved it up for the construction of small factories and rows of habitations for their employees. The course of the Wandle that had flowed through the grounds was bricked over, the tunnel connecting the two separate sections of the property (divided by the main road) was filled in. Not a tree, shrub, pool or grass-plot remains to mark the place of Nelson's home; in their work of obliteration the authorities have succeeded in erecting a stony mausoleum over what was once springing turf and moving water, and so in their own peculiar way, have devised a monument, the least fitting that could be, to Nelson's only home.

[1] Sichel, 511.   [2] NMM/NWD/9594/7/A.

CHAPTER XII

'THE PATHS OF VIRTUE'[1]

WHEN Nelson entrusted the upbringing of his daughter to Lady Hamilton he could not do so frankly and naturally, and say that obviously the child would be better with its mother: he had to find other arguments for doing so, explaining his choice by the brilliance of her gifts, and the virtue of her way of life. The sequel was hardly what he had envisaged: Horatia's growing years, as she passed from childhood to adolescence, were marked by nothing but deprivation and bitter experiences, as Lady Hamilton's fortunes foundered.

The space and beauty of her country home, the settled peace of the long periods she passed there with only her grandmother and governess in charge, with her pets for playthings, and the big garden for playroom, were gone for ever. The loss of Merton put an end moreover to Lady Hamilton's hospitality to Nelson's family, and deprived Horatia of the frequent companionship of her cousins, and the annual visits of her aunts. Contact with her aunts, indeed, was first reduced, and then ceased altogether. For the next few years she lived without the family ambiance which Nelson had intended to be hers.

In exchange were the excitements and upheavals, the restrictions and agitations connected with the succession of her mother's furnished homes which now constituted the background to her growing years. The financial pinch was felt physically as well as morally; there was not room in Lady Hamilton's lodging houses for more than the two women-servants (Dame Frances and Nan) and the foot-boy reported by George Matcham. Sarah and Cecilia Connor, however, became regular members of the household (Sarah had previously held several posts as governess in other houses) and were now required to make themselves useful in return for the benefits they had received. Worst of all, however, was the company Lady Hamilton kept—the hangers-on, blackmailers even, to whom Horatia now became accustomed. She later vividly remembered the freedom with which Harrison had access to the Richmond house, and his removal of Lord Nelson's letters with Lady Hamilton's apparent

[1] Nelson's letter of 8 Sept. 1803: P. ii, 341.

concurrence, an incident that could have meant little to her at the time.

The loan of Heron Court, which followed the Duke of Queensberry's refusal to buy Merton, laid the diminished household deeply under the Duke's obligation; he acknowledged this in the end by his legacies, not only to Emma, but to Sarah Connor as well. His influence extended to Horatia's education, on which he was ready to advise, and a French governess of his recommendation was appointed in place of Cecilia Connor, who had fallen out of favour with her employer. Emma made much play of Horatia's wonderful progress in French under the tuition of Mlle Roulanch (probably Roolants) and, indeed, boasted of her accomplishments at every opportunity, without considering what losses she increasingly sustained by the kind of influence to which she was now exposed.

Towards the end of October 1808, Lady Hamilton and Horatia stayed with Sir John and Lady Perring in the city, as a measure of protection perhaps from her creditors, until their demands were met. She wrote from there on 7 November to the Countess Nelson making as usual great play of her connections, though naturally omitting to mention such details as the fact that it was Sir John who headed the committee to deal with her creditors. To Countess Nelson she wrote: [1]

Horatia improves in Beauty talents and virtue every day She is a Glorious Child cou'd He have lived to see her alas that would have been too much happiness. Ann (sic) Bolton is at Cranwich she is not well at all but I hope country air will do her good. Lady Bolton is at Brancaster the Matchams are all well I heard from them Friday. I have been living in the Citty with Alderman and Lady Perring last week Horatia had a great dinner given to Her on Her birthday the Lord Mayor drank her health and She was put on the Table after dinner and she made a Speech which made them all cry their is more Hospitality in the Citty than any were tell my Lord his Vase is magnificent I was at Bushy a Day or Two before the Duke of Clarence went to Portsmouth and he asked after you all He has Built a Temple which is beautiful with our angel's Bust My love to my Lord and Lady Charlotte my mother's and Horatia's to you all ever believe me dear Lady Nelson your affectionate

Emma Hamilton

P.S. Tell Lady Charlotte to write me a long letter.

Whether the vision of Nelson's daughter trained to bring tears to the eyes of her mother's 'citty' benefactors favourably impressed Earl Nelson and his wife is open to doubt; they might excusably infer that whatever Lady Hamilton's complaints over the Codicil, she derived some very substantial benefits from the mere existence of Horatia.

[1] NMM/BRP/4.

It was at this time that Lady Hamilton evolved the most sensational of all her stories about Horatia's birth, the one which, because of its very daring, produced the most lasting effect, and which even half a century later needed the good sense of Horatia herself to refute for good. Lady Hamilton's tale, instigated no doubt by Nelson's foolish invention that Horatia was born abroad and confided to his care, was nothing less than that the Queen of Naples was her mother. Forgetting the many written statements to Mrs. Gibson that the mother was ill and out of London, and finally that she was dead, she traded on the known confidential relationship existing between herself, Nelson, and the Queen, to give credence to their role as intermediaries in disposing of the Queen's illegitimate child.

Her statement, cunningly bruited about, has been preserved in two particular documents, one of which was widely circulated at the time: this was written to Mr. Salter, Nelson's sword-cutler and jeweller, to whom Emma sold Horatia's silver-gilt cup at this time; and the other, thinly disguised, occurs in a letter to Greville, written in November 1808.

The statement to Mr. Salter (attached to the cup) read:

The Victor of Aboukir, the great, and good Nelson, bought this for his daughter Horatia Nelson, August 30th 1805. She used it till I thought it proper for her to lay it by as a sacred relic—Emma Hamilton.

She is the daughter, the true and beloved daughter of Viscount Nelson, and if he had lived, she would have been all that his love and fortune could have made her; for nature has made her perfect, beautiful, good, and amiable. HER MOTHER WAS TOO GREAT to be mentioned, but her father, mother, and Horatia had a true and virtuous friend in Emma Hamilton.[1]

To Greville she made a further mystifying allusion to the Queen of Naples and the 'charge she had laid on her'; mentioning a letter which she had just sent by hand by Madame Graeffer (the Bronté agent) Emma made the following statement:

I have begged Her Majesty by the love she bears or *once* bore to Emma, by the sacred memory of Nelson, by the *charge she has placed in me* . . . to be good to Mrs. Graeffer . . . I have given her an account of the Cruel neglect of the present possessor of dear Lord Nelson's honored Titles, Estates and Honours, neglect to me who was the maker of His family and neglect to Mrs. Graeffer. But why speak of such people.[2]

[1] Nicolas vii, 388.
[2] See above, letter to Greville: Sichel, 511. Horatia's comment on this story, made in 1874 to Mr. Paget (see below) was: ". . . Poor Lady Hamilton was not a strict adherer to truth and her statement implying that the Queen of Naples was my mother, was most incredible—had it been so, of course I should have passed as her husband's child . . .", NMM/NWD/9594/2.

The accusations against Earl Nelson even here in her correspondence with the Queen of Naples, not only indicates the degree of Emma's fixation, but may also explain her motive for inventing the story of Horatia's birth at this particular moment: was she not aiming it precisely at the Earl who was 'neglecting' her more and more, and trying to compensate by this tale of sorry grandeur for her own sinking fortunes?

In the Richmond home there was little domestic harmony; a strange document wrung out of her Connor relations at this time shows how Emma was turning on those around her. The document speaks for itself: (Elizabeth Harrison was the writer, Harrison's wife)

Mrs. Connor voluntarily acknowledges, that she and her children have been generously supported for many years by the bounty of Lady Hamilton, who has expended, on her account, as she believes, little less than Two Thousand Pounds, and still kindly protects them: and Mrs. Connor farther declares, that all the reports to Lady Hamilton of reflections on her Lady-ship, by Mrs. Connor; such as having sold the bed from under her, and the like scandalous aspersions; are totally false and unjustly intended to prejudice Lady Hamilton against her, to whom she the said Mrs. Connor now protests she can never be sufficiently grateful. To Mrs. Cadogan too, Mrs. Connor hereby acknowledges she is likewise indebted for the most kind and generous assistances.

Signed by Mrs. Connor, this
29th Decr 1808 in the presence of

Jane West   ⎫
Elizth Harrison ⎬ Sarah Connor[1]
              ⎭

As Horatia grew up, the subject of her birth became a cause not only of understandable concern, and of fertile inventions as has been seen, but also of friction in the home. Lady Hamilton and her mother very seldom quarrelled, as Horatia testified, but she remembered vividly into middle age a certain occasion when the two had a serious quarrel on the subject, during their residence at Richmond: Horatia had been punished for some childish misdemeanour and Mrs. Cadogan was pleading for her 'when Lady Hamilton became angry and said she alone had authority over me. Mrs. Cadogan, rather irritated, said: "Really, Emma, you make so much fuss about the child as if she were your own daughter"; when Lady Hamilton turned round much incensed, as I was present, and replied: "Perhaps she is." Mrs. Cadogan looked at her and replied: "Emma, that won't do with me—you know I know better".' [2] The presence of Horatia during this scene, as Mrs. Ward shrewdly noted later, caused both disputants to speak, and act, false roles.

[1] NMM/NWD/9594.
[2] NMM/NWD/9594/13–14. Mrs. Ward to Sir Harris Nicolas, 1846.

To Horatia's aunts and the outside circle of acquaintance, reports of Horatia's wonderful education were sent from Richmond. 'My dear Horatia!' wrote Mrs. Bolton on 23 April 1809, 'I am glad you have got such an accomplished governess for her. I am sure she will improve much under such instructors as she has.' Emma's constant complaints about the cost of Horatia's education made Mrs. Bolton add: 'but do not let your generous feelings for her induce you to do too much for her to your own injury, for remember your life is everything to *her*.'[1]

Mrs. Peirson had also received reports of Horatia's new governess, and wrote to Lady Hamilton on 25 May: 'I wish to hear something of Horatia; I suppose she is a compleat French woman by this time. Caroline sends her love to her'. Writing to induce Lady Hamilton to fix her expected visit to Ashfold that summer, Mrs. Matcham said:

We shall be happy to see Madom[lle] Roulanch and any part of your family; we beg Mrs. Cadogan will come with you. Be assur'd *we* shall be at all times delighted to *have you* here and accomodate you to the best in our power. The country is now delightful, and I trust we shall soon see you. Mr. M. and the girls beg to join me in every affectionate wish to you, etc ... P.S. Pray kiss Horatia for us; I hope she has not forgot her *aunt Matcham*.[2]

The extent to which Horatia's showy education was bruited abroad can be judged from a letter to Lady Hamilton from Lord Northwick—a governor of Harrow and former friend of Sir William Hamilton's—on the occasion of the school Speech Day to which her Ladyship was invited. This was an attention which must have been peculiarly gratifying to her at such a time of enforced 'retirement'. Lord Northwick wrote:

28th June, Harrow on the Hill.
I am delighted with your letter this momt recd, & look forward with impatience for the 6th July, when I shall have the pleasure of seeing you at Harrow. Your proposal of inviting Mrs. Bianchi is most excellent and you have indeed anticipated my wish tho' I should not have ventured to have proposed it as it might be construed into an intention of giving a Fete which I hope your Ladyship will have the goodness to explain to Mrs. Bianchi will not be the case—our little Party will be confined to a few of our Old Neapolitan Friends. The Duke of Sussex has very condescendly promised to join us, with, I hope, Lord Douglas; I told H.R.H. that I had written to you, which seemed to give him great pleasure.

Your amiable and most interesting Elève (if report says true) repays your care and solicitude by her improvements in every Grace—in every Charm—and could it be otherwise with such inimitable perfection before her? I am most anxious to see the progress she has made, and am much gratified by your Lady-

1 NMM/NWD/9594/7/A. 2 Ibid.

ship's acquiesceing in my wishes by allowing Horatia to accompany you. I hope it will not be too great an effort to be here by One O'clock in time for the Speeches, as I am sure your presence wd be the greatest possible incitement to our juvenile Orators—to use their utmost endeavours to be deserving of your commendation.[1]

Despite the reputed progress Horatia made in learning and accomplishments, it is noticeable that her relations who repeatedly asked to have letters from her were as repeatedly disappointed. How little there was to show for all the boasted accomplishments remains to be seen in the letters written in her late teens, when both spelling and composition were full of faults. Not only the awkwardness of an eight-year-old girl with her pen, but the unstable background of her home-life, made communication with her unsuspecting relatives difficult. Anne Bolton, for long Horatia's companion at Merton and separated from her as a result of the sale, wrote frequently from Cranwich to express her lasting affection and eagerness for news of her. 'I am now sitting in Tom's room opposite two of your pictures which he has nailed up in his room. I hear from him that Horatia is very much improved; pray, my dear lady, is it part of her education to forget me? I was in hopes she would have written to me; give my love and tell her so.'[2]

In the spring and summer of 1809 Horatia had an unspecified illness whose effects were lasting and unpleasantly recurring. The malady had probably a nervous origin. From both parents she inherited a highly nervous constitution. The ups and downs of her home life, the constant agitation of spirits to which Lady Hamilton was prone, the alternations between ostentation and secrecy, were not conducive to a regular, carefree childish life. Her mother's debts created a furtive atmosphere that placed a barrier between her and her friends. Repeatedly Mrs. Bolton sent pressing invitations for them to come to Norfolk; from May onwards she urged Lady Hamilton to name her date, a request repeated in every letter from Anne, but few and indecisive answers were received. For the first time in six years, Lady Hamilton paid no visit to Norfolk in 1809.

Anne, the closest to Lady Hamilton and Horatia, wrote on 26 July: 'My mother and myself have been anxiously expecting to hear from you this last month; fear you are not well, or have quite forgot your friends at Cranwich . . . as you well know, we have not much news here, mearly that the hen has sat, the cow calved, or that the crops are pretty good.'[3] 'I hope

---

[1] Ibid.
[2] Anne Bolton to Ly. H. 26 July 1809. NMM/NWD/9594/7/A.
[3] Ibid.

HORATIA DANCING WITH A TAMBOURINE, oil painting

you will allow that I am much better than you are in answering letters,'
she wrote again on 22 August:

I do not mean in the style but in the quickness . . . I was *extreemly* sorry to
hear poor Horatia has been so unwell. My mother sends her love and hopes that
you will come into Norfolk as you promised, as perhaps the change of air may be
good for Horatia, which I know will be a very great inducement to you . . . Hope
you will write quite soon and tell us Horatia is quite well, and what has been the
matter with her.[1]

Mrs. Bolton wrote:[2] 'How sorry I am for our dear Horatia. Give my kind
love to her, I shall be most happy to see her and you too before the summer
leaves.' By 29 September 'out doors it begins to look rather dreary', Mrs.
Bolton wrote as she urged Lady Hamilton to 'turn her thoughts towards
Cranwich, where you will be most cordially received. Tell Horatia we
shall be most happy to keep her birthday and Anne's together this year.
How long it is since we had the pleasure of hearing from you'.[3] A fortnight
later, having still had no reply to her invitation, Mrs. Bolton wrote again:
'What can be the reason my dear Lady, that we have not heard from you. I
was in hopes that you would have fixed your time for coming into Norfolk.
I long to see you; why not keep the birthdays together? I sent Mrs.
Cadogan a hare last week, and this day Tom sends you a brace of birds . . .
Do think seriously of coming.'[4] A last plea was sent by Anne on 26
November in which Horatia was urged to come on account of little Emma
Bolton who could now play half a tune on the piano 'and is so fond of it
she plays from morning till night . . . give her a little instruction'. Little
Emma, it appeared, often had Horatia's portrait 'down to kiss'.[5]

At the very end of the year Lady Hamilton left Richmond and took
furnished rooms again in town, in Albemarle Street. Young Lady Bolton,
going through town on her way to join her husband stationed at Cork, had
a disappointing experience trying to trace her whereabouts. She wrote from
Plymouth on 3 January 1810:

I cannot describe my disappointment at calling at No 36 Albemarle Street
and finding they did not know you. I then tried at No 44 the Hotel, but they
said they knew no such person. Poor Emma then began to look quite melancholy at the thought of not seeing cousin Horatia and her Godmama, and I
assure you, I looked quite as dismal—I was loth to leave the street without a
further attempt, and seeing a letter carrier we stopped him, feeling certain of

---

[1] Anne Bolton to Ly. H. 22 Aug. 1809. NMM/NWD/9594/7/A.
[2] NMM/NWD/9594/7/A.   [3] Ibid.
[4] Ibid.   [5] Ibid.

his knowing where you resided; but, unlucky as we were fated to be, he did not deliver the letters in that street . . . I feel so vexed with myself at having missed seeing you, when I was so near . . . Emma sends her best love to you, Horatia, and Mrs. Cadogan; when I told her just now how if we had gone two houses further we should have seen you, she looked very grave. At last she called out: 'Pray, mama, promise me to call as we go back to Cranwich' [1]

Emma's departure from Richmond appears to have been hastened by financial consideration, to judge from a letter from Sir Harry Featherstonehaugh:

Tho' I lament that there should be such a reason for quitting Richmond . . . because none such ought to exist had you common justice done you, yet your judgement is good in doing so, and at all events I shall stand a better chance of seeing more of you. I hope you received the first basket of game as well as the last. You shall certainly continue to have a supply from time to time. [2]

The very day Sir Harry was writing to Emma (14 January), the biggest disaster since the death of Nelson befell her; her mother suddenly died. Many references in the family correspondence of the last two years to Mrs. Cadogan's chronic ill-health, the recurrent attacks of bronchitis in winter and need of country air in summer, show that she had been failing; but for her death Emma had certainly not been prepared. The blow was a terrible one and she recovered from it far less easily than from the loss of Nelson. For her mother she had a disinterested love, dependent on no considerations of social success, pleasure, or glory, all of which had entered into her love of Nelson. While her mother had served her faithfully and in recent years had been her best and sanest critic and adviser, it was not for what her mother had done for her that she cherished her; they were two of a kind, indissolubly bound together, and between them there was no need for play-acting. Mrs. Cadogan was not a moral woman nor had she a high standard of conduct; but she had a great sense of loyalty and she understood her daughter's nature, and more than anyone brought out the best in it. Emma's loss was irreparable and she did not have to assume any attitude to express her grief; it was apparent enough. There need be little doubt that for Horatia also the loss was great. Mrs. Cadogan made herself beloved by all the young people in the family; the tributes to her kindness from Ann and Tom Bolton in particular sufficiently testify to her sympathetic as well as practical treatment of young people. Horatia's situation was much the poorer by her loss. Lady Hamilton was not a patient or consistently kind mother; she would soon be reproaching

[1] M.987.   [2] M.989.

Horatia for not being so good a daughter as she herself had been, but much as she revered her mother's memory she was unable to emulate her maternal gifts.

Mrs. Cadogan was buried in the church on Paddington Green[1] near Greville's former home where she and Emma had lived with him. Mrs. Bolton, learning of her death, wrote to Lady Hamilton on 27 January 1810:

I must write, tho' I have before written to Miss Connor, and hoped to have heard, but Cecilia said you were not only grieved, but very unwell. Do pray cause to be written only one line to say how your health is—miserable I know you must be. Dear Blessed Saint, was she not a mother to us all. How I wish I was near you, but that is impossible. I am afraid I shall never get so far from home again, but I know you have many kind friends around you. My dear Friend, endeavour to support yourself under this very severe trial, for the sake of dear Horatia. What can she do without you and many other friends amongst whom I rank myself. Do pray come to me as soon as the spring gets milder. Every one here will endeavour to soothe you.... Anne in particular, she is most grieved for her kind friend.[2]

Almost immediately after Mrs. Cadogan's death Emma moved lodgings again. From the letters of the period her address was over 'Bridgman's Confectioner', 76 Piccadilly, a choice again dictated by its proximity to the Duke's house at No. 138 (the Hyde Park end of Piccadilly). Emma's friends, Sir Harry Featherstonehaugh and Mrs. Bolton among them, were openly reckoning on her benefiting under the old man's Will. 'I am glad you are such friends with the duke', wrote Mrs. Bolton on 12 February. 'I hope you may continue so to his life's end, for, depend on it. Whoever is most in favor will then have the *Largest Legacy*.'[3]

In 1810 Lady Hamilton again failed to pay her customary visit to Norfolk. The scant news she sent her friends at Cranwich aroused their anxiety and prompted repeated invitations, but they were obviously unaware of her worsening financial position and of the true causes for her prolonged silences. Reading in the papers of the riots in Piccadilly following the arrest of Sir Francis Burdett in April 1810, Mrs. Bolton wrote, 'How are you in the midst of this uproar and Mob? Whenever we read or think of Burdett we speak of you . . . do leave it all and come to us we shall be so happy to see you and all your Party—it will be a change of scene for you at least . . . Give all our loves to Dear Horatia tell her all the Tea things are in order for her'.[4] On 19 May Mrs. Bolton wrote again: 'The

[1] Annual Register, 1810.   [2] M.991.
[3] NMM/NWD/9594/7/A.   [4] Ibid.

sun shines bright, and Anne is recovering after 3 months' confinement; [Anne had a chronic liver complaint] do come to us, who will be so happy to embrace you and dear Horatia bring as many of your family as is convenient. Do my dear friend, fix your time for coming.'[1]

In early September Lady Hamilton wrote to say she was going to Ashfold on a visit. Addressing her there on 9 September Mrs. Bolton wrote: 'Except coming to me I think you have done the wisest and best thing you could do: change of scene and the society of kind friends. I wish I could peep in upon you all.'[2] The promised visit was still eagerly expected by the Boltons until the end of year, but it never took place.

Of Lady Hamilton's reduced domestic circumstances, two letters from Sarah Connor written to her during her stay at Ashfold give evidence. Since Mrs. Cadogan's death Sarah had assumed the role of prudent housekeeper; while necessarily lacking Mrs. Cadogan's authority with Lady Hamilton, she would appear to have given good practical advice. Sarah's report on the crisis in Mr. Goldsmid's affairs was only too true; Abraham Goldsmid committed suicide on 28 September 1810, following a sudden fall in stocks which found him unable to meet a claim for £350,000 from the East India Company.[3]

On 10 September Sarah wrote:

Both of your's I got to-day, and will act according to your last, which I told Mrs. Domier. She seemed quite disappointed. For my own part, I cannot see why she should, except that I believe them to be very poor indeed. I am has much surprised has you to think that a hundred pounds should be owing in a few weeks. I am afraid that you have been paying rent for two good months before you took possession of your apartments. If so, I am sorry, for that is money all gone for nothing. No one will do it towards you—that is the way of this selfish world. The Duke sent to me to know by what coach I sent parcels to you which I sent to him, so I suppose he is going to send you something. Saturday I went to the play with Mrs. Billington, who, with Mrs. Bianchi, desires their love, and yesterday dined at Hammersmith [the Bianchis] and slept there; came to fetch the parrots, which went quite well and safe. You must excuse my freedom in the remark I am about to make, namely, in your being obliged to pay for the board when all will be away, except only servants, when I sett off. That has fretted me staying in town, as I thought it made you pay the same has when all was at home, but find that my absence nor yours makes no difference. This alters the plan of cheapness greatly in my opinion, for there never has been extravagant dinners but good plain joints for you. But you, dearest Lady Hamilton must be the best judge. If you think it right to consent to

---

[1] Ibid.   [2] Ibid.
[3] *Transactions of the Jewish Historical Society*, 225–45.

this arrangement, it must, I must candidly own, I do not nor whould not have this to vex you, it has me, but not knowing what Mrs. Domier and you agreed upon, in that case I am obliged to submit to you. I hope to join you soon. With love to all I remain, etc.[1]

On Monday, 17 September, she wrote again:

Your two last letters I got, and thank you for them, I found the codicils and took them to Lord Herdley [i.e. Eardley] but did not see him. It is now 3 o'clock and no Mr. Goldsmid is come, nor do I look for him now to-day, so when I shall get to you God knows. Their's one excuse for him—the clerk told me the other day that it was feared he should lose a large sum of money. It would not ruin him has he was so rich, but that the amount was so large. I hope it may turn out better than he expects. He is a good man; it's a pity he should suffer. The enclosed is, has you will find, from Mrs. Domier. She wants the weeks that we are all away to be paid the same, and that, she says, will make up for the pound-a-day not being enough when all is at home. What do you mean to do about coals? Has the weather is getting cold you will want fires when you come home. They are sixty pounds I shilling now, and will soon get to seventy.[2]

At last, on 23 December 1810, the Duke of Queensberry died, aged eighty-six. Lady Hamilton had declined invitations from Norfolk to spend Christmas at Cranwich so as to remain at hand, but in the event her expectations were only partially fulfilled by his legacy of £500 a year which, owing to a general contestation of his Will, she never enjoyed. Sarah Connor was another beneficiary, her devotion to her patroness being thus recognized. After his death Lady Hamilton moved house again, into lodgings at 16 Dover Street. Mrs. Matcham, hearing of the legacies, wrote to congratulate Lady Hamilton, and hoped that now 'with economy, it will enable you to live comfortably'. But that era was past for Lady Hamilton. The death of Greville the previous year had delayed the payments of her annuity pending the settlement of the Hamilton estate on the new heir, the Hon. Robert Fulke Greville brother of the deceased, and she had been borrowing on the anticipated quarters. Lord Mansfield, as a trustee of the Hamilton estate, wrote to warn her of the folly of such proceedings in January 1811:

Allow me to add that I hope you never anticipate the quarter *you expect to become due*, so as to occasion any pressing demand ... Excuse my saying thus much and adding a word of advice—that you should be *cautious* not to increase your expenditure till your affairs are settled, or your creditors will become very troublesome from the apprehension that you will spend the legacy bequeathed to you without their reaping the advantage they expect of being *first paid*.[3]

[1] NMM/NWD/9594/&/A (M.1001).   [2] Ibid. (M.1002).   [3] M. ii, 347.

13

By mid-April, despite the payment of her jointure, she applied to Mr. Matcham for the loan of £100; his belief in her ability to repay him sufficiently shows how uninformed the family remained of her true position. Mr. Matcham wrote from Ashfold

It is very fortunate that you applied to me at this instant; had you applied five days ago, I had not a hundred to lend, but having received seven hundred pounds three days since to be invested in the funds for Mrs. Matcham & the children, Mrs. M. has consented to withold one hundred pounds of that sum for you. I know you will repay it as soon as you can, but do not mention my having lent you any money. I wish not the trustees to be acquainted with it.[1]

Despite her legacy, Sarah Connor was shortly to leave Lady Hamilton's service for good. The break with Cecilia was already complete. The non-payment of her salary as Horatia's governess over many years was evidently not the only reason. In a final appeal written to Lady Hamilton on 26 July 1811 she made this plain:

Manly Place, Kensington Common, July 26th 1811.
I take the liberty once more to address your Ladyship concerning the sum of thirty guineas for teaching Miss Horatia Nelson, for which I had a voucher signed by your Ladyship. I merely mention this latter circumstance as a proof of your Ladyship's acknowledgements—by no means upon the ground of dispute, but as my qualification of appeal to your Ladyship in the present instance. My future Wellfare constrains me to renew the solicitations, having a situation of advantage submitted to me which I must be compelled, with grief, to resign unless your Ladyship supports my views by affording me, on account, the sum of ten pounds between this & next Monday—the time limited to consider the proposal.
This is the last resource I have. Being denied a character from your Ladyship, obliges me to give up the thought of applying any longer for a preparatory governess, which I had the honour of attending on dear Horatia. Excuse, dear Lady Hamilton, this familiar term, but it is what I most sincerely feel for you both. Could I forget for a moment the many obligations me and my family owe to your Ladyship, I hope God will forget me, and He is now the only friend I have.
Time will bring forth everything, & then I think your Ladyship will find you have been misinformed in many circumstances concerning me. Let me, dear Lady Hamilton, intreat a favourable answer, as it will release my mind greatly. Would it could relieve my heart from the sorrow that I feel at being deprived of a friend & guardian like you![2]

The eviction of the Miss Connors from the Hamilton circle was a loss to Horatia; they had been close to her since childhood, and from Cecilia at

[1] M. ii, 349.   [2] M.1024.

least she had received nothing but kindness. How complete was the severance can be judged from the wording of Lady Hamilton's new Will drawn up on 4 September 1811 which was necessitated by the deaths of Mrs. Cadogan and the Duke of Queensberry. Her final dispositions for Horatia were, happily, much improved. She left her to the guardianship of her uncle Matcham and of Mr. Rose, and begged that Horatia might be taken to live with the Matchams until she married—unexceptionable dispositions which, in the event, were all carried out. Less commendable was her plea to the Regent to provide for Horatia on the score of his great friendship for Nelson. The text of the Will is as follows:

I, Emma Hamilton of No 150 Bond Street London Widow of the Right Honourable Sir William Hamilton formerly Minister at the Court of Naples being in sound mind and body do give to my dearly beloved Horatia Nelson dau^r of the great and glorious Nelson all that I shall be possessed of at my death money jewells pictures wine furniture books wearing apparel silver gold-plated or silver-gilt utensils of every sort I may have in my house or houses or of any other persons' houses at my death any marbles bronzes busts plaster of Paris or in short every thing that belonged to me I give to my best beloved Horatia Nelson all my table linen laces ornaments in short everything that I have I give to her any money either in the house or at my bankers all debts that may be owing to me I beg that she may have I give to Horatia Nelson all silver with inscription with Viscount Nelson's name on or his arms I give to her wou'd to God it was more for her sake I do appoint George Matcham, Esq of Ashfold Lodge in the County of Sussex and the Right Honourable George Rose of Old Palace Yard Westminster my Ex^{ors} and I leave them Guardians to my dear Horatia Nelson and I do most earnestly entreat of them to be the Protectors and Guardians and be Fathers to the Dau^r of the great and glorious Nelson and it is my wish that H.R. Highness the Prince Regent or if before my death he shall become King, that he will provide for the said Horatia in such a manner that she may live as becomes the dau^r of such a man as her victorious Father was and as His Royal Highness often promised me that he wou'd have me remuner-ated when he had it in his power for the services that I have rendered to my King and Country and as I have never been remunerated nor ever received one sixpence from Government let me on my knees beg of His Royal Highness to provide for the said Horatia Nelson the only child of the Great and Glorious Nelson and I beg after my death that a copy of this my last will and testament may be sent to His Royal Highness the Prince Regent or if he is King it may be sent to His Majesty for his high worth honour and probity and the friend-ship which he had for Nelson will induce him to protect his child for me H.R.H. always shewed me the greatest kindness and for the sake of Sir William Hamilton whom His R. Highness so highly honoured that he will provide for the orphan Horatia when my head is laid low she will want protection therefore to God

Almighty to His R. Highness and to my Ex^ors do I most earnestly recommend her on my knees blessing her and praying for her that she may be happy virtuous good and amiable and that she may remember all the kind instructions and good advice I have given her and may she be what her great and immortal Father wished her to be brought up with virtue honor religion and rectitude Amen Amen Amen I do hereby annul all wills made by me formerly and I beg that this may be considered as my last will and testament written with my own hand this September the fourth 1811, Emma Hamilton—If I shall have any money in the Funds or landed property at my death I give to the said Horatia Nelson all and everything belonging to me and if she shall dye before she shall be able to make her will I give all that I have bequeathed to her to the dau^rs of Mr. John and Amy Moore my late Aunt and Uncle and now living in Moore Strt Liverpool and I pray to God to bless them but I hope my dear Horatia will live to be happy and marry well and I hope that she will make her will as soon as I am dead for I do absolutely give her all I have I still hope Mr. Matcham and Mr. Rose will see to the educating of Horatia and that she may live with Mrs. Matcham's family till she is disposed to some worthy man in marriage I forgot to mention that I also give Horatia all my china glass crockery ware of every sort that I have—

Emm Hamilton

Signed sealed published and declared by Emma Hamilton as her last will and testament in the presence of Thomas Coxe A.M.—William Haslewood of FitzRoy Square, Middlesex.[1]

The exclusion of the Miss Connors from this Will is the more cutting because the residue of Emma's property was left, in the case of Horatia's death, to other members of her family—the daughters of her uncle and aunt Moore—who had hitherto remained outside her immediate circle. No records remain of what became of Sarah and Cecilia later on.

In the July of 1811 Lady Hamilton paid what proved to be her last visit to Cranwich, and at Christmas that year took a leading part in a Nelson family celebration for the last time, when she was chief witness at the wedding of Eliza Bolton to her cousin Henry Girdlestone. Henry's courtship had not been smooth. On obtaining his degree at Cambridge he had taken Orders, and while waiting for a living had 'domesticated' with his uncle's family at Cranwich, assisting the Vicar, the ailing Mr. Partridge throughout 1810. So at home did he feel with the Boltons that he was not long in wishing to become a permanent member of the family and by the autumn proposed to his cousin Anne. She refused him, largely it would seem on the grounds that they had nothing to live on, 'to make the pot boil' as Mrs. Bolton put it, but even when Henry at last got the promise

<hr />

[1] Jeaffreson, ii. 305.

of a living at Litcham, only seven miles away, she did not change her mind. The speed with which Henry became engaged to Eliza, however, after Anne broke with him, would suggest that Eliza's love for her cousin was no sudden flowering. Anne's frequent illnesses had thrown Eliza and Henry much together, and by the autumn their engagement was announced. It gave great joy in the family circle and the marriage was planned to take place immediately after another major event in the Bolton family; their removal from Cranwich in November 1811. It had for years been what Mrs. Bolton most wanted, but no suitable place had been found. In 1811 the lease of Cranwich came to an end and it became a matter of urgency.

They were fortunate to find at last Bradenham Hall,[1] a house built in 1772 seven miles east of Swaffham, and two and a half miles from Shipdham. The property, though in a neglected condition when they moved in, was a far more considerable one than Cranwich, the choice of it being influenced apparently by the consideration that Tom, the prospective heir to the Nelson titles, must be furnished with a suitable residence: in due course he assumed the title of 'Nelson of Bradenham'.

Mrs. Bolton hoped that everything would be ready by Christmas and that she would then be in a position to receive Lady Hamilton. For the cousins, Anne, Eliza, little Emma Bolton and Caroline Peirson, the prospect of a visit from Horatia after a lapse of two years was still a special treat. 'I had, the other day, a few lines from Emma [Bolton],' Anne told Lady Hamilton: 'she writes very well when you come to consider she has only begun this last two months... How pleased she will be to see Horatia; she used often to talk to me about her, and tell me what fun they used to have in bed of a morning.'[2] After the move to Bradenham and in expectation of his cousin's arrival for Christmas, Tom wrote to Lady Hamilton: 'Emma is every day wishing for her cousin Horatia's arrival, sends her love, and wishes the day was arrived.'[3] 'My dear Cousin Horatia,' Anne wrote on 24 November: 'I flatter myself she will be as happy to see us as we shall her. Emma is often talking about her and wishing for her.'[4]

No news of the changed circumstances of Horatia's life had penetrated to Norfolk. The Bolton girls urged the inclusion of the Connors in the wedding invitations, and hoped Lady Hamilton would make room for Sarah in her 'coach', as Sarah had not the money, they regretted to learn,

---

[1] Bradenham Hall was later the home of the Haggard family, where Rider Haggard was born in 1856.
[2] NMM/NWD/9594/13-14.   [3] Ibid.   [4] Ibid.

to pay her fare. Of the change in Lady Hamilton herself the impression of an unprejudiced eye-witness has been preserved; it bears little resemblance to her public image of earlier years. On her birthday, 26 April 1811, she was seen walking through Greenwich Park with Horatia, one of the Connor girls, and 'some half-dozen children' by Major Pryse Lockhart Gordon who had known her at Palermo. She was taking them to the Ship Inn for a birthday celebration, but her slovenly appearance, with only a shawl thrown over her head, made her hardly recognizable to the Major and he hesitated to accost her.[1] There seems little doubt that she was already drinking heavily then, as her frequent 'bilious' illnesses, which she increasingly made an excuse for declining social engagements, betray.

Her last appearance on the Norfolk scene—at the house-warming party at Bradenham Hall and the marriage of Eliza—had of course to be in a major role: she was the guest of honour, and chief witness of the marriage, where her signature can still be seen in the registers of St. Andrew's Church.

The wedding took place on 27 December 1811 at West Bradenham in the church which lay only half a mile from the hall in the midst of fields, where Mr. Bolton's cattle were at graze. The marriage was solemnized by the Revd. William Bolton, uncle to both the bridegroom and the bride; the registry entry reads:

Henry Girdlestone of the Parish of Litcham in the County of Norfolk, and Elizabeth Ann Bolton of this Parish, both single persons, were married in this Church by Licence this 27th day of December in the year 1811, by me *William Bolton*, Ror, of Brancaster.
Witnesses: Emma Hamilton
          Thos. Bolton
          Ricd Watson (Parish Clerk)

Thus the year ended with two of Mrs. Bolton's fondest hopes fulfilled: the family had found a home worthy of her ambitions for Tom, and she had married another of her beloved daughters. Eliza, twenty-two at the time, had a long and happy life. After the miscarriage of her first child in 1813, she reared twelve more in the years to come. During the festivities that marked Christmas day and the marriage, there can have been few of the large party gathered at Bradenham who foresaw the disasters awaiting some of them in the immediate future. Not only did Lady Hamilton never return to Norfolk, but she never saw Mrs. Bolton again. For Horatia it marked the end of childhood. With 1812 she entered on the darkest period of her youth.

[1] Pryse Lockhart Gordon, *Personal Memoirs*, ii, 388–90

CHAPTER XIII

'WITHIN THE RULES—'

EVIDENCE about Lady Hamilton's activities becomes sparse in 1812. Few letters have been preserved, because few reached her in the many hiding-places she sought, and she herself avoided putting pen to paper for fear of betraying her whereabouts. (Her new companion, Miss Wheatley, undertook much of the correspondence with the family.) Her public appearances almost ceased, and acquaintances who called at her house at 150 New Bond Street found her 'from home'. How little the Boltons and Matchams even then realized her situation is shown by their repeated complaints at her silence, by their surprise at her many unannounced absences from home, and by their repeated invitations to her and Horatia to 'change air' and join them in the country. They still supposed her in the thick of 'the gaieties of London', as Anne Bolton spoke of them, and looked for her name in the social columns of the press. An incident that occurred in February 1812 showed how ignorant they were of her declined social standing.

Parliament was debating subsidies for the erection of breakwaters at Plymouth (an innovation at the time) and Rennie had been engaged to carry out the project. As it happened, the idea originated with George Matcham at Ashfold; he had experienced their use in India and advocated their construction on the English coast. In fairness to Mr. Matcham, his close friend Dr. Lawrence was determined to make his part known to government; not 'with a view to remuneration', as George Matcham wrote, 'but from honest pride of having it known I was the projector of a plan that has been so generally approved of'.[1] Dr. Lawrence urged that Mr. Rose should be approached, and proposed that Lady Hamilton should give him the necessary introduction. George Matcham wrote on 23 February: 'I have this moment received a letter from Dr. Lawrence urging me to lose no time in desiring you to speak to Mr. Rose. Dr. Lawrence lives at No. 5 Junction Place, Harrow Road. Pray write a line to him to see him as soon as you can . . . On referring to the Dr's letter, I find he says he will call on you on Tuesday at 2 o'clock.'[2] The Doctor's own

[1] Eyre-Matcham, 274.   [2] Ibid.

evidence of the interview that took place two days later reads: 'Lady H's ideas flow altogether in another channel . . . if I took a just estimate of her the five minutes I was at her house, she is one of those characters that promise everything and do nothing, nevertheless she is possessed of great good nature and has great abilities with much benevolence.'[1] It was a fair summing up of Lady Hamilton's character. She promised of course to approach Mr. Rose, but did not do so.

Partially enlightened of her circumstances by the Doctor, Mr. Matcham wrote again on 5 March:

I fear I have requested of you what might not be altogether pleasant. Do pray let me know if you think I should better apply to some gentleman who may be acquainted with Mr. Rose. I really should be very sorry to put you to the least inconvenience . . . I know the kindness of your heart, and I shall certainly be sorry if there is the least impropriety in what I have requested; but do not, my dear lady, omit writing me *one line by return of post*, as the delay would be bad.[2]

All through the spring and summer of 1812 the Matchams wrote urging her to fix her time for a visit. 'We are looking forward with great pleasure to our annual meeting at Ashfold,' Kitty Matcham wrote on 6 August, 'and hope the time is now drawing very near when we shall talk over the occurrences of the year . . . I hope, my dear Lady, to have some lessons in singing from you, and if you have any new songs or pretty EASY tunes for the harp ask Horatia to make a collection for me, as I have not had any this year waiting for you'.[3] There were further letters and on 8 September Kitty Matcham wrote: 'We have been anxiously expecting to have a line from you every day, & began to be fearful it is indisposition which prevents your writing. We were in hopes you would have been at Ashfold by this time . . . I am desired to request *one line*, letting us know how you are & when we may expect to have the pleasure of seeing yourself and Horatia here.'[4]

As with the Matchams so it was with the Boltons; Lady Hamilton left them without news. The growing anxiety of all was expressed by Anne Bolton who, after complaining of Lady Hamilton's long silence, wrote direct to Horatia on 26 November. Welcoming Horatia as a correspondent she said: 'My Mother sends her love to you and your Mama she hopes to see you both as soon as the gaieties of London will permit you. I know the snow will prevent our seeing you this winter . . . So good night my dear little cousin I shall remember you in my prayers.'[5] Among other matters, Anne mentioned in her letter that the Matcham children were all ill with

[1] Ibid.   [2] Ibid.   [3] NMM/NWD/9594/13-14.
[4] Ibid.   [5] Ibid.

whooping-cough. Before the end of the year Horatia herself was very ill with the same complaint. On learning this Mrs. Matcham wrote in haste to Lady Hamilton on 1 Jannuary 1813:

We are sorry to find our dear Horatia has had the whooping-cough so severely; but I trust the worst is over. The best thing you can do is to change air. Come down to us, where you will be quiet and, I hope, happy. As to medical advice, I do not think it necessary in this complaint. We have not even applied to our Apothecary. Susanna had it bad. [Susanna was nearly eleven at the time.] We took her one day to Horsham, and we found the ride gave a turn to the disorder, for the cough has not been so violent since. They are all now, thank God, quite well, except with violent exercise they sometimes have a fit of coughing . . . Do my dear Lady, let us hear from you soon; we are very anxious to know how our dear little girl is, to whom we all beg our love, and not forgetting to wish her and you many many happy returns of this season, likewise our best wishes to Miss Weatley. I am glad to find you are bringing your affairs to a conclusion, I need not say that none of your friends will rejoice more than we shall to hear that they turn out to your satisfaction.[1]

Mrs. Matcham's letter, addressed to Bond Street, found Lady Hamilton gone. She had been arrested at the suit of several tradesmen and removed with Horatia to the King's Bench prison. Like most people in her position at the time, she had been 'made free of the Rules' of the prison, which meant that she was on parole and could lodge outside the walls in one of the sponging-houses with which the district abounded. She found desolate enough accommodation at 12 Temple Place, Blackfriars Road, one of a terrace of houses abutting onto St. George's Fields. The prison itself faced the Borough High Street. Its walls were so high that no sight over them and across the surrounding fields was possible to the prisoners. Lady Hamilton's situation was a little less dreadful; she could walk out within the prescribed area, and even go to Church in the Chapel of the Magdalen Hospital facing her lodgings across the road. But for one of her temperament and background the horror of it was unrelieved. She wrote at once to James Perry, editor of the *Morning Chronicle* and her former neighbour at Merton, who had already befriended her in previous financial crises, sending her letter by her faithful Merton servant, Dame Francis: dated 3 January 1813 the letter read:

Will you have the goodness to see my old Dame Francis, as you was so good to say to me once at any time for the present existing and unhappy circumstances you wou'd befriend me, &, if you cou'd, at your convenience, call on me to aid me by your advice as before? My friends come to town to-morrow for the season?

when I must see what can be done, so that I shall not remain here, for I am so
truly unhappy & wretched, and have been ill ever since I had the pleasure of
seeing you on dear Horatia's birthday, that I have not had either spirits or energy
to write to you. You that loved Sir William & Nelson, & feel that I have deserved
from my country some tribute of remuneration, will aid by your counsel your
ever affectionate and grateful, etc, etc.[1]

When the gravity of her situation was realized, the Matchams' instant
reaction was to urge that Horatia be sent to them. Not only did they take
for granted the need to spare a twelve-year-old girl the misery of a
sponging-house but they feared for her health after her whooping-cough.
The weather was also exceptionally cold. But neither then nor later, when
the situation was repeated, did Lady Hamilton consent to part with
Horatia: so long as she had possession of Nelson's daughter she felt that
she had some claim upon society. In consequence Horatia was made to
experience the full measure of her mother's degradation over the next two
years.

'Your letter had made us very uneasy respecting the health of our dear
Horatia,' Mrs. Matcham wrote on 25 January:

God grant she is still doing well; this is very severe weather, and we have nothing
but coughing all over the house, My good man is far from well; his cough is very
bad. Do give our best love to our dear girl, and tell her we hope, as soon as the
doctors allow her to change the air, her uncle will go in the coach as far as Reigate,
take a postchaise from thence, which will give our horses time to rest, and she will
be at Ashfold Lodge before dark. I need not say, my dear Lady, what happiness
it would be to us to see you with her, but if you cannot manage to come, we will
endeavour to supply your place. You know she is one of our children, and while
we have a loaf for them she shall share it & with it our best affections. We have a
fine snow scene and not able to stir out of the house either in the carriage or on
foot.[2]

Mr. Perry was not inactive and used his best efforts at once to obtain Lady
Hamilton's discharge; deeply complicated as were her affairs (she had
pledged all her assets, including the Hamilton pension for years ahead) it
appears that as a result of his efforts and those of Alderman Smith she was
bailed out by mid-February and allowed to return to her Bond Street
house. She had been busy, just before her arrest, on two Memorials to the
King and the Prince Regent, reiterating yet again her old claims to a
government pension. In wording these she was helped by a new friend—a
Mr. Russell who with his wife had been introduced to her by Mr. Perry.
Her enthusiasm for him and his wife became unbounded and soon she did

nothing without consulting him. 'You don't know how many obligations I have to Mr. Russell,' she wrote to Mrs. Russell, adding that he had 'worked like a horse' on her behalf. Mr. Russell, who was not steeped in the long history of Lady Hamilton's petitions to government, was unable to check her ill-founded declarations in the memorial to the Regent regarding Canning's and Rose's *positive assurances given to Nelson* on his last departure from England to favour her claims to a pension. The effect upon both gentlemen of this falsehood was fatal to her cause, as Rose's 'Diaries' show. Canning had no part in the confidential last exchanges between Nelson and Rose on board the *Victory* (and wrote at once to remind Rose of it on 17 February 1813) and Rose, whom Lady Hamilton had not advised of her new petition to the Regent, was equally astounded at her inventions and emphatic in repudiating them. He wrote to her on 18 February:

Dear Madam—I had a letter from Mr. Canning last night . . . It is incumbent on me, therefore, to state to you that Mr. Canning was not a party to the conversation between Lord Nelson and me, and could not have heard a syllable of it . . . It is not merely to state that, however, that I now trouble you, but to apprise you that your recollection is not correct as to what I told you passed between me and Lord Nelson at the time . . . I did not know you were now bringing your claim forward again, till I received Mr. Canning's letter.[1]

Answering him from Bond Street on 4 March, Lady Hamilton had recourse to her usual methods, invoking pity for her weakness whilst hitting out hard against her enemies. She assured Mr. Rose that, had she not been so ill, she would have sent him a copy of her petition to the Regent. Of particular interst is her assertion that

a kind friend of mine has told me that the reason my claims have not been remunerated was owing to a most infamous falsehood raised against my honor and that of the brave and virtuous Nelson, which is false, and it shall be made known; for I will appeal to a generous public, who will not let a woman who has served her country with the zeal I have, be left to starve and insult.[2]

She concluded with the postscript: 'Mr. Canning has a short memory'.
On 6 March Mr. Rose wrote for the last time:

Dear Madam—I return the copies of your memorial, etc . . . in doing which it is impossible for me to avoid expressing my very deep regret at your having referred to Mr. Canning and myself for assurances having been given to Lord Nelson, on board the Victory 'that the promises made by Mr. Pitt in your favour should be fully realised', because the accuracy of that cannot be supported

---

[1] Rose's *Dairies*, i, 264 et seq.   [2] Ibid., 270.

by either of us. In a letter I wrote to you about a fortnight ago, I reminded you of what did pass in my last interview with Lord Nelson . . . and I must lament that your statement was not conformable to that.[1]

Lord Sidmouth's official reply on behalf of government, also dated 6 March, added nothing to the final repudiation of her many claims—the true and the false—contained in Mr. Rose's letter. She had lost the last vestige of interest she had once enjoyed with certain members of the government, even with such long-standing and long-suffering allies as Mr. Rose. What was worse, she had lost their good-will towards Horatia. This is clear from the subsequent statement made by Lord Liverpool to Mr. Haslewood that 'nothing could be done for Miss Nelson whilst she remained under Lady Hamilton's roof'.[2] The text of Lord Sidmouth's letter to Lady Hamilton makes everything quite clear:

Whitehall, March 6th 1813

Madam,

It is very painful to me, to acquaint your Ladyship, that after a full communication, with Lord Liverpool, on the subject of your memorial to his Royal Highness, the Prince Regent, I am unable to encourage your hopes, that the object of it can be accomplished. His lordship sincerely regrets the embarrassments which you have described, but upon comparing them with representations now before him of difficulty and distress, in many other quarters, and upon review of the circumstances with which they are attended, he finds it impossible so to administer the scanty means of relief and assistance, which, under the authority of the Prince Regent, are at his disposal, as to satisfy his own sense of justice to others, and at the same time give effect to your Ladyship's application.

I have the honour to be, Madam,
Your Ladyship's obedient humble
servant,
SIDMOUTH.[3]

Hers was not a reflective nature, nor one capable of judging causes and effects; she believed herself to be a victim of injustice and cruelty, and allowed herself to be over-whelmed by her misfortunes. Spoilt and successful all her life, her situation was all the harder to bear. She found no recourse but in drink, which only envenomed her violent temper and ill-health. For long periods she took to her bed and made no attempt to leave it.

The effect on Horatia of such a situation was inevitable and swift. From both parents she inherited a nervous and passionate temperament, and the evidence shows that she now openly rebelled against the treatment she

---

[1] Ibid., 271.   [2] Eyre-Matcham 282.   [3] P., ii, 631.

received from Lady Hamilton. To the first shock and disgust of her surroundings at Temple Place, she reacted vehemently. On 29 January she was twelve (though always taught to believe her birthday was 29 October) and perhaps for the first time found words to criticize her mother. It may be that she learnt of her aunt Matcham's invitation to Ashfold, and resented Lady Hamilton's refusal to let her go. Whatever the immediate cause—there could have been many—her first attempt at judging her mother was met by vehement reproaches and accusations of ingratitude. To crush Horatia more effectively Lady Hamilton did not hesitate to call in Mr. Russell, her new ally. Horatia's poor little letter of contrition, carefully written between traced lines, showed how unequal was the struggle between two such contestants. Addressed to 38 Norfolk Street, Strand, dated '6 O'clock JA 1813', it reads:

My dear Friend, Thanks for your valuable letter I hope it will correct me of such behaviour and trust me dear Mr. Russell I know my error and with my dear Mothers goodness to me (which after such conduct I did not deserve) correct a fault which would be detestable to evry one if ever again (which I hope will never happen) I by any means do wrong I will read your friendly letter and then I shall do wright again.

And believe

Dear Mr. Russell

Yours ever affectionately and Greatfully

Horatia Nelson.[1]

Neither Horatia's circumstances nor her temper appear to have improved as the year wore on: on two further occasions she brought down upon herself the most violent recriminations from Lady Hamilton.

It had been a habit with Sir William, when much tried by Lady Hamilton's temper and extravagancies, to write her notes of reasonable protest; she would write a reply on the back of them and so scenes were avoided. Reviving this habit with her own child now, between whom and herself it is evident an open rift had developed, she wrote a first letter on '18th April (Easter Sunday) 1813' which read:

Listen to a kind good mother, who has ever been to you affectionate, truly kind, and who has neither spared pains nor expense to make you the most amiable and most accomplish'd of your sex. Ah, Horatia! if you had grown up as I wish'd you, what a joy, what a comfort might you have been to me! for I have been constant to you, and willingly pleased for every manifestation you shew'd to learn and profitt of my lessons, and I have ever been most willing to overlook injuries. But now 'tis for myself I speak & write. Look into yourself well, correct

[1] NMM/NWD/9594/13-14.

yourself of your errors, your caprices, your nonsensical follies, for by your inattention you have forfeited all claims to my future kindness. I have weathered many a storm for your sake, but these frequent blows have kill'd me. Listen, then, from a mother who speaks from the dead! Reform your conduct, or you will be detested by all the world, & when you shall no longer have my fostering arm to sheild you, whoe betide you! you will sink to nothing. Be good, be honourable, tell not falsehoods, be not capricious, follow the advice of the mother whom I shall place you in at school, for a governess must act as mother. I grieve and lament to see the increasing strength of your turbulent passions; I weep & pray you may not be totally lost; my fervent prayers are offered up to God for you; I hope you will yet become sensible of your eternal wellfare. I shall go join your father and my blessed mother, & may you on your death-bed have as little to reproach yourself as your once affectionate mother has, for I can glorify, & say I was a good child. *Can Horatia Nelson say so? I am unhappy to say you CANNOT* No answer to this—I shall tomorrow look out for a school, for your sake & *to save you*, that you may bless the memory of an injured mother.

P.S. Look on me now as gone from this world.[1]

It is strange that in these letters Lady Hamilton openly avowed the relationship she had so often concealed in the past and was to deny again in the end.

Horatia clearly had enough ground for complaint in the confined and sordid atmosphere of the sponging-house, and her situation was undoubtedly aggravated by her mother's complete lack of self-control. That her young feelings were frequently hurt by Lady Hamilton was testified by Mr. Haslewood who later told the Matchams: 'I believe, when warm with wine and with anger, Lady Hamilton sometimes bestowed upon Miss Nelson epithets less kind & flattering than that of Lord Nelson's child.'[2] By the time Lady Hamilton's second letter was written—31 October 1813—the misery of their mutual relations appears to have been complete. Though much of importance occurred to Lady Hamilton between the writing of these two letters, the text of the later one is given here because of its relevance to the earlier one. It read:

Horatia,—Your conduct is so bad, your falsehoods so dreadfull, your cruel treatment to me such that I cannot live under these afflicting circumstances; my poor heart is broken. If my poor mother was living to take my part, broken as I am with greif and ill-health, I should be happy to breathe my last in her arms. I thank you for what you have done to-day. You have helped me on nearer to God, and may God forgive you. In two days all will be arranged for your future establishment, and on Tuesday at 12, Col. & Mrs. Smith, Trickey, Mr. & Mrs. Denis, Dr. Norton will be here to hear all. Every servant shall be put on their oath, for I shall send for Nany at Richmond—Mr. Slop, Mrs. Sice,

[1] M.1047.   [2] Eyre-Matcham, 281.

Anne Deane—and get letters from the Boltons and Matchams to confront you, & tell the truth if I have used you ill; but the all-seeing eye of God knows my innocence. It is therefore my command that you do not speak to me till Tuesday, & if to-day you do speak to me, I will that moment let Col. & Mrs. Clive into all your barbarous scenes on my person, life and honnor.[1]

This letter has to be read in the context of another letter, written only the previous day by Lady Hamilton to her new-found friend Mrs. Lambert; in what relates to Horatia they are contradictory. 'My ever Dear Mrs. Lambert,' she wrote:

Your Dear Kind letter gave me such pleasure & that this day week I shall have the pleasure of your company to stay with me for a few days is beyond my powers of utterance—Yesterday my Dear Horatias Birth Day His Royal Highness dined with me Mrs. B.[2] Mr. Perry of the morning Chronable Col. O Kelly & in the evening Col. Smith—We were very merry I wished for you . . . Horatias Love Love Love—She is attentive to her Studies & behaves very affectionately. Mrs. Francis begs her respectfull Duty & ever ever believe me
Your affectionate & grateful Emma Hamilton.[3]

The letter to Mrs. Lambert was in fact written from Temple Place, for Lady Hamilton had been committed to prison again at the end of June. In these dismal lodgings she somehow managed to hold her merry party.

Her discharge earlier in the year had brought her no security. Though she wrote to Mr. Rose from 150 Bond Street on 4 March and even appointed him a meeting there, she soon began to live a hunted life at the hands of her creditors. One of her frequent hiding-places was the 'luxurious Villa' at Fulham which Mrs. Billington built for herself with the savings from a sensationally successful career. Her fortune was assessed at £60,000 and if, after her retirement in 1809 she showed generosity to Lady Hamilton, the gesture might be said to be no more than due, since Mrs. Billington owed her triumph on the continent to the Hamiltons' introduction of her at the court of Naples in 1793. (It was due to them that she was appointed prima donna at the San Carlo and made her début there in 1794 in a work especially composed for her by Francesco Bianchi—'Inez de Castro'.) To the villa at Fulham were furtively conveyed the more precious of Lady Hamilton's possessions— the Nelson relics mainly—in the course of the summer when she lived in daily anticipation of the seizure of her goods. How little she confided in the Boltons and Matchams appears from Mrs. Matcham's letters expressing the family's surprise and disappointment at not finding her at home

[1] M.1051.   [2] Mrs. Bugge, The Duke of Sussex's mistress.
[3] NMM/NWD/9594/13-14.

on three successive calls they paid during a London visit early in May. Though Kitty Matcham wrote on 9 May to announce their intention and urged a reply in a postscript which said: 'If you cannot write yourself, let Horatia or Miss Wheatley give us one line by return of post,' no reply was sent. This was the more inexplicable to them because they had reported to Lady Hamilton the sad news received from Norfolk on 8 May that Mrs. Bolton was dying. Of all Nelson's family, Mrs. Bolton had been Lady Hamilton's best and closest friend, and nothing can demonstrate more clearly her desperate need to lie low than her total inactivity and silence during Mrs. Bolton's last illness.

She heard about it from Anne Bolton on 4 May, who wrote:

You will I know my dear Lady be grieved to hear of the severe illness of my dear Mother she has if you remember long been unwell lately she has been much worse—her complaint is extreem weakness indeed she has hardly any strength left & what little now she has seems daily to diminish. We sent to Norwich for better advice but I fear . . . God only knows how long she may continue with us . . . She is at present able to come down stairs you know her mildness at all times, but I think it is more visible at this time—*Thurs eve*. We have got my Aunt Girdlestone with us & also my Aunt Bolton, which is some comfort as the first is a good nurse.[1]

Anne concluded by begging Emma to write. Kitty Matcham did so too in her letter of 9 May: 'I write this to entreat you to let me hear by return of post whether you have a letter from Bradenham or not . . . I am sure you will feel for us too much to let us remain in an uncertainty, therefore, my dear Lady, with the hope of hearing from you etc, etc.'

After their fruitless visit to town Mrs. Matcham wrote on 19 May:

We were truly mortified to find you from home the three times we called . . . and would have staid a day longer on purpose to have taken a peep at you, but to say truth all our money was gone, & we were obliged to borrow of our bankers but, however, one expense we must incur, as I am afraid we must go to Bradenham to see my dear sister, if she makes a point of seeing us. In that case we shall certainly see you in passing through town, as we shall not sleep there. I am sorry to say the accts from Bradenham are by no means flattering to-day. I much fear she will never recover; but we must look forward with hope, and try to make her as happy as we can. God bless you & dear Horatia, and believe us at all times, yours affectionately etc.[2]

From Bradenham, where Mr. and Mrs. Matcham were shortly afterwards called, Mrs. Matcham wrote to her son George:

[1] Ibid.   [2] Ibid.

We compleated our journey within twenty-four hours, which delighted your poor Aunt, to think I could be with her in that time . . . she feels no pain, is perfectly cheerful and the happiest creature you ever saw. When they think she will exert herself too much to talk to me, she smiles and says 'then if you will let me look at her I shall be content.[1]

Mr. Haslewood, who had become a close friend of the Matchams at Ashfold, found the right words to speak of Mrs. Bolton when he heard of her death. He wrote to the Matchams: 'All who knew Mrs. Bolton's serene, benevolent and friendly spirit will reverence her memory and lament her loss.'[2]

Mrs. Bolton died on 13 July at Bradenham Hall, the home she had been so delighted to acquire only eighteen months before. She was fifty-eight, but had been failing for some time. Characteristically, she wished to be buried in her father's old church at Burnham Thorpe, and there the funeral took place on 19 July, the service being conducted by her father's successor, the Revd. Daniel Everard. Her grave is in the churchyard under the north wall of the church, and is marked by a simple slab of stone which says: SUSANNAH BOLTON / The Wife of / Thomas Bolton Esq / And Sister of / HORATIO VISCOUNT NELSON / Aged 58 Years.

The report of these sad events was no doubt sent to Lady Hamilton but it is doubtful if she received them. No letters on the subject have been preserved, and about a fortnight before Mrs. Bolton's death Lady Hamilton was not only back in prison but the contents of her Bond Street home had been sold to meet her creditors' demands. Not till September did Lady Bolton take courage to write on the subject of her mother's death which, though expected, left the whole family heart-broken.

I must write for the first time, and the longer I delay it, the worse it will be, for at present, she is always in our thoughts. Our house appears so melancholy, we miss her everywhere. She was always in the way to hear our little distresses, and to relieve them if in her power, if not, to sympathize with us. What a void has her death made in our once cheerful circle.[3]

To Lady Bolton had been born a second child, christened Mary Ann on 1 July at a most joyless moment. Telling Lady Hamilton how different the baby was from little Emma, she added:

Emma sends many loves and kisses to her cousin Horatia. She often speaks of cousin Horatia. She will write her one day soon, but she must wait till I am well enough to attend to her. I hope when you write you will be able to give me good accounts of your own health. You have been an invalid for a long time. I trust now you will find your health improve rapidly.[1]

From which it is evident the Boltons had no idea of Lady Hamilton's fresh arrest at the end of June.

The decision of three of her creditors to proceed against her in the course of June appears to have been a consequence of the failure of the last petitions to the King and the Prince Regent, the prospect of which had hitherto held them at bay. The Execution in her house, made by order of the Sheriff of Middlesex, took place on 8 July 1813. The Catalogue of the 'Sale of Elegant Household Furniture The Property of a Lady of Distinction'[2] shows that though much diminished from the time of her Merton splendours, she still possessed the nucleus of Sir William's library, including many rare books (Domesday Book in two volumes among them) and a fine collection of Italian works, and portraits and relics of Nelson. The furniture, described as 'Capital' was still the mahogany 'Grecian style' furniture of Merton, the draperies of French chintz, the china and glass including some of the presentation services given to Nelson. Every item bequeathed to Horatia by Lady Hamilton's latest Will of 1811, the silver-gilt utensils inscribed with the Nelson arms, the glass and china services, numbering some of them ninety-seven pieces (in particular a 'white and gold tea and coffee set of 50 pieces'), was included in the sale. But for the generous gesture of Mr. Perry, Alderman Smith and Mr. Salter (the silversmith who had already bought back Horatia's drinking-cup) these relics would have been sold at the auction and lost to Horatia. As it was Alderman Smith took them in guarantee for the money he advanced to Lady Hamilton, and had them packed in crates and stored in his warehouse in Southwark. Pathetic items among the Catalogue of 'Valuable Pieces' were Horatia's 'doll's bedstead', relegated to the 'Front Attic', her 'Pope-Joan' board, and 'Draft Board and Men'.

The beneficent role of Alderman Smith, Presiding Magistrate of the Borough Council whose offices were at Southwark Town Hall, which put him, both in the physical and legal sense, in close touch with Lady Hamilton's affairs, cannot be over-estimated. The list of his good offices towards her and Horatia, which began with his buying the contents of her Richmond house, including the coat in which Nelson was killed, is long and honourable, and only ended when he paid her funeral expenses.

Besides buying the Nelson relics at the Bond Street sale,[3] he paid Lady

[1] Ibid.　　　[2] Ibid.

[3] Monmouth, Nelson, Museum: Inventory of the Property of the late Lord Nelson, transfer'd by Mr. Alderman Smith to John Kinsey, Constable, Town Hall, Southward, June 1830.

Hamilton's bills at the sponging-house and, finally, by standing her bail, obtained her discharge. This was not, however, until she had spent a year 'within the Rules'. Without Alderman Smith to pay for her lodgings at Temple Place, Lady Hamilton and Horatia could not in fact have afforded to live 'within the Rules', and would have been confined in the King's Bench itself. The receipt for her expenses in the sponging-house delivered to Alderman Smith by the landlord as a final quittance on Lady Hamilton's liberation, shows that the apartment she occupied was let at a rent of 3½ guineas a week, that her bill for coals over a period of three months amounted to £7. 8s. 0d., that 'Washing & general expenses' over the same period were £1. 0s. 0d. The outstanding item on her account, one that was out of all proportion to the rest was the bill, written on a separate sheet, of Lady Hamilton's 'Breakages' during the same period which, enumerating one hundred and eighteen separate items amounted to £13 4s. 11d. The list,[1] revealing in its thoroughness, comprises china, ornaments, glass and crockery of every sort and use which, by its very enormity, excludes the possibility of accident. There can hardly be any doubt that the 'Breakages' were the consequence of those moments described by Mr. Haslewood when Lady Hamilton 'was warm with wine and anger'. To judge by the bill for breakages, these appear to have been frequent.

To Alderman Smith and his wife Horatia owed what few pleasures she enjoyed during her mother's imprisonment. From a letter written in October 1818 it is evident she was allowed to visit the Smith's home and play with their little girls, Fanny and Georgiana. 'I greatly fear,' she wrote then, 'your eldest daughter has forgot her old playfellow.'

The bill for the 'Hire of a Piano—15/- a month for about 10 months' shows that even at Temple Place Horatia was not left without the means of practising her music, even if she received no other education during the period, which was presumably the case. The piano, moreover, may have served on those surprising occasions when, even in the sponging-house, Lady Hamilton gave a party. Evidence of two such occasions is preserved, which shows that despite her misfortunes her taste for convivial company survived. On 31 July 1813, only a month after she was committed to prison, she wrote to Sir Thomas Lewis:

12 Temple Place: Saturday 31st July
My dear Sir Thomas, Will you come to-morrow to meet our good pope [this was the Abbé Campbell, one of her intimates] and Mr. Tegart [her doctor]. It is the first of Agust do come, it is a day to me glorious, for I largely contributed to its success and at the same time it gives me pain and grief thinking on the

[1] NMM/NWD/9594/34.

Dear lamented Cheif, who so bravely won the day, and if you come we will drink to his immortal memory. He cou'd never have thought that his Child and my self shou'd pass the anniversary of that victorious day were we shall pass it, but I shall be with a few sincere and valuable friends, all Hearts of Gold, not Pinch-back (sic) and that will be consoling to the afflicted heart of your Faithful Friend,

Emma Hamilton[1]

Prisoners had to provide their own board, and the few letters of the period to be preserved, show that the Matchams helped to keep Lady Hamilton and Horatia supplied in farm produce. 'Pray let us know the carrier's name of the waggon which passes your house,' George Matcham wrote Lady Hamilton on 21 November. 'We will supply you with potatoes all the winter, and send you a turkey by the first opportunity . . . Write as soon as ever you can, and give directions for anything our farm can supply.' It became a refrain with every letter from the Matchams, urging Lady Hamilton to write and keep them informed of her health and needs; only at very rare intervals did they receive any answers. Two of these show that Lady Hamilton was allowed to 'take an airing in the carriage' (no doubt within the area prescribed by the 'Rules') and Horatia received a birthday-present from the Matchams, a hat. In the box containing the hat Mr. Matcham enclosed a budget of family news, which gave Horatia great pleasure.

Lady Hamilton's neglect of the Matcham connection during the crisis in her affairs appears inexplicable—considering her desparate situation—unless she feared their interference on behalf of Horatia. She gave Alderman Smith the impression, which he later communicated to Mr. Haslewood, that Horatia had little consideration to expect from Nelson's family, and that unless he championed her cause she had few friends to look to. Receiving no replies to their letters to Lady Hamilton, the Matchams wrote frequently to Horatia, letters in which no doubt they repeated their former offers of adoption. In Horatia's replies may have lain the causes of Lady Hamilton's anger. The date of her October letter of remonstrance to Horatia written just after her official birthday would point to such an interpretation, since Horatia had just received three letters from the Matchams, and the birthday-present containing the budget of family news. Her heart was, understandably, not in Temple Place, but at Ashfold with her cousins, where Kitty was 'keeping school' during the holiday of the resident governess, Miss Owens. In the past Horatia had shared in this happy schoolroom life.

[1] Ibid.

But Christmas at Temple Place in 1813 was not the lugubri
friends of Lady Hamilton and Horatia might have supposed
Dillon gives some account of the dinner to which Lady Han
him. 'I found a letter from Lady Hamilton inviting me to d
he recorded.

Three years had elapsed since I had seen her ... When the hour approached, the rain was pouring down in torrents. I engaged a postchaise for the remainder of the evening, then started for the residence indicated.

Upon my arrival her Ladyship greeted me most sincerely. 'How did you know I was in Town?' I demanded. She acquainted me that a friend who had seen me at the Admiralty had told her, and that she was highly delighted to shake me again by the hand. I noticed a splendid display of plate on the table, and covers laid for four, but made no enquiries who the guests were ...

While we were thus occupied, I was surprised by the entrance into the room of H.R.H. the Duke of Sussex. Soon afterwards Mrs. B made her appearance [Mrs. Bugge]. The Prince was all kindness, and wondered I had not been to see him ...

The dinner being served, the conversation turned in another direction. I had to do the honours—carve, etc—The first course went off in complete order, and I could not help thinking that rather too much luxury had been produced. H.R.H. did not expect such an entertainment from the lady who received him. However, there was a sad falling off in the second course, and a great deficiency in attendance, as also of knives and forks. I had to carve a good-sized bird, but had not been supplied with the necessary implements. Time passed on, but no servant made his appearance. At last Lady Hamilton said: 'Why don't you cut up that bird?' I told her I was in want of a knife and fork. 'Oh!' she said, 'you must not be particular here.' 'Very well my lady' I rejoined. 'I did not like to commit myself in the presence of H.R.H. but since you desire it, I will soon divide the object before me. Besides, you are aware that, as a Midshipman, I learnt how to use my fingers!' Then, looking round, I found what I wanted, and soon had the bird in pieces. My reply produced some hearty laughter, and the repast terminated very merrily. After a sociable and agreeable entertainment, I took my leave of the company.[1]

In 1814, which saw the abdication of Napoleon and peace in Europe after twenty-one years, Lady Hamilton's misfortunes only increased. During the rejoicings that followed the news of the Emperor's abdication (it reached London on Monday 11 April), when the whole town was illuminated at night (though 'owing to the shortness of the notice and the hurry that prevailed, many persons were prevented from lighting with lamps and others obliged to abridge their design')[2]

---

[1] Tours, 253. The bird was presumably the one supplied from Ashfold.
[2] *Morning Chronicle*, 22 April 1814.

there was published anonymously *The Letters of Lord Nelson and Lady Hamilton*.[1] First advertised in of the *Morning Herald* on 21 April, Lady Hamilton at once recognized the danger it represented to her. Her immediate action in writing to Mr. Perry of the *Morning Chronicle* to deny all knowledge of the letters indicated that she knew their contents only too well; the 'Thompson' letters were among them, and she had every reason to dread the effects of their publication. Here at last for all the world to see was proof of what had hitherto only been surmised and whispered in the London drawing-rooms—the truth about her connection with Lord Nelson. In their 'Advertisement' the editors said of the writers of the letters that 'Their mutual attachment is so generally known, that for the Editors to have given notes . . . might not . . . have been deemed perfectly decorous', and added: 'It is the duty of the Editors to State, that every letter has been most accurately transcribed, and faithfully compared with *the originals in their possession.*' Their claim was true; the letters from which the book was compiled were the originals which Nelson years before had begged Lady Hamilton to destroy as soon as read. The poor woman's folly in disobeying him overwhelmed her now and struck the death blow to her reputation. Without seeing the book, she knew what it contained—a proof that, whatever her denials, she had been expecting the blow, and suspected the identity of the authors. Her account of the abstraction of the letters does not tally with that given later by Horatia. Her letter to Mr. Perry, dated 12 Temple Place, April 22nd, read:

To my great surprise I saw yesterday in the 'Herald' that Lord Nelson's letters to me were published. I have not seen the book, but I give you my honour that I know nothing of these letters. I have now been nine months in Temple Place & allmost all the time I have been very ill with a bilious complaint, brought on by fretting & anxiety, & lately I have kept my bed for near twelve weeks, nor have I seen any person except Dr. Watson & Mr. Tegart, who have attended me with kindness & attention, & to whoes care I owe my life. About four years ago my house in Dover Street was on fire, & I was going into Sussex for 3 months, & I left part of my papers in a case with a person to whom I thought I cou'd depend on. Weather this person has made use of any of these papers, or weather they are the invention of a vile, mercenary wretch, I know not, but you will oblige me much by contradicting these falsehoods, and you will much gratify your gratefull, etc.[2]

Mr. Perry did not publish Lady Hamilton's denial—how could he?—and within a fortnight the advertisement of the book figured in the columns of

---

[1] The Letters of Lord Nelson to Lady Hamilton/With a Supplement of Interesting Letters by Distinguished Characters/in Two Volumes/London: Printed by Macdonald & Son, Smithfield. For Thomas Lovewell & Co. Stains House/Barbican, 1814.

[2] M.1054.

his own paper among other novelties of the day, which included the first notice of *Mansfield Park* on 27 May.

The publishers had chosen the moment well for launching the *Letters*, while London was seething with patriotic fervour and popular excitement, and crowded with illustrious visitors, and the great hostesses were giving parties every night; the time was opportune for cashing-in on the name of Nelson and for setting the drawing-rooms humming with the revived scandal of his infatuation for the beautiful adventuress. The book, priced one guinea, was accessible to all ranks, and was elegantly produced in two slim octavo volumes.

The contrast between her former triumphs and present pitiable lot could not have been more forcibly impressed upon Emma. The daily papers, which she obviously read, told her of nothing but universal rejoicings, parties, receptions, balls. At the very corner of her street— opposite her in Great Surrey Street, where it abutted on Blackfriars Bridge Road—was the Surrey Theatre advertizing daily in the press a 'New National Interlude interspersed with Songs, Duets & Choruses entitled BRITONS AT BORDEAUX, and THE ALLIES AT PARIS—or THE DOWNFALL OF TYRANNY. A new Comic Song called the Devil and BONAPARTE' will be sung by Mr. Gilbert . . .'. Here on her doorstep was the kind of entertainment in which she revelled, recalling the countless occasions on which she had appeared after Trafalgar and regularly fainted in the stage box at the conclusion of 'The Death of Nelson' sung by her protégé, Mr. Braham; at such popular manifestations she was in her element. She read of the entry of the French King, Louis XVIII into London, on his way to Dover (after twenty-one years in exile) and of the levee he held at Grillon's Hotel in Albemarle Street at which he was 'supported' (both literally and metaphorically) by the Prince Regent and the Duke of York; of the cavalcades, processions, reviews, banquets, in all of which the Prince played the leading rôle in a quick-change succession of dazzling uniforms. Brought to the fore at last by the confirmed madness of his father, the Regent basked in the reflected glory of his countrymen's victories. This was the moment for which Lady Hamilton had been waiting for years when she would receive the fruits of his promised favour, the official recognition of her claims to a pension.

She did not immediately realise that with the publication of Nelson's love-letters to her the jealousy and detestation he had expressed for the Prince Regent would be made public too. This additional consequence of the ill-fated publication was only gradually borne in on her as her few remaining advisers pointed out the inevitable loss of the Prince's favour.

Too late she issued denials asserting to the Editor of the *Morning Herald* that 'Sir William, Lord Nelson and myself were too much attached to his Royal Highness ever to speak or think ill of him. If I had the means I wou'd prosecute the wretches who have thus traduced me'. It was all to no avail. The Prince read enough to draw his own conclusions and to withdraw his patronage. Few were left to doubt the authenticity of the letters, though speculation remained rife about their editors. James Harrison was considered the most likely from the opportunities he had when writing the life of Lord Nelson in 1806. A great favourite then with Lady Hamilton, she financed the book which was to show her in such an advantageous light and discredit Lady Nelson. Another candidate for the sorry distinction of publishing the letters was a secretary Lady Hamilton sometimes employed, a man named Clarke, whose handwriting is much in her correspondence. Whether Harrison, Clarke, or even Oliver, the opportunity had been open to anyone living in the immediate entourage of Lady Hamilton, given the imprudent and unguarded way in which she spoke of Nelson and of everything connected with him, and the great claims she made of having been at the centre of every major event in his career. Her lack of reticence was such that it hardly needed a calculating thief to get a sight of the famous letters. The financial destitution in which she had lived during the last few years would even suggest that she had been prepared to part with them for ready money on some understanding that they should not be published before an agreed date; her partner in the transaction had broken the contract.

This was a view of the case openly expressed by the *Morning Post* in its obituary notice on Lady Hamilton (26 January 1815) in which, after describing the vicissitudes of her life, it was said: 'It is, however, much to be regretted that she was induced to give those letters to the world, which were more calculated to display Lord Nelson's private opinions and feelings, than to increase the lustre of his public character. But she, perhaps, might urge the plea of Shakespeare's Apothecary—"My *poverty*, and not my *will*, consents".'

To the letters which so completely proved the liaison between Lord Nelson and Lady Hamilton, and their parentage of Horatia, Horatia's own reactions will be examined later. When in 1846 their undoubted authenticity was proved, she deeply deplored the fact. Of Nelson's duplicity towards Sir William, she exclaimed: 'Alas! that such a Master-mind should be subject to such weakness.'[1]

Whichever of her former familiars it was who came by the letters Lady

[1] NMM/NWD/9594/I.

Hamilton herself had no doubt that Harrison was the man responsible. After reaching Calais in August 1814 she wrote to Alderman Smith: 'I have begd of Sir Wm Scott to speak to you and the Lord Chancellor to lay an injunction on the scoundrels Harrison and Lovel [the printer] for the stolen letters and let me beg of you not to let one letter be taken from your House.'[1]

Lady Hamilton's first reaction to these accumulated misfortunes showed some revival of spirit, or at least a greater aggressiveness. A week after the fatal publication she wrote to Earl Nelson, on 29 April 1814.

> 12 Temple Place in the Rules of the King's Bench
>
> My Lord,
>   It cannot be more disagreeable to you to Receive a Letter from me than it is for me to write to you but as I will not have anything to say or do with Lawyers without I am compell'd to it I shou'd be glad to know from your Lordship weather the *first half year* of the Bronte pension which my ever Dear Lamented Friend the Glorious & virtuous Nelson left in His Will I was to Receive & which I never have Received I shall be glad to know how it is to be settled as now from my present situation which has been brought on not by *any Crime* but by having been too generous to the ungrateful I rather glory in being the injured and not the injurer and as every six pence is of the utmost consequence to me on account of Horatia Nelson's Education the beloved Child of my dear Nelson I do not in the midst of poverty neglect her Education which is such as will suit the Rank in life which she will yet hold in Society & which her great Father wish'd her to move in. I ask not Alms I ask not anything but right & to know weather I am to receive my due or not. Believe me my Lord Yours etc   Emma Hamilton.

That the Earl did not keep her long is shown by her receipt, dated 6 May,[2] in acknowledgement of '£225 on Bronté', to which she added a note that she 'had *not* before received the Bronté £500 in advance'.[3] (A necessary assurance in her case, where all the rest of her assets had been pledged in advance to moneylenders.) Despite this prompt payment, the Earl did not escape her usual censure. Time had only added to the list of his misdeeds in Lady Hamilton's estimation, and equally to the list of his obligations to her. Barely four months later she repeated to Sir William Scott (who of course was a personal acquaintance of the Earl) the long list of her complaints against him. Reporting on the then state of her affairs (after her escape to Calais), she said:

But, my dear Sir William, without a pound in my pocket what can I do? the 21st October, fatal day, I shall have some. I wrote to Davison to ask the Earl to let

---

Eyre-Matcham, 277.   [2] BM Add MSS 34992. Nelson Papers.
[3] Ibid.

me have my Bronté pension quarterly instead of half yearly and the Earl refused, saying he was too poor, although I got the good and great Lord Nelson that estate by means of the Queen of Naples. I set out from town ten weeks or more ago with not quite fifty pounds, paying our passage also out of it; think then of the situation of Nelson's child, and Lady Hamilton who so much contributed to the Battle of the Nile, paid often and often out of my own pocket at Naples for to send to Sir John Jervis provisions and also of Palermo for corn to save Malta, indeed I have been ill used. Lord Sidmouth is a good man and Lord Liverpool is also an upright Minister, pray and if ever Sir William Hamilton's and Lord Nelson's services were deserving ask them to aid me. Think what I must feel who was used to give God only knows, and now to ask! Earl & Countess Nelson lived with me seven years, I educated Lady Charlotte and paid at Eton for Trafalgar. I made Lord Nelson write the letter to Lord Sidmouth for the Prebendary of Canterbury, which his Lordship kindly gave him. They have never given the dear Horatia a frock or a sixpence.[1]

Immediately on the declaration of peace, but before the publication of the Nelson letters, young George Matcham called on Lady Hamilton on his way home from Cambridge. His report was that she 'and dear Horatia were so well'. Lady Hamilton's long silences left the family at Ashfold in constant doubt of her situation (an exceptionally severe winter, as appears from the Matcham letters, prevented their intended visit to her), so much out of touch with her as to suppose that she might shortly be released. On 18 April Kitty Matcham and her father wrote to Lady Hamilton. The latter was ready with a plan which the opening of communications with Europe had instantly prompted in his mind. His offer to Lady Hamilton to join them 'abroad in some city, town or village' shows that, as far as the Matcham family went, nothing as yet had changed in their kindly feelings towards her. The young Matchams were like their father, eager for travel. 'I wish we could have you with us,' Kitty wrote to Lady Hamilton. 'Papa says he would send the carriage to meet you anywhere. This news has given us all new life. What glorious intelligence it is. All the world are flocking abroad to more genial climates.' Mr. Matcham wrote:

We were all anxious my dear Lady Hamilton, to see you at Ashfold. The summons to Mrs. M. and myself to escort you and dear Horatia to this place would be most grateful to us . . . When our house is free of visitors, Mrs. M. and myself purpose going as far as your house, and staying with you a few hours. We shall not go into London, our only object will be to see you and talk over our future destination. The dear beautiful Ashfold is offered for sale. My other planted property I shall not dispose of, as it will be of no further expense to me, and may in time prove an advantage to my family. You will consequently infer that we

[1] NMM/NWD/9594/34.

seek another country. We do; but where, I cannot determine till I have some
conversation with my travelled friends, Write us frequently. I offer a joint wish
that we may all settle abroad in some city, town, or village.[1]

The nature of Lady Hamilton's affairs, which required the utmost
secrecy, prevented her taking the Matchams into her confidence even if
she had wanted to. When she herself crossed the channel soon after it was
without notifying the family. Through the generosity and activity of
Alderman Smith and James Perry, the demands of Emma's immediate
creditors were met and her discharge obtained by the end of June. This
did not mean that she was out of debt and able to live a free life; the
imminence of other claims which could not be met left her no choice but to
flee the country. Even her passage had to be undertaken from London
Bridge Wharfe, by a small vessel (the *Little Tom*) which took three days
crossing to Calais; to embark at Dover by the normal packet would have
meant risking re-arrest at the suit of other creditors. She made over her
few remaining possessions in an attempt to hold them off, except for personal relics—letters, ornaments, family portraits— which she confided to
Alderman Smith and his wife and to Mrs. Billington, who kept them in
her Fulham house. It was with £50 in her pocket that, with Horatia, she
left England for ever, on the last day of June or the first of July.

It is understandable that, on reaching foreign soil, her mood should not
be one of heartbreak but of revived energy and hope. The long, dismal
sojourn in the Temple Place sponging-house made the continental
sunshine and bustle appear doubly exhilarating. At Calais, where English
tourists were flocking by the hundred, she could forget she was a bankrupt
and share in the general excitement at the ending of the war. She was
caught up in the spirit of holiday that animated all, and in that mood wrote
to Mr. Rose only four days after arriving in Calais.

Hotel Dessin (sic) Calais, July 4th
We arrived here safe, dear Sir, after three days' sickness at sea, as for precaution we embarked at the Tower. Mr. Smith got me the discharge from Lord
Ellenborough. I then begged Mr. Smith to withdraw his bail, for I would have
died in prison sooner than that good man should have suffered for me, and I
managed so well with Horatia alone that I was at Calais before any new writs
could be issued against me. I feel so much better, from the change of climate,
food, air, large rooms and *liberty*, that there is a chance I may live to see Horatia
brought up. I am looking out for a lodging. I have an excellent Frenchwoman
who is good at everything for Horatia and myself, and my old dame who is
coming, will be my establishment. Near me is an English lady, who has resided

[1] M. ii, 369.

nty-five years, who has a day school, but not for eating and sleeping.
he morning I take Horatia; fetch her at one; at three we dine, and
evening we walk. She learns everything—piano, harp languages
ly. She knows French and Italian well, but she will improve. Not
t those of the first families go there. Last evening we walked two
miles to a fête champetre pour les bourgeois. Everybody is pleased with Horatia,
The General and his good old wife are very good to us, but our little world of
happiness is in ourselves. If, my dear Sir, Lord Sidmouth would do something
for Horatia, so that I can be enabled to give her an education and also for her
dress it would ease me, and make me very happy. Surely he owes this to Nelson.
For God's sake, do try for me, for you do not know how limited [I am] I have
left everything to be sold for the creditors, who do not deserve anything, for I
have been the victim of artful mercenary wretches, and my too great liberality
and open heart has been the dupe of villains. To you, Sir, I trust, for my dearest
Horatia, to exert yourself for her, and that will be an easy passport for me.[1]

Nothing could make Lady Hamilton believe, not even Lord Sidmouth's
unequivocal rejection of her claims in March 1813, that her credit with the
government was utterly gone, and any intervention of the well-disposed
Mr. Rose a useless gesture. To a woman who had known her triumphs, it
was impossible to realise that she herself was the main obstacle to any help
being given Horatia.

[1] Rose's *Diaries*, ii, 272-3.

CHAPTER XIV

CALAIS

THE news of Napoleon's abdication was scarcely announced before the first wave of English tourists crossed the channel. The opportunists lost no time in cashing-in on the spirit of holiday which prompted a war-weary generation to enjoy its new-found freedom. In the first week of the peace the *Morning Chronicle*, which recorded daily the numerous departures of the leaders of fashion, carried the following advertisement: 'TO THE NOBILITY & GENTRY WHO PROPOSE THE TOUR OF FRANCE. An Englishman of respectability intends leaving England to reside in Calais the latter end of the present week, where he is establishing a Repository of Horses & Carriages for the Accommodation of the English Nobility & Gentry, and to facilitate the travelling to Paris . . .'.

Calais, as the Gateway to Europe, was not only the English debtors' goal in the flight from their creditors, but a gay resort crowded to capacity in that early summer of 1814 with pleasure-seekers on the way to Paris and further afield. In Calais there was only one place for 'persons of rank' to stay—Quillan's and Dessein's Hotel as it was known at the time from the names of the two partners who owned it; and there, as of right, Lady Hamilton took rooms for Horatia and herself. For a time she could, and did, cut a figure among the other tourists—the 'General and his good old wife' among them.

'Everybody,' as she wrote to Mr. Rose, 'is pleased with Horatia'; Nelson's daughter was still an asset on which she could draw, despite her own financial and physical ruin. By the time she reached Calais, Lady Hamilton was indeed a very sick woman, with barely six months to live. The dropsy from which she died in the following January had been provoked, and would be hastened still further, by her now inveterate 'intemperance'. Of Horatia, however, she continued to boast, so long as there was money enough to mix with the travelling English. 'Lord Cathgart past 3 days ago,' she wrote to Greville's brother on 21 September. 'Horatia improving, in person and education daily. She speaks French like a French girl, Italian, German, English . . .'. To Sir William Scott, in an earlier letter, she had written more frankly of the impossibility of maintaining the cost of Horatia's education at the present rate. With £50, which was all she brought from England, and nothing more to come until Horatia's annuity was paid on 21 October, it was not surprising that the brief Indian summer of living at hotels and sending Horatia to a finishing school had to end. Her only recourse were Horatia's annuity (£200) and her own pension on Bronté (£500). These had not been mortgaged to her creditors.

Before the end of August the move out into the country two miles from Calais was made. Lady Hamilton's remaining letters were dated from there.

The allegations against Earl Nelson continued and were still further amplified in yet another letter to Lord Sidmouth (of which a draft remains) dated 7 October 1814, the tone of which is almost hysterical. By then it is clear that nothing was left of the £50, and she still had a fortnight to wait until further funds became due. The interest of the letter lies in the statements concerning Horatia. The text reads:

Common of St. Piere (sic) October 7th 1814

My Lord,

It is with the utmost anguish & regret I write to you, Sir William Scott was so kind knowing my services to my Country to speak to your Lordship in behalf of myself and Horatia the DAUGHTER of the Glorious and virtuous Nelson if there is Humanity still left in British Hearts they will not suffer us to die in famine in a foreign Country for God's Sake then send us some relief let Horatia who will be fourteen the 29th October finish her education, let her be provided for, at present we have not a shilling in our pockets, altho' I spent all I had on the family of Earl Nelson. He never takes notice of HIS BROTHER'S CHILD altho' He KNOWS WELL she is his Child I will not teaze your Lordship any more only to say if Horatia will be provided for, & believe my Lord your grateful

Emma Hamilton

my direction is Chez Desin.[1]

Horatia described in later years their exact movements at Calais: 'On her arrival,' she wrote, 'for many weeks she had apartments in Quillan's Hotel. Thence she went to a house she *hired* two miles from the town situated on the "Commune de St. Pierre" in consequence of some misunderstanding with the Landlord she remained there only one night and took lodgings in an adjoining farm house for some months. Afterwards she took part of a house in the town [No. 27 Rue Française] belonging to a

[1] NMM/NWD/9594/34.

Mons. Damas where she died. These were the only houses she occupied during the time she was in France.' [1]

To Alderman Smith Lady Hamilton wrote from the farm at St. Pierre in August: 'I am got into a farmhouse 2 miles from Calais and Live Comfortably'. With food as cheap as she described in a letter to the Hon. Fulke Greville (21 September) comfort might have been a reality for her and Horatia. By then the faithful 'Dame Francis' of Merton days had joined them. 'The best meat here five pence a pound,' she wrote. '2 quarts of new milk 2 pence, fowls 13 pence, a couple of ducks the same. We bought 2 fine turkeys for four shillings, an excellent turbot for half-a-crown, fresh from the sea, partridges five pence the couple, good Bordeaux wine, white and red for fifteen pence the bottle, but there are some for ten sous, helfpence.' The pastoral life, inexpensive as it was, had still to be paid for, and the purport of Lady Hamilton's letter, as of all her last letters, was to ask for money. Her ignorance of business left her utterly unaware of the consequences of her previous financial transactions with her creditors, to whom she had made over her Hamilton annuity. Her letter to Fulke Greville, the present administrator and heir of her husband's property, reveals this.

Common of St. Pierre, 2 miles from Calais.
Direct for me chez Desin   September 21st 1814
   You know that my jointure of eight hundred pounds a year has been now for a long time accumulating. If I was to die, I should have left that money away, for the annuitants have no right to have it, nor can they claim it, for I was dreadfully imposed upon for my good nature, in being bail for a person whom I thought honourable. When I came away I came with honor, as Mr. Alderman Smith can inform you, but mine own innocence keeps me up, and I despise all false accusations and aspersions. I have given up everything to pay just debts, but annuitants never will. Now, Sir, let me entreat you to send me a hundred pounds, for I understand you have the money. I live very quiet in a farm house, and my health is now quite established. Let me, sir, beg this favour to your etc.[2]

On 27 September Fulke Greville replied

                                                          Gt Cumberland Street
                                                          Oxford St.
   Madam—Your letter of Sept 21 I received only by yesterdays post. It is now some time since the regular payments from me of your annuity of eight hundred pounds a-year were very unexpectedly interrupted by a notice addressed to me by professional persons, and on the ground that you had made over the greater

---

[1] Letter to Mr. Paget of 2 Nov. 1874: *Blackwood's Magazine*, May 1888.
[2] M. 1055.

part of the same for pecuniary considerations received by you, and in consequence warning me not to continue the payment of your annuity otherwise than to them to the extent of the claims.

Not hearing from you in the long intermediate time which followed respecting your not receiving your payments as usual, I could scarce doubt the unpleasant statement I had received. Still I have demurred making any payments when called on, and under existing circumstances I must not venture to make payments *in any direction* until this mysterious business is made known to me, and whereby my acts by legal authority may be rendered perfectly secure to me. This done, of course I shall pay arrears, and continue all Future payments *whenever they shall be due* with the same precision and *punctuality* as has hitherto *always* been maintained by me, and which were attended *to the Day* until thus interrupted. But now, *my own Security* requires that I should clearly *know how this mysterious business actually stands*, e'er I shall deem it prudent or safe for me to take a step in a case where I am resolved not to act on doubtful reports. I am, Madam, Your obedient humble servant, Robert F. Greville.[1]

The press still did not leave her in peace; she could provide an occasional paragraph for gossip columns until the end. From the 'Village of St. Pierre' she wrote fresh denials to the editor of the *Morning Herald* on 14 September:

Mr. Editor, I was surprised to observe that the Morning Herald, with other newspapers, had published that I fled from my bail. This is false; and I had had Ellenborough's discharge, Mr. Alderman Smith, who became my bail, never lost a shilling by me. I have left in England [all] which I possessed to pay my creditors, retaining only that sufficient for Horatia and myself to subsist upon at a farmhouse. My innocence, I trust, will support me against all calumnies that have been raised against me. I have taken on oath and confirmed it at the altar that I know nothing of those infamous publications that are imputed to me. Many letters were stolen from me by that scoundrel, whose family I had in charity so long supported. I never once saw or knew of them. That base man is capable of forging any handwriting; and I am told he has obtained money from the Prince of Wales by his impositions, Sir W. Hamilton, Lord N. and myself were too much attached to his Royal Highness ever to speak or think ill of him. If I had the means I wou'd prosecute the wretches who have thus traduced me. I entreat you to contradict the falsehood concerning my bail, and also the other malicious reports I have alluded to in this letter, which will much oblige the much injured

Emma Hamilton[2]

Had anything like a true harmony existed between Lady Hamilton and Horatia, had their 'little world of happiness' really existed within themselves as she claimed in her letter to Mr. Rose, her last days might have

[1] M., 1056.   [2] BM Add. MSS 34992.

been less miserable. As it was the country-life—despite the cheap food and comfortable lodgings—palled; her addiction to drink, which every disappointment only increased, made havoc of their small resources, and reduced their stock of comforts still further: the brief revival of health and spirits that her escape from prison had brought, did not last the autumn. They returned to Calais, taking lodgings in the house of M. Damas at 27 Rue Française. These were so mean and cramped that Horatia's accommodation consisted only of a bed within an alcove of her mother's room.

When in years to come doubts were expressed to Horatia of her being of an age—nearly fourteen at the time—to understand what was going on around her, and of her memory serving her clearly of the actual facts, she answered: 'You say that at the death of Lady Hamilton I was but 14—true but circumstances form an almost child's character into that of a woman and that was unfortunately my case . . . Alas my dear Sir the time I spent in Calais is too indelibly stamped on my memory ever to forget.'[1]

'Circumstances' had indeed transformed the child Horatia into a careworn adolescent, faced with the starkest realities and fears. Within a week of their moving to the Calais lodgings Lady Hamilton took to her bed, a dying woman. Surrounded by strangers, and not particularly friendly strangers because of their want of money, Horatia's outlook was even worse than it had been in England just before they were arrested. A new confinement was imposed on her in which she was virtually alone, for Lady Hamilton lying often unconscious on the bed was already as good as gone; impotent to improve their situation, Horatia sat by her side. She described those days during which she never ventured out.

Lady Hamilton took little interest in anything but the indulgence of her unfortunate habit, and after the first week of her removal to the lodgings she hired in Calais at Monsieur Damas, but once she left her bed . . . at that time I never went out no one could have called unknown to me and I hardly ever during the day left her room, my own almost opened into it. For some time before she died she was not kind to me, but she had much to try her alas to spite her, and I was too well aware of the state of her finances, so much so that I applied to Lord Nelson to advance me a portion of my dividend for use in providing for necessaries for the house.[2]

That Horatia was no longer an ineffectual child is shown from the fact that the application for money to the Earl (and probably to Alderman Smith) was made on her own initiative. She was forced to act because Lady Hamilton had sent to the pawnbrokers her last jewels, some dresses

[1] Letter to Mr. Paget, referring to his of 8 Nov. 1874. NMM/NWD/9594/2.
[2] Ibid.

15

and an 'Indian Shawl' together with all Horatia's trinkets, family pictures, mementoes. Horatia recorded,

She was in great distress and had I not unknown to her, written to Lord Nelson to ask the loan of £10 and to another kind friend of hers, who immediately sent her £20, she would not literally have had one shilling till her next allowance became due. Latterly she was scarcely sensible, I imagine that her illness originally began by being bled whilst labouring under an attack of jaundice whilst she lived at Richmond. From that time she was never well, and added to this, the baneful habit she had of taking spirits and wine to a fearful degree, brought on water on the chest.[1]

This was the time, no doubt, when seeing death at hand she appealed to Lady Hamilton to tell her the truth about her birth. 'On her death-bed, at Calais I earnestly prayed her to tell me who my mother was but she would not influenced then I think by the fear that I might leave her.'[2] It was to Horatia's credit that she did not leave her but stayed to the end. The opportunity was given her, as she told afterwards; 'Latterly her mind became so irritable by drinking that I had written to Mr. Matcham, and he desired that I would lose no time in getting some respectable person to take me over and that I was to come to them, where I would always find a home. After her death, as soon as he heard of it, he came to Dover to fetch me.' Without pretending to have dearly loved Lady Hamilton, Horatia usually spoke of her with compassion. She paid one important tribute to her memory the fairness of which stands as her own personal valediction of the dead woman.

With all her faults—and she had many—she had many fine qualities, which, had she been placed early in better hands, would have made her a very superior woman. It is but justice on my part to say that through *all* her difficulties she *invariably* till the last few months, expended on my education etc, the whole of the *interest* of the sum left me by Lord Nelson and which was left entirely in her control.[3]

Lady Hamilton died on 15 January 1815 at 1 p.m. She was not buried until the 21st, the delay being no doubt caused by her known desire to be buried in England, and the fact of her destitution which made such an expense impossible. In the event, she was buried in the burial-ground outside the town (formerly known as the 'Duchess of Kingston's Garden') and in use till 1816, the expenses being borne by the English Consul, whose name, by a strange coincidence, was Henry Cadogan. This gentle-

[1] Letter to Sir Harris Nicolas, April 1846. NMM/NWD/9594/13-14.
[2] Ibid. In a further letter of 7 May 1846 Horatia told Sir Harris that Ly. H. declared she had left a written account of the facts to be delivered later to her.
[3] Ibid.

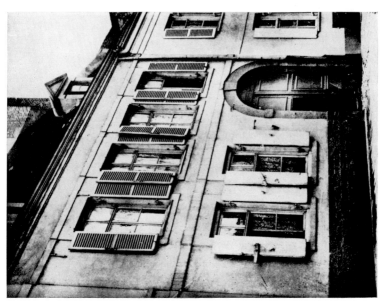

b. ROOM WITH ALCOVE WHERE LADY HAMILTON DIED

a. HOUSE IN CALAIS WHERE LADY HAMILTON DIED

man and his wife stood by Horatia, paying not only for the funeral expenses, but for the articles at the pawnbrokers, for which Horatia still held the tickets. From Mr. Cadogan's account, later presented to Horatia's guardians, Mr. Haslewood and Mr. Matcham, it appears that he had lent Lady Hamilton money and paid her 'Wine and Spirit bills' to the amount of £77. Altogether he laid out on her behalf £116, which in addition to the £28 10s. 0d. for the funeral expenses were fully refunded him later.

The details of the Undertaker's Account, which specified 'An oak coffin, casked, church expenses, priests, candles, burial ground men sitting up, dressing the body, spirits, etc, etc £28 10s. 0d.', conclusively disprove the sensational story circulated years later by an English resident in Calais about the funeral. When Dr. Pettigrew was writing his *Memoirs of the Life of Lord Nelson* which appeared in 1849, he was contacted by a Mrs. Hunter who was in Calais in 1815 and claimed to have rendered Lady Hamilton numerous kindnesses during her last illness. Her statements, both as regards her claim to feeding and nursing Lady Hamilton and concerning the funeral, were pronounced by Horatia to be 'utterly fabulous'. Mrs. Hunter alleged that Lady Hamilton was buried in a 'deal box without inscription', for which she herself made a pall 'out of a black silk petticoat'. She also claimed to have scoured Calais to secure the services of an Irish Half-Pay Officer to read the burial-service, without which, she said, there would have been no religious service, there being then no English clergyman resident in Calais. The Undertaker's bill sufficiently disposes of most of Mrs. Hunter's story, even without Horatia's denials; and Horatia moreover gave definite evidence that Lady Hamilton was buried by a Roman Catholic priest, she having been converted for some time to that religion. 'The service was read over her body by a Roman C. priest,' she wrote, 'who attended her at her request during her illness. Lady H. had, ever since she had been in Calais, professed herself a Catholic.' 'Lady H. for a long time had openly expressed herself as being a Catholic,' Horatia further attested, 'that must be between her God and herself but had I lived so long with such a decided free thinker as Sir William Hamilton professed to be it is not surprising that she should not have any fixed principles of religion.' [1]

Lady Hamilton did not, apparently, lack followers at her funeral; it is said that all the captains and masters of the many vessels in the harbour at the time followed her bier, in a last gesture of respect for Nelson's Emma. [2]

[1] Correspondence with Mr. Paget, Nov. 1874. NMM/NWD/9594.
[2] Gamlin, ii, 237.

The news of the death did not reach England until 25 January when it was reported in several papers (though not in *The Times* until the next day). The *Morning Post* reported:

DEATH OF LADY HAMILTON—from the Gazette de France of January 20th. *Calais January 17th*. The celebrated Emma, widow of Sir William Hamilton *died* here yesterday. This lady had been intimately connected with Lord Nelson. By a codicil to his will, written an hour before the battle of Trafalgar, he confirmed all the legacies he had made to her Ladyship. This document was found in the possession of Lady Hamilton: and, pursuant to her last request, her body will be conveyed to England.

The news published in the morning papers interested two readers in particular: the Hon. R. Fulke Greville, and Lady Hamilton's last creditor, represented by his lawyer Mr. Lloyd, who was pressing his claims against her in Chancery. The need to establish the bona fides of her death was therefore pressing, and Fulke Greville lost no time in writing the same day to the Mayor of Calais to confirm the news. He received an answer on the 31st, signed by the Mayor, 'L. Michaud, Maire de Calais Chevalier de la Légion d'honneur', stating that Lady Hamilton had died on the 15th. The record of her death, entered at the Town Hall of Calais reads: 'A.D. 1815, janvier 15, Dame Emma Lyons, agée de 51 ans, née a Lancashire, à (sic) Angleterre, domiciliée a Calais, fille de Henri Lyons, et de Marie Kidd, Veuve de William Hamilton, est decédée le 15 janvier 1815, a une heure après midi au domicile du Sieur Damy (sic) Rue Française.' (The Calais papers which reported her death as having occurred on the 16th were therefore wrong.) For Fulke Greville, the matter was closed. The creditors sustained no loss either, since they had had the perspicacity to insure Lady Hamilton's life with the Pelican Insurance Office, and could on producing the evidence of her death pocket the money. Though the creditors sought information from Mr. Greville concerning any relatives Lady Hamilton might have left none were in a position to meet her liabilities, and when her Will was proved in April 1816 she was declared to have died insolvent.

While the press on the whole contented itself with announcing the mere fact of Lady Hamilton's death, the *Morning Post* published a 'Commentary' on 26 January which could leave its readers—among them Nelson's family—in no doubt whatever what sort of life Lady Hamilton had led. Nothing more clearly demonstrates her complete loss of social standing than such a public attack on her character. Secure in the existing laws which exempted him from libel, the editor did not spare Lady Hamilton and for some of his allegations there had never been any evidence; he reckoned that the dead favourite had indeed no friends. Under the heading of THE LATE LADY HAMILTON the article read:

The origin of this Lady was very humble, and she had experienced all those vicissitudes in early life which too generally attend those females whose beauty has betrayed them into vice, and which unhappily proves the chief means of subsistence. Few women, who have attracted the notice of the world at large, have led a life of more *freedom*. When, however, she became such an object of admiration as to attract the attention of Painters, she formed connections which, if she had conducted herself with prudence, might have raised her into independence if not affluence. ROMNEY, who evidently felt a stronger admiration for her than what he might be supposed to entertain merely as an Artist, made her the frequent subject of his pencil. His admiration remained till the close of his life in undiminished ardour. The late CHAS GREVILLE, well known for his refined taste in VIRTU, and who was a prominent character in the world of gallantry, was the PROTECTOR, to use the well-bred language of the polite circles, of Lady Hamilton, for some years; and when his uncle, the late Sir William Hamilton wanted to take abroad with him a *chère amie*, he recommended the LADY with so good a character that Sir William took her with him and having a reliance on her fidelity, married her. Sir William returned to this country for the purpose of getting her introduced at Court, in order to procure a similar honour for her at the Court of Naples, but found it impossible for him to enable her to pass over the chaste barrier which defends the purity of British Majesty. Sir William, therefore, returned to Naples, and the Lady, by her own talents, and assiduity, recommended herself so well to the King and Queen of that Kingdom, that she became a great favourite with both, and particularly with the latter. The *friendship* between Lady Hamilton and our great Naval Hero, Nelson, is too well-known to need any record in this place. It is, however, much to be regretted that she was induced to give those letters to the world, which were more calculated to display his private opinions and feelings, than to increase the lustre of his public character. But she, perhaps, might urge the plea of Shakespeare's APOTHECARY, 'My *poverty*, and not my *will*, consents.'

In private life, she was a humane and generous woman, intoxicated with the flattery and admiration which attended her in a rank of life so different from the obscure condition in her early days, and obliging to all whom she had any opportunity of serving by her influence.[1]

[1] *Morning Post*, 26 Jan. 1815.

CHAPTER XV

MR. MATCHAM'S WARD

HAD Lady Hamilton died only a few weeks later, after Napoleon's escape from Elba on 25 February and the resumption of hostilities between France and England, Horatia might have found herself like many other English nationals at the time, interned in France for the duration of the campaign. Even so she was not free to go as she pleased. Despite the surety given by the English Consul, Mr. Henry Cadogan, Lady Hamilton's creditors at Calais were not to be put off by promises of payment from England, and during the inevitable delay before Mr. Matcham's instructions could be received Horatia remained virtually a prisoner. On Mr. Matcham, as her guardian, now devolved all the liabilities incurred on her behalf, and he instructed Mr. Cadogan to retrieve Horatia's trinkets and mementoes pawned by Lady Hamilton, for which Horatia, the unhappy messenger on such errands, still held the 'duplicates'. Lady Hamilton's personal debts, like her bill for 'Wines and Spirits' totalling £77, and her funeral expenses, as already mentioned, were not Mr. Matcham's concern, and were met once again by Alderman Smith. The lapse of a week between Lady Hamilton's funeral and Horatia's final departure for England on 28 January is thus explained by the fact that she could not leave Calais until the creditors were satisfied. This was plainly stated in the report on the event which appeared in *The Gentleman's Magazine* for March 1815. Even so, according to Mrs. Gamlin's[1] evidence, when Horatia finally crossed the channel under the escort of Mr. Cadogan she went disguised as a boy.

The Gentleman's Magazine commented:

The article in page 183 relative to the interment of Lady Hamilton we have since been assured is inaccurate. Her body was not refused Christian burial. . . . The fact is that Lady Hamilton having incurred many very considerable debts at Calais and its neighbourhood, no person would undertake to furnish her funeral, and she was on the point of being buried in a spot of ground appropriated to the poor, when an English merchant resident in Calais [Mr. Cadogan] considering the services she had formerly rendered her country and the wretched

[1] Gamlin, ii, 237.

situation of the daughter of Lord Nelson (who in compliance with the wishes of her father had never left Lady Hamilton) offered to become responsible for the charges of her funeral, which was respectably performed at the cimetière at Calais; all the English gentlemen in Calais and its vicinity to the number of fifty attending as mourners. The merchant above alluded to, finding that a process was commenced to detain the person of Miss Horatia Nelson for Lady Hamilton's debts, conveyed that young lady on board a vessel for England, and on her arrival placed her in the hands of Mr. Matcham, the late Lord Nelson's brother-in-law, with whom she is now residing.[1]

However horrible the Calais experience had been for Horatia she had not been without moral comfort through the kindness and generosity of the Cadogans. A letter from Mrs. S. F. Cadogan to Mr. Haslewood written after Horatia's arrival in England, and after the resumption of hostilities between France and England, shows this plainly. From Dover on 2 April 1815, she wrote:

Your letter to Mr. Cadogan on the subject of Miss Nelson's pictures, little ornaments, gold cups, etc. I have fortunately been able to save with some of my own property and shall feel very great pleasure in forwarding the same to my Amiable friend Miss Nelson. Some time since I had the pleasure of receiving a letter from Mr. Matcham which my good Gentleman immediately answered, but we have discovered through a friend at Calais that all letters written by Mr. Cadogan, or directed to him, have been opened at the Calais Post Office, from what reasons we are not acquainted, all letters relating to the late Lady Hamilton were always detained, and Mr. Matcham's letters were on that subject, which induces Mr. Cadogan to suppose they shared the same fate.

Mr. Matcham requested me to receive what duplicates of Miss Nelson's I could, which I have done, and taken the Ornaments from the Pawn brokers and that he would pay the Amount of these Articles etc etc to any hands that Mr. Cadogan chose to name . . .[2]

At Dover Horatia was met by Mr. Matcham. The entry in young George's journal, recording her arrival, could not be more laconic: 'Friday January [28] The Squire arrived with Horatia from Dover.'[3] Mr. Cadogan would appear to have gone straight on to London, where in the course of the next few days he saw Alderman Smith and Mr. Haslewood, Mr. Matcham's solicitor, who lost no time in discharging the debts incurred on his client's behalf at Calais. Mr. Cadogan's receipt for the funeral expenses is dated 4th February and reads: 'Recd, Feby 4th 1815 of J.J. Smith Esq the sum of twenty-eight pounds ten shillings, being the

[1] "Lady Hamilton's death and funeral", *Gentleman's Magazine*, March 1815.
[2] Eyre-Matcham, 278-9.   [3] Ibid., 277.

amount of the funeral expenses for the late Lady Emma Hamilton at Calais, in France, as paid by me. (Signed) Henry Cadogan.'

Horatia, when she arrived at Ashfold on the eve of her real fourteenth birthday, 29 January, was a very different person from the carefree child the Matchams had known before. There was no doubt how deeply she had been marked by her tribulations. Her health was affected after two years' privations, lack of exercise and fresh air. She had, by her own account, never left Lady Hamilton's sick-room from the time she took to her bed a week after arriving at M. Damas's lodgings in the previous autumn. Mr. Haslewood, with whom Horatia stayed in Fitzroy Square within ten days of reaching England, remarked on her condition to Mr. Matcham: 'Miss Nelson appeared not to be in good health while she was here. The kind of life she has passed through during the last two years must have given a shock to her constitution. But I trust, the invigorating breezes of Sussex will restore her bloom and increase her strength.' [1] Mr. Haslewood had been an ardent advocate of 'Sussex breezes' ever since he had bought Slaugham Park in 1809.

By the terms of Lady Hamilton's last Will, dated 4 September 1811, Mr. Matcham and Mr. Rose were appointed Horatia's guardians, and on Mr. Matcham's instructions Mr. Haslewood acted on Horatia's behalf in the important matter of her inheritance. Her annuity from Nelson had not been touched, but there remained the nominal legacies made to her by Lady Hamilton, and Horatia's own scant possessions—relics of her father, china, family portraits, miniatures, some of them left in the keeping of Mrs. Billington and others with Alderman Smith. The rest had been pawned at Calais. To trace her possessions in England, and especially any documents or letters proving her identity, Mr. Haslewood now approached Alderman Smith.

I apprehend he will not have the least reluctance to give up every paper he has which concerns Miss Nelson [Haslewood wrote to Mr. Matcham]. I will see him again in a few days, and in the mean time, will write to request him to separate from the "sacred deposits" [i.e. Lady Hamilton's personal papers] every letter and other paper which belongs to Miss Nelson to any member of the family of the Late Lord Nelson or to myself; that they may be ready for me to bring away.

I collected from Mr. Smith's conversation, that he was reluctant to communicate what he knew, or rather what he suspected (for I believe he *knows* nothing) of Miss Nelson's history—from an apprehension of exposing her to neglect, if not to ridicule or contempt.

[1] Ibid., 280.

He formed, as I told him, a most erroneous judgement of those who prided themselves in the title of the great Lord Nelson's friends, and above all a most erroneous judgement of you, if he thought that any of us could neglect, much less despise, one who, whatever might be her extraction, was most dear to our illustrious friend; if she were not, in herself, unworthy.

I will press this upon him more closely, and have little doubt but that I shall extract all he knows and imagines, the conclusions he has formed as to Miss Nelson's birth and the grounds of them. It is, to say the least, highly improbable, that Lady Hamilton should confide to Mr. Smith a secret which she carefully concealed from yourself and Mr. Rose. But, I believe, when warm with wine and with anger, Lady Hamilton sometimes bestowed upon Miss Nelson epithets less kind and flattering than that of Lord Nelson's child. But all this would prove nothing. [1]

Haslewood's statements at this time are of the utmost importance when viewed in the light of those he made later, both to Sir Harris Nicolas and to Horatia herself. In 1846 he declared himself bound by honour *not to divulge the secret that had been confided to him*. In 1815, on the contrary, he positively told Mrs. Matcham, who appealed to him to tell her the facts if he knew them, *that he knew nothing*.[2] He declared himself eager, moreover, to establish the truth and questioned all those who, by their intimacy with Lady Hamilton, might know something. After seeing Alderman Smith a second time he wrote Mr. Matcham again:

Fitz Roy Square, 15th Feb: 1815

Thus long have I deferred writing in the hope of having something satisfactory to communicate concerning your interesting ward. I will no longer be silent, though what I have to say is not so satisfactory as I could wish. First concerning Miss Nelson's birth. When the will was deposited in Mr. Smith's care, Lady Hamilton said—'the documents which prove Horatia's parentage are deposited in the hands of Mr. Haslewood, sealed up and not to be opened until I shall be no more.'

I need not say, *this was not true*. But the relation of it by Mr. Smith, has recalled to my mind, what I had forgot, that, at the time of executing her will or shortly afterwards, Lady Hamilton said to me—'I have a packet, concerning that dear child, which you must permit me to deposit with you.'

I made no objection. But the words which I considered merely as idle talk, made no impression on my memory. I am however now led to hope, such a packet is in existence and will be found among the papers left in France.[3]

Going on to the long-deferred question of a pension for Horatia in compliance with Nelson's dying wish, Mr. Haslewood showed that he had let

---

[1] Ibid.   [2] NMM/NWD/9594/13-24. Horatia to Sir Harris Nicolas.
[3] Eyre-Matcham, 281.

no time elapse before taking it up at the highest level. He wrote further to Mr. Matcham:

Next concerning Lord Nelson's appeal to his country on behalf of his adopted child. This has been taken up by Lord Liverpool; who says nothing could be done for Miss Nelson whilst she remained under Lady Hamilton's roof; but now that she is released from that unfit situation, the last request of the great Nelson must be remembered. Mr. Rose, who claims to be joint guardian with yourself to Miss Nelson, has had several interviews with Lord Sidmouth on the subject. And the latter has repeatedly spoken upon it to Lord Liverpool. All concur in thinking, something should be done. Mr. Rose has strongly urged, that, in addition to Miss Nelson's private fortune the country should bestow on her an annuity of £300 a year.

Lord Liverpool conceives, that Parliament will think this too much, and has named £200 a year. But Mr. Rose and Lord Sidmouth have warmly contended for the larger sum and I have little doubt but they will be successful.

Miss Nelson should, I think, be introduced to her other guardian and I hope, in a few days, to be able to say, your old quarters are at your service. At present, Mrs. W. H. and two of the children are confined with erysipelas, which has been quite epidemic in London . . . Lord Liverpool has applied to the French Government for Lady Hamilton's papers, which his Lordship will deliver to those whom they may be found to concern.[1]

Lord Sidmouth's reply to Mr. Rose's application on Horatia's behalf has been preserved. Dated Whitehall, February 5th 1815, it is of particular interest for its open reference to Horatia's being Nelson's child, and reads:

My dear Sir—You may rely upon my best efforts to obtain an allowance for the poor girl who, I conclude, is really the daughter of Lord Nelson. I fear, however, that it will not be possible, at least at present, to reach the Amount you have named. Lord Liverpool told me a short time ago that He was completely dry. I do not believe that his Reservoir has since receiv'd a considerable (if any) supply.

> But I will *do my best*.
> Believe me to be, dear Sir,
> Most truly yours,
> Sidmouth.[2]

The only conclusion to be drawn from Haslewood's conflicting statements made in 1815 and in 1846, is that Nelson himself confided the facts to him as a sacred trust never to be divulged unless Lady Hamilton released him from his vow by revealing the truth herself. As time passed and it became apparent that she had not done so in any document or declaration, Haslewood felt his hands tied and his lips sealed for ever. In

---

[1] Ibid., 282.　　　[2] Gamlin, ii, 249.

his quixotic resolve to keep faith with the dead Nelson, Haslewood did not measure the burden he laid on the living Horatia, whose life was permanently darkened by the unresolved mystery of her birth.

Towards the end of March Mr. Matcham received a tantalizing letter from the banker Coutts who wrote to say he had 'some papers of importance entrusted to him by the Duchess of Devonshire . . . to take care of for Horatia Nelson'. Here, Horatia's eager friends might suppose, were the papers so anxiously awaited that would pierce the mystery of her birth; in them, it might confidently be supposed, Lady Hamilton's promise to Horatia on her death-bed had been kept.[1] Without delay, Mr. Matcham drove to town with Horatia in the frank expectation of their hopes being justified. Some echo of their disappointment is found in young George's entry in his journal for 22 March, in which he noted: 'Wednesday March 22nd (1815), The Squire went to London with Horatia Nelson for some papers entrusted to Mr. Coutts. They proved to be two letters from the late Lord N: the last dated Oct 20 1805, to Horatia, to whom he calls himself Father.'[2]

The two letters, dated 21 October 1803 and 19 October 1805 (the eve of Trafalgar) were entrusted by Lady Hamilton to the Duchess of Devonshire on her flight from England, to be handed to Mr. Coutts, her onetime banker; she considered them too precious to take abroad. (The incident is related in the Duchess's journal.) Apart from their intrinsic sentimental value, and the fact that Nelson called himself her father, the letters revealed nothing about the identity of Horatia's mother. It can well be supposed that Horatia had personal reasons enough to be 'disinclined', as she honestly confessed to Sir Harris Nicolas years afterwards, to believe that Lady Hamilton was her mother; she had too often seen a side of her character, never revealed to Nelson's family, which was too painful to acknowledge.

A reflection of the deep emotional disturbance she had been through in the last years with Lady Hamilton can be seen in the miniature painted of her by Cosway, in which her costume—the powdered hair, high stock, frilled bodice—suggests that it was done after her return from Calais.[3]

Horatia had to be present at the opening of Lady Hamilton's Will.

[1] See above, p. 208, footnote 2.
[2] Eyre-Matcham, 283.
[3] The miniature must have been painted before 1821 when Cosway died. The fact that Cosway painted the Hon. George Rose among other notable people, might explain the choice of him to paint Horatia. The dress, and Nelson's locket round her neck, seem designed to emphasise her connection with Ld. Nelson at a time when Mr. Rose was furthering her claims to government help.

A note relative to the Probate granted was entered in March of the following year, and said:

Probate granted 6th March 1816.

The registration of the Will is accompanied by a memorandum stating that George Matcham Esq and the Rt. Hon. George Rose *having* disregarded the court's citations to accept or refuse probate and execution of the will, and Horatia Nelson, a minor, having in like manner disregarded the court's citation for her to accept or refuse letters of administration etc, etc, two gentlemen (William Tabor and George Goodwin) were called to substantiate and confirm the proceedings, etc. etc. N.B. A proceeding made necessary by the insolvency of the deceased, and the possible action taken by her creditors.[1]

The testatrix being declared insolvent, it goes without saying that none of the provisions of Lady Hamilton's Will were executed. But for Nelson's legacy, made in anticipation of just such an emergency and vested in a trust on her behalf, Horatia would have been left a penniless orphan. He had foreseen the eventuality when hurrying to make the settlement: 'I will not put it in my own power to have her left destitute; for she would want friends, if we left her in this world. She shall be independent of any smiles or frowns.'[2]

The recovery of her personal belongings, the gifts received from her father, the silver and china services engraved with the Nelson coat-of-arms, the family portraits and miniatures, proved in the event to be a long and disillusioning task.

Happily for Horatia, in 1815 she was young and resilient, and with the beginning of a new life the worst effects of her recent trials could be effaced. Only occasionally, when some matter relating to Lady Hamilton's nefarious transactions called for action on her part, did the shadow of the past fall again upon her.

There could have been no greater contrast between that past and the home-life to which she was now introduced at Ashfold. 'You know she is one of our children, and while we have a loaf for them she shall share it and with it our best affections', Mrs. Matcham had written of Horatia in January 1813 on first hearing she was with Lady Hamilton in the sponging-house. 'She is our dear girl.'[3]

Glimpses of life at Ashfold afforded by the Matcham letters show a warm-hearted cheerful household, in which a singularly kind and civilised attitude existed between parents and children. George Matcham and his wife were cultured and kindly people who entered into their children's

---

[1] Jeaffreson, ii, 305.
[2] See above: letter dated 14 March 1804. Nicolas, vii, 382.
[3] See above: Chapter XIII, letter 25 January 1813.

HORATIA NELSON, miniature by Richard Cosway c. 1815

b. HORATIA'S DRESS AS A YOUNG GIRL

a. OBVERSE OF HORATIA'S DRINKING CUP

LADY HAMILTON'S LETTER CONCERNING THE CUP

occupations and personalities with zest and sympathy. Towards Horatia that sympathy and indulgence was even greater than towards their own daughters, so family tradition claimed.

At Ashfold Horatia found her five girl cousins again (ranging in ages from twenty-three to eleven) and none of them as yet engaged, and the four boys, whose education was mostly given at home. Tolerance, good-breeding and kindness were the family's characteristics. The Matcham's world, like the world of their contemporary Jane Austen, was conditioned by rural surroundings and a limited society; its occupations and interests derived from country pursuits and its pleasures were dependent on good-neighbourliness. The young people's radius of experience seldom extended beyond Horsham on the one hand and Handcross on the other, except for the summer excursions to the coast. Their balls and parties were mostly impromptu affairs, organized between neighbours. They visited the more distinguished of these: the Sergisons of Slaugham Place (the lords of the manor) and the cadet branch of the family at Cuckfield Place; the Graingers (who had once owned Ashfold) and the Lawrences from whom they had bought it; the Pilfolds, and the Haslewoods. They were on good terms with the rector (the Reverend Robert Ellison who was incumbent there from 1800 to 1838) and were punctual in attending his charming old church above the village green; and indeed they conceived so great an affection for its rural calm that when, many years later Mr. and Mrs. Matcham died in London, they left instructions to be buried in its church-yard overlooking the Sussex woods and fields that had once compassed their home.

Without being a wealthy man, Mr. Matcham could live on his £3,000 a year in the comparative retirement of Ashfold in 'gentlemanly style'; the house was unassuming but the estate was rich in timber. At heart the master of Ashfold remained young, and his unspoilt, genial nature speaks out of the hastily-scribbled verses he addressed to his wife, on presenting her with their first carriage:

> For twenty years and more my dear
> We've walked and drove and rode together—
> And forty-seven now sure requires
> A little shelter from the weather.
> So ride at ease, and without harm
> now for the first time since our marriage
> And since the price need not alarm,
> From your old husband take this carriage.[1]

[1] Eyre-Matcham Papers, by courtesy of the family.

By the time Horatia joined them most of the girls were out of the school-room, and Miss Owens's only remaining task was to 'bring on' Susanna the youngest and persuade her of the pleasures to be derived from arithmetic. Horatia Nelson's irregular education did not compare with that of her cousins in scope and thoroughness, but she was in some ways both more advanced and more backward than they. In terms of experience the same might be said. She had seen a Christmas Pantomime and the Elephant at Drury Lane, but she had also lived 'within the Rules' of the King's Bench, a less avowable experience.

At Ashfold, as in most cultured homes of the period, music was the great study of the young ladies, and the main beguiler of the gentlemen's evening hours.

Horatia became what every young lady of the period strove to be, 'a talented musician' and 'an accomplished needlewoman'. She became also something rarer in the women of the day, an avid reader of something more solid than novels; her later choice in books showed a wide range of interests in literature, travel, and poetry that did credit to George Matcham's well-stocked library. As a result of Lady Hamilton's efforts she spoke five languages fluently.

As a member of the Matcham family her prowess in languages was very soon put to the test when her uncle decided to take them all abroad when peace finally came. George Matcham, ever 'the most unsettled man alive',[1] must have been one of the very first English civilians to cross the Channel purely for pleasure after the Battle of Waterloo. It had long been a cherished plan of his to take the family abroad when conditions allowed it. Something of the problems entailed by such an early incursion into the militarized zone of Paris can be gathered from a letter to George Matcham from a Mr. Grenside of whom he had made inquiries, and who was taking the same road. Dated July 1815 and addressed to Ashfold, Mr. Grenside's letter reads:

If you take the early Coach on Thursday, I mean the Dart, which drives into the City, I should be obliged by your calling on me at No. 26 Mark Lane which is only five minutes walk from the Inn. We can then take a Coach and after leaving your Port Mantua at my House in Henrietta Street, proceed to the French Ambassador's House where Passports are obtained and can immediately take places for Saturday morning so that we may hope to reach Paris before the Duke of Wellington has marched Southward—which appears probable—I am told we shall most likely be detained one day, after applying for Passports, which induced me to mention Thursday but if it is inconvenient to you to set off so soon, I

---

[1] Lady Nelson said this of him.

a. VIEW OF ASHFORD LODGE, Horsham, the Matcham's home

a.   *b.*

PORTAITS OF MR. & MRS. GEORGE MATCHAM, Horatia's Uncle and Aunt

will thank you to write a few words by return of Post . . . I have not had any opportunity of making . . . enquiries about the Diligences but shall inform myself on that subject between this and Thursday.[1]

The pattern of continental travel once set, Mr. Matcham decided to let Ashfold in their absence, and take an annual trip abroad (combining business with pleasure) while young George stayed in London to pursue his legal studies (he became an advocate at Doctors' Commons). On the eve of the family's second and longer trip taken in 1816, Horatia wrote to Alderman Smith on the subject of her possessions still not restored to her. Dated 16 May 1816 her letter reads:

Dear Sir,

As we purpose quitting England in a fortnight I should feel myself greatly obliged to you to give to Mr. Salter those various articles you have so kindly taken care of for me among which are several miniatures. I have felt much anxiety with regard to those Pictures tho' of little value but was quite relieved from all apprehension on that score when I found by my good friend Mrs. Smith's letter to our departed friend they were under her care she was good enough to say in her letter to Lady Hamilton at Calais if my poor Lady liked she would forward them to her there—this letter came to me since my arrival at Ashfold sent me with a parcel of letters by Mrs. Cadogan of Calais or I should have done myself the pleasure before to have thanked Mrs. Smith for her goodness in taking care of them. Mr. Salter has been so good as to offer to forward things to me before my departure for the Continent. I have inclosed the letter to him not knowing whether you were in town or Country you mentioned to me you had some articles of mine when I saw you at the opening of the will but when we left England last autumn I neglected to write to you.

Wishing you and Mrs. Smith every happiness,
I am dear Sir,
Your obliged and obedient Ser^{yt}
Horatia N. Nelson.[2]

Stacked in Alderman Smith's sugar warehouse, and increasingly inaccessible after lying there so long, Horatia's mementoes of her illustrious father remained lost to her for several years. They were, as she said, 'of little value', except to her, since they represented the one tangible proof remaining of her life with Lord Nelson; she held to these objects as though they gave her what was otherwise denied—a sense of identity. But the fact was that Alderman Smith's situation had deteriorated, and while he had accepted the Nelson relics at a time when they represented a guarantee against his generous loans to Lady Hamilton, he could no

---

[1] Eyre-Matcham Papers.   [2] NMM/NWD/9594/34.

longer afford to part with them without recouping himself for his losses. Hence the delay in restoring them to Horatia.

Horatia's surviving correspondence tells us something about the family's trip abroad in 1816, which lasted from May to October. Lisbon was the objective, and there Mr. Matcham established connections with wine, fruit and vegetable exporters, and the party stayed long enough to make friends among the English colony and the British officers in the garrison stationed there. With her girl cousins Horatia walked, danced, dined and made up picnic parties into the surrounding countryside, the beauty of which together with the climate gave to the summer an atmosphere of enchantment. No attempt was made by the liberal-minded parents to prevent the girls corresponding with their recent escorts. With one of these, a Mr. Newcomb of the Commissariat department of the Treasury, Horatia entered into a regular correspondence. From Mr. Newcomb's references to the conquests she had made at Lisbon it can be gathered that the beauty she inherited from her mother was already making its mark. A married man with two little girls, Mr. Newcomb permitted himself to adopt the language of gallantry, and as an incurable gossip-monger he was a useful purveyor of news.

'I wish to God you had all remained in Lisbon a little longer', he wrote to Horatia on 2 October 1816.

I am quite sure your Uncle would have found many good opportunities of disposing hospitably of his money . . . No doubt since your arrival you have been enjoying all the pleasures and amusements of a Brighton or a Worthing or some other watering place equally agreeable. How has travelling agreed with you. I hope you are none the worse for your long journeys.[1]

Mr. Newcomb reported too on the movement of the military in Lisbon and, evidently in reply to direct questions on the whereabouts of certain officers, quoted the list of those still garrisonned there. On 17 January (1817) he replied to Horatia's queries concerning a 'Colonel Browne':

how long he is likely to remain there I cannot tell, nor can I learn anything about his private affairs further than his reported attachment to the daughter of the late gallant Admiral with whom he became enamoured when the young lady was at Lisbon a short time back and it is not at all surprising that he should be over head and ears in love with such a damsel. I am told his attachment remains unalterable, and that he has spoken of it to many of his friends . . . Mrs. Newcomb and Caroline join me in best wishes and regards to yourself, Miss Eliza [Horatia's cousin, aged twenty] and every branch of that excellent family.[2]

[1] NMM/NWD/9594/34.   [2] Ibid.

Horatia later spoke of herself as 'a giddy girl' at this time, one to whom
Mr. Haslewood might be excused for not communicating an important
secret. Certainly she blossomed out in the genial atmosphere of the
Matcham household and enjoyed her liberty.

A major event in the Matcham family in February 1817 altered their
views on the desirability of keeping Ashfold: this was the marriage of
young George and his decision to settle on his wife's property in Wiltshire.
By a strange sequence of events George's destiny was decided for him
by his uncle, Earl Nelson, who in the course of 1814 had acquired under
the trust set up by the government for that purpose the estate of Standlynch near Salisbury which, in compliance with the terms of the grant,
was re-named 'Trafalgar'. Still resident at Canterbury (where his stall
obliged him to live a part of every year) the Earl was slow to furnish the
new house and moved in only gradually. In default of a son, he now
looked to the young men of his family for advice and help in ordering his
property, especially to Tom Bolton whose experience as a farmer was
invaluable to him. In a kindlier spirit than had ever existed between him
and his sisters' families, he now convened both Tom and George to
Trafalgar. Barely established there and acquainted with his new neighbours, the Earl introduced his nephews among them, with the avowed
intention of match-making on their behalf. While Tom resisted such an
encroachment on his liberty, 'young' George obliged by falling violently
in love with the young lady of his uncle's choice, Miss Harriet Eyre,
heiress of the New House estate at Downton, adjoining Trafalgar. How
instrumental the Earl was in forwarding his nephew's suit can be seen
from 'young' George's letters of the time. In the late autumn of 1816, the
Matchams on their return from Lisbon were in London occupying a
rented house at 64 Baker Street, Portman Square, from where George
wrote to his prospective mother-in-law, the widowed Mrs. Eyre, on
19 November 1816: 'I have lost no time in communicating to my Father
the particulars of my present situation, and after having considered the
state of our respective circumstances, I venture to propose the following
terms, which I trust will meet your approbation and enable me to claim
the hand of your inestimable daughter'. After explaining that his father
would resign property in his favour that would ensure him an income of
£500 a year, he added:

With the five hundred a year before mentioned and the three you have con-
ditionally promised, our income will amount to eight hundred a year, a sum
sufficient for the comforts of life, but my Uncle, desirous of removing any
16

possible objection, and wishing that his nephew should commence his establishment in a manner not wholly inconsistent with the merit and expectations of your daughter, has generously offered me two hundred a year to complete the thousand. With this ample provision, I trust, my dear Madam, that your maternal solicitude will be quieted, and that you will allow me to claim the treasure on the possession of which the happiness of my life must in future depend. I shall in no way resign my profession [the law] . . . as it is my Uncle's intention to exert his influence in my favour so soon as I am qualified to hold an office of emolument . . . My Uncle who desires me to present his regards to the whole family, allows me to say that, if our arrangements can be so soon completed and I can obtain your consent and that of my dear Harriet, he will with pleasure come from Canterbury to New House about the end of January to exercise the functions of his profession. Without this voluntary offer, I should not have so soon presumed to mention the subject, but he has encouraged me, and I could certainly not resist the temptation of proposing an offer the most acceptable of any he could ever perform . . .[1]

To Harriet herself George wrote by the same post: 'My Uncle received me with great kindness, and has proposed everything I could reasonably expect'. His own mother, he adds, 'is to give us the carriage'.[2]

Mr. and Mrs. Matcham gave more than a carriage to the young couple: on the day before George's wedding (19 February 1817) they settled on him an estate at Handcross, adjoining but separate from Ashfold, called 'Hoadlands', three-quarters of which was woodland but which included a residential cottage, where the family stayed during subsequent visits to Sussex.

Earl Nelson was as good as his word, and performed the marriage so cordially promoted by all parties on Thursday, 20 February 1817 at the parish church of the bride, All Saints, Whiteparish. The *Salisbury and Winchester Journal* for 24 February reported the event: 'On Thursday last was married at Whiteparish, in this county by his Uncle, the Right Hon. and Revd. Earl Nelson, George Matcham jun. eldest son of George Matcham, Esq. of Ashfold Lodge, Sussex, to Miss Harriet Eyre, eldest daughter of the late William Eyre, Esq. of New House.'[3]

Not content with uniting them himself, the Earl abandoned 'Trafalgar' to the young couple for the first year of their marriage. He was seldom resident there as yet, and while Mrs. Eyre still occupied New House with her younger daughters, Charlotte and Julia, Trafalgar became the young Matchams home.

These events and the consequent break-up of the Ashfold household

<hr />

[1] Eyre-Matcham Papers.   [2] Ibid.
[3] *Salisbury and Winchester Journal*, 24 Feb. 1817.

explain Horatia's own departure for Norfolk at the very time of 'young' George's marriage. Though she was later invited to Trafalgar, her presence at the Matcham marriage is unlikely; the Earl could hardly have welcomed it at the time. His own very marked change towards his sisters' families, from whom he had been virtually estranged for years thanks to the machinations of Lady Hamilton, was clearly imputable in part to her death, but he showed no inclination, then or later, to espouse her daughter's cause. By February Horatia had left to join the Boltons, and although she remained in close touch with the Matchams and visited them on their annual returns to England, for the next seventeen years Norfolk was her home.

CHAPTER XVI

NORFOLK ROOTS

MANY changes had taken place in the Bolton family since the Christmas of 1811 when Horatia last visited them for the marriage of her cousin Eliza to Henry Girdlestone at Bradenham Hall. The new home, so much coveted by poor Mrs. Bolton, hardly survived her death; after many indecisive attempts to keep it going without her vital presence Mr. Bolton sold it early in 1815 and moved to Burnham Market. There the family was back on home ground. Nelson's father had been incumbent there (jointly with Burnham Thorpe) and at one time had taken lodgings, close to his church, so as to leave the old rectory at Thorpe to Nelson and his wife during his long inactivity on shore between 1787 and 1793. Burnham Thorpe was only two miles away; Wells was six; Brancaster, where the Revd. William Bolton and his family still lived, was only four. The family roots were deep, and the faces they passed in the village and in the lanes about were those of friends, or the children of friends.

The house where the Boltons settled—a handsome, rambling Queen Anne house behind high walls opposite the church—was recommended to them by friends; it was known at that time as 'Burnham Polsted House', and pleased them at once. Tom Bolton, writing to his cousin George Matcham in May 1815 from Plymouth, said his sister Anne (whose health continued to give the family much anxiety) liked the 'new house very much indeed'. Susanna was now her father's housekeeper; capable as ever she acted as his amanuensis, accountant, and shrewd business confident. Mrs. Bolton had said of Susanna years before when she had broken her right arm in a fall from a horse: 'Susanna can do more with one arm than most people do with two', and she had always admired her level-headed daughter. But Susanna lacked some of her mother's warmth of heart, and it was doubtful whether the home would ever be the same without Mrs. Bolton. Sharing it at the time of Horatia's arrival were Anne, her former closest friend, Lady Bolton and her little girls. (Her husband's name remained on the Navy Lists until 1829, but he was virtually retired.) Emma Horatia had now a little sister, Mary Ann, born 1 July 1813, and in the July following Horatia's arrival at Burnham a third daughter was born to Lady Bolton, Ellen Catherine, who in later years married a Girdlestone cousin—Horatio—one of Eliza and Henry's numerous progeny. The Girdlestones were living at Norwich in 1817 where Henry was curate and later rector of the parish of Colton St. Andrews. Nearest to Horatia in age was Caroline Peirson, only a year her senior, who was a frequent visitor at her grandfather's rectory at Brancaster, and with whom she soon re-established the fond relationship of their childhood.

Burnham Market (the 'mother-parish' of the seven Burnhams) was the principal market town in the area. Its tree-lined, straggling main street stretching from the church of Burnham Ulph at one end to Burnham Westgate at the other, was bordered along its whole length by dignified Queen Anne and Georgian houses, whose pillared porticos, bow-windowed fronts, high-shouldered roofs and clustered chimney-stacks, presented every variety of architectural style within the period. Between the lanterned doorways, the chain-posts and the small cobbles of the side-walks linking the solid gentlemen's houses, the small shop-fronts were squeezed—the apothecary's, the cobbler's, the saddler's, the herbalist's— while the main food purveyors were stall-holders on the green which ran down the centre of the street and where regular markets were held two days a week. The Boltons' house, a solid structure dating from 1700, stood at the Westgate end of the town, overlooking St. Mary's Church. It had both a secluded and a dominant position, being the first (or last) house in the town and lying back from the road behind high walls. Access to it was through a gate in the side. At the rear was a long garden shaded by lime-trees, wth a giant mulberry-tree in the centre of its lawn. French-windows gave access to the two ground-floor parlours, the modest entrance-hall, and the graceful staircase beyond. Upstairs, the rooms were oak-panelled and beamed, with lattice-windows overlooking the roofs of cottages which bordered the highway in those days. Horatia's room (called the 'Nelson Room' since that time) looked out directly towards the tower of St. Mary's Church. Here were all the elements of home, such as Horatia had already found at Ashfold.

Society was not lacking at Burnham, especially to the relations of Lord Nelson. Besides such old family friends as the Revd. Dixon Hoste, Rector of nearby Holkham, whose younger son, Sir William, had been one of Nelson's *Agamemnon* midshipmen, and whose nephew Derick owned the land round Burnham, there was the family of Sir Mordaunt Martin at Burnham Polsted Hall, just across the green from the Boltons. Sir Mordaunt, a retired Admiralty Court Judge of Jamaica, an old friend of the Nelson family (particularly of the Matchams who had been his neighbours at Barton Broad early in their marriage) was Lord of the Manor of Burnham. With the Matchams he had kept up a correspondence after their move to Bath and his lively letters show how closely he followed the family's rise to fame and how he celebrated, almost with a personal pride, every victory of Nelson's, not only with verbal fireworks, but with bonfires and banquets on the green at Burnham, and in the best parlour of the 'Pitt Arms', the main hostelry in the place. (The 'Pitt Arms', incidentally, was not called after England's Prime Minister, but after the local architect, Thomas Pitt, who built the Hall into which Sir Mordaunt moved in 1780). Sir Mordaunt was a man of immense patriotism and benevolence, of strict integrity and practical good-sense. A keen agriculturist, it was he who introduced potatoes into Norfolk and modern farming methods on his estates. Sir Mordaunt had married a daughter of the former Rector of Burnham, Dorothea Everilda Smith, by whom he had an only son and six daughters. Dorothea's sister Susanna had married the Revd. John Glasse, her father's curate, and *her* son, another Revd. John Glasse, married his cousin, Anna Maria Martin, one of the daughters of Sir Mordaunt and Dorothea. There was thus a double family link between the Martins and the Glasses which ultimately provoked a family tragedy. When Sir Mordaunt died in 1815, just before Horatia's arrival on the scene, his son Roger, who had spent many years in India, soon achieved notoriety of his own by the open scandal of his life, in which his cousin, the upright and lovable rector of Burnham, the Revd. John Glasse, became tragically involved. The rector and his family lived next door to the Boltons, at Burnham House, and were on the best of terms with them, both as neighbours and parishioners. Mr. Bolton acted as his rector's 'Warden' (always a personal choice of the rector) and Mr. Glasse's concern for the new addition to his neighbours' family is early apparent in his preparation of Horatia for Confirmation. Horatia's last years under Lady Hamilton's care were hardly conducive to such an event, and even at the Matchams their frequent absences abroad delayed it further. A memento of the occasion finally celebrated at Burnham has been preserved; a book given to Horatia by Mr. Glasse, which he inscribed for her:

> Horatia Nelson Nelson,
> from her
> Very sincere friend
> John Glasse,
> Burnham
> March 16th
> 1817

The title of the book was:

A Short & Plain Instruction
for
The Better Understanding of the Lord's Supper
Necessary Preparation Required for the benefit of
Young Communicants
1815 [1]

Like the majority of the young women of her time, Horatia kept a
Day-book of 'Private Thoughts'. One such which has been preserved,
dating from 1818, shows how the religious training of Mr. Glasse was
directing her mind. Not that these pages hold anything original, either in
expression or thought; the rhetoric of the period in which they are expressed prevents a more personal note being struck, but what does emerge
is the freshness of the mind they mirror, the earnestness of the young
writer's intention. Writing on 'The Death of a Friend' and wondering
whether, by showing 'the grief we feel' we are not 'offending our Maker'
and 'doubting the truth of his divine word which promises a reunion
with the objects of our affection in another and a better World than this,
provided we walk in his paths', Horatia prays:

Forgive us Oh! Lord, forgive the childish regrets this temporary parting occasions. Grant *me* to be as good, as pure, as truly religious as she was and (when it is
thy Will to take me to thyself) to be as well prepared as she appeared to be, for
no joys this world can give are worthy to be put in Competition with thy Kingdom. Thou knowest what is best for me and if it be thy Will that I should continue here let me always walk in thy ways and let my deathbed be cheered with
the hopes which thy infinite Mercy has held forth. Signed: Horatia Nelson Oct^b
27th 1818. [2]

Mr. and Mrs. Glasse had two sons then at the University, William
and Mordaunt, and in their absence had living with them the rector's
curate, Robert Ferrier Blake, a young man from the other side of Norfolk,
who appears to have lost no time in falling in love with Horatia. Considering Horatia's growing beauty and the daily proximity in which the
young people lived this was not surprising. What is surprising is that
Horatia immediately accepted Robert Blake, and more surprising still
considering her youth (she was only sixteen and a half) and the little time
she had been in Norfolk, was the consent the Boltons gave to the engagement. The Matchams, who went abroad again in August, also gave theirs,

[1] By courtesy of Marshal of the R.A.F. Sir William Dickson, great grandson of
Horatia Nelson.
[2] NMM/NWD/9594/34.

and appeared indeed not to favour a long engagement for Horatia. In the family view an early 'establishment' for her was desirable. Her circumstances were not ordinary: though she was the acknowledged daughter of the national hero, her birth was nevertheless illegitimate, and her relatives and friends could not aspire to a very advantageous 'settlement' in life for her. Mr. Blake offered her with his devotion the 'shelter' of his 'cloth', and it was too good an offer to turn down. What Horatia really felt in the affair was not apparent (possibly not even to herself) until later.

Meanwhile she was quick to announce the event to her friends. On receipt of the news Mr. Newcomb, back in London, wrote to her on 28 July 1817:

You talk, my dear friend, about changing your name, I hope in God it will be to your advantage, for heavens' sake, do not be in too great haste, consider well before you give yourself away, not that I have the least doubt but your own good sense and discretion will enable you to make a good and deserving choice. I pray pardon, but your welfare is so near to my heart I cannot forbear saying thus much.[1]

From Paris, where the Matchams settled until the following May, Kitty Matcham wrote to her new sister-in-law, Mrs. George, on 30 October:

We had a letter from Burnham last week, but no mention of any wedding being fixed on. Horatia has paid another visit to Mr. Blake's family and is still better pleased with them. I wish that match was concluded as they appear to gain nothing by waiting. I hope *nothing* will be lost—at present the love is lasting we are informed, and I trust it may continue, but you know delays are dangerous.[2]

Mr. Blake's financial situation, however, apparently made a long engagement necessary. He was twenty-eight and had as yet no living. Ordained deacon in November 1815 and priest in November 1816, he had been Mr. Glasse's curate since November 1815, earning the customary pittance of the curates of the time. Though it would appear from Kitty Matcham's letter that Horatia had already been received by the Blake family, the result of this second visit seems to have brought home to them the desirability of putting off the marriage until their son was in a better position to support a wife. This, at any rate, was the tenour of a letter Horatia, showing considerable spirit in a girl of sixteen, sent to her guardian Mr. Rose at the time asking him to procure Mr. Blake some preferment, or the small government pension for herself that had already been mooted. On receiving her letter, Mr. Rose wrote to the Prime Minister:

[1] Ibid.   [2] Eyre-Matcham Papers.

Mudiford, October 29th
1817

My dear Lord,—I am most deeply concerned at the situation of the writer of
the enclosure recommended to my best attention by the Hero in parting from
him when he last sailed from Spithead (at which time I had never seen her)
and strongly recommended to his Country in his very last moments. She will
not have wherewithal to buy Cloathes on the death of Mr. Matcham. She is, it
seems, engaged to be married to the gentleman she mentions, but his friends
refuse their consent unless some modest preferment can be procured for him;
he is now a Curate. Do you think the Chancellor could be moved for him?
supposing a Pension of £200 a year be quite impossible.[1]

As in 1815, Mr. Rose's application achieved nothing except some
expressions of official sympathy. It was, in the event, Mr. Rose's last act
of kindness for his young ward; he died the next year without having
secured for her the long sought-after pension, and his death was a severe
loss to her.

Meanwhile the engagement held, and the young couple, undaunted
by the delays of government, derived what comfort they could from the
close neighbourliness in which they lived, and sent a thousand hopes and
speechless messages every day over the high flint and brick wall dividing
their homes.

The curate's parochial duties lay mainly with the parish of Burnham
Norton, one mile out of Burnham Market, whose ninth century church
of St. Margaret was the oldest of the Burnham group of seven parishes,
and in many ways the one with most character. Its round Saxon tower of
flint and stone is a local landmark still, and the interior preserves an
impression of undisturbed antiquity. In the registers, Mr. Blake's many
entries witness to his busy ministry there. While an occasional supplementary fee came his way in taking duty at Brancaster or Deepdale, the
living for which he and Horatia waited to advance their prospects did not
come.

The Matchams showed little inclination to return to England, and
indeed were seriously contemplating leaving England for good. The
family's frequent letters home showed how settled they were in the
Paris of the Restoration, which offered so many attractions to the throng
of English tourists. Under the guidance and help of their old friends,
General Blanckley and his family, who lived there much like Thackeray's
old Anglo-Indians on their half-pay, the Matchams found a house on the
outskirts of Paris at Boulogne-sur-Seine, where for a rent of £116 a year

[1] Gamlin, ii, 245.

they lived in style. It was, young Eliza Matcham wrote home on 11 September 1817, 'so immense that it quite resembles a Mrs. Radcliffe House with immense Coach House and Stabling'. A carriage to take the family into Paris could be hired for £5 a week, and allowed them to visit the theatre, the opera, the great picture 'Gallery', the parks, the site of the Bastille, the palaces at St. Germain and St. Cloud; and to 'return home of an evening with a relish for a comfortable dinner and quiet evening'. In company with one of the Blanckley girls, Horatia and Susan Matcham attended a weekly boarding-school where they found themselves 'very comfortable'.[1]

The frequent mention of the Blanckleys, the General (a former consul-general at Algiers), his wife, their son and daughters, throughout the Matchams' travels, their irruption in varying countries and places where-ever the Matchams happened to be, was eventually explained by the growing romance between Harriet Matcham and Captain Edward Blanckley, R.N., whose marriage in Naples in April 1819 only shortly preceded the marriages of Kitty and Eliza. Travelling about Europe with a family of charming daughters, Mr. and Mrs. Matcham could not expect less, or hope for more.

In May 1818, after a visit from young George and his wife, the Matcham party left Paris for Italy, arriving in Rome 'particularly fortunately on Horace's birthday' (21 June), where the heat was so excessive that they fled to Naples. There they settled until the following May in a house overlooking the bay and in full view of Vesuvius. With match-making in the air, the travellers were concerned at the irregular posts reaching them from England and were particularly anxious for news of Horatia. 'From Norfolk we never hear', wrote Kitty from Naples on 14 July 1818, 'but perhaps our letters miscarry. Do you know whether Horatia is likely to be married this year?'[2]

Horatia's intentions were evidently unchanged, as she wrote to her friend Mr. Newcomb, for he answered her on 11 July (1818), 'It gives me no small pleasure to perceive by the tenor of your letter that you were still in the same mind on that most important subject, Matrimony, and that your expectations of happiness were not lessened by your more perfect knowledge of him who I hope will by and by be all the world to you'.[3]

Questioned by his family about Horatia's matrimonial plans, George Matcham arranged a meeting with her during that August when he and his young wife had occasion to visit Ashfold. They were about to set-up house-keeping on their own at last, had acquired a house near Romsey

[1] Eyre-Matcham Papers.   [2] Ibid.   [3] NMM/NWD/9594/34.

(Woolley House) and were urged by Mrs. Matcham to fetch 'any articles remaining at the Farm' as Ashfold was still called. It would seem that Horatia joined them there escorted by Tom Bolton, and discussed her future plans with her cousins. She also took the opportunity to pack up the books and music and other few possessions she had left there, putting them aside until such time as she was married, when George undertook to have them sent to her.

While in London Horatia stayed with the Salters in the Strand. It seemed an appropriate time to retrieve the rest of her small patrimony, and she made a further application to Alderman Smith. His first reaction was to give it her, and he wrote a letter to that effect, which she acknowledged rather breathlessly on 21 October 1818:

My dear Sir, I received your kind letter last week and have availed myself of your kindness in offering to give those things you had of mine to any one I may appoint. Mr. Salter has some things he is going to forward to me and I should feel very grateful if you will give them to him when he apply's believe me I shall never forget the kindness I have experienced from both yourself and Mrs. Smith to whom I beg to be most kindly remembered and also to all your family although I greatly fear your Eldest daughter has forgot her old playfellow. Pray accept my sincere acknowledgements for your unmerited kindness and believe me Yours obliged Horatia N. Nelson.[1]

But reconsidering his rights in the matter Alderman Smith decided that he must have a security for the return of the articles and dashed Horatia's hopes once again: 'I greatly regret', she wrote him, 'you see the necessity of a security for the China. My Uncle Matcham is abroad therefore he could not enter into any for me . . . from him and from Lady Hamilton and Mr. Salter I always understood that on my coming of age they were to be delivered to me'.[2]

Mr. Newcomb, ever on the pounce for a crumb of news, wrote to enquire about the trip to London and Horatia's immediate plans on 7 September 1818: 'When are we to have the pleasure of hearing from you, I hope soon. I can assure you we are very anxious to learn the particulars of your voyage and journey to London (and else where) I trust Mr. & Mrs. Matcham, yourself, and all the family are well, be pleased to remember us most kindly to them all.'

A month later Mr. Newcomb was asking if there

were any chance of seeing you in Town this winter? or have you made up your mind to reside entirely and exclusively in the Country, but I [suppose] that will depend *upon circumstances*. How long is it your intention to continue your old

---

[1] Ibid.   [2] Ibid.

signature, I beg pardon, but when I should like to know, is it to be superseded for *another*? You must forgive my curiosity, but as yet I remain in ignorance of the *name* you are likely to assume.[1]

Horatia's reluctance to name her fiancé to Mr. Newcomb may have been due to a fairly natural disinclination to feed his curiosity, but it could also argue a want of enthusiasm on her part for the approaching event. As the weeks passed, indeed, it became clear that she was in a state of considerable uncertainty about almost everything. Tom Bolton wrote on her behalf to 'young' George on 18 November 1818: 'Horatia is not going to marry immediately, but probably will take place early in the spring as Mr. Blake gives up his curacies here at Xmas when it will be quite time enough for her music and books to be sent'. On his own matrimonial disinclinations Tom gave his cousin a piquant commentary: 'I probably might have visited Trafalgar this summer', he admitted, 'but my Uncle so pesters me and all around him with matrimonial schemes and speculations that I am determined to avoid it'.[2] So successful had the Earl been in promoting the marriage of one nephew that he was even then busily plotting to ensnare the other, and for all the resistance he put up Tom Bolton did in due course, and to his lasting happiness, fall a victim to his uncle's 'matrimonial schemes'.

To the Earl, the architect of the Eyre–Matcham marriage, 'great satisfaction' was indeed given by the birth of the young couple's son (christened Horatio Nelson Eyre) at Woolley House on 16 April 1819. The event preceded by only a few days another family celebration, the marriage of Harriet Matcham to Captain Edward Blanckley at Naples on 24 April 1819. Leaving her there (where her husband was temporarily stationed) the Matchams set off by sea for Marseilles and arrived in happy time to receive the news of their grandchild's birth. Kitty Matcham wrote to her brother from there:

My dear George—We were made very happy yesterday by the arrival of a Letter from Harriet containing a copy of yrs which brought the welcome intelligence of dear Mrs. Geo: safe confinement . . . Pray present our hearty congratulations to your dear wife upon this event and say Papa ordered a couple of Bottles of Champagne on receiving the news—it happened so fortunately to arrive at dinner time.[3]

Harriet Matcham's marriage started a succession of other marriages, some of which were directly the outcome of her own.

As to Horatia Nelson's immediate prospects, Mr. Blake could not leave

---

[1] Ibid.   [2] Eyre-Matcham Papers.   [3] Ibid.

Burnham in pursuit of preferment till his curacies had been filled; and this was dependent on the ordination of his successor, Philip Ward, which took place on 8 November 1818 at the church of St. Martin-at-Tours-at-Palace in Norwich. Philip Ward, as the registers of Burnham Norton Church attest, had been taking the occasional service there since July; he was, therefore, already known to Mr. Glasse, and to the Boltons as well, before he officially took up his duties at Burnham at the end of the year.

How far his appointment affected Horatia's engagement to Mr. Blake is difficult to determine. Did Mr. Blake leave Burnham because of Philip Ward, or because there already existed differences between him and Horatia? At all events, by the spring of 1819 the engagement was definitely broken off, and her aunt Matcham informed of it. Mrs. Matcham, who reached Paris in June, found the news awaiting her there and wrote to her son George on the 22nd:

We are very much concerned to hear that the match is broken off between Horatia and Mr. Blake. A letter we received here from her, mentions his bad temper to be the only reason, and that it has the full concurrence of all her friends [i.e. the Boltons]. Poor, dear Girl, her lot in life I fear will not be so quiet as we could have wished, and she is very young, and I am sure there is no fault in her, only a few childish foibles, which I daresay time has remedied.[1]

If it was for Philip Ward that Horatia threw over Mr. Blake she certainly did not act in haste. Perhaps she had learnt her lesson: it was three years before she got engaged again. Mr. Blake, whether the victim of his own bad temper or of his rival's superior charms, left Burnham early in 1819 to be curate of Bradfield St. Giles, where in 1820 he was appointed rector.

---

[1] Ibid.

CHAPTER XVII

'ADMIRED HORATIA'

PHILIP WARD, a graduate of Trinity College Oxford, came to Burnham with glowing testimonials. He had previously spent a year in the parish of his uncle, the Revd. Philip Smyth, at Worthen in the diocese of Hereford, where his conduct was 'highly approved'. Ordained deacon on 8 November 1818 at Norwich, his Ordination as priest followed in November 1819 when his sponsors were the three Burnham Rectors who had come to know him in the past year, and who vouched for his learning and good behaviour.

Born in 1795 at Trunch, near North Walsham, of which parish his father and grandfather were in turn incumbents, he came of a line of clergy on both sides of the family. The Wards were of Norman origin, and they migrated from Derbyshire to Norfolk in the early eighteenth century. Philip's father, the second Marmaduke Ward, married Eleanor, daughter and heiress of Philip Smyth of Gimmingham Hall, a manor of great antiquity, once in the occupation of John O'Gaunt. As the Smythes were descendants of William of Wykeham they could claim the privilege of 'Founder's Kin' and send their sons to Winchester. There Philip Ward and his two brothers, William and James, were accordingly sent in 1804. Philip entered Trinity College in January 1813 and took his B.A. degree in 1817.

His sponsors were right in speaking of his learning; he was, both by taste and profession, a scholar, and widely enough read to educate his own sons in due course, and prepare them without other schooling for the university and other professional careers. He was a man of sensitive feelings, a lover of poetry, and capable of expressing himself in pleasant and witty verse. In addition he was good looking (a family trait for his three sisters were known as the 'Norfolk Graces') which no doubt helped to promote his cause with Horatia Nelson. Time and experience were to develop his naturally sympathetic and affectionate nature, and those generous traits that made him universally respected. Philip lodged, like his predecessor at Burnham, with his rector Mr. Glasse, in the house next to the Boltons.

With his advent the whole tone and tempo of Horatia's life seem to have become enlivened; the reports of her doings are more numerous, the impact she made on people and the admiration she aroused more evident; and, as the natural consequence of all this, her happiness increased —of this she made no secret. Mrs. Matcham, writing from Paris to her son George in November 1819 commented: 'Horatia N. writes me word she never was so happy as at present; whether there is another Lover in the way I know not, but should think some other motive than the one assigned must exist for that match being off. From Mr. Bathurst, the Bishop's son, we find it was entirely on her side'.[1] Certainly the verses addressed to Horatia in May 1819 (purporting to be written by a visiting 'Miniature Painter') are evidence of the flowering of her beauty and of her spirits, and seem to argue considerable relief at the breaking-off of her engagement. It is evident that the writer of the verses knew something more about Horatia than her looks, for he quotes her favourite books, and is struck by her resemblance to her famous father. The verses were addressed:

Burnham—May the 31st 1819

Miss Horatia Nelson
Burnham.
An humble address from a Miniature painter to Miss Horatia Nelson.

> Fair Lady, this address forgive,
> From one who aims by art to live
> a Painter of the human face
> In trait expression form, and grace,
> Your patronage most humbly prays
> For Miniatures, while here he stays—
> Grant him with skilful hand to trace
> The features of your charming face
> Whether in serious mood or gay;
> The tints he'll delicately lay,
> And you'll appear, as best you chuse (sic)
> The Tragic, or the Comic Muse—
> Whether you love the quizzing mood
> Of which each Dandy is the food,
> Or dwell entranc'd on some sweet Book,
> In Marmion, or Lalla Rookh,
> And love to read of gallant Knight
> For damsel fair impell'd to fight—
> A pair whom nought but death can part,

[1] Eyre-Matcham Papers.

His prize her smile—her heav'n his heart—
But pardon, Lady fair, these lines
In which no muse poetic shines.
But sh^d thy features once impart
The flame of glory to my heart,
In tints and lines divine I'll trace
TH' expression of thy angel face—
The painter from thy deathless name
Will reap an everlasting fame—

                                    Anon[1]

The continuance of this happy state of things appears from further verses addressed to her in the following spring on the occasion of her first visit to Wells, the nearby and then fashionable seaside resort. Not since her childhood, when visiting Brancaster with Lady Hamilton had Horatia been at the sea. The genuine stir her appearance made at the theatre there can be seen under all the elegant bombast of the lines; signed 'Henri', they may well have been the offering of her cousin Henry Girdlestone (a native of Wells), who had a great admiration and affection for her. The verses, addressed to 'Miss Nelson', were left at her lodgings 'at Mr. Webber's, Wells'.

To Miss Nelson on her Visit to Wells
Welcome admired Horatia, to our Wells—
Thou pride of Burnham, and thou Belle of Belles!
Dull is that breast, that does not sigh for thee—
To love thee is but sensibility!
Oh for the Poets pen, the Muse's fire,
To say how much, how deeply I admire
Thy looks enchanting and thy graceful mien
By none with justice told, or safely seen—
In Wells, or Burnham, or where'er you rove,
The Graces follow with the God of LOVE—
With you in vain for Fame a FISHER tries,[2]
You conq'ring win all hearts, and charm all eyes—
You steal attention from the Actor's skill,
The play forgot, you captivate the will—
In you transcendently becoming shine
The genuine virtues of the Nelson line!

[1] NMM/NWD/9594/27.
[2] Fisher was the theatrical manager responsible for the seasonal productions in Norfolk.

Spirit with ease and gaiety combin'd—
The feeling heart with the unconquered mind,
Great Nelson prostrate laid a world of foes—
Thy charms have prostrate laid a world of BEAUX!

Henri [1]

Wells, May 11th 1820

The Bolton family seems to have returned to Wells again later in the summer; its distance of only six miles from Burnham made it an easily accessible as well as healthy resort, and the continued delicacy of Anne and the needs of Lady Bolton's growing little girls made it an obvious choice. During her stay at Wells in July or August Horatia made acquaintance with a young lady from Norwich, who maintained some correspondence with her over the next couple of years. The letters tell us something about Horatia, though they tell us yet more about the writer, whose affectation of learning, worldly wisdom, and superior manners, recall Jane Austen's Mrs. Elton in *Emma*. The first letter comments on the opening of the trial of Queen Caroline which began on 17 August 1820. It is signed simply 'Marianna', without surname or address.

In conjunction with your wish and also in observance of the promise I tacitly made when we parted, je mis la plume à la main . . . Norwich, since, our return, has been most dull and monotonous . . . from the majority of the noblesse being absent and likely so to continue whilst they can receive much enjoyment and advantage from the purer and more healthful breezes sent from Neptune's noble and expansive ocean, and participate in those gaities and new born pleasures for which a watering place is so justly celebrated. I presume the distance of six miles which Burnham is to Wells, has neither damped nor quelled the spirit and independence of mind you manifested when you entered upon and kept up a political debate and inquiry with Mr. Bloom . . . The Queen has nevertheless my warmest wishes for a full acquittal of all the charges of which she stands so deeply arraigned.

Although my acquaintance with you is but of short duration to sanction the liberty of 'pointing a moral', yet the interest and friendship I feel for you you will, from the goodness of your nature pardon such a presumption. Namely the inclination and desire you but too strongly manifested in playing off practical jokes; and although done in the gaité de coeur and height of youthful, buoyant spirits, whereby no anticipation of anger or mischief could arise, yet, 'great events may from trivial causes spring'; so much so as to displease and conciliate ill-will where by observing the line of demarkation deference to age and those customs and rites of society point out and prescribe, might by such especial observance have won the affection and excited those sentiments which the knowledge of your many estimable qualities have fully entitled you to receive

[1] NMM/NWD/9594/1-5.

17

and ever to command. What I have said is not the Chimera of the day nor the
fastidiousness attendant on the sincerity of a few years, but the result of reasoning
cool and dispassionate which an intercourse and insight into the world allow
me to offer and suggest for your attention. And although it may come within
the air and fashion of a rebuke, yet I feel assured you will neither consider it as
such, but give to its true and only interpretation—*a little friendly advice*—
administered by the hand of one in whose breast you have awakened every lively
sentiment which absence can neither depress nor yield to its sometimes too force-
ful instrument of erasement! Charlotte begs to unite with me in most affectionate regards. to Mr. and the Miss Boltons present our best compliments, also to
Sir William, Lady and Miss Emma Bolton when you see them. Marianna.[1]

There is no doubt that in the Boltons' entourage—as Marianne would
have spoken of their circle—Horatia was evolving from the shrinking
girl at Calais into a young woman of character, capable of speaking her
mind. At a time when a broken-off engagement was judged as the action
of a 'jilt', Horatia had the courage to go through with it. That her family
did not condemn her is evident from Mrs. Matcham's comments.

The Matchams were again settled in Paris.

Apart from Mr. Matcham's business enterprises (export of fruit, olive-
oil and wines from France and Spain) there was another matter of interest
to detain them there. This was the prospective marriage of Kitty to a
naval friend of Captain Blanckley's, Lt. John Bendyshe, whose introduction to the family Mrs. Matcham joyfully reported to George in July
(1820) as news which

will give you as much pleasure as it does us. Our dear Kate is going to be
married to a young man who appears worthy of her, which is saying a great deal
for him. He made his bow only yesterday. He is the son of Mr. Bendyshe, who
has good estates in Cambridgeshire . . . Mr. & Mrs. Blanckley have known him
for years and say a better creature never lived. Thank God, our dear Girl has the
prospect of being as happy as she deserves to be.[2]

The marriage took place at the British Embassy on 10 August 1820. A
comment upon this, and on the family situation generally, has been preserved in a letter from the bride's young brother Horace (Horatio Nelson,
Lady Hamilton's godson), aged seventeen at the time. The feebleness of
the writing, and Horace's references to his health, are a reminder that
the poor boy had been an invalid for years; he died shortly after their
return to England in 1821.

Dated 21 August 1820, his letter reads:

[1] NMM/NWD/9594/34.   [2] Eyre-Matcham Papers.

I hope my Dear George you will excuse me for not writing to you before . . . you will have had the whole account of Kitty's wedding I will therefore not trouble you with an unnecessary detail. I need only say she was in excellent spirits when she took leave of us, Kitty offered to take me with them [to Switzerland] if Papa and Mama would have spared me but they did not like to trust me out of their sight. I should have liked it above all things but perhaps after all it is better I did not go for being now under the care of Dr. Marshall who pretends he can cure me it would not have been fair to have quitted him. As to myself, I shall be very thankful if I grow no worse but enough of that—We were delighted to hear of the birth of your daughter [Catherine Eyre Matcham, born 2 August 1820] and should like to see your young gentleman and lady—perhaps we shall pay you a visit next summer.[1]

The Matchams' longed-for return took place in 1821. It followed closely upon other family matters of importance whose effects were to reunite once more the widely-scattered branches of the Nelson family.

Earl Nelson had not relinquished his match-making plans for his nephew (and heir) Tom Bolton, however much the latter may have hoped to elude them. Tom was making himself a figure of fun to the rest of the family, taken up as the older generations were with matrimonial schemes to benefit the younger. 'Why doth not Tom marry?' his uncle Matcham had written from Naples on 8 February 1819. 'Years roll and he should not wait for the application of Old Bachelor.' The equal pressure now brought to bear by George Matcham junior, in conjunction with the Earl's renewed attack, brought about the desired result in February 1821, when Tom, after several visits to Trafalgar and Woolley, married Frances Elizabeth Eyre, the cousin of Harriet, George's wife, and sole heiress to the Brickworth and Landford estates neighbouring Trafalgar. The event was celebrated by his brother-in-law Sir William Bolton, in punning rhymes upon his fiancées's name.

> In classic times when Ovid strung his lyre
> To tell how Cephalus sought his lovely Air
> (For we, like jealous Procris think 'tis clear
> In 'Aura' more was meant than met the ear)
> With numbers soft, melodious, refin'd,
> He charms the sense, & lures the willing mind.
> The gallant youth displays in Attic grove
> And o'er the scene unfolds the purple light of love.
> A modern Cephalus, remote from town,
> With 'Aura Veni' quick his game brings down,
> No zephyr here eludes his soft embrace

[1] Ibid.

But 'solid flesh' attracts him face to face,
Wash'd in Pactolus stream her Robes unfold
And crush the puny youth with solid gold.
To tell this tale some Norfolk Naso starts
Skilled as he thinks in poetry and arts,
And wends his heavy flight to God knows where
To paint the loves of 'Bolton' and 'Miss Eyre'.
In vain the luckless wight his Muse uprears
His pinions sink, he flounders midst the 'spheres',
In meagre impotence his doggerel drags along,
And to *his subject* kindly suits his *Song*.[1]

As with George Matcham, the Earl officiated at his nephew's wedding, which took place at the bride's parish church of St. Andrew's, Landford. Sir William Bolton, cousin and brother-in-law of the groom, was best man. Miss Eyre returned with her husband to Landford House, a massive red-brick Carolingian Mansion adjoining the church, and so began what proved to be a supremely happy union. Tom was understandably missed by the family at Burnham, where his kindness to his sisters, nieces and cousins—and especially Horatia—had been so much valued.

Horatia's own prospects had, however, by that time, taken a decisive, and equally happy turn, her engagement to Philip Ward being by then an open secret. From her seaside acquaintance, Marianna, Horatia received a bouquet of mixed metaphors:

You say 'I suppose you have heard of me lately', could I but otherwise hear when so interesting a subject as Monsieur Cupid weaves and introduces the theme? May the Voyage which you have in perspective be replete with the radiant amber smiles and tints which a happy sufficiency fails not to produce . . . I met Miss Ward [2] the other evening at a rout, when we mechanically as it were aspirated your name, which she did I assure you with no small degree of pleasure. She requested me to say when I wrote to you, not only to present her best respects but that she proposed addressing you by letter, which intention, I assured her would be received with courtesy and satisfaction.[3]

The marriage of Tom Bolton and his establishment in Wiltshire gave him at last the position that his fond mother had dreamt of since his boyhood. Characteristically, he made others benefit by his good fortune. Together with Sir William Bolton, he assumed the trusteeship of Horatia's affairs, the death of Mr. Rose and the continued absence of Mr. Matcham abroad leaving her without advisers on the investment of her small capital. This Tom conscientiously undertook. He made a material

---

[1] *Norfolk Chronicle.*   [2] Eleanor, Philip Ward's sister.
[3] NMM/NWD/9594/34.

contribution, moreover, to Horatia's prospects, by appointing Philip Ward his honorary chaplain, a post that carried a salary and called for a minimum of duties. Horatia's prospects as 1821 advanced, therefore, were better than ever in her life. On his side, Philip was not without prospects either as heir to his mother's capital (she herself being co-heiress with her sister to the Gimmingham estate). The consent of Hora-tia's family to her engagement was secured in the summer of 1821, the presence of the Matchams in England at the time allowing them to judge of the situation for themselves and to confirm the good opinion of Philip Ward already formed by the Boltons. Though the Matchams' chief objective and pleasure in returning to England was to visit George in his new home, they rented a furnished house in London as had become their custom, as a central situation for family reunions. For Horatia the opportunity to renew relations with her unmarried girl cousins, Horatia and Susan Matcham in particular, led to a lasting affection between them.

A deep shadow was cast over the Matchams' return after three years by the deterioration in Horace's condition. Pessimistic though Horace himself appears to have been about Dr. Marshall's treatment in Paris, the tragic outcome was evidently not expected so soon. He died on 11 October in London of 'an enlargement of the heart',[1] and was buried at Slaugham in the grave of his brother Frank, whose death had saddened the family's first summer at Ashfold in 1808. No wonder that after the loss of Horace Mrs. Matcham said she could no longer 'bear the thought of Ashfold' and urged her husband to dispose of the place for good. The fact that young George Matcham and his wife were about to take posses-sion of Newhouse, her father's home, was another factor, and Mr. Matcham decided that when his foreign commitments permitted him to live permanently in England again he would settle near his son. The sale of Ashfold, and even the sale of their previous home in Bath which had hung fire all these years, kept the Matchams in England till the mid-summer of 1822, until after Horatia's marriage.

The anticipation of this event was made the object of further 'badin-age' by Horatia's seaside acquaintance, Marianna, who wrote to her on 11 December 1821: 'Apropos of Cupid's procedures and Hymen's silken, and more fastening bands, when am I to offer you ma douce amie my congratulations on so joyful an event? "On dit" you are seen on a Sunday to walk dressed in the neat, sober style of a primitive curate's wife with a bible under one arm and a prayer book under the other, to that Kirk in which the beauty, sublimity and beneficial affects of which

[1] *Gentleman's Magazine*, 1821.

both books treat, are I doubt not properly elucidated and sweetly enforced by him to whom sooner or later you will give the tender name and confiding epithet of husband! To your "Caro Sposo" elect present our best compliments and accept the affectionate regards of Charlotte and of her who subscribes herself, Yrs very sincerely, Marianna.' [1]

Horatia's wedding was arranged for 19 February 1822, three weeks after she had come of age. All her Norfolk kinsfolk rallied. For the occasion her uncle, the Revd. William Bolton, came over from Brancaster to officiate; with him came his daughter Mrs. Peirson and Caroline, who of all Horatia's cousins was the nearest to her in age, and was now chosen to be her bridesmaid. Caroline had grown into a very handsome young woman, with classically regular features. The Bolton family was complete with the possible exception of Tom in Wiltshire with whom, in any case, the honeymoon was to be spent. In addition to Mr. Bolton, there was Sir William and Lady Bolton, their three little girls (always great pets of Horatia's), Susanna and Anne and, if the demands of her ever-increasing family allowed, Eliza and her husband from Norwich. Henry Girdlestone retained into old age a strong affection for Horatia. In the absence abroad with his regiment of Philip's brother Captain James Ward, his sister Eleanor acted as his witness and signed the registers. For the time being, the newly married couple were to make their home with Mr. and Mrs. Glasse, with whom Philip had lodged ever since his arrival at Burnham. While the arrangement saved them the expense of furnishing a home of their own at this stage, it had also the advantage for Horatia of being next door to the Boltons, and for Philip of living 'on his job'. The Glasses' house, moreover, was so roomy and rambling that the young couple could be assured of complete privacy. It still shows signs of having been two houses at one time, before the lower floors were connected by communicating arches. There began a new life for Horatia.

On the morning of 19 February 1822 Horatia walked across the road to Burnham Westgate Church where her uncle, the Revd. William Bolton waited to marry her to Philip Ward. The entry in the church register reads:

1822

Philip Ward, Clerk of this Parish,
Bachelor,
and Horatia Nelson Nelson of this Parish,
Spinster,
were married by Licence on the Nineteenth day of February 1822
By me William Bolton, Officiating Minister

[1] NMM/NWD/9594/34.

Signed   Philip Ward
                                    Horatia Nelson Nelson
In the presence of   Ellen Ward
                                    Caroline Peirson

The event was reported in the *Norfolk Chronicle* for 23 February:

Marriages. Tuesday last, at Burnham, by the Rev. William Bolton, the Rev. Philip Ward, son of the late Rev. Marmaduke Ward, of Trunch, to Horatia Nelson Nelson, adopted daughter of the late Admiral Lord Viscount Nelson."

The marriage was also announced in the *Gentleman's Magazine.*

PART THREE

HORATIA NELSON WARD

CHAPTER XVIII

DOLCE DOMUM

MARRIAGE to a provincial clergyman was not the obvious destiny Horatia's friends would have predicted for her a few years back. Marianna's taunts at her altered demeanour as a curate's betrothed sufficiently betray her friends' awareness of the incongruity of the choice. Horatia's early training and experiences were, indeed, not the ideal preparation for such a lot and had she stayed with the Matchams her 'settlement in life' would doubtless have been different. A 'settlement' like that of her cousins who married naval officers would, on the surface, have appeared the most suitable for her, affording her the life of constant change to which she had been accustomed. Her lively temperament had so far shown little sign of a reflective mind, though she had character and courage in plenty, and considerable intelligence. Yet it might still be doubted whether she had the making of a good clergyman's wife in her. The clergy of the period (to judge not only from the fiction of the day) were not particularly edifying and were either sanctimonious, or worldly and place-seeking (Earl Nelson was a good example of the kind), but the chance that threw Philip Ward in Horatia's way seems to have been singularly fortunate, as he was neither priggish nor subservient and, though he remained poor all his life, he had principles, a lively mind, a good intellect, and, what mattered most to Horatia's happiness—a feeling heart. While it was the man she married, and not his 'cloth', time would bring out the best in him as a clergyman and develop in her the qualities of endurance and sympathy that made of her a good clergyman's wife. It is fair to say that, in all the conflicting factors of her life, the one certain good that befell her was her marriage. Horatia was not only lucky in her husband, but in the love that the children of her marriage brought her.

Passing through London on their way to Wiltshire the bridal couple found the Matchams there and also 'young George', on business at Doctors' Commons.[1] A family reunion obviously took place. To introduce Philip to her family and friends was the first and most natural of Horatia's

---

[1] George Matcham wrote his wife 23 Feb. 1822 of the arrival in town "of Mr. Ward and his bride". Eyre-Matcham Papers.

desires on the occasion. She also called on Alderman Smith to urge once again the return of her family relics. The Smiths lived at that time at Bennet's Hill, Doctors' Commons. She also visited her other old friends, the Salters, prompted in part by the desire, shared by Philip, to meet all those who might possibly be able to furnish clues to her origins. In Horatia, certainly, the wish to solve the mystery of her birth increased tenfold with her marriage. It became one of the constant preoccupations of her life, and grew to prey on her mind with increasing intensity.

Several branches of the Nelson family were settled near Salisbury. At Trafalgar, in the parish of Downton, lived the Earl himself; at Romsey was young George Matcham pending his move the next year to nearby Newhouse; and at Landford Tom Bolton and his bride, Frances Eyre, where Philip and Horatia were invited to spend their honeymoon. Tom Bolton had already in mind a plan to offer Philip the living of Landford (now in his gift) at the next vacancy. Unfortunately for Philip the vacancy was not yet, he himself was still bound to his curacies at Burnham for a year, and when the time came he was not free to accept Landford. Tom therefore offered it to his cousin and close college friend, Henry Girdlestone, who held the living for nearly forty years. In compensation to Philip, Tom appointed him his honorary chaplain. To Horatia, Tom showed the same steadfast friendship, springing from his essentially kindly nature, throughout his all-too-short life; and this was afterwards continued by his widow. The Wards were received with every token of affection on their first visit to Landford. The great Charles I house stands on rising ground off the main road to Romsey immediately above the church of St. Andrew's. The building is of red brick, picked out with stone (as is Trafalgar House) and came into the possession of the Eyre family of Brickworth in 1628 and was inherited by Tom's wife on her father's death in 1815. Tom and his wife had no children yet (their first child, the subsequent 3rd Earl Nelson, was born 7 August 1823).

Meanwhile the presentation of the Wards to the head of the family, Horatia's formidable uncle, Earl Nelson, had to be made and the visit to Trafalgar House undertaken. The Earl had only seen Horatia at Merton during the Admiral's last days in England, though he may possibly have caught sight of her on the few subsequent occasions after Nelson's death when he called on Lady Hamilton at Clarges Street. There could, therefore, be no question of their recognizing each other. Though Lady Hamilton had not scrupled to denounce his alleged neglect of 'His Brother's Child' and declared he knew perfectly well who Horatia was, there is in fact no proof that the Earl did. Like Hardy, he may have suspected Lady

a. PORTRAIT OF REVD. PHILIP WARD and *b*. MINIATURE PORTRAIT OF HORATIA at the time of their marriage, 1822, by Sir Charles Ross

Hamilton of exploiting Horatia for her own ends. The sum total of his benefactions to Horatia, so far, were the £10 he sent her to Calais, when she wrote asking him for a loan at the time of Lady Hamilton's last illness. Horatia later recalled with something like amusement that the Matchams had absolutely forbidden her to repay the loan when she reached Ashfold.[1]

In receiving Horatia now the Earl was doubtless influenced by the attitude towards her that the Matchams and Boltons had adopted since Lady Hamilton's death. Since that time, Horatia had received every advantage enjoyed by their own daughters, and had moved in good society. She had, as her grandson Hugh Ward later recalled, been much admired wherever she appeared, and she evidently made a good impression now. Furthermore, the shrewd old Earl, scrutinizing the young couple before him, obviously judged they were intelligent—as well as handsome—since, in due course, under a guise of generosity, he laid a great burden on their abilities, and was not disappointed in them. He could, on occasion, assume a very genial manner, and presumably adopted one now in welcoming them to Trafalgar.

Trafalgar House, the nation's gift to the dead hero's heirs, presented a startling contrast to the house Nelson had bought for himself at Merton —the home he believed Horatia would inherit. On entering Trafalgar she might truly reflect how different her situation would at that moment have been had Lady Hamilton not thrown away Merton to pay her debts, and measure more fully still the extent and nature of her loss. She would not have become, as Nelson dreaded she might, 'dependent on any smiles or frowns' for her provision.

The sheer scale and size of Trafalgar (the Doric portico built in imitation of the Temple of Apollo at Delos was 14 columns wide) made it less a home than an exhibition-piece, and the Earl, for all his love of grandeur, could not give it a feeling of being lived-in. It was too much the product of its designer-architect, the city magnate Sir Peter Vanderput, who built it in 1733 as a bravura-piece. Its situation was, of course, splendid, standing on the crest of a hill in acres of parkland, only six miles out of Salisbury off the Romsey Road. The trustees appointed by government in 1806 to buy an estate to be annexed to the title of Nelson, eventually paid £120,000 for it, a sum which Nelson, paying his modest £9,000 for the ready-furnished Merton, might have thought rather a high price to pay for death and glory. Could he have been a witness of the reception

[1] Horatia to Sir Harris Nicolas 13 April 1846. NMM/NWD/13.

there of his daughter by his brother, the thought must have crossed his mind: who, in fact, was his rightful heir?

That Philip and Horatia had expected to stay longer in Wiltshire, possibly even to settle there, would appear from a letter Philip wrote to Alderman Smith while at Landford. Dated Landford House, 22 March 1822, it reads:

Dear Sir,—

Since we had the pleasure of seeing you in Town, circumstances have occurred which will demand our continued presence in Burnham I fear for some time. This will I trust be a sufficient excuse for our again troubling you. We have determined to take London in our way into Norfolk on purpose to request the favour of you at that time to unpack the china, if you can without any great inconvenience to yourself. We shall be in Town on Saturday and purpose leaving it again on Wednesday at the furthest: perhaps you will be kind enough to fix a day previous to that for what you think necessary to be done. If you will be kind enough to favour us with a few lines by the twopenny post—28, Norfolk Street, Strand, it will be sure to be delivered to us on our arrival. Mrs. Ward unites in best compts: and believe me,

Yours truly,
P. Ward.[1]

The draft reply by Alderman Smith to Philip's letter reads:

March 1822

I called yesterday morning at 29, Norfolk Street Strand and was informed that you had not arrived in Town. In respect to unpacking the China it will be attended with very great inconvenience and danger I am fearfull after so many years laying in my Warehouse much will be [damaged] and as it is my intention to sell it in Auction [in] the course of the spring I will inform you of the time and give you the opportunity of selecting out the Service you are anxious to possess with the Arms of Nelson which I will be ready to put under the advice and approbation of Mr. Salter.

JJS[2]

Alderman Smith's liberalities towards Lady Hamilton entitled him, no doubt, to sell what he had received from her in surety; but the right of Lady Hamilton to sell Nelson's household effects and personal belongings destined for his daughter might well be queried by Horatia, the chief sufferer in the transaction. Had the appointments of only two or three of the Merton rooms been saved for her from the wreck, the home she could not yet furnish would have been more speedily hers. Meanwhile,

[1] NMM/TRA/9421.   [2] Ibid.

she clung tenaciously to the few remaining relics of her father, as her frequent applications to Alderman Smith showed.

As the year advanced, the need for a 'living' and a home of their own became more pressing for Horatia and Philip with the expected birth of their first child. He was born on Sunday 8 December 1822 at Burnham, and was named Horatio Nelson. All the admiral's kith and kin were calling their eldest sons Horatio Nelson—the Boltons and Matchams and Girdlestones—but in Horatia's case the gesture had a deeper significance, asserting her son's rights to bear his grandfather's name. In this context, it is noteworthy that she called none of her daughters Emma.

With marriage, and motherhood, Horatia achieved at last a name and a family of her own. She was just twenty-two on the day of her son's christening, 29 January 1823. Philip, who entered the births of all his children in his black Bible, noted that his son was privately christened on the Tuesday following his birth, and publicly baptised at Burnham Westgate Church on 29 January. The godparents were Tom Bolton, Captain James Ward, and Mrs. Matcham, a choice which showed perhaps where Horatia's truest friends lay. (Neither Mrs. Matcham nor Captain Ward were in England at the time.)

With the coming of spring, the child with the illustrious name had a choice of gardens—his parents' and the Boltons' next door—in which to sleep in the sun, and no lack of doting aunts and cousins to watch over him. Horatia's cup of contentment might be thought to be full, but the birth of a son increased, rather than lessened, her longing to prove her origins. She pursued every trail that might lead her to the truth, and thus, when in need of a nursemaid for the baby Horace, eagerly engaged Bet Allen, niece of Nelson's old body-servant Tom Allen, as a potential link with the past. Time, which never lessened Bet's devotion to her nurslings, showed how right Horatia had been in engaging her, though for quite other reasons than the one that prompted her.

Tom Allen, who was a Burnham lad, born in 1764, had filled with immense pride the role of his Captain's 'Wally-de-Sham', and served him with a fierce, protective, heroic devotion, especially when he was wounded or ill. He had as many faults as virtues, and was drunken, self-opiniated, hard-headed, and an inventive liar. Despite all of which, when Merton was bought, Nelson engaged Tom's wife as dairy-maid, and helped Tom retire on his prize-money. After Trafalgar, with his £95, Tom retired to Burnham, but ran through his little fortune very soon and fell on hard times. Learning of his plight, Sir William Bolton took him into his employment, so that when he came upon the Burnham scene again and found Horatia and her husband eager for every iota of evidence concerning her birth, he was prompt, with an old sailor's ingenuity, to spin them a yarn. Tom was a strange mixture of truth and guile, and found Mr. and Mrs. Ward fair game for his inventiveness. The statement he made to Philip and which Philip later reported to Sir Harris Nicolas when he was editing Nelson's Letters in 1844, was crammed with inconsistencies and errors, not to say falsehoods. By then however Tom was dead and could no longer be consulted. On Sir William's death in 1830, Tom, who was presumably a widower by then and alone, was admitted to Greenwich Hospital by Hardy, the then Governor, and given a post of 'pewterer' at a salary of £65 per annum till his death in 1838. Tom's fidelity to his master was not forgotten, and Hardy paid for a headstone to be erected to his memory.

His statement of the facts concerning Horatia's birth published by Sir Nicholas Harris Nicolas was as follows:

One day towards the latter end of January 1801, while Lord Nelson was living in Half-Moon Street, and he was dressing for dinner, a female who appeared to be very near her confinement, and much agitated, came and enquired for Lord Nelson. He (Allen) recognized her as the sister of a merchant in Genoa, who had a brother a Lieutenant in the Navy. On Allen's informing Lord Nelson he immediately desired him to call a hackney coach, and to say nothing concerning it to the servants. He got into the coach and drove off not returning for a couple of hours. Allen also said that she came over in the Seahorse, Sir W. Fremantle, who was acquainted with the whole story. He further added, that he heard afterwards that she died in her confinement.[1]

Sir Harris's comments on these statements were that they were nearly all erroneous: 'the Seahorse was not commanded by Capt. Fremantle in 1800 nor did she arrive at that date.' (The *Seahorse* had been Fremantle's ship in 1797 at the Teneriffe engagement at which Allen was present.) Furthermore, 'Lord Nelson quitted London 13 January 1801 for Plymouth and did not return to town till 24 February when he remained for only two days. He sailed 2 March from Spithead for Yarmouth and the Baltic. Haslewood', concludes Sir Harris, 'declares the statement is not true'.[2] By 1844, when this disproval of Allen's statement was made, Horatia had learnt far more about her birth than she knew in the early 20's at Burnham when Tom Allen told his story to Philip.

Allen's cock-and-bull story was certainly not the invention of malice. He may truly have believed Horatia was neither Nelson's nor Emma's child. He was not the only one to think so. Hardy himself did not believe

---

[1] Nicolas, vii, 369.   [2] Ibid., 370.

it, and his reasons, related by Sir Nicholas Harris Nicolas are revealing:
he had applied to Lady Hamilton directly in 1812 and received the reply:
'My dear Sir Thomas, Let me only say to you *that which is true*. Horatia
is our dear Nelson's daughter. May God bless you. Emma Hamilton.'
Hardy (who lived till 1839) was still not convinced, and as late as 1835
told Locker (the son of Captain William Locker, Nelson's 'old sea-daddy')
that neither Nelson nor Emma were the parents. He believed Emma
claimed it as Nelson's 'in order that she might claim some pension of
provision for it'.[1]

Hardy's incredulity, born of his deep distrust of Lady Hamilton, had
by his own admission ill consequences for Horatia. In 1850, when a
National Appeal was launched by the *Morning Chronicle* (8 May) to raise
a fund for her, Hardy was quoted by the Organiser of the Appeal as
having been completely taken in by the 'Thompson' myth, and finding out
too late that Horatia was Nelson's own daughter. When he did discover
his mistake he said 'Had I known at the time of Nelson's death, the facts
which have since come to my knowledge, Mrs. Ward would have had a
Pension'.[2] There can be no doubt that with his prestige Hardy could at the
beginning have prevailed on government where others failed. When it was
too late he appears to have lost no opportunity of helping the Wards,
approaching Melbourne more than once to obtain preferment for Philip
—in default of the unobtainable pension.

The failure for so long to gain recognition cast the shadow of material
care over Horatia's otherwise profoundly happy married life. As the
family grew, with the nineteenth-century pattern of annual increase, and
Philip's stipend remained stationary, Horatia's initial loss multiplied.
She had seen too much of her mother's conduct in financial distress,
however, to imitate her public clamour, and maintained a dignified
reserve about her troubles. From the outset, she and Philip had to accommodate themselves to modest conditions.

In the summer of 1823 he was offered his first preferment, the living of
Stanhoe which was in the gift of Mr. Derick Hoste of Barwick House,
lord of the manor, and cousin of Nelson's Captain Sir William Hoste.
It was a rectory (valued at £16 per annum at the time) but with no parsonage house; none was built until 1861, but a pro-parsonage served
for the incumbent's use. Meagre as the prospect sounds, in 1823 when the
offer was made to the Wards it was worth something, when glebe lands
and tithes brought in provisions enough to stock a parson's kitchen all the
year round.

[1] Ibid., 386.   [2] *Morning Chronicle*, 8 May 1850.

Stanhoe was four miles south-west of Burnham, and both the church (All Saints) and the little pro-parsonage lay back from the road, screened by trees and surrounded by fields, in a most inconvenient position; the parsonage, indeed, could only be approached by a lane, deeply muddied in winter, and not easily accessible in any weather. The inconveniences were obvious, yet it was something for the Wards to call their own, and as such it could be seen through romantic eyes. The little house, scarcely more than a cottage, had a garden round it, and trees, and the hedgerows like all those in the district were starred with dog-roses in June. More important still, in the shrewd eyes of Mr. Bolton viewing the turnip-fields covering their land, they had saleable produce—he who has turnips lacks for nothing, he could tell them.

It was a beginning, however modest; and their acceptance may have been made the more readily from the reflection that Earl Nelson, whose grandeur they had so recently witnessed, had begun his career in the church as curate of Stanhoe!

As the registers show, Philip performed his first duties at Stanhoe on 11 July 1823, a propitious time of year for the removal of his little household from Burnham. They settled down and made lasting friends in the district, Mr. Derick Hoste among them. The short distance from Burnham allowed Mr. Bolton to ride over frequently to advise and help them, not only on their root-crops but on Horatia's investments, as their few remaining letters show.

In the following April their first girl was born, whom they called Eleanor Philippa, and whom Philip christened on the day of her birth (15 April 1824) in his own church, and for whom his sister Ellen Ward and Horatia's favourite cousin, Caroline Peirson, stood sponsors.

The Matchams were over in England once more, for the marriage of their daughter Eliza to yet another naval officer—Lieutenant Arthur Davies, son of a very old family friend, the Revd. Henry Davies, Rector of Ringwood, the Matchams' former home, with whose children the Matcham children had grown up. As usual on their shorter visits to England Mr. and Mrs. Matcham rented a furnished house in town, from where the wedding took place on 6 May (the bride's birthday) at St. Pancras Church.

Eliza's marriage took her far from her family. Her husband who had been invalided home from the West Indies in 1816, and was appointed to the Water Guard Service at the time of their marriage, emigrated with her shortly afterwards to Tasmania (Van Dieman's Land at the time) where he colonized land at New Norfolk. In 1849 he was appointed Emigration Agent at Hobart. They had a numerous family.

A very depleted Matcham family (only two boys and two girls now remained with the parents) returned to Paris in July 1824 and from a letter written from there to Horatia by her cousin Horatia Matcham, it would appear that a meeting had taken place either in London or Norfolk giving Horatia Ward the opportunity to introduce her little family to her aunt and uncle. The letter is of particular interest for its mention of 'the old Viscountess Nelson', with whom the Matchams had for some time past renewed friendly relations. The Viscountess stayed frequently and for long periods with her son and his wife in the Champs Elysees where, like so many English people of the time, Josiah conducted a very successful business, and his children grew up. No kinder or more sympathetic grandmother than 'the old Viscountess' lived; she was often left in charge of her grand-daughters, while the parents travelled further afield for Josiah's affairs. With Mrs. Matcham in particular, Mrs. Josiah Nisbet was on the most affectionate terms; no trace of the former divisions was allowed to spoil the amity of the present time. Viscountess Nelson was prepared to forget and forgive so much else than her in-laws' defection that it was made easy for them to resume the old ties as though nothing—and no one—had come between them. Since the Matchams had adopted Horatia they must have learnt much about Lady Hamilton as a mother and begun to see her in a new light. The mention of the Viscountess Nelson in a letter to Horatia raises the inevitable query: how did the Matchams mention *her* to the Viscountess? Horatia Matcham's letter, dated 20 July 1824 from Paris, was addressed:

Mrs. Ward/Stanhoe Parsonage/Nr. Docking/Norfolk/England.

As my dear Cousin Horatia was so kind as to request me to become one of her numerous correspondents, I cannot feel otherwise than happy in performing my promise of writing to her on our arrival in paris where we have been about ten days.

After describing their journey, stay at Calais, and visit to Chantilly, the writer reports that the family settled in the Rue Cadet in a house of a French Marquis 'who lives on the 2nd floor', and goes on to say:

We see the old Viscountess Nelson almost every day, we have drank tea with her once and are going again this evening. Mrs. Nesbitt unwell and expects to increase her family very shortly. We went last night to Mr. & Mrs. Page of Tilgate I believe you have seen them at Ashfold . . . I suppose Mrs. Peirson and Caroline are by this time arrived at Burnham, if they are, will you remember us very kindly to them? I hope your little boy has by this time recovered his health and beauty, the little girl I daresay improves much . . . Please direct to Mr. Delisle 3 Rue Blanche.[1]

[1] NMM/NWD/9594/34.

Mr. Delisle, the Matchams' banker in Paris, appears also to have been Lady Nelson's and to have been in the confidence of both parties. He rejoiced in their resumed relations. Not content with expressions of good-will, Lady Nelson used her influence with her old friend the Duke of Clarence to find the Matchams' son-in-law, Captain Blanckley, 'a situation in which flags are to be obtained'.

On the Matchams' next visit to England in 1826, spent mostly with 'young' George's family, it was the turn of Horatia Matcham to marry. The marriage took place from New House and was celebrated at White-parish Church on 6 July 1826, the bridegroom being Lieutenant Henry William Mason, R.N., of Beel House, Amersham, Buckinghamshire.

A couple of letters from Philip Ward to the Boltons, dating from this period, show to what extent Mr. Bolton and Tom watched over Horatia's interests to make the most of her small capital. One reads:

Thomas Bolton, Esqre
Landford House,
Nr. Rumsey.
Wilts
Dear Bolton,
Your father having suggested to me and Horatia that it would be much to our advantage, during the present height of the funds, to sell out, and having just been informed that Mr. Glasse is in want of 1600 on Mortgage at 4½ per cent, we have been induced to apply to you, as one of the trustees of Horatia's property for permission to carry this into effect. I dare say, before you have read thus far, you will have found out that I am no man of business; but at all events you will find by a letter from your father, that we act by his advice. He has made it evi-dent to me, that could all Horatia's money be sold out and put on Mortgage even at 4 per cent, it would make a very comfortable addition to our income. Your father begs me to say, that should you give permission he will order a power of attorney to be sent down to you. Horatia joins with me in kind regards to Mrs. Bolton and yourself, as well good wishes for the health of your son and heir.[1]
Yours very truly
Phil: Ward

Stanhoe Nr. Docking
December 6th 1824
Your father says that, after the next dividends are paid, he supposes the funds will be about 94; consequently, it will require about £1700 stock to make up the £1600.[2]

[1] Horatio Nelson, 3rd Earl Nelson, born 7 Aug. 1823.
[2] NMM/TRA/9421/36.

The re-investment of Horatia's money had been advised by Mr. Bolton in view of the family's yet further expansion and their imminent move to the altogether more important 'living' of nearby Bircham Newton.

Philip took his last duty at Stanhoe on 19 February 1825, between which date and the birth at Bircham Newton of their third child, Marmaduke, on 27 May, the move was made. At Bircham the parsonage was a far more roomy and well-situated house than the one at Stanhoe. It stood above and opposite to the church, on the brow of the hill, approached by an avenue of Spanish chestnut trees. Behind the house was a large garden, with a grass-plot studded with beech trees. Here Horatia had room for her rapidly growing family. After Marmaduke (whose godparents were Mr. Bolton, Sir William Bolton and Mrs. Glasse), there was John James Stephens (born 13 February 1827, whose godmother was Lady Bolton), Nelson (born 8 May 1828, whose godfather was Mr. Salter and his godmothers Mrs. Salter and Emma Horatia Bolton), and William George (born 8 April 1830), one of whose godmothers was Susanna Matcham. That made six, and in the following years Horatia had four more, Bet Allen remaining with her throughout.

Soon after settling into the new home at Bircham Newton, Philip had further occasion to write to Tom Bolton on the subject of Horatia's trustee money administered by him and Sir William Bolton. Addressed Brickworth House/Rumsey/Wilts, it read:

Dear Bolton,

Horatia and myself are much obliged by your readily acquiescing in our wishes in relation to the money being sold out and put on Mortgage. Your father has been so kind as to interest himself—unless you object or Sir William [Bolton] we should prefer having it all sold, where safe and suitable Mortgages have been found. Your father is still on the look out for us. You have heard of course of our change in residence; we like it much; but perhaps in the course of your peregrinations about Burnham you may have seen our parsonage; if so, I need not describe it to you.

With our best regards to Mrs. Bolton, the children and yourself,

Yours very truly,
Philip Ward

Bircham Newton   30th August
Nr. Docking   1825[1]

What cares the growing family brought can be seen from a further letter from Philip to Horatia's trustee on the spot, old Mr. Bolton, who had forgotten to pay her dividend and had gone across half Norfolk to stay with his nephew the Revd. Horace Bolton at Oby.

[1] Ibid.

My dear Sir,

I called at Burnham yesterday, hoping to have found you, but found you were at Oby and were likely to remain for some time there. I have therefore taken the liberty of troubling you with this letter to inform you that our interest was due from you on the 4th inst; and that, as Horatia is near her confinement and as money is a necessary article at such time you would much oblige me by giving me an order to draw for it with Fakenham Bank. I understand from Horatia that I am to look to Chapman for the Interest of the £300; but perhaps you would oblige me by writing to that effect, in your answer to this, in order that if necessary I may show it to Mr. Chapman. With our united best regards to yourself and Horace. Believe me I should not press for an early answer did I not want the money for this ready-money *job*.

Very truly   Yours
Philip Ward[1]

Bircham Newton
Nr Docking. Tuesday Morning.

The expected child, John James Stephens, was born shortly afterwards, on 13 February 1827.

Though the Burnhams lay inland, the coast was visible from every vantage point, and it was true maritime country in the sense that the majority of the population looked to the sea for their living, or were employed as guardians of the coast against sea-encroachment—or smugglers. An appeal to Horatia made at this time from a Mr. Southey, whose son was a coast-guard Captain who had been reprimanded because of a recent successful raid of smugglers, is some indication of the regard in which she was already held in the region as a strong and fair-minded woman, above the formalities of her time, and eager to right a wrong. She had frequently to take major initiatives on her husband's behalf, to judge independently, in a manner unusual in the women of her class and time. Her business letters show she was a capable woman, seeking no privileged treatment for being of 'the weaker sex'. As the evidence concerning her is examined, the image grows of a woman of strong courage, of unaffected conduct, of humane feelings. In these she was equally matched by her husband, whose finest tribute as a parson was that 'towards the poor he had always a listening ear for their troubles, a sympathetic heart for their sorrows, and an ever-open purse for their wants'.[2] Under such a guiding influence, the home that gradually took shape under Horatia's hands was characterized by a breadth of sympathy extending beyond the compass of its roof-tree and the white bars of its gate.

---

[1] Ibid.   [2] *Maidstone & Kentish Journal*, 22 Jan. 1859.

The home itself certainly teemed with life—not only with the children but with the numerous dogs that Horatia always kept, and the ponies in the paddock, and other animals. The little leisure she had she spent in reading. To our modern judgement, Horatia appears to belong rather to the emancipated women of Maria Edgeworth's later tales than to the elegant wits of Jane Austen's society, to which, by so much of her naval and clerical background, she might have been expected to belong.

CHAPTER XIX

THE GIBSON LETTERS

IN 1827 there came home on leave from India Philip's brother, Captain James Ward, of the 81st Regiment of Foot (the Loyal Lincoln Volunteers). He was three years younger than Philip, but since their Winchester days they had always been close friends. The most natural arrangement, now that both their parents were dead, was for the Captain to spend his leave with his brother. Horatia's welcome of him, her hospitality which, in the event, extended over a year, was so cordial that the Captain was anxious to prove his gratitude. In the following year Horatia received a letter from a Mrs. Johnson, a name unknown to her, who explained that she was the little crippled girl, Mary Gibson, daughter of her old nurse and her playmate in childhood. The provisos of Nelson's bequest to Mrs. Gibson (an annual pension of £20 paid by Mr. Haslewood on condition she never made any attempt to contact her former charge) had effectually severed all connection between Horatia and her old nurse, and, of course, Lady Hamilton had reasons enough for not re-opening the connection; Horatia had therefore not even heard that Mrs. Gibson was dead. In 1818, presumably when her death occurred, her daughter had made a first attempt to contact Horatia, and had written her a letter which she never received. Since then, she had married and had two little girls, Emma and Mary Ann, and prevailed at last on Mr. Salter to give her Horatia's address. Mrs. Johnson's letter, like all her subsequent conduct, showed that she was completely trustworthy, and Horatia keenly welcomed the communication. She remembered Mary with affection, recalled her deformed appearance perfectly well and wished instantly to see her if possible, and invited her to Norfolk. How much might not Mrs. Johnson know that was hidden from her? Mrs. Johnson was not at liberty to leave home then, but a suggestion was made by Captain Ward who, having to go to London on business, offered to visit Mrs. Johnson on Horatia's behalf. Thankfully accepting his offer, Horatia awaited his report. He wrote her two letters after his visits to Mrs. Johnson, which, together with Lady Hamilton's letters to Mrs. Gibson which his visits elicited, constitute the main dossier in the evidence relating to Horatia's birth. What no one knew, barring Lord Nelson, Lady Hamilton, and the doubting readers of the 1814 edition of *The Letters of Lord Nelson*, was here fully revealed in the letters of Lady Hamilton to Mrs. Gibson. They corroborated all the details in Nelson's letters to Lady Hamilton regarding the birth of their child at the end of January or early February 1801.

Captain Ward visited Mrs. Johnson for the first time on 18 September and wrote to Horatia next day:

Dear Horatia,

I have seen Mrs. Johnson, and she is the little deformed woman who you recollect. She appeared very much pleased at hearing of you although the poor creature was under great affliction, her husband whom I understand was a most respectable man and comfortably off, was then nearly dead. I have, since, called twice and found he is no more, so that probably I may not see her again for some days. I sat with her an hour and she gave me the following information about yourself which probably you have heard before.

Lady Hamilton brought you to her mother's house in a hackney coach one night and placed you under her charge telling her that she should be handsomely remunerated. She was un-attended, and did not give the nurse any information as to your parents. The nurse declared at that time you were no more than eight days old. This was (I forget which) either in the month of January or February, and nurse could never make out why your birthday was kept in October. You remained with nurse till you were five or six years old. Lady Hamilton constantly visiting you and showing all the affection of a mother towards you. Lord Nelson was frequently her companion in her visits to you and often came alone and Mrs. Johnson says playing for hours with you on the floor and calling you his own child. Mrs. Johnson has some letters that passed between Lady Hamilton and Lord Nelson. She did not tell me how they fell into her mother's hands. She promised to let me see them and to send them down to you if you pleased, but she has not read them since her mother's death and does not recollect that there is any information in them. There is a full signed picture of you at 5 years of age hanging up in the room—'tis an excellent picture in good preservation and very much resembles your children. She wrote to you some ten years ago but supposed that you never got the letter. She learned your present address from Mr. Salter whom she says appeared very cautious in giving her any information about you.

Pray write soon, and tell me if you wish me to see Mrs. Johnson again, or to hear further. If it is practicable I wish to purchase a company and go on half pay. There is no prospect of either Battalions coming home.

Signed J. Ward.[1]

[1] NMM/NWD/9594/1.

After further visits to Mrs. Johnson, at Horatia's request, Captain Ward wrote to her again:

Dear Horatia,

I have been out of Town for a few days or would have seen Mrs. Johnson before—however, I saw the poor widow yesterday and she has given me the letters to forward to you. I was disappointed in finding they are only letters from Lady Hamilton to Mrs. Gibson. No doubt they will be interesting to you and Phil although nothing particular appears can be gathered from them—All mystery. I told her of your invitation, and at present she cannot avail herself, but she told me she would again write to you, and probably you will arrange it better between you. She has 2 daughters, the eldest 9 years of age, named Emma. I fear she is left in very poor circumstances. I told her of your wish to be of assistance to her, and she tells me that her husband's Master who is a most extensive hat manufacturer is very kind to her. She is very sure that it was in the beginning of January that you were placed under the charge of her mother. She never remembers any person being admitted to you but Lady Hamilton and Lord Nelson. Nor heard anything from old Oliver. I am sorry you should think it necessary to apologize and talk of trouble which, to me, has been a pleasure—besides, you forget how much I am indebted to you for housing and cherishing me for these last 12 months. I met an old Friend of the 48th the other day who took me home with him into Essex for 4 days which I enjoyed very much, but I cannot say my health is benefitted by it . . . Best love to Philip and the children.

Yours affectionately

J. Ward.[1]

This letter was endorsed: 'The enclosed hair is yours preserved by Mrs. Gibson—cut when you were 4 years old'. [This was no doubt at the time when Horatia was taken from her nurse for good.]

The letters, the relics, the lock of hair, the portrait of Horatia given by Lord Nelson, were all eagerly acquired, and as eagerly scanned.

It is understandable that Horatia's first concern was to find out who, besides Lady Hamilton and Lord Nelson, visited her in infancy, and the evidence of Mrs. Johnson on this point is of major importance, since it disposes of Mr. Haslewood's statement that Horatia's mother visited her frequently while at Mrs. Gibson's whilst in the same statement denying that Lady Hamilton was her mother. There was, patently, no one else.

The mention of 'Old Oliver' in this connection is significant, when his confidential role in the Hamilton ménage is remembered. He was, as Nelson openly stated, the bearer of the all-important letter of 1 March 1801 in which he acknowledged Horatia was his and Emma's child; he may well have been the bearer also of many of Lady Hamilton's letters to Mrs.

[1] Ibid.

Gibson—many of which were not franked. He may, as the anonymous *Memoirs of Lady Hamilton* reported, have been in the hackney coach with her on the occasion Horatia was confided to Mrs. Gibson's care.[1] How much more he knew that was incriminating to Lady Hamilton can be gathered from his threats to expose her in 1808, when the benevolent Dr. Lawrence took him in hand to deter him from his project.

That Oliver believed himself justified in his enmity, and in a position to injure Lady Hamilton, appears from his letter to Mr. Matcham of 4 February 1809. Thanking him for the help given him by Dr. Lawrence, he continues:

The worthy Doctor has expressed your wishes for my rule and government with respect to Lady Hamilton. Her Ladyship, Her Mother, who has all along been my inveterate foe and the vile Miss Connors; let them defame, revile and discredit me ever so cruelly; now that I know your pleasure, I shall neither address Mr. Rose, the Lord Chancellor or anyone (as I ought in justice to do) since you disapprove . . . I shall not mention her name when I am asked about Her, much less seek to justify myself.[2]

The thirty-eight 'Gibson Letters' acquired by Horatia, which contained 'nothing particular' in Captain Ward's estimation, held the key of course to Horatia's mystery, had she only realised the fact, and not been deterred by the many contradictory statements purposely put out by both Lady Hamilton and Lord Nelson to confuse the issue. One of the first notes in Lady Hamilton's handwriting to Mrs. Gibson, said:

Horatia Nelson Tomson
Born October 29th 1800
Father and Mother being dead are unknown to Mrs. Gibson[3]

This was followed by a note in Lord Nelson's hand, which said: 'Mrs. Gibson is desired on no consideration to answer any questions about Miss Thompson nor who placed her with Mrs. Gibson as ill tempered people have talked lies about the child'.[4]

Mrs. Johnson's clear recollection that Horatia was brought to her mother in January or early February 1801 was completely confirmed by the postmarks on Lady Hamilton's letters to Mrs. Gibson, the earliest of which was posted 7 o'clock, 7 February. But for Mrs. Ward in 1828 the 'Gibson Letters' were crammed with enigmas, and a thousand questions remained to be asked of Mrs. Johnson. Horatia would appear to have arranged a meeting with her (probably in Norfolk) when the widow was

---

[1] See *Memoirs of Lady Hamilton*, 304–5.
[2] Oliver to Mr. Matcham 4 Feb. 1809. Eyre-Matcham Papers.
[3] NMM/NWD/9594/1.   [4] Ibid.

invited to bring her little girls to Bircham Newton, for later (after the
public Appeal in the press of the 1850's) 'Emma' Johnson, then Mrs.
Lewis, re-established contacts with Horatia and recalled her happy memories of that time. Both Emma Lewis and her sister Mary Ann died
relatively young, leaving young children.

Horatia's contacts with Mrs. Johnson only confirmed her good opinion
of her former playmate; years later, when discussing her revelations with
Sir Harris Nicolas, she emphasized that 'Mrs. Johnson was of the most
respectable character and in good circumstances, and had no pecuniary
or unworthy motive for communicating these facts'.[1]

Whilst caught up in the pursuits of past events, Horatia continued to
make her contribution to the future. On 13 February 1827 her fourth
child was born, another boy, called John James Stephens. His christening
was delayed until the summer to allow a family gathering at Trunch,
Philip's former home. In May 1828 Horatia had yet another son, Nelson;
so that Captain Ward found a houseful of children when he came on leave
to Bircham Newton, which does not appear to have troubled him at all.
Children became so much a pattern of Horatia's life, and a necessity for
her happiness, that even in old age she had to adopt a delicate grandchild
in need of country air to fill her days. In a period of high infant mortality,
she was lucky not to lose more children than she did (her Aunt Matcham
lost four infants and two grown boys out of fourteen children), but her
first sorrow struck her at Bircham Newton when John James died in
January 1829, having barely attained his second year. The funeral was
conducted by Mr. Glasse, Philip's former rector, and something of the
pathos of that first loss can be felt today in seeing the little oval tablet
the parents placed to his memory in the bare chancel wall.

SACRED
to the memory of / John James Stephens
Fourth child of
Revnd Philip Ward
And Horatia Nelson / His wife
Who died Jan^{ry} 4th 1829
Aged two years.

John James's brief life was connected with a somewhat romantic circumstance. He was called after a Mr. John James Stephens, a wealthy Lisbon
glass manufacturer who was totally unknown to Horatia, but who left her
a bequest in his Will for £500, moved to do so, apparently, by her being
Lord Nelson's 'Adopted Daughter'. Relating the incident to Sir Harris

[1] Nicolas, vii, 370.

Nicolas Horatia said that Mr. Stephens was 'a resident Merchant of Lisbon', and commented: 'I wish I had known of his kind intention as I would have called on him when I was at Lisbon [1816] he died worth immense riches . . . I forget the large sum Probate on the Will amounted to'.[1] Though Horatia did not know Mr. Stephens, he may have seen her or heard about her during her stay in Lisbon, when her connection with Lord Nelson was an open secret. His death occurred on 12 November 1826 at Lisbon and prompted her to call her third son after him.

The totally unexpected bequest was the more welcome because almost at the same time Horatia suffered a further check to her hopes of a government pension, first sponsored by Mr. Rose, and after his death by Canning. Canning's goodwill in the matter was still more important when he became Prime Minister in April 1827, and he was encouraged by the fact that George IV was known to be well-disposed towards Horatia. A Petition to set out her claims on the government was actually in train when, quite suddenly, Canning died on 8 August 1827. He was succeeded by Lord Goderich, and not realising the loss to her cause occasioned by Canning's death Horatia sent the documents in her case to the new Prime Minister. On 31 August 1827 she got the following reply from Downing Street:

Madam,

I am desired by Lord Goderich to return to you the enclosed, it being an original Document. The Great Pressure of Public Business will prevent his Lordship from immediately taking into consideration your letter.

I have the Honor

To be Madam,

Yr Obed[t] Ser[vt]

B. Balfour.[2]

Horatia's childhood had been embittered by the repeated mortifications suffered by Lady Hamilton in pursuit of her 'just claims' to a government pension, and it seems that the frustration of her hopes now decided Horatia never to open the matter again. When the question was reopened, more than twenty years later, it was prompted by Horatia's friends, and not countenanced by herself.

Help came to the Wards, however, from a quite unexpected quarter shortly afterwards, through a surprising gesture on the part of Earl Nelson.

Earl Nelson had never done with surprising his family. On 13 April

[1] Letter of 28 March 1846. NMM/NWD/9594/13–14.
[2] NMM/TRA/9421/36.

1828 his Countess died—Emma's one-time 'jewell' and bosom's confidante. Though the friendship dissolved in acrimony, the acrimony had
mostly been on Emma's side. The poor Countess, even before the chasten-
ing blow of her son's death, had extended the olive branch to her foe,
though the gesture was unavailing. At seventy-one her widower felt
himself neither too disconsolate nor too old to found another family,
and within a year announced to his astounded relatives his re-marriage to a
young and extremely handsome widow, Mrs. Hilaire Barlow, daughter of
Rear-Admiral Barlow. As the Earl made perfectly plain to his entourage
in announcing his nuptials, he did not take this step merely to secure a
charming companion in his old age but in gleeful anticipation of yet
'dishing' the young collaterals by bringing 'the title back into the authentic
line' and producing an heir himself. In this he was disappointed.

He had not abandoned any of his ambitions, it would seem, when, in a
gesture of apparent benevolence, he offered Philip Ward a 'living' in his
gift, at Tenterden in Kent. As Canon of Canterbury (he was Canon
of the 5th Stall) it fell to his turn, in regular rotation, to nominate to a
vacancy in the Chapter's gift, 'the Nomination to take effect as from the
next Chapter Meeting on the 23rd June following'.[1] It does not appear
at what stage in the proceedings Philip's patrons, the Dean and Chapter of
Canterbury, made it clear to him that the appointment carried an obligation on his part to enter, on their behalf, into a suit with his principal
parishioners to obtain a commutation of the tithes. Had he realised the
strain and costs of litigation which such an attempt would bring him
over the years it is unlikely he would have accepted the living. At the
time the apparent benefit to himself and his family made the offer appear
not only acceptable but like a benefaction on the part of the Earl.

The living of Tenterden, which carried a stipend of £200 per annum
and vicarial tithes estimated at £450 per annum, was an obvious boon to
a struggling clergyman with a large family. The fifth son, William George,
was christened on 29 June 1830: it was a family occasion because Nelson,
born two years before, was also christened on that day and among the array
of godparents assembled was Susanna Matcham whose parents were at
last re-settled in England. She was godmother to the infant William, with
whose future destinies her own became closely bound. He married her
adopted daughter and niece, Catherine 'Toriana' Nelson Blanckley
(left orphaned by the premature death of Harriet Matcham Blanckley,
Susanna's sister). Mr. and Mrs. Salter were present at this christening
as godparents to Nelson, with two of the Boltons, Horatia's little cousin

[1] Chapter Act Books, Canterbury diocesan archives.

Emma, and Sir William's younger brother from Brancaster, Horace, the Rector of Oby. It was a gathering of friends and of the family in all its ramifications, in final tribute to the Wards who were so soon to be lost to their Norfolk kin. Some of them would return to their native county—Marmaduke Ward, aged five on the occasion, would return to live with one of the godmothers, Mrs. Young of Burnt Street Wells (who was born a Bolton), with whose husband, the family doctor, he would in due course pass his medical articles. The presence of the Salters at the christening would suggest that Alderman Smith had at last unpacked Horatia's possessions from his warehouse, and remitted them, as agreed, to the Salters for conveyance to her; certainly these relics of Lord Nelson were taken to Tenterden.

Philip Ward, inducted Vicar of Tenterden on 14 August 1830, did not take up residence there at once. The Vicarage was in bad repair and indeed remained unfit to live in for some eighteen months after his family arrived. The Tenterden Church Registers show that Philip did not take up his duties until the following April and it is very likely that the family did not move from Norfolk before then.

The last winter at Bircham was saddened by two deaths in the Bolton family. On 9 October 1830, Anne's life of protracted illness—already foreshadowed in the Merton days—at last came to an end. Anne had been the first in the Bolton family to show kindness to her 'dear little cousin Horatia' at Merton, sharing her birthday parties with her, and writing to her from Cranwich during the unhappy years that followed. Only two months later, on 10 December, Sir William Bolton died at the age of fifty-three. With the departure of Tom for Wiltshire, Sir William had been virtually the head of the family, and also trustee for Horatia. His obituary in the *East Anglian* of 21 December provides some background to a rather shadowy figure in the Nelson circle; it said:

On Thursday last at Cossey, Capt. Sir William Bolton, R.N. eldest son of the Rev. William Bolton and one of the few surviving Norfolk heroes who accompanied Nelson to his deeds of fame. It might be the honor (sic) of Sir William Bolton that he became, in some sense, the adopted child of his chieftain; but he had a plume of his own. A combination, perfectly unique, of the sailor, the scholar, and the gentleman; he lived, the delight of his comrades, and of his social circle; he died with the devoutness of the christian.

A strange occurrence that followed very shortly after the Wards' departure from Norfolk should be related here, since it brought to a decisive end Philip's connection with Burnham Market. Ever since the death of

Sir Mordaunt Martin in 1815 his son, Roger, the new Lord of the manor, had lived at Burnham Polsted Hall. He was, by reason of the double inter-marriage between his family and the Rector's, first cousin to the Revd. John Glasse, Philip's friend and former Rector. He did not marry, and in September 1831 it was brought to Mr. Glasse's notice that he was having, like many landlords of his day, extra-marital relations with his house-keeper, Miss Mary Anne Clarke. Impelled by a double sense of duty—that of a relative and pastor—poor Mr. Glasse set out to visit his cousin at the Hall to put an end to this flagrant scandal. It was Tuesday 13 September. Sir Roger, he soon found, did not mind in the least having his sins exposed and he was totally impervious to his cousin and Rector's opinion; as the argument was prolonged, he asked only one thing, to be rid of his company. Nothing that Mr. Glasse could say could shake his resolution; the lady was necessary to his pleasure, and would remain in the post where he had placed her. Unaccustomed, perhaps, to dealing with colonial gentlemen, Mr. Glasse was first incredulous, and then stricken to the soul with the failure of his mission; and, realising how hurtful to his flock at Burnham Sir Roger's example would be, he took the respon-sibility for it upon himself, walked home to Burnham House, and killed himself. The effect of such an action, committed by a parson, at that time, can well be judged. His long record of faithful service, however, and de-cent life, prevailed to save his memory from contumely, and he was given christian burial in his own church on 23 September 1831. The situation was the more envenomed that his widow was the sister of Sir Roger.

How she felt towards him can be fairly guessed by her almost imme-diate sale of Burnham House and departure for London. The Glasses' former home (and the Wards' as well) was bought by the new incumbent, the Revd. Bernard Gilpin. Poor Mrs. Glasse bought a house at 30 Cam-bridge Street, Connaught Square, where in later years one of her regular visitors was Horatia, who stayed with her whenever business or other occasions brought her to London. The unrepentant Sir Roger lived till 1854, when the estate passed to his nephew, William Bulkeley Glasse, the son of his injured sister, but even then subject to the life-interest being paid to Miss Mary Anne Clarke!

When the time for the Wards' departure from Bircham came, in the early summer of 1831, they had been married nine years, had five children living, and were expecting a sixth in July. They were going a considerable distance, to a county neither of them knew, and leaving behind the family and friends who had made that corner of Norfolk their home. Into the coach stacked high with their household goods, when the family had taken their places and the dogs were settled, stepped Bet Allen the children's nurse, carrying in her arms—not the youngest baby—but a Delft plate belonging to Lord Nelson which, so an old Catalogue of Nelson Relics[1] describes, she 'carried by coach all the way from Burnham Thorpe (sic) to Kent so that it should not be broken'. Having lost so much and found her own again so hardly, Horatia understandably clung to the few possessions that proved her right to the illustrious name.

[1] Catalogue of the Loan Exhibition of Nelson Relics in aid of "Save the Victory Fund." Spink & Son Ltd., King St. St. Jame's 1928 Item. "Delft Plate. This plate was carried personally by Bet Allen, niece of Tom Allen (Ad. Ltd. Nelson's body servant) by coach from Burnham Thorpe into Kent, so that it should not be broken."

CHAPTER XX

TENTERDEN

THE Wards arrived at Tenterden to find the Vicarage uninhabitable and were given, meanwhile, accommodation elsewhere in the parish. This was in a house in High Street, near the 'White Lion' Inn, which had a large garden. Its position, almost opposite the old Tollgate, was full of novelty for the little Wards who had hitherto lived in retired parsonages, away from the stir of men. To their unaccustomed eyes the long High Street, bordered with genteel residences on both sides, was a source of perpetual wonder; especially when the man from the Tollgate came out to open the barriers for the drays, country carts and gentlemen's chaises that, on busy days, seemed perpetually passing through. In many respects Tenterden High Street was like Burnham Market, for it had the same array of old houses, Plantagenet, Tudor, Georgian, bordering the side-walks; but Tenterden was much longer than Burnham, and seemed stretched out between its two extremities at East and West Cross, like a hammock between two trees. The comparison arises even today in a place that, winter and summer, has a perpetual air of spring gardens about it. Tenterden in 1831 had the same essential features as today, except for the Toll house and gates that are gone; but there was the same elegant little Town Hall—only finished in 1792—with its delicate columns and fine wrought-iron balcony; the same old Inns with their steep tiled roofs, the 'weatherboarded' shopfronts, and the narrow alleys leading off into a maze of gardens behind. But Tenterden resembled neither Burnham nor any other place the Wards had known in the unique glory of its church tower which dominated the whole locality. Hidden out of sight as the main bulk of the building is, behind the steep roofs and closely-serried house-fronts of the High Street, the presence of the church makes itself known only by its soaring tower; standing on ground 200 feet above sea-level, and itself a good 120 feet high, the tower can be seen from the Channel. Up there, since the days of the Armada, fire-balls hanging from the pinnacles have warned populations inland of the enemy's approach, and signalled to friendly ships at sea the proximity of shelter.

The area was, of course, intensely rural at the time. Sheep-farming

TENTERDEN HIGH STREET IN THE 1830'S

was the chief activity, and the seasonal sheep-fairs (like the surrounding orchards and hop-gardens) were an integral aspect of the scene. Communications were still by stage-coach when the Wards arrived, with the 'Tally-ho' leaving for London every morning 'at a quarter before 7' from the Woolpack Inn, whose situation, incidentally, was very convenient for the Vicar and his wife on their journeys to London, since it lay at the foot of the churchyard wall where the church path abutted on High Street. There was one post in and one post out every day, at seven in the morning and evening. In the early 1840's, when Horatia had frequent occasion to travel to London, she welcomed the good train service that allowed her to make the journey up and down in the same day; and in 1846 improved postal services followed: 'We have now two deliveries of letters in the day', she told Sir Harris Nicolas.

Philip's Tax Returns for September 1832 show that, even after eighteen months residence in the town, his Vicarage was not yet in repair or fit to live in. The costs for this, as for so much else as he shortly found, would predominantly fall on him. Its position was agreeable, since it lay back from the High Street, in a large garden (he had three to four acres of 'Glebe') and had its own bricked walk communicating with the churchyard. Standing on high ground, there were splendid views of the surrounding Weald of Kent. Though not a particularly attractive building, with its weather-boarded front, it was roomy, and the garden was safe for the children to play in. Such as it was, it would be the family's home for the next twenty-eight years.

To Horatia, the unfit condition of the house was an additional problem when, on the 10 July, she gave birth to another, her sixth, son 'at 25 minutes past 2 p.m. on Sunday', as Philip recorded in his family Bible. The child was christened 'Edmund Nelson', after the Admiral's father; but he did not live long like his namesake, and died the following year.

His death on 13 February was followed by a happier event at the end of the autumn, when Horatia's eighth child and second daughter was born on 24 November and called after her mother, Horatia Nelson. That the Wards soon made friends among their parishioners appears from the names of the godparents to these first children born at Tenterden—Mrs. Croughton and Mrs. Curteis respectively. The families, both of ancient standing in the place, were intermarried, and would shortly form close ties with the Wards. During the protracted Tithes suit with his parishioners, Philip found their friendship and support all-important.

His position was not enviable. In a parish numbering 3,300 souls, he was without the aid of a curate (because he could not afford one) and, pending the suit in process of law during which no tithes were paid, could not count on a larger stipend than £150.

Once the vicarage was habitable, the pattern of family life could be established. Philip taught his sons, and Horatia her daughters. A birthday note to her eldest, Ellen, remains to show how one of her problems was to cope with the hot-temper, which together with their splendid heads of auburn hair, her daughters appear to have inherited from their grandmother. The note, dated 15 April 1833, accompanied a present given on the occasion. It reads:

My dear Ellen,

I give you as a birthday gift a writing desk which was given to me when I was a little girl of the same age that you are now. You are now nine years old and are old enough to be a comfort to your papa and me and an example to your brothers and little sister and you must pray to God to assist you in subduing your temper and making you a good, mild little girl. May God bless you my dear child and make you everything your papa and I can wish and that you may be so is, my dear Ellen, the sincere prayer of your affectionate Mother,

Horatia N. Ward.[1]

While Philip was awaiting a visitation from his Archbishop and the Commission from Canterbury to instruct him on the line to follow in his impending suit, Horatia returned to Burnham for a family celebration in September 1833, taking with her the two youngest children, William, aged three and a half, and Horatia. A letter written to her on the occasion by her eldest, the ten-year-old Horace, has been preserved and appears a creditable performance, and one which speaks well for his master and father, the patient Philip. Written between ruled lines, in a firm, regular hand and totally uninhibited by punctuation, young Horace's purview of the domestic situation, interspersed with typical reports on the family pets, affords an image of the new circle at Tenterden, and evokes the old one in Norfolk.

My dear Mamma,

I hope you are quite well & William and baby poor Hester Croughton has recovered her senses Papa told me to tell you to ask Mr. Derrick Hoste and Mr. Henry Blythe [curate at Burnham] to send him some game back by you. Mungo has got three kittens Mrs. Warterman begs to be remembered to you Mrs. Frank sends her love to you and wants you to give her love to Miss Howlet and ask her to send her a letter back by you and Papa says you are to send him a letter soon tell William that Ann will take care of his spaniel bitch Bowman is now getting the garden ready for the Archbishop and Mrs. Jerry Curteis asks to be particularly remembered to you and hopes you will not be long. We have all

[1] NMM/NWD/9594/1.

had colds Mr. Twig [Curate of nearby Newenden] is to have the colt I think
Nelson Marmaduke Ellen and myself all send our loves to you Mary and Mr.
Blythe Miss Banyer and Maria Frost and all the rest of them.

I remain dear mamma

Your affectionate son

Horatio Nelson Ward.

S.P. (sic) Ann and Bet send their love to William baby and Mary.[1]

In Philip's accompanying letter, the first references to the pending law-
suit, and the visit of the Commissioners from Canterbury, are made.
The firm of solicitors engaged by him, on the advice of Earl Nelson, were
Messrs. Fladgate, Young & Jackson, of 12 Essex Street, Strand, to whose
proposals he here refers.

My dear Horatia. I find you have heard from Jackson and that the day for the
Commissioners is the 23rd Inst. He speaks of the attempt at the Compromise, as
best *after* the Commission. I have written to ask him whether it would not be
more advisable *before* it? I have been looking for a letter from you for these few
days past. *You* are in the land of news—*we* are not—therefore you must be the
chief scribe. We have had most stormy weather, and the old limes creaked
again—but the house and all was safe and sound—the hops have suffered much
from the gale, but, I trust, our friend George (who always talks of you) as little
as any of the neighbours—all very kind . . . I hope my check was received.

With my best love to you, and kind regards to all who ask for me or care
about me. / Believe me,

Your ever affect. Husband

Philip Ward.[2]

The occasion for Horatia's visit to Burnham was the marriage of her
cousin Emma Horatia Bolton, Lady Bolton's daughter and Nelson's and
Emma's goddaughter, to Henry Foley, M.D., which took place at Burnham Westgate Church on 16 September 1833. A life-long devotion had
bound the bride, ever since they met as tiny girls at Cranwich, to her
'dear cousin Horatia', whose presence on this occasion was the fulfilment
of a long-standing promise. The bridegroom, then practising at Windsor,
was of a Brancaster family, his mother Mary Cooper being a collateral
of old Mr. Nelson's of Burnham Thorpe. After their marriage, the couple
lived mostly abroad, though Emma Horatia returned to end her days at
Burnham, living with her sister Mary Anne and her Aunt Susanna at
Bolton House, till her death in 1869.

The Tenterden Tithes suit was not a singular case but one of many
being contested at the time, before the passing of the Tithes Act in 1835-6

[1] Ibid. Letter dated 6 Sept. 1833.
[2] Furley, Robert: *History of the Weald of Kent*, 1874, ii, 648.

brought the whole question of parochial dues under revision. It was distinguished from the others merely by its duration, and the unrelenting character of the landowners who fought it. On Horatia's return from Burnham she and Philip found themselves immediately caught up in the details of the case, from which they emerged, after a ten-years' contest, considerably the poorer in pocket and in health; the only immediate gainers being the Dean and Chapter of Canterbury.

Briefed by his Archbishop (the former Bishop of London, Dr. Howley) and the Canterbury Commissioners, Philip launched the campaign for the commutation of the tithes, acting in all good faith and under a deep sense of obligation towards them, and without a doubt of its success. In this he reckoned without the power of the landowners in his parish. They contested the proposal from the outset. The Dean and Chapter, who stood to gain £821 15s. 8d. per annum (as against Philip's £450) instructed him without a qualm to go to law, and Philip, who had once written to Mr. Bolton that he was, all too recognisably 'not a man of business', accepted their advice, without a thought for safeguarding his own interests. Receiving from Earl Nelson instructions to engage his own family solicitor to act for him, Philip never paused to ask the Earl who was to pay the costs; in the end Philip found that he and the landowners were left to pay between them the total sum. This amounted, on the landowners' side to £6,600 and he must have been in debt to almost the same amount. He had, furthermore, throughout the ten-years' suit to forgo his tithes which, at the settlement, were estimated at £2,865 16s. 5d. for arrears payable to him by the landowners; a sum which was, of course, absorbed in the enormity of his own share of the costs.

The suit was not only a financial drag on the Wards throughout, but a mental strain which took its toll of Philip's health. A sensitive, scholarly man, his was not the temperament to sustain a prolonged, aggressive role; but in the event he found his strongest ally in his wife, who took the main burden of the dispute on herself. The historian, Furley, relating the circumstances of the suit in his *History of the Weald of Kent*, had this to say of Horatia's services to her husband: 'Earl Nelson strongly advised Mr. Ward to fight the case and employ the best legal advice, for the sake, not only of himself, but of the Canons of Canterbury; he does not appear to have helped with the means to do so. Horatia was a great help to her husband in the affair, taking frequent journeys to London for interviews with lawyers and counsel during the whole suit; it was mainly due to her efforts that a satisfactory compromise was reached'.[1]

[1] Furley, Robert: History of the Weald of Kent, 1874 et seq ii 648.

What emerges from the case, besides Horatia's outstanding abilities in defending her husband's and children's interests with spirit over a number of years, is the attitude of the landowners towards their vicar, whom they might be supposed to view with antipathy after so long a battle. This, surprisingly, was not the case; they showed they liked and admired him, and even the most aggressive among them, the largest landowner of all Mr. Virgil Pomfret of Morghew, who had the most to lose by the compromise, bore his discomfiture with the overheard reflection: 'Hang it all! Ward's a gentleman!' as a conclusive, if not consolatory proof that things might have been worse.

Throughout the years of harassing litigation Horatia's domestic cares and obligations were not lessened; the family continued to grow. In May 1834 her seventh son, Philip, was born; and in January 1836, her third daughter, Caroline Mary (called after Caroline Peirson in all probability): these children proved to be her last. She had now a family of eight children five boys and three girls, who all attained adult age.

Apart from attendance at local Dame-schools, the boys were educated at home by their father, money for school-fees being altogether lacking. This did not, in the event, militate against the eldest, Horace, who went to Pembroke College Cambridge, took his B.A. degree in 1847 and entered the Church; nor Marmaduke, who in due course returned to Norfolk and lived with Dr. and Mrs. Young at Wells, where he passed his Articles and went on to Glasgow University in 1848, and took a medical degree. Nelson Ward was articled to a Tenterden Solicitor, Mr. John Scratton in 1844, whose garden adjoined the Vicarage; with him he remained for five years before going up to London and entering a firm of solicitors in Lincoln's Inn Fields. Nelson Ward's subsequent career was most successful. The 'little ones' of the family, William and Philip, were not so early off their parents' hands and, with their sisters, formed part of the home circle for many years.

Bringing up such a big family at home was not without its social, as well as financial, trials for a clergyman with liberal views, liable to the incursion of his superiors. On the occasion of a visit from his Archbishop to Tenterden, when Philip was expected to put him and his chaplain and his servant and his coach-horses up for the night, a grievous contretemps arose as a result of the children's freedom and Horatia's love of animals. The Archbishop arrived late in the evening and was ushered to his room (with his servant in attendance) without seeing the rest of the house or more members of the family than the Vicar; but he knew something of the size of the Ward family, and that there were many boys at home (an arrangement he no doubt deprecated). When in the early morning he was greeted by what he considered outrageous language coming from the garden below, he threw up the window of his bedroom prepared to castigate the offenders. What he heard, and heard distinctly, from the floor below was a raucous voice shouting up to him: 'Well, old file, how are ye?' The Archbishop related his own story years later, and declared that, however disagreeable the situation was, he felt it his duty to tell the Vicar that his sons must be reprimanded and taught 'respectful manners'. He waited his opportunity all through breakfast, but none of the culprits appeared at that meal. Directly afterwards, Horatia invited him to join her in the pleasant drawing-room where, on entering, he saw in the window-recess a parrot's cage. He nevertheless still considered it his duty to advise Mr. Ward to enjoin on his sons to teach their parrot better manners. If Marmaduke Ward, who went to sea as a ship's surgeon, later remembered that story he probably had plenty of occasions for thinking the Archbishop lucky in the good-manners of their parrot.

Both the elder girls, Ellen and Horatia, were delicate, especially Horatia, whose frequent illnesses in her early teens—usually designated as 'inflammation' when not more specifically named, as when she had cholera at thirteen—kept her mother at her bedside sometimes for weeks together. It is a sad commentary on so much of Horatia's life that, writing to Sir Harris Nicolas in November 1844 and enquiring after his sick children, she could say: 'I wish I was nearer to you to offer to assist Lady Nicolas in nursing. I am sorry to say that I have had sufficient practice to make me a good one'.[1]

A favourable issue to the Tithes suit could not always be confidently expected during the long-drawn-out deliberations, and a time came when evidently Philip considered resigning the living and looking for a less troubled one elsewhere. In this, as in all his efforts, Horatia seconded him, noting the possible vacancies in the Church as they occurred. Such mutations were not obtainable without patronage, and she had to put forward, yet again, her diminishing claims on the government in pursuit of preferment for her husband. Captain Sir Thomas Hardy was one of the faithful friends whose support she enlisted in 1838. His shakily-written reply, dated Greenwich Hospital 11 May 1838, reveals his declining strength; he died in the following year:

Dear Mrs. Ward,

I have more than once requested of Lord Melbourne to give a living to Mr. Ward, and I shall have great pleasure in again requesting of his Lordship to

[1] Letter dated 7 Nov. 1844. NMM/NWD/9594/13-24.

present Mr. Ward to the living of Wareham, but I am sorry to inform you that I have not the least interest with the Government, tho' I consider that your Claims on the Public are sufficiently strong to claim the attention of Lord Melbourne.[1]

Earl Nelson, who had pitched Philip into the interminable lawsuit, did not live to benefit by its issue. He died at his London home on 28 February 1835. It was announced in the Annual Register: 'In Portman Square, aged 77, the Rt. Hon. and Rev. William Nelson, first Earl Nelson. He was the elder brother of the hero of the Nile and Trafalgar. He was succeeded in the title, pursuant to the patent, by his nephew, Thomas Bolton, junior, Esq., son of his elder sister, Susannah.'

The funeral took place at St. Paul's, where the poor old Earl whose life had been one pursuit of advancement was buried amid the ashes of greatness, near his illustrious brother, and beside his own beloved son.

He had busied himself to the last with aggrandising his family, and had succeeded in alienating the title of Bronté from his heir, Tom Bolton, in favour of his daughter, Lady Charlotte Bridport,[2] to whom on his death the title passed. The kindness with which Tom's wife wrote of his demise is the more creditable. She wrote to her sister-in-law Susanna Bolton at Burnham on the event:

Rumsey 3 MR 1835.

My dear Sister,

Since your Brother closed his letter to you he has received one from Lord Bridport announcing poor Lord Nelson's decease which took place about one O'clock on Saturday morning without much apparent suffering. He is to be buried at St. Paul's on Monday next the 9th inst. when your Brother will of course attend to pay his last tribute of respect to his memory.

You will I am sure excuse my adding more at present than kindest regards to our Sister and nieces and our relatives at Wells.

Believe me   Yr affec^t
F. E. Nelson.[3]

His death was not unexpected, and left no-one shattered, save perhaps his kind daughter, but the tragic passing only ten months later of his successor, Tom Bolton, was a calamity that left the family incredulous. Charles Matcham, who had emigrated to Australia some years before, and was sheep-farming in Sydney, wrote to his mother on hearing the news that he believed the report incorrect: though it was announced in the papers, he believed it still referred to the 'Revd. Dr.', and was 'most shocked and unwilling'[4] to believe its confirmation in the family letters.

[1] Ibid.
[2] She married the Hon. Samuel Hood, 2nd. Baron Bridport at St. Marylebone, 3 July 1810.
[3] NMM/GIR/9590/1.   [4] Eyre-Matcham Papers.

Tom Bolton had everything to live for; a devoted wife, and seven children, whom he deeply loved. His eldest and second sons, Horatio Nelson and John, were aged respectively twelve and ten when they were fetched from school at Chichester to attend his death-bed. An extract from the diary of Mrs. Jones—a close family friend and witness of the event—gives the details of Tom's last days. He was at Brickworth House, near Landford, and gathered about him those he loved and trusted best—among them Dr. Beatty, who had treated him for years.

In the autumn of 1835, urged by Lord Nelson and the Girdlestones to visit Wiltshire I went first to Landford [the Girdlestones' rectory] but here again both sickness and sorrow followed me. Dr. Beatty came to Brickworth but no real encouragement could he give us. My friend requested him to come to him— none, he was sure, *could* nurse, as his dear little sister Anne's 'Child'. Once I drove with him to desolate Trafalgar, he was always calm and humble-minded, was sure that he should not adorn the title—But one morning he was said to be so much worse that he desired Dr. Watson might be summoned as well as the lawyer from Salisbury. From that day he was nursed in turns— . . . I and Mrs. Girdlestone [Eliza Bolton, his sister] always together, one sitting up, the other lying down. It was my night in my own room when on November 2nd I was hastily summoned to his bedside and found him apparently dying . . . His two eldest boys had been sent for from Chichester School—he lingered through the day quite conscious and in the evening breathed his last supported by Henry Girdlestone and myself.[1]

Tom Bolton, who had never sought greatness, was spared the splendour of a funeral at St. Paul's, and was buried on 9 November in the little chapel at Trafalgar (the chapel of Standlynch), where his memorial can be seen today. The sylvan setting was far more in keeping with his essentially simple character and rustic tastes. After the enumeration of his titles, Tom Bolton's real claims to be remembered were recorded:

In fulfilling the duties of his life and station, he invariably preserved and fostered the attachment of his family, and obtained the regards and confidence of those with whom he acted. His conduct towards his dependents was considerate and indulgent, towards his neighbours and associates honourable and consistent, towards his wife and his children and his relations, peculiarly kind and affection- ate. And in sustaining during a lingering illness the slow but certain approaches of death, he exemplified in an eminent degree to those around him the piety, patience and fortitude of a Christian. He died, leaving 5 sons and 2 daughters, Nov. 1st 1835, in the 50th year of his age.[2]

Philip Ward was invited to the funeral and stayed at Trafalgar a week. Horatia, who was also invited, could not leave home, expecting the birth

[1] NMM/GIR/9590/1.   [2] Standlynch Chapel, Downton, Wilts.

of her daughter Caroline. With Tom Bolton's widow, the kind connection that had existed between him and Horatia from the first, and which later had been extended to Philip, was maintained. The new young Earl, Horatio, confirmed Philip in his post of chaplain, and Philip visited him at Trafalgar on many occasions.

Nelson's immediate family circle, even the younger generation with which he had delighted to surround himself, was fast thinning out. In the two preceding years both his brothers-in-law had died: Mr. Matcham on 3 February 1833; and Mr. Bolton on 17 October 1834. The announcement appeared in the Annual Register: 'At Burnham Market, Norfolk, in his 83rd year, Thomas BOLTON, Esq. This gentleman married Susannah, eldest sister of Admiral Lord Nelson and his son Thomas Bolton, Esq., of Brickworth, the present high sheriff of Wilts, is heir presumptive to the titles of the hero of Trafalgar'.

The Matchams had finally settled in England in 1828 and rented a house in Holland Street, Kensington, from where their remaining daughter, Susanna, was married on 24 April 1832 to Alexander Montgomery Moore, of Co. Tyrone. With her departure, there remained with them only their son Nelson, who was a barrister-at-law practising in Gray's Inn. George Matcham's last journeys were confined to visits to young George at Newhouse, where the happiest moments of his declining years were spent riding about the estate on a pony, with a bevy of grandchildren always at his heels.

The obituary notice of George Matcham in the *Gentleman's Magazine* for March 1833 spoke of his happy disposition and hearty old age. The long tribute to his honourable course in life ended with these words:

His conduct on every occasion was marked by a total disregard of self-interest very rarely witnessed, whilst his anxiety for the welfare of his family, which occupied his mind from their earliest connection with him to his latest hour, must ever be held by them in affectionate remembrance. They had, indeed, the satisfaction of seeing that his sound integrity, unwearied kindness, and unostentatious piety, were rewarded even in this life by an old age passed without infirmity of body, depression of spirits, or weakness of mind, and that his existence was closed even without a sigh.

After George Matcham's death Mrs. Matcham continued living at Kensington with her son Nelson. She had suffered a double loss, with the death of her daughter Kitty Bendyshe only a year before. The Bendyshes were living at Kneesworth near Royston, on their Cambridgeshire estates, during Kitty's last illness and there her parents stayed with her to the end. What with Charles Matcham in Australia and Eliza in Tasmania, Mrs.

Matcham's family circle was still further reduced in August 1838 by the early death of her daughter Harriet Blanckley, at Plymouth. It was then that Susanna stepped in, and adopted Harriet's youngest child, 'Toriana', who eventually married William Ward. Mrs. Matcham spent more and more time with her son George at Newhouse. Her death on 28 March 1842 brought to an end the living Nelson connection with which so much of Horatia's life had been bound.

With the conclusion of the Tenterden Tithes-suit in 1841–2, Horatia herself was moving into a new phase of her life, in which the living present was already giving way to the historic past. With the shaping of this she was to bear an unexpected part in the publication of the Nelson Letters.

Meanwhile the well-wishers of the Wards rejoiced with them on the compromise reached over their law-suit. Dr. Beatty, whose interest in Horatia dated from the death of Nelson, when he was one of the few witnesses to his dying thoughts filled with her, and who in recent years had made personal contact with her, acting as godfather to her son Nelson in 1832, was among the first to congratulate her on the news of a settlement. From his club in Pall Mall, he wrote:

8th April 1841.

My dear Mrs. Ward, It was with great satisfaction, and indeed sincere pleasure, that I heard by the contents of a letter from Lady Nelson [Tom Bolton's widow] that Mr. Ward had at length secured a favourable issue to his Suit with his Parishioners; and although he was constrained to bring the matter to trial at the Assizes, I trust that the termination has been of an amicable nature, rather than in any spirit of hostility, by the party defeated. I hope Mr. Ward and your family are quite well, and that their comfort and yours will be materially increased by the late decision; it must at all events relieve you and him of much domestic anxiety.

Yours most truly, etc
Wm. Beatty.[1]

To Philip and Horatia the settlement of the suit could not be a matter for unalloyed rejoicing; it had cost them too much. Philip had urgently needed the help of a curate in his parish work and had not been able to afford one. His application in 1837 to the Curate's Aid Society, though sympathetically received by the Archbishop, and even with some eulogy of his merits, of 'his personal worth and his zeal in discharge of his duties', had failed to procure him a grant until considerably later. In the meantime he engaged his own nephew, the Revd. Charles Green, son of his eldest sister Mary, at his own expense to help him out.

[1] NMM/NWD/9594/1.

The trials through which he and Horatia had passed, while undermining his health and her nervous energy, do not appear to have weakened the strongest sentiment of their lives, their love for each other. He continued to mark her birthdays with presents of books, and a few of these volumes remain, with the inscriptions in them; in 1840 he gave her the *Arabian Nights*, in five volumes, and in 1841 Smollett's translation of *Gil Blas*. In the former he wrote: 'Horatia Nelson Ward, the gift of her affectionate Husband, on her Birthday 1840'; and in the latter: 'Horatia N. Ward, a Birthday Present Oct 29th 1841. P. Ward'. The inscriptions remain to show that, despite the revelations of the Gibson Letters, Horatia's birthday was still kept on the fictitious date. Her husband's choice of books for her also goes to show that, evangelical clergyman though he might be, he did not attempt to confine her reading; while the verses he wrote on her birthday in 1842 after twenty years of married life remain as a tribute not only to her enduring qualities but to his own as well.

> What tho' each year may steal away
> Some charm of form or face;
> Some sparklings of a brighter day
> Affection still can trace:
> What tho' that envious Time may try
> (Tho' almost try in vain)
> Some lesser rivets to untie
> Of beauty's fairy chain;
> Yet while the heart remains the same,
> Affectionately kind:
> If not so *bright*, so *fine* a flame
> Will linger still behind—
> While Time o'er *that* will have no power—
> If sanctified by grace:
> It will not feel the varying hour
> That withers from a face.
> Oh! may this heart be thine to-day
> And never leave thee, dearest!
> May each fresh birthday give it play
> And make *it* burn the clearest!
> And may such birthdays long be thine
> And mine their joy to share:
> While *beauty* fades, may patience shine
> And guide us every-where!

Oct 29. 1842
P.W.[1]

With good Wishes.

[1] Ibid.

CHAPTER XXI

EDITING HISTORY

THE death of Mrs. Matcham in 1842, following on that of her husband in 1833, of Mr. Bolton in 1834, and of Earl Nelson and Tom Bolton in 1835, removed from the public and domestic scene the closest relatives of Lord Nelson, all those who might in any way be directly affected by a publication of his private papers, upon which task Sir Nicholas Harris Nicolas embarked in April 1843. This was not intended to be a 'Life' in the accepted sense, but as complete a collection of Nelson's letters as could be made available from the scattered sources thirty-eight years after the Admiral's death. Sir Harris had not deliberately awaited the deaths of the sisters and brother before attempting the work, for he anticipated no objection on their part, but his task was certainly lightened by the co-operation of the second generation of the family, particularly by that of Lady Charlotte Bridport and her husband, who laid at his disposal all the family correspondence inherited from her father. Sir Harris received equal help from the sons of Nelson's first commanding officers in his career, Captain Locker and Lord Hood, from whom the letters of his early years at sea were obtained; while the Admiralty supplied the official documents, Nelson's 'Dispatches', which gave the public for the first time the measure of his resolute character in action. This was the first attempt of its kind. The early biographies—incomplete and ill-informed as they all were, with the exception of Southey's *Life* in 1813—had culminated in the scurrilous edition of *The Letters of Lord Nelson to Lady Hamilton* anonymously published in 1814, which received no more than it deserved—a *succès de scandal*. The book's failure, Horatia liked to believe, was complete; speaking of the work to Sir Harris later, she said that the letters it published "cannot sully his fame, as I firmly believe most of the readers of that unfortunate publication of Mr. Harrison's disbelieved them—better so'.[1] This was an opinion she came to modify as time went on.

Sir Harris was accustomed to work of this kind, having, after a short career in the Navy, compiled and edited many books of antiquarian

[1] Letter of 21 Aug. 1846. NMM/NWD/9594/1.

interest (*The Remains of Lady Jane Grey, The Memoirs of Sir Christopher Hatton*, and others). A member of The Royal Society, a barrister of the Inner Temple, a Member of the Society of Antiquaries, Chancellor of the Order of SS Michael and George, his contacts were wide and his knowledge various; a lifelong enthusiasm for Nelson prompted the present work. He envisaged it on a grand scale from the start, but the response he received to his advertisements in the press for Nelson manuscripts, far exceeded his expectations, finally numbering 3,500 letters, which ran into seven volumes. The first volume appeared appropriately enough on 21 October 1844, and the last on 1 August 1846.

The Editor had not been prompted, he declared in the Preface, by any ambition to rival the success of the Wellington 'Dispatches' published in 1835, but solely because 'he was long since convinced that full justice had not been done to Nelson and that such justice could only be rendered by Nelson himself'. Nelson was not nearly so popular a figure in the 1840's as Wellington (as the Matchams frequently realized in Paris after the peace) but the publication of his letters brought about a great revival of his fame. Their sincerity, humanity and passion captivated the country. He was indeed one of the great letter writers, fervent, frank, always vivid. And when it is remembered that the letters published by Sir Harris Nicolas exclude the private correspondence with Lady Hamilton, the fire that animates them is the more remarkable; it is proof that in all his dealings Nelson spoke from the heart. Their impact on the public was immense, and more than anything else since his spectacular death at Trafalgar immortalized his name.

As might be supposed of any editor working so conscientiously as Sir Harris, no avenues of possible research were left unexplored, and before even the first volume was published in October 1844 (which brought Nelson's life up to the year 1794), Sir Harris had established contact with Horatia and had a first meeting with her in London. This took place (as she later recalled) on Wednesday 2 October 1844, in the Strand, at Mr. Veale's, from where they proceeded to Sir Harris's house in Torrington Square. After that the correspondence of Horatia and Sir Harris follows step by step the editor's explorations into the facts of her birth and her own re-discovery of her past. In this sense the editing of her father's letters holds an important place in her own biography, and was fraught with more consequences to herself than she could anticipate; though there can be little doubt that she entered on the task with the great hope of solving the mystery of her birth.

Horatia's personal knowledge of some of the prime movers in the

Nelson drama was, of course, invaluable to Sir Harris Nicolas. A first meeting with her obviously convinced him that he was dealing with a woman of intelligence and character, and though in many instances she proved herself wrong in her judgements and biassed in her conclusions her honesty was as apparent as Nelson's own. At that first meeting he asked her to take home and study carefully the 1814 edition of the Nelson Letters, whose authenticity, in the absence of the original holographs, remained in doubt, and on which she gave him her opinion in due course. She instantly furnished him with the evidence relating to her birth, of whose existence he was ignorant—the thirty-eight letters from Lady Hamilton to Mrs. Gibson, the baptismal certificate from St. Marylebone, and Nelson's four letters to herself, which Sir Harris, acknowledging her contributions to the finished work, described as 'the most touching letters ever written by a father to his child'.[1] Sir Harris had, of course, long since seen the Codicils to Nelson's Will, copies of which were by then entered in Somerset House, including the eighth and last written on the eve of Trafalgar, and was fully aware that Nelson had considered Horatia to be his daughter. Lady Hamilton in her several Wills, likewise had openly spoken of her as such. To Sir Harris, therefore, the letters published in the 1814 edition, which included the 'Thompson Letters', were evidence of the first importance if only their authenticity could be proved.

Horatia's comments on these letters were, therefore, the more important as they influenced his judgement, at least temporarily. On 4 November 1844 she sent Sir Harris her detailed comments on the book. She never hesitated to ascribe it to Harrison, author of the first *Life of Lord Nelson* in 1806, a work which Sir Harris described as disgraced by its disparaging and unjust allusions to Lady Nelson. Of Harrison, Horatia wrote: 'Harrison was a needy man who thought he might oblige Lady Hamilton to give him a certain sum by the threat of publishing letters which he had in his possession—and when this failed—he immediately turned his head to concoct a set of letters from those in his hands which would bring him in a handsome remuneration'.[2] Horatia was convinced that he added to and altered the original letters, and where this would not do, he invented. 'I compare this correspondence,' continued Horatia, 'with Lord Nelson's letters to his wife before they married, and how cold in comparison those to Lady Nelson appear'.[3] Supposing 'a man of 26 to express himself with greater affection and warmth than a man of 46', Horatia refused to believe that the letters to Lady Hamilton were by

[1] Nicolas, i, xxv.   [2] NMM/NWD/9594/13–24.   [3] Ibid.

him—the difference in the two styles of love-letters being altogether too great. 'That Harrison had papers of Lady Hamilton's to make a selection from I know,' Horatia went on, 'as in 1809 when we were at Richmond a large box, quite as large as the one which holds Lord Nelson's letters in your study, was sent to his house'.[1] The published letters, she concluded, were 'in great part fabrications by Harrison'. Her inability to accept the truth they revealed was based on her belief that 'such a man as Lord Nelson was incapable of such deceit', that 'such a man as Lord Nelson' could not use 'such duplicity as to express devotion to Sir William Hamilton, and speak of setting an example to others'.

Horatia's incredulity did her credit, it sprang from a highly-developed sense of honour. That she was Nelson's illegitimate child she accepted, but the explanation she clung to still exonerated him from the long deception practised on Sir William Hamilton, whose friend he declared himself and under whose roof he had lived. In rejecting Lady Hamilton for her mother, she always hoped to prove that Nelson's infatuation, ending in her birth, had been a passing affair, never repeated, during his seven-year service in the Mediterranean without once seeing his wife. This was an interpretation that Horatia could accept, and which relegated Lady Hamilton's role to that of guardian to Nelson's illegitimate child.

Horatia furthermore doubted the authenticity of the verses supposedly composed by Nelson that figure in the 'Thompson Letters', for the double reason that 'I have never heard Mrs. Matcham say (and I think she would have done so) that she ever saw or heard of him writing any', and that Harrison 'was a versifier—I will not call him a poet, and used to be employed occasionally in writ^g verses for me to repeat, so I have no doubt he introduced some of his own here, the *style* is certainly Mr. Harrison's'.[2]

Confronted with the frenzied outbursts of jealousy in Nelson's letters against the Prince of Wales, Horatia again rejected their authenticity; she was 'amazed that Lord Nelson should express himself coarsely to a female friend, when all his letters to his *male* friends are so gentlemanly'.[3]

On the very next day, 5 November, Sir Harris wrote to Horatia about a new development in his researches caused by the appearance on the scene of a dealer in manuscripts, antiques, and furniture, a Mr. T. A. Evans, who had responded to Sir Harris's advertisement with the offer of a great number of Nelson Letters. Evans later published his own account of what he claimed took place between him and Sir

[1] Ibid. [2] Ibid. [3] Ibid.

Harris, and in due course between him and Horatia.[1] His account is scurrilous (though he took care and advice not to make it libellous), but in the main it agrees with the facts as confirmed by the correspondence of Sir Harris and Horatia. Briefly, they were these: Evans, who had an antique shop—called 'The Old Curiosity Shop' at 17 Maddox Street, Hanover Square—received a visit in August 1844 from a man who offered to put him in touch with a person (who proved to be a Mr. Kinsey,[2] Constable of the Borough Town Hall) who had Nelson manuscripts for sale. He had worked for Alderman Smith, from whom he had obtained several documents relating to the Alderman's transactions with Lady Hamilton, and of his loans to her upon the security of her furniture. Evans was concerned, of course, with making money; it was his business. On learning from Kinsey that Nelson's coat was still in the possession of Alderman Smith's widow, whose address he was given in return for a promised share in the profits, he determined to acquire it. With the double prospect of doing business with Mrs. Smith, and of selling letters to Sir Harris, Evans bought all the letters Kinsey offered him, which amounted to hundreds—and approached Sir Harris, who very naturally asked to see them. Evans's story was that he sent a list of the letters and inadvertently included among them Mrs. Smith's address, thus putting Sir Harris in the way of contacting her and outwitting him in bidding for the coat. Evans's case, which rested on the supposition that neither Sir Harris nor Mrs. Ward knew where Nelson's coat had been stored all those years, had no foundation. Horatia had, of course, always known where the coat was, and told Sir Harris of it at their very first meeting on 2 October 1844. She had corresponded with Mrs. Smith about it ever since the death of Alderman Smith in 1835, deploring her inability to buy it. The matter was of secondary interest to Sir Harris, whose chief concern was to acquire the hoard of letters brought him by Evans. Among these were ten, tied up separately, addressed to Lady Hamilton and signed 'Horatia'. Telling Evans that he had better contact Mrs. Ward about those, he wrote to Horatia telling her the whole remarkable incident. She answered him by return on 7 November 1844; and commented rightly on the 'strangeness that these letters and at *this time* have been offered to you. These letters I should very much like to see—so much so that if Horatia [her young daughter] is well enough and willing to part

---

[1] A Statement of the Means by which THE NELSON COAT . . . was obtained by Sir Harris Nicolas, London 1846.

[2] On Ald. Smith's death his widow sent several crates of Ld. N's letters etc. to the safe-keeping of Kinsey at Southwark Town Hall. Nelson Collection, Monmouth Museum.

with me I think I shall run up to Town on Monday for a couple of days. Possibly I may form a guess were they came from'. How delicate her daughter Horatia was, aged twelve at the time, is apparent not only from this letter, but throughout the correspondence with Sir Harris, especially during the spring and summer of 1846, when three successive and 'severe illnesses' kept Mrs. Ward at her bedside for weeks.

Among the letters mentioned by Sir Harris as received from Evans were numbers from the Boltons and Matchams to Lady Hamilton (eventually published in Alfred Morrison's invaluable collection in 1894) and one of so singular and arresting a nature as to be especially intriguing to Sir Harris; it was Sarah Snelling's note to Lady Hamilton written in May 1801, regarding the child received from the Foundlings. The obvious conclusion he drew was that it related to a twin of Horatia's. Horatia's comment on the subject is therefore the more important since the letter's prima facie interpretation would support his view, and no other:

My opinion I will give you . . . I have heard Lady Hamilton say that she attended the service at the Foundling with Mrs. (afterwards Lady) Nelson, Sir William Hamilton and several others. It was then the Custom to have the foundlings Xened either during or after the service and for some reason which I do not remember, Lady Hamilton did on this occasion stand godmother to one of these infants. I remember some years after going to hear a blind girl play who was organist there of the name of Jane Frere. She had published some Sonatas. Lady Hamilton bought a copy and gave it to me. She dated it when we got home June 20th 1808. I perfectly remember her *then* telling me this circumstance of her having answered for a Child there, and her enquiring of Mrs. Johnston who was then Matron and Superintendent of the Hospital after the children were Xened, that she was named Emma. I have therefore little doubt but that the Child named in the letter was that same one . . . Lady Hamilton was *much* too cunning and cautious had she taken away a child from this place for any sinister purpose in contemplation ever to allow the person with whom she placed it to know whence it came . . . Besides else, what became of this child? I never heard of any person of the name of Snelling.[1]

In the hope, perhaps, of disproving the existence of such a person, Horatia got Philip to write to the Vicar of Chertsey, the Revd. Mr. Cotton, to ask whether a Mrs. Snelling had indeed ever lived within his parish. The Vicar's answer was more conclusive than the Wards had expected, for he wrote to say that Mrs. Snelling—and her husband—were alive, living in Chertsey still, and had two grown-up sons.[2] Mr. Cotton

---

[1] Letter of 7 Nov. 1844. NMM/NWD/9594/13-24.
[2] NMM/NWD/9594/1.

gave Philip, moreover, all the particulars relating to Mrs. Snelling; her maiden name was Field, she had been employed as servant to a lady named Pembroke till her marriage to Snelling, who was a sawyer, and confirmed that she had received children from the Foundling Hospital, altogether four children—three boys and one girl—the name of the girl being Emma Hamilton.

One would expect this to have prompted further investigations on Horatia's part—a visit to Sarah Snelling to question her on whatever light she could throw on Lady Hamilton's connection with the child committed to her care. But there is no evidence that Horatia did anything of the kind, or took the matter further.

Sarah Snelling was perhaps bound by oath to reveal nothing relating to the Foundling infants committed to her care. Even so the clue was the clearest of any that had been uncovered, and the fact that Horatia did not follow it up seems to suggest that all clues leading to Lady Hamilton were too unacceptable to be pursued. Meanwhile, Horatia tried to convince both Sir Harris and herself of the unimportance of the clue. 'Lady Hamilton was always remarkably fond of visiting these kind of places', she wrote. 'Hardly a month passed but we used to drive to the Magdalen or the Blind School and any other places of this kind . . . I have written to the Boltons and George Matcham respect[g] these letters and will send you the substance of their answers. Will you retain them till then?' [1]

George Matcham's answer to Horatia's letter, dated 15 November 1844, is interesting mainly for his comments on the old Viscountess Nelson and his doubts whether the public retained any interest in Nelson. 'My dear Mrs. Ward'. he wrote her from Newhouse, near Downton,

I am very much obliged to you for your communication relative to the letters addressed to the great Admiral—but it is not my intention to apply for them. With regard to those of my own parents: I am quite certain that they can contain nothing which will injure their reputation in any way whatever because as they were guileless and honourable in all their actions, their letters will, I am convinced, bear the same character. If there is any that would interest me it is that of the Viscountess Nelson which might probably tend to show the provocation she cast on her husband and the difficulty of living with her in ordinary comfort.

I hope Mr. Ward and all your olive branches are quite well the latter I presume, sprung up into tall men and women. If you or any of them visit this part of the country: I hope you will not forget this place and that we shall be very happy to see you here.[2]

[1] NMM/NWD/9594/13-24.   [2] Ibid., 9594/1.

Presumably on the Monday suggested, 11 November, Horatia travelled up to London and stayed with her old friend, Mrs. Glasse, in Cambridge Street, Hyde Park Square. She dined with Sir Harris and his wife, and learnt from him the whole story of the letters offered by Evans. Later, in the evening, Evans himself called on her by arrangement, and showed her the bundle of ten letters tied together, addressed to Lady Hamilton and signed 'Horatia'. Evans, in a printed statement, related the circumstances of the interview which took place at 7 p.m. 'in the front drawing-room' of Mrs. Glasse's house, and described Horatia as 'a portly-looking Lady, apparently between forty and fifty years of age ... and I was instantly struck with the strong resemblance she bore to the portraits and miniatures of Lord Nelson'.[1] He took great umbrage from the fact that she wore a heavy gold chain round her neck, as she had been described to him by Sir Harris as 'the wife of a poor country clergyman, with a large family, and though she much wishes to have the letters, it is not in her power to give a large sum for them'. Though Horatia saw his defamatory pamphlet two years later, her sense of humour was equal to most contingencies, and the only detail that interested her was his comment on her resemblance to Lord Nelson; this struck her greatly: 'do *you* think there is any?' she asked Sir Harris in a latter of 28 March 1846. 'It is a singular fact that my children are reckoned strikingly like Mrs. Henry Girdlestone by her sisters (she was a daughter of Mrs. Bolton). . .'.[2]

According to Evans's narrative, he showed Mrs. Ward the letters which 'she wanted, she said, only to destroy them—they were of no value', and asked £1 for them. Upon her saying that she could not afford that, he asked 10s.—'the price of his cab-hire', meaning to humiliate her. Evans was not concerned with history, or even with partial truths; all he wanted was to make money. Horatia's letters, probably written as a child from Merton while Lady Hamilton was at Clarges Street, which would be so precious to her biographer, had no interest for him; what he wanted was to ascertain from Horatia particulars about Mrs. Smith, with whom he intended doing a 'deal'—to buy Nelson's coat so as to re-sell it at a good profit. Because the matter went against Evans, and the coat was secured for the nation through the intervention of Horatia and Sir Harris Nicolas, Evans accused them of dishonest collusion, in first extracting all the information regarding the coat from him and then out-bidding him. He ignored, of course, Horatia's long association with Mrs. Smith and interest in buying the coat ever since 1835.

[1] *A Statement of the Means by which THE NELSON COAT was obtained* ... op cit.
[2] NMM/NWD/9594/13-24.

Horatia had written to Sir Harris before going up to town, saying she would 'much like on Tuesday to go down to Mrs. Smith's if you will accompany me—perchance we may learn more. She has not yet answered my letter . . . My time will be so short that I must make the most of every minute.' [1] With Sir Harris, therefore, she drove out to Twickenham and called on Mrs. Smith. Her price, £150, was beyond even Sir Harris's means, but his hope and intention, as later carried out, was to start a national subscription to buy the coat and place it at Greenwich. Mrs. Smith herself was anxious that the coat should be secured for Greenwich, and agreed to defer selling it to Evans or anyone else for a further month.

Evans's account of his own visit to Mrs. Smith is interesting for the details he gives of her situation which, he declared, 'did not correspond with her reputed poor circumstances'. On calling at the house in Park Road, Twickenham, he was 'admitted by a footman in livery, and I found her in a room elegantly furnished and decorated with many articles of taste and vertu' (as a dealer in antique furniture, Evans had an eye for good pieces). 'There was no attempt at deception, no appearance of being in straitened circumstances, and so much candour in her manner, that I began to suspect Mrs. Ward to be, what events have since proved the fact, an artful, cunning woman, with some sinister object in view in her representations relative to the widow'. Mrs. Smith showed him the coat and named 200 guineas as the price, which, Evans declares, 'he agreed to pay'. 'Then Mrs. Smith said she was not free to sell it as she had already promised it to a lady who had applied before.' Evans contested this and argued 'that *no one* for forty years had known of the coat, except Kinsey'. On his asking Mrs. Smith who the applicant was,' she replied: 'Mrs. Ward, the daughter of Lord Nelson'. Evans, who saw a plot in everything, alleged that Horatia had promised to help Sir Harris get the coat, on condition that he got her the ten letters relating to her. He did not hesitate to accuse Sir Harris to his face in a further interview, of making use of Kinsey's list (inadvertently sent him) which revealed the whereabouts of the coat. From this conviction he could not be moved; he demanded back all the letters loaned to Sir Harris, and threatened to expose him in the press.

While Evans threatened and fulminated, the alleged plotters pursued their course. Horatia visited Mrs. Smith again in December, after which visit Mrs. Smith wrote to her:

Now my dear Mrs. Ward, the very candid statement you have made me respecting the Coat is such that I will wait till the middle of next month. I perfectly

[1] Ibid.

agree with you, that if it should so happen that it cannot belong to the family, it should to the Nation, as the most valuable relic . . . It is strange that so many persons are anxious to possess that which has remained so many years in my possession, unsought.[1]

The story of the coat ended shortly after the publication of the first volume of Nelson's *Dispatches and Letters*, which was greeted with unanimous praise. The re-awakened interest in Nelson far exceeded even Sir Harris's hopes; he was proved to have been fully justified in his undertaking. In the altered climate of opinion, he was not only encouraged to pursue his task—and his ceaseless search after authentic Nelson letters —but in his wish to secure Nelson's coat for the nation. On 26 June 1845 he drew up a Statement for insertion in the press to open a public subscription but before circulating it, he sent a copy to the Prince Consort. By return of post he received an acknowledgement from the Prince's secretary, dated 28 June, which informed him that the Prince 'wished to purchase these relics on his account, and it will be a pride and pleasure to him to present them to Greenwich Hospital'. Furnished with the Prince's cheque for £150, Sir Harris immediately paid Mrs. Smith, received the coat (and waistcoat), and himself delivered them to the Prince at Buckingham Palace.

Mrs. Smith was quick to report the good news to Horatia; her satisfaction, furthermore, prompted her to make a fresh search among her late husband's papers (possibly at Horatia's repeated request) and to find, most opportunely, though somewhat belatedly, a document about which she wrote to Horatia on 9 July. It had been endorsed by Lady Hamilton and Mrs. Smith reported:

I read it and found a confirmation of what I never doubted—Your being his— Nelson's—child. I thought it might be a satisfaction to you because in this document she speaks with certainty of your being *Lord Nelson's daughter*, and what advantage could she gain at the time she wrote this of telling a falsehood because she must at that time have been living in prosperity, however dreadful her after life was. I wish I could in any way have satisfied you further, but I cannot. The Lady must have been highly respectable—or why should it be shrouded in mystery? Excuse me. I have known you long and believe me, there is no one who has been more anxious except yourself to tear aside the veil which leaves one part in obscurity.[2]

(Mrs. Smith, apparently, took Horatia's view of the case that Lady Hamilton could not be her mother).

Already, the whole purpose and direction of Horatia's investigations

[1] Letter dated 16 Dec. 1844. NMM/NWD/9594/1.   [2] Ibid.

for Sir Harris Nicolas were centred on the question of her mother's identity. While Sir Harris, studying the 'Thompson' letters in Harrison's edition, was strongly inclined to believe it was Lady Hamilton, Horatia always contested the fact. The proof she sought by which to refute the idea conclusively always eluded her; she had no proof, only her strong, her intense antipathy to the idea. This was so apparent to Sir Harris that she herself referred to it: 'I am sure you thought I shut my eyes against the fact', she wrote to him on 20 May 1846, 'because I was disinclined to it.'[1]

As Sir Harris advanced the great work, and the contents of the last volume were under review, a decision had to be reached on the place of Horatia in her father's life, and what statement the editor was to make regarding her birth. He was resolved on taking the 'bull by the horns' and dealing frankly with the matter (in the end he gave twenty-eight pages to it) and wished, naturally, to reach an agreement with Horatia on the statement to be made. Searching among the last survivors of Nelson's intimate circle who might yet be able to furnish the clue both he and Horatia so ardently sought, Sir Harris decided to consult Mr. Haslewood, now retired and living at Brighton, who, as Nelson's solicitor, should be the repository of family secrets if anyone was.

Having to consult him on the question of Nelson's separation from his wife, of which Haslewood was the eye-witness, Sir Harris resolved to put the question regarding Lady Hamilton straight to him as well. He told Horatia of his intention, and received from her a letter on the very day Haslewood wrote to him about Nelson's last meeting with his wife. 'Mr. Haslewood,' wrote Horatia, 'knows *nothing*. Mrs. Matcham had a long conversation with him on the subject—he told her that he really knew nothing—had he done so, he would not have hesitated one instant to communicate it to her.'[2] Haslewood surprised both Sir Harris and Horatia, however, by declaring (verbally, during a visit from Sir Harris) that he *did* know something, but was bound in honour not to reveal it. Such a statement, in flagrant contradiction of all his previous assurances to the Matchams, Mr. Rose, and Horatia's other friends in 1815, could not fail to astound Horatia. 'If you knew more of Mr. Haslewood', she wrote Sir Harris on 25 April, 'you would think that he had more of the fox about him than you now give him credit for. More on that subject when we meet . . . I shall possibly be in town on the 27 but may, I fear, be detained till the 4 May—Will this do?' The delay, as she explained to Sir Harris on 7 May, was caused because 'in the night of Tuesday poor

[1] Ibid.　　[2] Letter of 13 April 1846. NMM/NWD/9594/13-24.

Horatia had a large abscess broke and I was up with her all night'. The
health of her daughter Horatia throughout that spring and summer continued to give her constant anxiety. Reverting to Mr. Haslewood's
innuendoes, she continued further to Sir Harris in the same letter:

I still can hardly bring myself to believe that Mr. Haslewood knows anything, if
he does why not tell you when he saw you at Brighton—as well as now, if bound
by any promise it would be equally binding, now as then—and why impart to an
utter stranger what he refused, or at least told that he was ignorant of, to tell to
Lord Nelson's sister and the person most concerned in it, myself—and again, I
cannot credit that Lord Nelson would have confided to Mr. Haslewood that
which he never revealed to his own family or even Mr. Davison, a man whom he
esteemed very highly, for you must remember that Mr. Haslewood's connection
with Lord Nelson was not that of a friend, but that of lawyer and client.[1]

From Hastings, where she took her daughter later in May, Horatia
wrote again to Sir Harris, re-affirming her conviction 'that Lady Hamilton
was not and could not have been my mother'—and wondering, rather
sarcastically, whether 'Wm. Haslewood, Esq., of Kemp Town, Brighton,
could be persuaded to communicate his knowledge *under a promise of
inviolable secrecy?*'[2] Informing her that the proof of the seventh volume
had gone to press, Sir Harris wrote: 'As to Haslewood, you really know
quite as much of him in this matter as I do. He seemed to me to think
it a point of honour not to divulge more than I have told you. I think
a little time hence you may fairly appeal to his feelings to communicate
to you a fact in which you have so deep an interest'. In pursuance of this
advice, Horatia wrote to Haslewood after the publication of the last
volume of the Letters, in September, an appeal of which the rough draft
has been preserved.

23rd September

My dear Sir,
    So many years have passed since I had the pleasure of meeting you that I feel
some hesitation in again recalling my self to your recollection. I have just read the
7th Vol. of Lord Nelson's Letters and dispatches and find by a paragraph in the
Appendix that you are acquainted with the Secret of who my Mother was.
Believe me, my dear Sir, I am actuated by no idle curiosity but by an earnest and
natural desire to know to whom I owe my being, when I implore you to impart
the knowledge to me—it shall be if you wish it under the seal of confidence. I
am sure you will forgive my importunity when I beseech you not to withhold
that information so highly interesting to me. What you would have been unwilling
to disclose to a giddy girl I hope you will not fear to trust to the discretion of a

[1] Letter of 25–6 April 1846. NMM/NWD/9594/13–24.
[2] Letter of 20 May 1846. NMM/NWD/9594/13–24.

woman of forty-six. I am quite sure that although you were requested to preserve a mother's secret, that injunction was never intended to extend to her own child. Apologizing for the liberty I have taken, Believe me, dear Sir,

Very sincerely yours,[1]

Mr. Haslewood's reply was dated Brighton, 26 September 1846, and was written in a very feeble hand.

My dear Madam,
    I dare not write so fully as I could wish on the topics referred to in your kind letter of the 23rd, lest the secret which I am bound to keep should be rendered too transparent. Thus much only may be said without incurring much risk—Your Mother was well acquainted with Lady Hamilton; and saw you frequently during your infancy: but soon after her marriage she went to reside at a considerable distance from London—Lamenting that I cannot be more communicative I remain always, my dear Madam, faithfully yours,

Wm. Haslewood.[2]

It seems extraordinary to the modern investigator that so contradictory and weak a statement should have satisfied Horatia in any way. She knew from Mrs. Gibson's evidence that no one, with the exception of Lady Hamilton and Lord Nelson, ever visited her in infancy; she also knew Lady Hamilton's statement to Mrs. Gibson that 'Father and Mother being dead' no questions relative to the child were to be answered. While Haslewood's letter only confirmed Horatia's unshaken conviction that Lady Hamilton was not her mother, the identity of the real one remained as obscure as ever; this was all that Haslewood's secrecy produced. The alternatives were not very wide, and Horatia had considered them for years. Lady Hamilton's written statement to Mrs. Salter that 'HER MOTHER WAS TOO GREAT TO MENTION' had—as she intended—confused the issue successfully, but Horatia was too realistic to accept the veiled allusion to the Queen of Naples. 'Mrs. Salter's paper has, I own, surprised me', Horatia wrote to Sir Harris,

and Lady Hamilton having always declared that she would leave an account behind her when she died, of the facts of the case, make me think more of it than I otherwise should do—the person might be too great to mention, but not the Queen of Naples ... I have always, and if you remember told you that I never for an instance gave credence to the story of the Queen of Naples and of *course* to a certainty none of her daughters—but my opinion has always been that either a foreigner or at any rate some one from abroad was the person.[3]

[1] NMM/NWD/9594/13-24.   [2] Ibid.
[3] Letter of 7 May 1846. NMM/NWD/9594/13-24.

Having taken her stand, Horatia was not to be dissuaded from it; and together with Haslewood's verbal and written statement that Lady Hamilton was not the mother of Nelson's child, Sir Harris Nicolas had no option but to bow to their pressure. Whatever his reservations—and he had several—he published the statement sponsored by them.

It is significant, however, that if Horatia was not prepared to accept the birth of a second child to Lady Hamilton, though mentioned in Nelson's letters of 1804, Sir Harris had his doubts, and wrote to the parish clerk of Merton to ask whether the death of a child called 'Emma' had been entered in the registers of burials there.[1] The answer was negative, and Horatia persuaded Sir Harris to omit mention of this 'apocryphal child' from his book.

Sir Harris Nicolas therefore concluded, and published, the following findings to his investigations into the whole question of Nelson's relationship with Lady Hamilton, and the paternity of Horatia.

It is here proper, in common justice to Lord Nelson and to Lady Hamilton, to state, that great doubt has been created in the Editor's mind, after considering all the documents to which he has had access, and knowing the opinions of persons likely to be correctly informed on the subject, whether the intimacy between Lord Nelson and Lady Hamilton was ever, in the usual sense of the word, of a criminal nature. This proposition will probably startle most persons, because a platonic affection, under such circumstances is very unusual, and because the early career of Lady Hamilton is not favourable to an opinion of her virtue in after life.[2]

Nelson's virtue, however, and that of his whole family, 'his nice sense of honour, his feelings of propriety, and his love of truth', the Editor claimed, should place his actions above suspicion. Moreover, the fact that his whole family, father, sisters, brother, were led by him to accept Lady Hamilton, that he left her the 'sole guardian of his child', should exonerate him from such a charge. That such suspicion generally existed, and that 'it has been generally supposed that Horatia was the daughter of Lord Nelson by Lady Hamilton', the Editor frankly admitted, but in the same breath quoted the evidence of Haslewood, which he accepted as conclusive 'The Editor is authorized by Mr. Haslewood', he wrote, 'long the confidential friend and professional adviser of Lord Nelson, to declare in the most positive manner, that *Lady Hamilton was not its mother*. The name of the mother is known to Mr. Haslewood; but he is prevented by a sense of honour from disclosing it.'[3]

[1] The reply from the parish clerk, a man named Bond, was dated 2 May 1846. NMM/NWD/9594/13-24. [2] Nicolas, vii, 389. [3] Ibid.

There can be little doubt that relief, as well as gratitude for the great task accomplished, influenced Horatia's thanks when the seventh volume reached her. She wrote to Sir Harris on 21 August 1846: 'I am, indeed, we are all, delighted with the last vol.—you have said all that was proper and judicious. How can I thank you sufficiently. I have not yet finished the book. I have only been able to read during intervals of watching my invalid.'[1]

Haslewood's statement, given such priority in the Editor's conclusions regarding Lady Hamilton, and eliminating Horatia's worst fears of a revelation she dreaded to hear, could not shelter Nelson's daughter from learning, at this late stage, truths even more bitter to accept. Sir Harris's volume had gone to press in the first week of May 1846, and was published on 1 August of the same year. It had barely had time to circulate when Sir Harris was approached by John Wilson Croker, sometime Secretary to the Admiralty, with the original letters published in the 1814 edition, reckoned to have disappeared after their sale to him in 1817, and whose authenticity was now glaringly apparent. Croker, who must have seen Sir Harris's repeated advertisements in the press for Nelson manuscripts, had presumably withheld them for reasons of his own. For Horatia, who had resolutely disbelieved in their authenticity, or at least had believed them grossly tampered with by Harrison, the discovery was grievous. This was a revelation that affected not merely her birth, or the identity of her mother, but the character of Lord Nelson, of the father whose great name she had borne with such pride. It was his fall from grace that grieved her most. 'Most correctly have you judged when you said I should be much shocked to find that those wretched letters are Genuine. Alas! that such a master-mind should be subject to such weakness', she wrote on 21 August 1846.

Of what a strange medley is the human mind constituted. I cannot however help rejoicing (I hope nor from any love of dissimulation) that these letters did not come under your notice till after the 7th Vol. was published. Had you seen them earlier you would have felt bound to take some notice of them. *Now* they cannot sully *his* fame as I firmly believe most of the readers of that unfortunate publication of Mr. Harrison disbelieved them. Better so . . . Thank God they did not fall into our friend Evans' hands![2]

Horatia supposed that Croker had, purposely, kept the letters back till the book was out, but wrote to Sir Harris that if the matter was a secret she did not press to be told. Even in her disillusionment over Nelson's

[1] NMM/NWD/9594/13–24.   [2] Ibid.

broken faith—and it is noteworthy that what she most deplored was not
his unfaithfulness to his wife but his deception of Sir William Hamilton—
she was impressed by his just and generous character: 'One thing', she
wrote to Sir Harris, 'is I think very remarkable, Lord Nelson's love of
justice in his Will—even at the time he did not *love* his wife his anxiety to
make such a provision for her in his Will was great'.[1]

Despite the revelations of the Croker letters, Horatia's basic conviction
remained unshaken: 'Still I do not alter my opinion', she wrote to Sir
Harris on 21 August 1846, 'that Lady Hamilton could not have been
my Mother. I do not recollect one letter in which I am named as a
Mutual tie between them, or any allusion of that kind'. Only three years
later, Dr. Pettigrew, in his *Memoirs of the Life of Lord Nelson* would
publish Nelson's letter of 1 March 1801, which by then he had acquired
from Croker, the wording of which could leave no one in doubt that
Horatia had been a 'Mutual tie between them':

Now, my own dear wife, for such you are in my eyes and in the face of heaven,
I can give full scope to my feelings. You know, my dearest Emma, that there is
nothing in this world that I would not do for us to live together, and to have our
dear little child with us. I love, I never did love, anyone else. I have never had a
dear pledge of love till you gave me one, and you, thank God, never gave one to
anyone else . . . Kiss and bless our dear Horatia—think of that.[2]

Sir Harris Nicolas, who died prematurely in 1848, 'worn out with work',[3]
barely two years after the completion of his monumental task, did not live
to see the publication of Dr. Pettigrew's work. His own summing up
of the facts regarding Horatia's birth was disproved on the evidence of
the Croker letters. But the effect of their publication was far less conclusive than it might have been, because of Pettigrew's unscholarly
treatment of his material, and his failure to give the sources of his evidence. Even after reading his book, Horatia might remain unconvinced,
as indeed proved to be the case. That so intelligent a woman, unremit-
tingly pursuing the truth, should have turned so blind an eye to the
evidence of her being Lady Hamilton's daughter can only be explained
by the intense revulsion such a thought aroused.

After her long collaboration with Sir Harris she seemed to be as far
away from discovering the truth as ever. But one lasting benefit she did
receive for Sir Harris commented on Nelson's dying bequest of his
daughter to the beneficence of his King and Country and wrote, 'This

[1] Ibid. [2] See above, p. 24. Also Pettigrew ii. 639.
[3] *Cornhill Magazine*, May 1906. E. S. P. Haynes, *Lady Hamilton and Horatia*.

solemn bequest has, however, to this day, been utterly disregarded'.[1] This statement brought Horatia's situation, more than forty years after Trafalgar, before a public that had for so long ignored it, and stirred a sympathy for her in the hearts of Englishmen which would at last have its effect.

[1] Nicolas, Preface, vol. i. p. x.

CHAPTER XXII

BELATED BOUNTY

LIKE Sir Harris Nicolas, Dr. Pettigrew was a man of enormous industry and varied interests, and work never daunted him. Not content with his career as a busy lecturer in the London Hospitals and a large private practice in Savile Row, he was a founder member of various antiquarian and literary societies—the City Philosophical Society, and the Archeological Association in particular—whose meetings were held at his house. His interest in Nelson was life-long, and derived from his father who was ship's surgeon in the *Victory* even before Nelson's time. Dr. Pettigrew's fault as an editor was a want of precision, due no doubt to the multiplicity of his interests; he was particularly careless in his acceptance of Mrs. Hunter's evidence about Lady Hamilton's death at Calais, and in his account of the Earl's conduct over the last codicil. His decision to publish Nelson Letters so soon after Sir Harris Nicolas's work was partially influenced, no doubt, by the sudden death of Sir Harris in 1848 and also by the death of Mr. Haslewood, which in a sense allowed him to tackle the disputed issues afresh. He totally disagreed with Sir Harris and with Horatia, with whom he made no attempt to discuss the problems before publishing his book. With Croker's collection of the original letters in his possession, Dr. Pettigrew could publish without fear of public denial the texts hitherto believed spurious. 'The examination of the entire correspondence', states Dr. Pettigrew, 'leads me to adopt a totally different opinion [to Sir Harris] and one which permits of no question as to the parentage of the child Horatia'. The Thompson Letters, and in particular the letter of 1 March 1801, sent by private hand 'and containing an absolute and distinct avowal of the parentage of the child, sets the question completely at rest and beyond dispute'.[1]

Once published, the fact was treated like current news and publicized in the world press. Philip Ward received a letter from a Mr. Edward Lombe, resident in Florence who, because he had estates in Norfolk, considered himself entitled to write to him: 'In Galignani's Messenger of the 18th inst I have just read of a letter to the 'Times' published by the 'Observer'

---

[1] Pettigrew, ii, 639.

and signed 'Anti-Cant'. It states that your wife is the Daughter of Lord Nelson and Lady Hamilton'.[1]

Unwelcome as the notoriety might be, in the altered climate of opinion produced by these various revelations Horatia's friends felt themselves emboldened for the first time to come forward on her behalf, to make her situation known, and to secure a pension for her either from the court or the government. Horatia herself strongly deprecated such an attempt; as those who came in contact with her found, she was proud and reticent, and preferred obscurity to the exposure of her wrongs; but she was overruled by the ardour of her supporters, and above all by the needs of her family. In 1849 she allowed a committee to be formed by an inner circle of friends.

The Wards' financial position—even after the settlement of the Tithes suit—remained painfully inadequate for their needs, with five sons to educate and launch in life, to say nothing of their three daughters. Philip's stipend amounted to £200 a year, and Horatia's income from the money left in trust for her by Nelson also totalled some £200.

The prime movers in organizing the committee were Captain Henry Lancaster, R.N., the Revd. John Hoole (a friend of Philip's), and James Walker, Esq. They sought out the right supporters from every walk of public life, from the Prince Consort to the Lord Mayor, from the great city bankers to the public press, and engaged their specialized and varied knowledge and influence. As might be expected in the formation of such a body, the names of Nelson's officers figure largely at their head, beginning with Captain Lancaster himself, the Vicar of Merton's son and a life-long friend of Horatia's, the same who sailed with Nelson as a boy in the last memorable action. The boy of 14 had fulfilled Nelson's prediction in one of his last letters home: 'Tell Mr. Lancaster that his son will do very well', he had written. Captain Lancaster had served principally in the Mediterranean and retired after 1815 on half pay. It was in keeping with the family's devotion to Nelson that one of the first subscribers to the 'Horatia Fund' was Mrs. Ullock, Captain Lancaster's sister. Another of the Trafalgar survivors, Captain James Robertson Walker (a boy like Henry Lancaster at the time) took a leading part in securing sponsors for the Appeal. Writing to Horatia after the event, the Revd. John Hoole told her of his active agency: 'You do no more than justice to Mr. Walker's agency in this matter', he wrote on 16 June 1855. 'He engaged, in great measure, the interests of Sir Edward Codrington, and entirely Captain Shepherd [Chairman of the East India Company]

[1] NMM/NWD/9594/29.

Captain Nelson also, who moved Richard Green, the Smiths of Newcastle; Sir James Graham, and in chief part, the Lord Chancellor. He also suggested the application to the Prince; and finally influenced Mr. Hume'.[1]

As the text of the Appeal, when finally drawn up, showed, these were among the prominent names of its earliest sponsors. Admiral Sir Edward Codrington, like Admiral Sir Thomas Bladen Capel, had both served at Trafalgar (the gallant conduct of Lieutenant Codrington in the *Orion* indeed gaining him a gold medal on the occasion).

The application to Prince Albert was made at Mr. Walker's suggestion before the Appeal was published in the press in May 1850. His reply has been preserved, and is interesting as showing the attitude adopted by the Establishment towards Horatia: a benevolent desire to be practically helpful, without publically admitting her claims. The Prince's secretary wrote:

Buckingham Palace / March 16th 1850

Dear Sir,

I have received the commands of His Royal Highness the Prince Albert to inform you, that although his Royal Highness does not feel that he could with propriety head the public subscription for Mrs. Ward, not being able to separate himself from the government, yet in his private capacity his Royal Highness was anxious as far as lay in his power to assist Mrs. Ward in the education of her children. The prince has at present a presentation to Christ's Hospital, and has directed me to request that you will have the goodness to offer this presentation to that lady in case any one of her sons should be of an age (between 7 and 10) to which he would be admissable.

Believe me,
Sincerely yours,
C. B. Phipps.[2]

In her reply, presumably sent to Captain Lancaster to whom most of the correspondence about the Appeal was addressed, Horatia gave an account of the present situation of the family. The only one as yet to earn his living was her eldest son, Horace, who had gone to Pembroke College, Cambridge, taken his B.A. degree in 1847, and was at that time acting as his father's curate at Tenterden. Helped by the Curate's Aid Society, Philip was able to pay him an independent salary that was not deducted from his own. Horace continued to help his father till 1853. Horatia's letter, which was undated and written during her stay in London on the business of the Appeal, reads:

[1] Ibid.   [2] Ibid.

21

My dear and Old Friend,

Many, very many thanks for your kind letter; it was only put into my hands as I was starting for London, and I was too much knocked up to answer it till this evening, I thank Prince Albert much for his kind intention, but my children are all too old to avail themselves of his offer, the youngest boy [Philip] being sixteen in the early part of May. You ask the ages and occupations of my children—Horace 27 the 8th December last, is now his father's curate and has been so for two years. Ellen 26 in April. Marmaduke 25 in May, now an assistant surgeon at Melville Hospital, Chatham. Nelson 22 in the early part of May I *greatly fear* will have an appointment in India: he has served his time to a solicitor. William, 20 next April has a cadetship to India. Horatia 17 last November, Philip 16 in May, Caroline 14 last January. I have written the above with some trouble as alas! I am neither in mind or body, as in the days of yore. Thank you very much for all your exertions, and believe me that whatever the result may be, the kind feelings which have dictated them have sunk deep into my heart.

When I return and have quiet and rest, I will write again,

Yours sincerely and truly,

H. N. Ward.[1]

A matter of great concern to Horatia was the offer of a Cadetship made by Captain Shepherd, Chairman of the East India Co., to her son Nelson, who had not yet completed his articles with the Tenterden solicitor, Mr. John Scratton, entered into in 1844. He had the prospect of a successful career in the law (as indeed proved to be the case) if he could complete his time, and if the offer of the Cadetship could be transferred from him to his younger brother, William George. This was happily effected two years later, and in 1852 William went out to Madras in his brother's place. All Horatia's sons, at various times in their lives, brought her comfort and pride, but with Nelson she lived on closer terms for a greater number of years than with any of them, eventually making her home with him; the decision to keep him in England was therefore a fortunate one.

On 8 May 1850 the Appeal on Horatia's behalf appeared on the front page of the *Morning Chronicle*; a more prominent position could not have been given to it. It was followed by a list of subscriptions already received and, more important still, was given an additional boost of a leading article of a column and a half on the centre page, the tenor of which suggests it was the work of Joseph Hume, M.P., one of the most active members of the committee. The texts of these statements make extraordinary reading today, when public pronouncements are both more discreet, less emotional, and of a less high moral tone! Yet their substance

[1] Ibid.

was based on nothing but the truth. The Appeal was headed: NELSON MEMORIAL FUND / FOR HIS DAUGHTER HORATIA, and read:

'I also leave to the beneficence of my country my ADOPTED DAUGHTER, HORATIA NELSON THOMPSON, and I desire she will in future use the name of Nelson only. These are the only favours I ask of my King and Country, at this moment, when I am going to fight their battle. May God bless my King and Country, and all those who I hold dear.'

Such were Nelson's words on the morning of the MEMORABLE TWENTY FIRST OCTOBER 1805, when, in sight of the Combined Fleets of France and Spain, off Cape Trafalgar. Again, after receiving his mortal wound and almost with his expiring breath, he said, 'Remember, I leave my Daughter Horatia as a legacy to my Country—Never forget HORATIA—THANK GOD I HAVE DONE MY DUTY—'

Nearly five and forty years have elapsed, and this request has never been complied with. Although large sums were bestowed on Nelson's family, and though we have raised and still are raising monuments and statues to his memory in various parts of the Kingdom, yet this nearest and dearest desire of his heart, uttered in the agonies of death by the greatest of naval heroes, remains to this day unfulfilled by the Government of the country.

Nelson's Horatia still survives, the exemplary wife of an excellent clergyman with a small income and a large family. Will the British nation now at length perform the long neglected duty, or still refuse to entertain this last claim on their gratitude, till reparation be no longer possible, and regret unavailing?

The following gentlemen, who will be glad to receive an addition to their number, have agreed to act as a committee for the purpose of promoting the above object, and of investing the amount that may be subscribed, in such a way as may be considered most beneficial for Horatia, and her family:

Admiral Sir Edward Codrington, G.C.B., Chairman
Lord Londesborough
Admiral the Hon. Sir T. Bladen Capel, K.C.B.
Sir William Burnett, Director General of the Medical Department of the Navy
Sir J. Duke, Bart, M.P.
Colonel Sir Duncan Macdougall
Rev. W. S. H. Braham
Rev. J. White
James Walker, Esq., LL.B., F.R.S., L & S
T. J. Pettigrew, Esq, F.R.S., F.S.A.
Rev. J. Hoole
T. Phillpotts, junr, Esq, 11, Bentinck Street, Manchester Square Hon. Sec.

Then followed a list of bankers throughout the British Isles, including Scotland, to whom contributions could be sent; and a list of the first subscribers. These, naturally, comprised all the members of the committee headed by Sir Edward Codrington with £25, the Lord Mayor with five guineas, Mr. Walker with £25, the Revd. J. White with £50. Names of old friends of the Nelson family, like Baron Goldsmid who, with his wife, each gave £10; the total of these preliminary subscriptions reaching £199 7s. 0d. before the appeal was launched.

In the leading article the case was treated from the moral point of view. It was felt by Horatia's friends that all moral condemnation of Nelson's conduct must be forestalled, his 'delinquency' admitted, 'all possible misconstruction' of the bounty appealed for on her behalf eliminated, so that the gift to Nelson's daughter should not on any count be regarded as a condonation of Nelson's 'sin'. In 1850, such a clarification of the moral issues at stake, had to be made—for the Prince Consort's sake if not for Horatia's.

Nelson Memorial Fund

In another part of this journal our readers will observe an appeal to the public on behalf of Nelson's daughter, and some may have felt disappointed that nothing of the kind has appeared before. That Lord Nelson had bequeathed a child to the care of his country was as well known forty years ago as it can be at present. And the light which Mr. Pettigrew has recently thrown on the previously doubtful history of the mother cannot materially have increased, as it has certainly not detracted from, whatever claim she might have on that country's attention. It may seem, therefore, not very easy to account for the little notice taken of her at her father's death, and the apparent indifference of the public ever since to her existence.

It must be borne in mind, however, that the people at large, when they lost Nelson, were unacquainted with the codicil to his will; and the narrative of his dying moments, since so familiar to us, was then unpublished. They knew little about Lady Hamilton, and less about her child. What they did know was not of a character to interest them in her favor. And her friends, or rather her flatterers, who should have been her advocates, suddenly fearing to incur defilement by longer association with the unclean, consigned her to debt and exile. They had their own fortunes to make, which were not likely to be promoted by the introduction of a new claimant. A pension for the fair thief who stole the King of Spain's letter and paid £400 from her own purse to get it safely conveyed to Lord Granville, would have been compounding for a felony; and any provision for the orphan might have been a slice from the rich pudding of the earl.

When the last wishes of Nelson became better known, the bounties of the state had already been distributed, and it was thought prudent to let well alone. Funeral pomp and monumental marbles had gratified the national vanity, as well as done honour to the departed hero. Nor were worthier feelings than these without influence in producing the same result. With the warmest affection for the memory of Nelson, many men, of generous and holy impulses, feared that any attempt to carry out his dying bequest might appear to offer a possible sanction to that coward sophistry which seeks to shelter guilt under the authority of a great example. They wept over Nelson's death and Nelson's folly, and were honestly grieved in believing that any public notice of Lady Hamilton or his daughter might give encouragement to crime. Thus, what with the selfishness of some, and the piety of others, the Court and the Ministry, the Admiralty and the House of Commons, Nelson's kindred, and Nelson's countrymen, agreed to suffer the dying voice of the deliverer of the land to pass by them as the idle wind which they regarded not. They bestowed abundance of honours, which he did not ask for; the only thing he did ask they refused.

During the preceding centuries Court favours had been distributed in so indifferent a spirit, that many may complacently contemplate a time when statesmen were so zealous for the honour of religions . . . as to withhold every tribute of affection from the infant Horatia, through the apprehension of indulging in too licentious a liberality . . . Since no motives but motives of piety could justify such seeming heartlessness, let us rest content that future historians should be able to point to the era of Nelson as the zenith of Ministerial Morality, no less than of England's Glory.

'The evil that men do lives after them'—lives on the hearth of their own homes, even to many generations. This is no potential sentiment. It is every day's experience . . . Let us pause, therefore, to mark the operation of the decree in the case of so great a man as Nelson; one in whom it would have been unusually dangerous that we should notice an exemplar. Whatever triumphs he might have achieved for his country, through his connection with Lady Hamilton, it was essential that there should be no triumph to his crime. See him, then, picturing to a bewitched fancy everything which the fondest father could desire for his babe. She was to be the image of her mother, to captivate the heart of his nephew, to succeed, by marrying her cousin to all the honours which Trafalgar might earn, and thus to secure to the only blood of Nelson and Bronte, the title of which its founder was so proud. If all else failed, one thing, he was at least secure of, 'the beneficence of his country', and to that he committed her. The result is well known, and a pregnant homily it is. The brother becomes the short-lived heir of Trafalgar. His son, the Horatio designed for Horatia, dies too. Lady Hamilton, having served her generation, is cast to the dogs, Bronte is severed from Nelson and, as for his own beloved child, 'My dearest Angel—' and her dowry, 'the beneficence of my country', five and forty years of total neglect, exhibited by an entire nation to the last solemn prayer of their most admired and petted hero . . . have amply sufficed to vindicate the unalterable supremacy of the Divine law.

'The father hath eaten a sour grape and the children's teeth are set on edge.' No one, we think, will henceforward presume to speculate on the impunity of a kindred delinquency by the example of Nelson. His one crime tarnished the lustre of his brightest deeds, and brought sorrow on his offspring. But be it remembered, the penalty is no longer due. It is a penalty *paid*. NOT SO OUR DEBT; and the most scrupulous conscience need no longer hesitate to discharge it. No future admiral is likely to adopt the hint of abandoning a daughter to his 'King and Country'. Nor will any man be suspected now of apologizing for Nelson's sin, by a public and honourable notice of Nelson's daughter.

It is, no doubt, in perfect confidence of immunity from all possible misconstruction that H.R.H. Prince Albert has been pleased to offer to Mrs. Ward a presentation to Christ's Hospital. And though the gift has been unavailable, the example is not lost. Encouraged by such auspices, a committee has been formed of which the two distinguished commanders who shared Nelson's triumphs have taken the lead for raising an Horatia Fund, that the grand-daughters of the Hero of the Nile may be no longer penniless. The City seems likely to follow the example of the Court, and among the committee of the contributors we observe already the names of the Lord Mayor, Sir J. Duke, Baron de Goldsmid; and something, we may conclude, will now be done worthy of the cause and worthy of the country.

But there is for the young what is of more value than money—an opportunity to work. Nelson would have been the last man to wish to rear a race of pensioned saunterers. And his grandsons, who, like himself, have been educated in the retirement of a country parsonage, are, it is to be hoped, as zealous to distinguish themselves by their own exertions. To one the opportunity is already offered. The Chairman of the East India Company, upon hearing of their claim immediately presented their mother with a Cadetship . . . Mrs. Ward has two other sons seeking employment, and Mr. Shepherd will surely not be the only patron, as he has the honour of being the first, to remember the services of their grandfather to England and India.

. . . Had Nelson survived Trafalgar, the wealth and honours accumulated on his successors would have enabled him to leave his child out of the danger of neglect. And, in reading the history of the period, it is impossible not to see, that had his relations been less engrossed with their own interests, and had they made any appeal to the nation on behalf of his little girl, when men's minds were in that fever of excitement which arose on the news of the last fatal victory, scarcely any contribution would have been thought extravagant . . . What the heart of 1850 may be it is vain to speculate. The appeal is now before the public . . . Horatia Nelson Ward has not herself courted—she has deprecated—public notice. It is the public who have drawn her forth from a dignified and uncomplaining, if not contented, retirement. Let them show that it has been for a worthier purpose than to make the daughter of the immortal Nelson the idle sport of curious gossip. Nor let us . . . suffer the object of his constant thoughts, the idol of his tenderest love . . . to go down to the grave . . . in the bitterness of a bruised spirit, insulted by the affectation of pious but empty condolence, and summoned into an unwelcome notoriety, only to be discarded.[1]

[1] *The Morning Chronicle*, 8 May 1850.

Once launched, the Appeal had to take its course—and a slow course it proved to be. From time to time Horatia received progress reports from her two most active agents, Captain Lancaster and the Revd. John Hoole. While the subscriptions slowly came in, the main purpose of the Appeal was being achieved by the direct action of the chief committee members in securing appointments for the young men, Nelson's grandsons. The cadetship offered Nelson Ward by the Director of the East India Company, was transferred to his younger brother William, who sailed for India in 1852 to join the 36th Regiment. In the following year Philip Ward, though only nineteen, received a cadetship through the recommendation of the Prince Consort, for the 25th Bengal Native Infantry, and sailed for India likewise. His departure in November 1853 was kindly watched over by Captain Lancaster who wrote to Horatia on 29 November from his home in Connaught Square:

My dear Mrs Ward / Philip is not wanted on board before ¼ before 11 on Friday morning in the East India Docks, and if he will call here before he goes he will get his Letter of Credit for £50 on the E.I. Co's Treasury at Calcutta and also another letter of Introduction I hope. With best regards to all your Circle, believe me always—

Yours faithfully, Henry Lancaster.[1]

Marmaduke, working as assistant surgeon in the naval hospital at Chatham, was given an appointment as surgeon to the Navy on the recommendation of Sir William Burnett, Director General of the Medical Department of the Navy, one of the Appeal Committee, and took up his appointment in 1853.

By then a further impetus to the whole business had been given by the energetic action of a new member on the committee, Sir Edward Bulwer Lytton, M.P. for Hertfordshire, whose outlook was characteristically more grandiose than that of the naval gentlemen who had hitherto conducted the business of the Fund. Sir Edward aimed high and enlisted his colleagues behind him to make a direct approach to the Prime Minister of the day, Lord Aberdeen. Captain Lancaster kept Horatia informed. He sent her a copy of the Circular that accompanied the Appeal, 'by which you will perceive we are getting on with subscriptions, and I am happy to be able to inform you that we have found a warm sympathizer in Sir Edward Bulwer Lytton, M.P. for Hertfordshire, who, I hope to have on the Committee, and who is disposed to bring the subject before Parliament.

[1] NMM/NWD/9594/29.

'Nelson drank tea with us last night, and told us you meant to avail
yourself of our bed shortly with a view to see the Autographs at Pettigrew's. When you fix your time, please let us have a line of notice for a
week, in order that we may have the Coast clear. Excuse haste...
Henry Lancaster.'[1]

The reference to seeing the 'Autographs at Pettigrew's' shows that
by then the doctor, who had joined the Committee for the Horatia Fund,
was in touch with her, and anxious to prove the authenticity of the Letters
he had published in his work.

By 21 July Bulwer Lytton's plan was carried into effect, and a deputation of the committee was received by Lord Aberdeen, which Captain
Lancaster described to Horatia in a letter of the same day.

I have great pleasure in writing that Lord Aberdeen viewed the thing in the
proper light, and in a more generous manner than Mr. Hume. He quite admitted
the principle of the necessity of recognizing the Claim ... I think he received us
in a kindly spirit and that Good will come of it. He said he would speak to Mr.
Gladstone about it ... Our deputation consisted of Sir Edward Bulwer Lytton,
Joseph Hume, Mr. Chichester and Fortescue. Mr. Charley Attwood (who came
in ill health all the way from near Darlington on purpose), Mr. Walker, Mr.
Johnson, Mr. Pettigrew, Sir W. H. Dillon, Mr. Hoole and myself ... Mr.
Gordon would have been with us, but was to undergo an operation to-day under
Chloroform! He desired me to say everything that was kind to you on his
behalf.[2]

About Mr. Gordon and his devotion to her cause, Horatia would shortly
hear more. The deputation stated its objective to the Prime Minister as
being 'A Grant of Public Money for the Adopted Daughter of Lord
Nelson'. They laid the facts of the case frankly before him: what they
wanted was preferment for Mr. Ward, and they solicited in particular the
then vacant living of Sherborne in Dorsetshire for him. They explained
that Mrs. Ward's 'family consisted of Mr. and Mrs. Ward, three daughters
and five sons'. It was a situation that spoke for itself, and Lord Aberdeen
was left to think it over.

It was discussed at Cabinet level with a view to laying it before the
House, but 'The Cabinet decided that it would not be expedient on the
part of the Government to make any such proposition to the House of
Commons'. What Lord Aberdeen suggested in his letter of regrets to the
Committee was that he would 'make an application for a pension of
£300 p.a. on the Civil List of Her Majesty'. The Queen, he explained,
had £1,200 per annum at her disposal out of which to grant pensions in

[1] Ibid.   [2] Ibid.

cases of hardship. Her Majesty in due course expressed her pleasure
to grant the pension, and Mrs. Ward was notified of it, a choice being
offered her of an annual pension for herself of £300, or an annual pension
of £100 for each of her daughters. Horatia's decision, sent to Lord Aberdeen on 26 July 1854, was in character: she accepted the offer that benefitted her daughters, 'to prevent distress in the event of her own death'.
Specimen signatures of her three daughters were asked for, and sent.
On 20 September 1854, Lord Aberdeen's secretary wrote to Horatia
finally on the matter:

'to acquaint you that the Queen has been pleased to approve of a Pension of
Three Hundred Pounds (£300) per annum being granted to your daughters,
upon the Civil List. As it will be necessary that Trustees should be appointed
to receive the pension, I have to request that you will communicate the names of
two Gentlemen to act in this capacity.

Signed: James H. Cole.[1]

How favoured Horatia's daughters were by comparison with others who
received pensions on the Civil List can be judged by the case of Captain
Sir William Hoste's daughter who, on her father's death, was 'left in a
destitute situation', and was granted a pension of £50 per annum by the
Queen in 1856.

The Nelson Appeal Fund remained open for a while longer. The
devoted band of helpers continued to send in progress reports to Horatia:
Mr. Hoole wrote her indignantly on one occasion: 'I am sorry to tell you
that notwithstanding all Mr. Walker's and Captain Lancaster's exertions,
the Times charged us for a trumpery bit of space for an advertisement
£5!'[2] By midsummer 1855 the Fund was closed, and Mr. Hoole wrote to
Horatia: 'It grieves me to have to publish to the world that 1400 odd
pounds is all the response to our repeated appeals! But we must consider
the Appointments and Annuities as the *real* result, the 1400 only as the
oil for the wheels'.[3] The exact sum received was £1,427 13s. 5d. Horatia
asked that £1,000 might be invested in the names of her three sons in the
Services—Marmaduke, William, and Philip—whose careers were little
likely to enrich them, and for the remaining £400 to be invested 'in the
funds'. The real result of the Appeal, as Mr. Hoole said, could not be
reckoned by the money collected, but by the interest roused and the help
secured 'in Appointments and Annuities' benefitting her children. With
her daughters endowed with modest dowries, her last keen anxiety on
her sons' behalf was allayed when both Horace and Nelson were given

[1] Ibid.   [2] Ibid. Letter of 30 June 1855.
[3] Ibid. Letter of 16 June 1855.

appointments that established them for life. In March 1853 Horace was offered the living of Radstock, in Somersetshire, which was in the gift of the Countess Waldegrave who, as a daughter of the singer Braham who had so often performed at Merton, was a veritable link with Horatia's childhood. Braham, who made a fortune singing 'The Death of Nelson' up and down the country (with the proceeds of which he built the Theatre in King Street, later known as the 'St. James's'), had a true devotion to Nelson's memory and had enjoined on his daughter to do anything she could to serve Horatia if the occasion presented itself. When the living fell vacant, the Countess wrote to Horatia on 19 March 1853: '102, Eaton Square. Frances, Countess Waldegrave is happy to have it in her power to be of some service to the daughter of Nelson.' [1] The living was worth £350 per annum and represented riches to the Wards. Horace, who had served as his father's curate since January 1848, took up his new post in August 1853, married there four years later, and spent the whole of a long and happy life in the service of his Radstock parishioners.

The Braham connection had altogether been very active in the matter of the Appeal: two of Braham's sons, both clergy—the Revd. W. S. H. Braham, and the Revd. S. Braham—served on the Committee; a half brother, the Revd. J. White contributed one of the largest sums received by the Fund, £50. A drawing of the old Vicarage at Tenterden as it was in the first days of the Wards' arrival was made by Meadows-White, another brother of the Countess Waldegrave, on the occasion of a visit he paid there in 1834, which would suggest that the resumption of relations with the Braham family was of long-standing. [2]

Nelson Ward was equally fortunate: in the same year, 1853, he was given a Clerkship in the Chancery Registrar's Office on the appointment of the Lord Chancellor, Lord Cranworth who, as plain Robert Rolfe, revealed himself to be a second cousin. He was the grandson of Alice Nelson, sister of Nelson's father, who married the Revd. Robert Rolfe, later Rector of Hilborough—a connection he preserved when raised to the peerage in the title he chose, Baron Cranworth of Hilborough. By this appointment to the Chancery Courts Nelson's future was assured. He rose to the highest position himself, in due course—Registrar of the Chancery—and was able in later years to provide his widowed mother with a comfortable home.

One more benefit to Horatia and her family can be traced directly to the Appeal: this was the legacy bequeathed her by Mr. James Adam Gordon, one of the keenest members serving on the Committee. He

---

[1] NMM/NWD/9594/29.   [2] Braham himself lived until 1856.

died the year following the deputation to the Prime Minister, which his operation had prevented him attending. Capt. Lancaster wrote on 12 March 1854 to acquaint Horatia with the fact:—

Doubtless you have seen in the Times the death of your worthy friend Mr. James Adam Gordon. It took place on the 4th at his seat in Somersetshire. But, as I am not aware that I have already informed you that you are beneficially interested under his Will, the object of this note is to tell you that on one of my visits to him in Albemarle Street he told me that he had arranged his affairs and that he had charged his heir to pay you £1 per cent on the amount of his inheritance— now, seeing that he had four Estates in Scotland and England—besides West Indies Property, I should expect that this will amount to something worth having. You had no one more earnest in your interest than that excellent Man.[1]

In his enthusiasm Captain Lancaster rather overshot the mark of Mr. Gordon's intentions; the one per cent referred not to the estate as a whole, but to the legacies. The terms of the bequest show plainly that the bequest was made in consequence of the Appeal, and were as follows:

Whereas the last legacy of a Nelson to his country has been so ungratefully ignored And whereas I have done my humble best to carry it out in my lifetime, I hereby desire that every Legatee under this my last will and codicil shall also contribute one per cent out of their legacies to Mrs. Horatia Ward and her children nor will they grudge it if they recall the life and deeds of Nelson, without whom they would never have had the other ninety-nine parts to enjoy.[2]

Mr. Gordon's legacy, made transferable to Horatia's children, was the sole asset she had to leave at the time of her death.

[1] NMM/NWD/9594/29.
[2] Mr. Gordon's Will, Somerset House. Codicil dated 27 Aug. 1852.

CHAPTER XXIII

PHILIP

FROM its inception in 1849 to the close of the Appeal Fund in June 1855, six years had passed. Irrespective of the objectives gained, for Horatia the period had been one of almost ceaseless strain, physical and mental. There had been constant journeys to London to consult with the members of the Committee; visits to sympathizers to make and to receive; information to supply in an endless stream of correspondence. The publicity given to the Appeal had not all been agreeable; it brought, inevitably, emotional stresses, as the privacy of her life in its past affections and present anxieties was exposed to the curiosity of the world. For her, as for Philip, the Appeal followed too soon upon the long exhaustion of the Tithes suit. When the return to normal life could be made, the change—both in themselves and in their home surroundings—had to be recognized: they were no longer a young couple, and their children were gone. Despite the obvious advantages gained by the Appeal, there had been loss—and the hardest to bear in that closely bound family was the departure of their sons, three of them to great distances. Letters from India took from four to five months. Young Philip, 'out of the goodness of his heart', sent money regularly home to his parents in a gesture that was not devoid of pain for them.

Horace departed for Radstock. Nelson set up house-keeping at Hatfield with a couple of fellow-clerks at the solicitors in Lincoln's Inn where he worked, William Johnson and Thomas Attree. His presence at home was therefore only a pleasant prospect for week-ends, especially in the cricketing-season when he was sure to come. He was an enthusiastic cricketer and had early got a team of village boys together, with the equally keen support of Mr. Croughton of Heronden, where matches were a feature throughout the summer. In the depleted Vicarage, only the girls remained.

Nelson's Hatfield house, however, was soon made to serve a double purpose: it was somewhere for his parents to stay when on business trips to London, and a holiday home for his sisters. The closeness of the family ties is nowhere more apparent than in these frequent exchanges between Tenterden and Hertfordshire.

Happily, during their mother's deep absorption in the business of the
Appeal, young Horatia's health was no longer a constant anxiety; she
grew up blooming and beautiful; in fact, she was so charming to look at
that the farmers' daughters, her contemporaries, could not take their eyes
off her at church. She quite distracted them from following the service,
as one of them frankly confessed in later years. Horatia had inherited
the abundant chestnut hair and the vivid colouring of her maternal grandmother, which together with much else of grace and sweetness that her
grandmother had never known made her irresistible. So, at least, her
brother Nelson's friend William Johnson thought, when he came down
to Tenterden at week-ends, or when Horatia visited Nelson at Hatfield
and helped him keep house. These sisterly visits, begun no doubt in a
spirit of pure helpfulness to set a bachelor's home in order, took on another
character as time passed, and acquaintance between the young people
ripened; while Ellen helped her mother at home and Carry minded her
lessons, Horatia was found to be indispensable at Hatfield.

Sometimes her father accompanied her, as his letters show. Philip's
letters are the true reflection of the quiet domestic scene that was his
world, a world not so very different from that of Francis Kilvert and
Charlotte M. Yonge—the world of his family and his parish. His home
affections were deep and abiding, his tastes simple, his nature cheerful;
he was essentially and appropriately a man of peace. As with his children,
so with his remaining brother and sister: the early ties of love never
slackened. His sister Ellen, after a late and unfortunate marriage to her
father's curate, the Revd. William Rees, Master of North Walsham
Grammar School, had been widowed at the end of a year and, urged by
Philip, joined the family at Tenterden in 1835. 'Uncle James', Philip's
brother, rose to the rank of Lieutenant Colonel of the 81st Regiment, and
was never far removed from the family circle on his returns to England.

With the surviving members of the Matcham family, much depleted
by the mid-century, Horatia and her husband preserved cordial relations. Their chief contact was through Susanna, Mrs. Moore, who lived
at Gipsy Lodge, Upper Norwood. She had one son and the adopted
daughter, 'Toriana' Blanckley. From Tasmania, Eliza Matcham (Mrs.
Arthur Davies) and her family returned to England in 1848, and with
them the Wards also renewed old contacts. The young people of the two
families became friends, especially Ellen Ward and Kate Davies who
were of an age, and visits were exchanged between the two homes. All
these domestic happenings are reflected in Philip's letters of the 1850's.

From Hatfield he wrote home on 23 July 1851:

My dear Horatia,

I rather expected to have heard this morning respecting next Sunday [about a substitute to take his services]. If you have made any arrangements, let me know as soon as you can, as it is important.

I have seen Mr. Gibbs the Dentist and I have bargained for the new teeth. It is *possible* that I may have them fitted in on Saturday—but further fittings would be far better, to ensure more security and comfort. So that if next Sunday could be cared for it would be better. Carry will have told you all about our adventure. Nelson is quite well. Uncle James will be in Town—all the better for his trip to Devon. Mrs. Moore [Susanna Matcham] is not in Town. I saw Arthur Davies yesterday at the Exhibition[1] and told him about your parcel.

Your affect -h. Philip Ward[2]

Kate Davies was staying at Tenterden when Philip wrote to Horatia from London after a visit to Susanna:

You will be surprised to hear that James and I did not arrive here till yesterday at $\frac{1}{2}$ past 7.

He met me at the Station in London and I persuaded him to come here with me—but as his *linen* was at the wash we were obliged to wait till the Tuesday—and then on the Tuesday we discovered that Ellen was to come up to meet Mrs. Frank so we managed to be with them at the Shoreditch Station for nearly an hour. All here are well—and we are very happy. . . . Mrs. Moore was very kind and I left her and all the party with regret. I was glad to hear from Ellen that things were going on better at Tenterden and that Nelson and Kate are home and perhaps if they had not been out the storm never would have broke out. James will not return with me, as he would rather be with us *alone*. With best love, in which all here join.[3]

The great strain of the Tithes suit left Philip a tired and weakened man. The occasional signs of exhaustion, viewed as a passing fatigue, were treated with the typical therapy of the day: a visit to the sea. Hastings was the family panacea and favourite resort (Horatia took her delicate little girl there to recuperate after each illness), the more so that their friends and parishioners, the Croughtons of Heronden, made long visits there and on occasions urged Philip to join them for a rest. The Croughtons were keen travellers, and went abroad most years, taking their own carriage and four with them; but with the outbreak of the Crimean war they had to forgo their trips abroad, and spent the winters of 1854–5, and 1855–6 at St. Leonards. On the earlier occasion they took Philip with them. An additional strain on Philip after Horace's departure was the lack of a curate, which meant that he had to take the full duty himself.

[1] The Great Exhibition, Kensington Gardens.
[2] NMM/NWD/9594/1.   [3] Ibid.

Meanwhile, further though not unexpected family changes occurred. There was little surprise indeed when William Johnson, after setting up on his own as Solicitor in New Inn, proposed to Horatia Ward. The friendship of Nelson had paved the way to her parents' consent—and to Horatia's heart. They were married at Tenterden on 17 August 1858. It was a very happy occasion, as remains apparent even today in the register entry that was signed by the entire family. Horace came over from Radstock to perform the ceremony, leaving Philip free to give away his daughter. Happily for Philip, who was so fond of his daughters, his favourite Carry remained at home, though in view of her good looks and high spirits she was not likely to remain there long; she was twenty-two and already much admired, and confidently expecting to be shortly engaged to a local young man. Ellen, alone of the girls, was without admirers; her destiny was to become, like Jane Austen, a much beloved aunt, in which role she shone.

In the lull following Horatia's marriage, Philip's fatigue became recognized for what it was—a condition of the heart—and he engaged a curate, Richard Powell, to help him with his work. The Christmas season approached, with all the extra calls it laid on him, which he carried out as usual. Three days after Christmas he had a particularly heavy day of burials and christenings as his registers show. He went home—so ill that a doctor was sent for at once, and was ordered complete rest. The presence of Richard Powell made this possible, and he stayed in bed to satisfy Horatia. He made good progress and after a fortnight was considered well enough to resume his duties. He was so much better that on Sunday, 16 January, he insisted he would take the morning service, and got up to get dressed. Only then, when he suddenly collapsed, was the truth realized; he had time to say he thought he was dying, and before the Doctor could be fetched he was dead.

The *Maidstone Gazette* for 25 January 1859, reporting the event with the shock that its suddenness provoked, said: 'His kind and Christian ministration has endeared him to all classes of his parishioners, by whom his death is deeply regretted'. The *Maidstone and Kentish Journal* had something more specific to say about this charitable man:

The sad and unexpected event has cast a gloom over the whole parish, for the deceased gentleman was equally loved by dissenters and churchmen. In him the poor have lost one who had always a listening ear for their troubles, a sympathizing heart for their sorrows, and an ever-open purse for their wants. All have lost a kind friend, and a truly christian Minister.

What his family lost could not be put into words. His brother James, more than a year after his death, said he could not yet realize that he would never see Phil coming towards him again.

After attending the funeral on 22 January (which was taken by the neighbouring Vicar of Appledore, Mr. Kirby), James wrote to the Davies's and the Moores who could not be present:

There was a full attendance at the funeral notwithstanding it was such a sad day. Mrs. Ward's intention at present is to reside somewhere near London, and Nelson will live with them. I understand Ellen Rees, our dear old sister, will go with them and so have her room . . . Horace has been with them at Tenterden since Poor Philip's death and all seem to lean on him, they say his kind manner is perfectly beautiful. Nelson has not yet returned from Tenterden, so I am not able to give you so many tidings as you would wish, but perhaps Ellen will have sent you every information. Horatia [Johnson] tells me her mother is going through her trials wonderfully, but that her nerve is somewhat shook.[1]

Horatia's sorrows, borne with characteristic courage, did not come singly; she had hardly to measure the loss of Philip before she was faced with losing her home as well. Almost before Philip was buried, she had to make up her mind where to go; the new Vicar must necessarily displace his predecessor's family, however deeply that family's roots were planted in the old place. Caroline had never known any other home; and Caroline's grief took on such dimensions now that Horatia had not time to consider her own. Things had not worked out as the brilliant Caroline had expected; the lover who had won her heart had withdrawn. Only the family knew why, even before Philip took to his bed, Caroline was ill. She had apparently had a riding accident and injured her leg; the cause was immaterial, but it was enough. The loss of her father, following on that other grief, was her death-blow. Barely a month after seeing Philip die, Horatia had to watch at Caroline's death-bed. Her death was certified as 'Mortification of the leg', but the family knew she had simply no wish to live. She died on 19 February and was buried on the 24th.

After that, what could Tenterden hold for Horatia? Nothing that she could not take with her: her remaining daughter, two faithful servants—Bet Allen and the man, Walter Honeysett—a couple of ponies, and her dogs. The destruction of her world was final; the suddenness of its removal was so grievous that she could never be persuaded, even years later, to revisit Tenterden. Twenty-nine years of her life had been spent there, yet she could never think of it but as the tomb of her happiness.

[1] NMM/NWD/9594/1.

CHAPTER XXIV

PINNER

NELSON busied himself at once on his mother's behalf. After the break-up of his bachelor establishment at Hatfield following the marriage of William Johnson and Horatia, he had moved to lodgings in Woburn Place. The need to make a home for his mother somewhere within reach of London where his work lay, decided him now to move out to Pinner, which combined the attraction of a semi-rural residence with good train-services to Town. He took a house in West End Lane—a lane in reality as well as name—characterized by its many bends and twists, its old buildings (Tudor barns still stand there today), its quick hedges, its shady trees, open fields, and absolute seclusion. Nelson was right in thinking that what his mother most needed was peace and quiet. Her arrival at Pinner was as unobtrusive as could be, and at no time during her residence there was her relationship to the illustrious admiral bruited abroad—even when certain family events had to be reported in the local press. She was merely the widow of the late vicar of Tenterden. Her new home, the charming West End Lodge, a pre-Restoration structure belonging to a family named Street in 1659, had enough garden, stabling and surrounding fields, to isolate the small family party that moved in there in the spring of 1859.

Ellen Rees did not after all accompany them; she decided to remain at Tenterden, where she had her friends and her home in High Street. She did not long survive Philip, dying at Tenterden in 1862, aged seventy-eight. The death of their far younger brother James in the same year while on service overseas, was a great sorrow to Horatia and her children, as 'Uncle James' had been a part of home for many years, and his devotion to Philip as deep as theirs.

Nelson Ward now assumed the headship of the family. As Deputy Registrar of the Chancery Courts, rising later to be Registrar in Chief, his routine was undeviating, travelling to and from Town morning and evening and deciding, the more he knew the place, to take root in Pinner. Across the lane from West End Lodge was a property that caught his eye known as West House, whose formal gardens, parterres and water-piece, charmed him so much that later when he had a family of his own he took a lease of it.

Meanwhile, Horatia's life was totally transformed; she was no longer the harassed parson's wife, the busy mother, the public figure even, with constant calls on her time; her occupations were gone. For a period at least, her active mind turned in on herself and her love of reading and music stood her in good stead. Her main outings in those early days were confined to the Sunday services which took her to the magnificent old parish church standing at the top of High Street. Pinner had many points of resemblance to Tenterden, the dominating position of the church for one, and the bow-windowed shop-fronts, the old Inns, the overall rustic ambience of surrounding gardens and clustered trees in the adjacent lanes.

There were, of course, the other centres of her interest: her sons in India, Horace in Somerset, and Horatia Johnson in London; and happily the need for new exertions came before the end of the year, when her daughter had her first child, a boy, William Horatio, born November 1859. The Johnsons lived in Gower Street, Bedford Square, at a quite accessible distance from Pinner, and Mrs. Johnson's record of ill-health required a return of something like the old vigilance and care, which it now became Horatia's chief happiness to provide. She watched over her daughter with a new devotion, all the stronger that a second life depended upon hers. Her daughter's extreme delicacy was only fully realized, however, when a second pregnancy put her life in danger. (She suffered from Bright's disease it was later found.) Then it was that her mother's dormant energies and courage were revived; despite her situation and her age when the infant was born—5 April 1861—and declared by the doctor too frail to be reared in the airless city, she came forward at once and offered to bring him up at Pinner. She meant indeed to bring the child up entirely as her own, and this arrangement, which relieved her delicate daughter of a great care and saved the infant, was still more beneficial to Horatia herself, since it restored to her a purpose in life. The little boy, christened Philip, flourished under her care, and became a source of un-alloyed happiness.

The children's old nurse, Bet Allen, resumed her former functions, and Ellen Ward began her career as devoted aunt.

Presumably because he saw in its big garden the possibilities of a cricket pitch, Nelson Ward urged a move, in 1862, to a house in Church Lane which had recently been restored, and appeared to him a much better home for his mother; this was New House (later known as Elmdene) which had an agreeable position on a bend in Church Lane. It was a double-fronted house with two gables, twisted Tudor chimney stacks and attractive dormer windows. Its chief charm, perhaps, lay in its entrance-hall which was characterized by delicate columns, a large adam-style fire place, and an ornate balustrade to its staircase. The garden was directly entered from the hall by a french window at the back.

Provided with the ideal cricket-ground in New House garden, Nelson Ward set about doing for the boys of Pinner what he had done for the boys of Tenterden, drilling them into a team. His enthusiasm had for years been a family joke, and when, after the inevitable delays, Lieutenant Philip Ward of the 30th Punjab Regiment heard the news in India, he wrote to banter his brother on becoming 'one of the cricketing celebrities of Pinner'.

The residence at New House also brought Horatia the friendship of a near neighbour, Mrs. Sophia Kelly, wife of the local doctor. Horatia often visited her at 'Chestnut Cottage', a converted Elizabethan house and formerly the home of John Smart, the painter. In the Kellys' hands it became a charming place with its timbered and whitewashed front, trellised walls and straggling garden abundant in fruit trees. In Mrs. Kelly she found a kindred spirit, both cultivated and kind. She was a daughter of Mrs. Sherwood, the authoress, who had died in 1851, and whose un-finished *Autobiography* she edited and published in 1854. Mrs. Sherwood's residence in India, where her husband was an army paymaster, made her intelligent and lively account of life in the military compounds of India of especial interest to Horatia, with two sons out there. The friendship ripened into warm affection, and when Mrs. Kelly was widowed in January 1868 and her husband's successor, Dr. Dove, took over the practice and the house, she moved so as to become a next-door neighbour of Horatia's.

Gradually, in these fresh surroundings, Horatia regained something like her old serenity. The family took root in Pinner, and Nelson began to find other interests than the promotion of a local cricket team: he made the acquaintance of the family of Mr. George Bird of Pinner Hall, to whose daughter, Jessie, he became engaged in 1863. The marriage took place on 12 May 1864, at St. Mary's, Bryanstone Square, and was per-formed by the bridegroom's brother, Horace Ward, who came up from Radstock for the occasion. The marriage was in every way a happy one, not only for those chiefly concerned, but for Horatia, who found in her daughter-in-law a woman of most kind and considerate feelings. Jessie's interest in her new family was keen, and led her to record for posterity all the facts she could glean about its historic past, collateral branches, and topographical connections.[1] Jessie's gesture in asking Ellen Ward to be her bridesmaid, though she was forty by then, was an instance of her generous sentiments towards her new family. Though Nelson set up a separate home for his wife and himself, he invariably called on his mother on his way home from the city of an evening, and very often found Jessie waiting for him there.

1864 brought Horatia further happiness, when in the autumn her sons William and Philip returned from India. William had become a Major on the Madras Staff Corps and was home on his first leave. After visiting his mother, he went to stay with his brother Horace in Somerset. During a holiday at Clevedon he met and fell instantly in love with Catherine (Toriana) Blanckley, Harriet Matcham's daughter who had been adopted by her aunt Susanna Moore. William did not delay, and secured his happiness literally 'on the spot'. He married Toriana at Clevedon on 15 November 1864, and took her back to India with him. Toriana had five little girls during the next seven years born in India, and a sixth in Pinner in 1873, after William had returned to England for good and settled near his mother.

William was still in England in September 1864 when Lieutenant Philip Ward arrived on leave and joined his mother at New House. He had seen active service during the Indian Mutiny and though not wounded came home on sick leave, affected by the climate, it was first supposed. He had been out in India twelve years and had a liver complaint. After staying with his mother a while, he started a round of visits— to his sister in London, to Horace in Radstock, and then to Paris for the winter. He was noticeably unsettled, and did not return to England till the spring, when on his arrival at Pinner his mother realized he was very ill. She and Ellen nursed him throughout the spring and summer, but on 12 September he died. He was buried in the new cemetery in Paine's Lane on 16 September 1865. The youngest of Horatia's sons, he was only thirty-one. He had always shown a practical concern in his mother's affairs; as a young cadet he had sent money home regularly to his parents, and when Horatia received Mr. Gordon's legacy Philip sent a procuration home, witnessed by two fellow-officers, waiving his personal rights to any part of the inheritance. Though his Estate was very small, declared 'Under £800' under the Letters of Administration taken out by his

---

[1] The present author is much indebted to Sir William Dickson, grandson of Nelson Ward, for the loan of Jessie's family records which are the main source of evidence relating to Horatia's life at Pinner.

brother Nelson, he left it to his mother. He was concerned for her future, and though certain of Nelson's care of her, pointed out to her before dying that her continued residence at New House would be a drag on him and urged her to move to a smaller house.

His death at New House was sufficient reason for Horatia to wish to move, and she joined Nelson and his wife at Woodridings to the north of Pinner. The Woodridings estate, mentioned in the Manor Rolls of Henry VI's reign, had just been laid out as a new residential quarter, and consisted of eight pairs of semi-detached identical 'Villas' in 'the Italian style'. Each pair lay in its own garden approached by a separate drive, and was to be let for £50 a year. Nelson Ward had moved there on his marriage, to 'Onslow Villas' and now took 'Beaufort Villas' next door for his mother. She occupied one villa and sub-let the other to a Mrs. Martin, who kept a dame-school where in due course Philip Johnson and Nelson's boys started school. 'Beaufort Villas' were flanked by beautiful chestnut trees whose cream-coloured blossom were a feature of the garden every May, long remembered by old residents. Here, in early 1866, Horatia set up her last home. In due course, all her living children except Horatia Johnson and the Revd. Horace settled round her at Woodridings, William taking 'Cornwall Villas' when he returned from India for good, and Marmaduke coming to live with her permanently when he retired. It is a note-worthy fact that Horatia's sons, grown men as they were, all chose to live near her when they retired, and that their wives lived in perfect harmony with her, finding her not only interesting but stimulating company. The grandchildren grew up around her, graduating from rides on her great retriever dog to rides on the old ponies in her paddock. During certain summers when Nelson Ward and his wife took holidays abroad, Horatia and the other grandmother, Mrs. Bird, were left in charge of the expanding nursery, with happy consequences for all. As the family spread beyond the capacity of 'Onslow Villas', Nelson realized his dream of acquiring West House, opposite their former home in West End Lane, and moved there in 1873. It was no distance from his mother's, and he still called in on her on his way home from Town. Mr. Jervis, a nephew of Lord St. Vincent, took 'Onslow Villas' and set up a boys' school there, where the young Wards and Philip Johnson graduated in due course from Mrs. Martin's. (Philip Johnson went on eventually to Epsom College.)[1] Nothing was therefore altered in the boys' daily routine of eating their dinners at their grandmother's at 'Beaufort Villas' next door.

[1] He graduated at Edinburgh University, and lived to be 89.

In the summer of 1870 Nelson and his wife took a house at Tenterden for the holidays and convened all the other members of the family to join them there; Horace brought his family from Somerset, and Horatia Johnson brought hers from Town. The experiment was a great success, old friends at Tenterden welcoming them wholeheartedly and the place casting its old spell on them again. They united in urging Horatia to join them, but nothing would persuade her to go; she and Ellen felt there were only painful memories for them there. For her, it was increasingly difficult to live in the past and devoting her life more and more to her grandchildren she looked steadfastly towards the future. With William's expected return in 1872, bringing his wife and a bevy of little girls with him, Horatia's cup of contentment looked like being filled.

While waiting to move into 'Cornwall Villas', near his mother, William rented a house for the summer on the Uxbridge Road, and it was on some errand connected with his installation there that Ellen Ward set out from home, on the afternoon of 6 August. She walked up High Street, and as it began to rain, put up her umbrella, and so did not see the horse and cart bolting across the street straight at her. There were no passers by to shout a warning—the rain had driven everyone indoors, so it was after-wards explained—before she was knocked down and trampled under the great horse and dray. The accident occurred outside the old 'Queen's Head', the main inn of Pinner. The commotion brought the men out and she was carried inside, but it was loo late; she was already dead.

It is a comment on the obscurity that Horatia and her family had achieved at Pinner that the local press, reporting the accident, spoke of Ellen merely as 'A lady (Miss Ward of Woodridings)', without connecting her family in any way with Nelson.

Ellen was forty-eight. Her life had been spent in the service of the family, with very little independence of her own. It was as she liked it, feeling fulfilled in the second generation of little Wards and Johnsons, who came to rely on her as the indispensable aunt. She was buried beside her brother Philip in the Paine's Lane cemetery.

After Ellen's death the daughters-in-law tried to fill the void left in Horatia's life. Toriana, like Jessie, proved to be most devoted, and through Toriana Susanna Matcham arrived in Pinner to look after Toriana when her sixth girl was born on 17 August 1873.

Susanna was the last of the Matchams to meet Horatia—the last, in-deed, of all her Nelson connections. 'Young' George died 18 January 1877, and Horatia outlived even his sons. By the time she died in 1881, a third generation of Matchams had inherited New House who knew no-

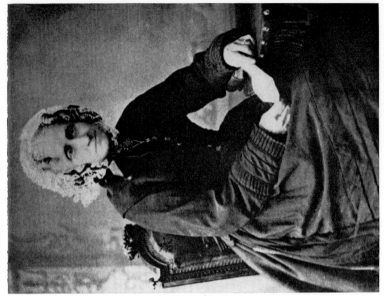

b. HORATIA, the last photograph

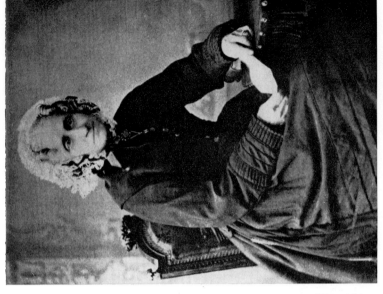

a. THE WIDOWED HORATIA, photograph 1859

thing about her; the then owner wrote, surprised at the mention in the press of her connection with Nelson, that he 'had not known Nelson had a daughter, though he believed that the Admiral had adopted a young person named Thompson of whom he had heard'.[1]

Lady Charlotte Bridport the old earl's daughter, died 29 January 1873. Lady Bolton died before her twin Susanna, with whom she spent her latter years at Bolton House. She died there in 1857, and Susanna in 1864. Susanna, to whom the house had been left by their father, left it to her favourite niece, Lady Bolton's daughter Mary Anne, who lived with her for years and never married, and Mary Anne was joined there by her widowed sister Emma Horatia Foley. They lived together until Mary Anne's death at Christmas 1864; Emma Horatia died in 1869. The whole family was buried in the churchyard of Burnham Westgate, where Sir William Bolton had preceded them. The old house passed to Susanna's nephew, William Bolton Girdlestone, Eliza Bolton's son.

Eliza and Henry Girdlestone, who had taken root at Landford, had a family of twelve children. Eliza died in 1861, but Henry lived to a great old age, dying on 1 February 1871, aged eighty-eight. Henry Girdlestone had followed Horatia's history with unflagging interest and affection, and wrote to Philip Ward after the Appeal was launched in 1850 commenting on Mr. Haslewood's statement concerning Lady Hamilton, to suggest a novel solution to the identity of Horatia's mother: what about Miss Knight, he wondered?

She was highspirited and romantic—Did Horatia ever remember seeing her? I should like to see a print of her (but is there one?) All I remember when young [was] hearing that some officers of the Mediterranean Fleet expressed a sudden astonishment at seeing the child, as if Struck with a likeness to someone well known.

Whoever Her Mother was, Horatia must wish with her, to keep her secret inviolate. Give my dearest love to her. Affect ᵞ Yours, H.G.[2]

Henry's view was the one finally adopted by the Ward family, however reluctantly it was accepted by Horatia in her heart of hearts; she never ceased searching for further proof that Lady Hamilton was not her mother and was never fully satisfied.

A re-opening of the whole case occurred in 1874 when once again she was roused to take up her pen and go over the old ground that had yielded

---

[1] Letter from the late Revd. Hugh Nelson Ward to Carola Oman. Quoted by courtesy of Lady Lenanton (Carola Oman).
[2] NMM/NWD/9594/2.

nothing in the sixty years since the death of Emma. The occasion was the publication of a book of essays, 'Historical, Judicial, and Literary' by John Paget, called *Paradoxes and Puzzles*, which included an investigation on Lady Hamilton. The author rejected Pettigrew's disclosures, based on the Thompson Letters, but swallowed whole Mrs. Hunter's spurious stories of her services to Lady Hamilton at Calais. These were too blatant for Horatia to let pass, and she wrote to Mr. Paget on 2 November 1874:

My dear Sir,

It was only last week that I had the pleasure of reading your 'Puzzles & Paradoxes', or I should have written earlier to you. Will you forgive me for taking up your valuable time by requesting you to read the following denial of Mrs. Hunter's account of Lady Hamilton.

Having been with Lady Hamilton during the entire period of her residence in Calais, from the moment of her landing to the day of her funeral, I can most positively affirm that neither Mrs. Hunter nor Monsieur de Rheims were ever known to her.

On her arrival, for many weeks she had apartments in Quillac's [Quillan's] Hotel. Thence she went to a house which she *hired* two miles from the town, situate in the Commune de St. Pierre. In consequence of some misunderstanding with the landlord, she remained there only one night, and took lodgings in an adjoining farmhouse where she remained some months. Afterwards, she took part of a house in Calais belonging to a Monsieur Damas, where she died. These were the only houses she occupied during the time she was in France.

Although often certainly under very distressing circumstances, she never experienced actual want, or received assistance from *any one* of the kind which Mrs. Hunter imagined she afforded.

Lady Hamilton was buried in a coffin, not 'put into a deal box' and was followed to the grave by many captains whose vessels (packets) were at that time in the harbour. The service was read over the body by a Roman Catholic priest who had attended her at her request during her illness. Having been a personal witness of what I have stated, I thought you would permit me to relate the facts to you.

                                    Yours very sincerely,
                                    Horatia Nelson Ward.[1]

In his reply, dated 8 November, Mr. Paget suggested that Horatia, being only fourteen at the time of Lady Hamilton's death, might not have known all that went on—found it probable, indeed, that 'the circumstances related in Mrs. Hunter's account might have taken place without your being acquainted with them, and indeed that from motives of delicacy

                                    [1] Ibid.

they might have been purposely concealed from you'. He clung to Mrs. Hunter's account, even to the 'box' coffin and the Irish half-pay officer officiating at the service; above all, he clung to Mrs. Hunter's 'main facts, namely, the monstrous ingratitude of the Country and the base and disgusting conduct of Lord Nelson's brother . . . to the Eternal shame of both'.

Horatia had sent him a copy of Haslewood's statement regarding her mother's identity, on which he commented:

I infer from your note that you agree with Sir Harris Nicolas that Lady Hamilton was *not* your Mother. There have been many suggestions as to this subject, one that the Queen of Naples was your Mother, which the dates appear to me to make impossible . . . Another, that your Mother was the sister of a merchant at Genoa—died at your birth. This is inconsistent with Mr. Haslewood's statement that she saw you often during your infancy . . . It is also inconsistent with Lady Hamilton's statement that she was some person 'too great to be mentioned'.[1]

Taking up each of Mr. Paget's arguments in her reply, Horatia showed Mrs. Hunter's claims 'still to be utterly fabulous'. On the score of her youth she said: 'I was but 14—true—but circumstances form an almost child's character into that of a woman and that was unfortunately my case. . . . Alas, my dear Sir, the time I spent in Calais is too indelibly stamped on my memory ever to forget'. With calm good sense she examined the Queen of Naples evidence:

Poor Lady Hamilton was not a strict adherer to truth and her statement implying that the Queen of Naples was my mother was most incredible—had it been so of course I should have passed as her husband's child. Many other things that I could mention would destroy I think with you the idea of Lady Hamilton being more to me than a guardian which if we meet I will tell you, but they would lengthen this already too long letter too much.[2]

In a reference to Sir William Hamilton, Horatia unwittingly put her finger on the clue to the riddle that had haunted her all her life: in his cynicism and indifference to his wife's conduct lay the explanation of Emma's boldness in giving birth to a child under his very roof—what every commentator in turn had found impossible to credit. 'Lady Hamilton for a long time had openly expressed herself as being a Catholic', wrote Horatia, 'that must be between her God and herself—but had I lived so long with such a decided free-thinker as Sir William Hamilton professed to be, it is not surprising that she should not have any fixed

[1] Ibid.   [2] Ibid. Letter of 10 Nov. 1874.

principles of religion. . . .' If Horatia had had a little more insight into the eighteenth century 'enlightment' and Sir William's moral code she might have found the answer to her problem. Born at the turn of the century, her belated moral teaching reflected the changed outlook of the nineteenth century and Sir William's attitude and behaviour were quite alien to her.

Mr. Paget, in the hope of fuller discussions on a theme so interesting to him, invited Horatia to visit him and his wife—'we could give you a bed'. Thanking him, she replied: 'I am sorry to say I am at this time so lame that I am hardly able to go upstairs, but when the warmer weather comes, I will gladly avail myself of your kindness'.[1]

The lameness was becoming more than an impediment to walking out or going upstairs; arthritis was gradually crippling her. She became confined to the sofa in her drawing-room and it was there, surrounded by her dogs, occupied in reading or with embroidery, that her grandchildren increasingly found her.

One great consolation time brought, and that was the return of her son Marmaduke who, after a career as naval surgeon in the East India and China Stations, secured an appointment as Inspector of Hospitals and Fleets in Home Waters, and lost no opportunity of being with his mother. This was especially necessary after Ellen's death, when he realised her need for cheerful companionship. In Marmaduke, Horatia found, indeed, a companion of exceptional warmth of heart, devotion, cheerfulness and generosity; the family united in saying of him that he was the most good-natured man that ever lived, unselfish to a fault. He never married, but took up residence at 'Beaufort Villas' even before his full retirement in 1879, and shared Horatia's life, with the old servants and the dogs, asking for nothing better than such a home. Being a doctor he could watch over and treat her arthritis, which he did with devotion, though powerless of course to stay the progress of the disease.

Hugh Nelson Ward (Horace's son) who was eighteen when his grandmother died, remembered her in old age as tall and thin, possessing a strong sense of humour, a keen wit, a liveliness of mind that altogether surprised him. She was excellent company, very well read (she spoke five languages), and always busy, as long as her hands could work, with embroidery or in making marionettes. Though the house was a museum of Nelson pieces—his pistols over the fireplace, his coat of arms on the china—no mention was ever made of her relationship to him.[2]

---

[1] Ibid.
[2] Correspondence of the Revd. Hugh Nelson Ward with Carola Oman.

The anomaly of her situation appears even in her last semi-official approach to the government, when she wrote to Disraeli on behalf of a grandson (Horace's son Philip) as 'the adopted Daughter of the late Admiral Lord Nelson', soliciting his influence to 'obtain a nomination as a Naval Cadet for my grandson Philip Ward, the son of my eldest son the Rev^d. Horatio Nelson Ward of Radstock. . . . The boy much desires to go into the navy, a fact which no doubt your Lordship will kindly take into account as natural in *my* family'.[1]

Disraeli might sardonically have queried why, if Mrs. Ward were only the 'adopted' Daughter of Lord Nelson, the blood of seamen should flow in her children's veins? The solicited cadetship was more than justified, however, in the eventual career of Admiral Philip Nelson Ward.

Marmaduke's comforting presence could not protect his mother from the last strokes of ill-fortune that, despite the many and great griefs she had already suffered, pursued her still. William died in 1876 after only a short illness contracted on his last voyage home—the chills of England were fatal to him after a lifetime in India; Horatia Johnson could not rear her children (except the two boys) and the death of her six-year-old Marjorie Horatia was an intense sorrow for mother and grandmother alike. Her own very delicate health made her visits to Pinner more and more infrequent; they were regarded as 'Red Letter Days' at Beaufort Villas.

Devoted and adroit attendant as Marmaduke was, Horatia needed increasing help as she become more crippled, and in her last year she engaged a lady companion, a Miss Louisa Packe, who came from Rochester. The household at Beaufort Villas, which still consisted of Bet Allen and Walter Honeysett and had never altered since the move from Tenterden, was shaken by a tragic occurrence in the winter of 1880. After taking his master's shaving water in to him as usual, and speaking about a heavy fall of snow in the night, the faithful Walter went out and, in a sudden access of madness, committed suicide. He had been ill with 'flu, but he was considered quite recovered, and nothing in his previous steady reliable conduct could have given warning of such an eventuality. Fortunately Marmaduke was there to deal with the situation.

Walter's loss, and Horatia's increasing infirmity, made some additional help necessary in the house, and a nurse was engaged. She was not needed for long. Without any certifiable 'cause of death' other than 'Old Age', Horatia died on Sunday, 6 March 1881. Marmaduke was with her to the end.

[1] Letter dated 8 Aug. 1878. NMM/NWD/9594/2.

The family inserted the notice of her death in the Tuesday's *Times*: 'On the 6th inst, at Beaufort Villas, Woodridings, Pinner, Mrs. Horatia Nelson Ward, widow of the late Revd. Philip Ward, Vicar of Tenterden, Kent, in her 81st year.' The funeral took place on 11 March, all her living children and the older grandchildren attending.

On 10 March the following Editorial appeared in the *Times*:

Our obituary column on Tuesday contained the name of a lady who ought not to be allowed to pass out of life without a few lines by way of remembrance. In this lady, Mrs. Horatia Nelson Ward, who died on Sunday, at Beaufort Villas, Woodridings, Pinner, Middlesex, in the 81st year of her age, many of our readers will recognize Lady Hamilton's little daughter, Horatia, the same whom her reputed father, Lord Nelson, bequeathed with his dying breath to the care of his country. Born in the last year of the last century she spent her infancy and childhood at Merton. In the garden of Lady Hamilton's villa there was a little streamlet (which she called 'the Nile') and a pond, dammed up and crossed by a rustic bridge. The banks of this pond were the little child's playing-grounds; and Nelson writes thus to her mother: '. . . and I also beg, as my dear little Horatia is to be at Merton, that a strong netting, about three feet high, may be placed round the Nile, that the little thing may not tumble in.' Lady Hamilton continued to live at Merton for three years after Nelson's death, when pecuniary difficulties overtook her, and she went abroad, and ultimately died in poverty. Her daughter Horatia, in due course of time, married the Revd. Philip Ward, sometime Vicar of Tenterden, Kent, but was left his widow about 20 years ago.[1]

The obituary understandably provoked the family to a sharp riposte. This they asked the son of the late Sir Harris Nicolas to send. His statement issued in the *Times* of 15 March, while eluding all the main issues, attempted to establish one fact only, that the unavowable Lady Hamilton was not Horatia's mother. It read:

To the Editor of the 'Times'

LORD NELSON'S DAUGHTER HORATIA

Sir—In the Times obituary of March 10th the late Mrs. Horatia Nelson Ward is spoken of as 'Lady Hamilton's little daughter Horatia'.

All the facts relating to Mrs. Nelson Ward's birth and early life were carefully collected by the late Sir Harris Nicolas and are printed pp. 369-396 of the 7th Volume of the 'Nelson Dispatches and Letters'. Sir H. Nicolas commences this account by the statement that he was authorized by the late Mr. Haslewood, long the confidential friend and professional adviser of Lord Nelson, to declare in the most positive manner that Lady Hamilton was not Horatia's mother; that the name of the mother was known to Mr. Haslewood, but that he was prevented

[1] *The Times*, 10 March 1881.

by a sense of honour from disclosing it. Against the presumption that Lady Hamilton was the child's mother, it has also to be considered that at the probable date of its birth Lady Hamilton was living with her husband at his house in Piccadilly surrounded by an establishment of servants.

I am, dear Sir, Your obedient servant,

N.H.N.[1]

London, March 12th.

On the question of Horatia the *Times* proved itself incorrigible, and when Horace Ward died, only seven years after his mother, the whole debate was opened again in a long obituary in their issue of 23 March 1888. Reporting the death of the Rector of Radstock, the article recalled that his mother was the 'little Horatia' whom Lord Nelson bequeathed to the care of the nation, and added: 'whether she was his natural daughter by Emma Lady Hamilton, or the daughter of Lady Hamilton by one of her other admirers, and his adopted child. In any case, whoever may have been her father, when she grew up she married Mr. Philip Ward, and the gentleman now deceased was her eldest son'.[2]

Hugh Ward wrote to the editor of the *Times* on the same day:

I was astonished to read in the obituary column of the 'Times' of to-day . . . the following sentence: 'His mother etc . . . ' I am beyond measure astonished that it should be again offered to the world, in spite of the solemn statement made by Mr. Haslewood to Horatia that . . . she certainly did not owe her being to Lady Hamilton . . . Apart from this, Lady Hamilton herself never claimed to be the mother of the child; in fact, she left behind her an emphatic denial of her right to the relationship, and the frequent unkindness she displayed towards Horatia in her latter years would not lead one to bestow it gratuitously upon her.[3]

As to the curious suggestion that she was 'the daughter of Lady Hamilton by one of her other admirers', the Revd. Hugh disposed of this very astutely when he recalled Nelson's plan to marry Horatia 'to his nephew and heir'— a plan 'that would have been absurd and incredible had her father been an unknown admirer of Lady Hamilton'. He concluded, hoping to silence speculation for good and all, 'It is a question which can never be settled with any certainty. Lady H. has left it upon record that Horatia's mother was too great to be even mentioned'.[4]

Horatia herself, after her last correspondence with Mr. Paget on the subject, had maintained an unbroken silence. Hugh Ward, who was eighteen when she died, testified that the subject was never, at any time, mentioned in her home. He described her as having 'searching eyes' and

---

[1] *The Times*, 15 March 1881. [2] *The Times*, 23 March 1888.
[3] *The Times*, 29 March 1888. [4] Ibid.

'a deep smile', the features which the remaining photographs of her so eminently confirm. They show, with the sad smile and the marks of grief, the enigmatic expression of a baffled woman who carried her own mystery, unresolved, to the grave.

When she came to die, the local press, which had never had any encouragement from the family to speak of her in any connection, let alone an historic one, did not even report her funeral; and the *Times* was rapped over the knuckles for its pains in giving her an obituary. Publicity was the last thing sought by her family, and when she was buried, with Philip and Ellen in Paine's Lane Cemetery, it was as the 'Adopted Daughter of Vice-Admiral Lord Nelson'. Happily, the lettering on her grave was discreetly altered later and the truth allowed to prevail, the word 'Beloved' being substituted for 'Adopted'.[1]

As the BELOVED DAUGHTER of Lord Nelson, she has her place in history, and in the hearts of Englishmen; that is her claim on our interest. Whatever wrongs Nelson committed towards his wife—and they were great; and whatever the folly of his infatuation for Lady Hamilton, as a father he showed himself at his best, and as a private man found his fulfilment in Horatia.

[1] *Country Life*, 1 Dec. 1961.

APPENDIX A

HORATIA'S WILL[1]

'A FEW LINES will express what I wish. I leave to MARMADUKE PHILIP SMYTH WARD and ELEANOR PHILIPPA WARD the money produced by the legacy left me by MR. GORDON as I have the power to bequeath it to any of my children I may choose to name. I also desire that the furniture, plate, linen and books should be theirs so long as they feel disposed to use it and at their death or when they cease to require it may be divided amongst all my children with the exception of such things as I may hereafter name in a Codicil.

H. N. WARD No. 2. Beaufort Villas, Pinner
December 21st 1869

Signed in the presence of her and of each other:

[2]ANN WESTON, spinster Tenterden
MARGARET ADAMSON, Rye,
spinster.

The death of Eleanor Philippa Ward on 6 August 1872 left M.P.S. Ward sole beneficiary, and on 20 April 1881 he was granted Letters of Administration of the personal estate of HORATIA NELSON WARD late of No. 2 Beaufort Villas, Woodridings, Pinner, MX, deceased who died 6 March 1881, widow.

After Horatia's death, Marmaduke went to live with his sister Horatia Johnson at her home 6 Gower Street, and sold and divided for the benefit of the family the furniture etc left under his mother's Will. 'He kept little for himself, and was a most generous and upright gentleman in all his dealings', his family said of him. In his sister's house he had his own sitting-room, bedroom, etc. He was on a visit to his brother the Rector of Radstock when he was suddenly taken ill and died there on 4 November 1886. He was buried in the Churchyard at Radstock at the top of the hill, against the West wall. When the Rector died, two years later, he was buried beside him.

Horatia Johnson inherited her sisters' pensions on the Civil List, and received the full £300 till her own death in October 1890. She was buried at Brookwood, with her husband.

[1] From the original document at Somerset House.
[2] Miss Weston was an old friend at whose house in Tenterden Nelson Ward and his family stayed on their annual visits.

APPENDIX B

BOLTON FAMILY

Revd. Thomas Bolton, Rector of Hollesley, Suffolk, m. Martha Bird
d. 1772

Samuel Bolton of Coddenham, Suffolk, m. Ann Minster
1730 | 1776

THOMAS BOLTON
1752–1834
m. SUSANNA NELSON
1755–1813

REVD. WILLIAM BOLTON
1754–1840
m. Mary Woodthorpe

Anne Bolton,
m. Dr. H. Girdlestone
of Wells

Henry Girdlestone
1782–1871
m. Eliza Bolton

Revd. Horace
Rector of Oby
m. Mary Blyth
1832
d. 1873

Mary Ann
1778–
m. Capt. C.
Peirson

Caroline
1799–
m. J. Cooper
collateral of the
Nelson family

Sir William
Bolton
1777–1830
m. his cousin

Anne
1791–1830

Eliza
1789–1861
m. her cousin
Henry
Girdlestone

12 children

George
d. at sea
1799

Samuel Bolton, 1750
of Akenham,
m. Mary Dykes of
Ipswich

Tom, 2nd Earl
Nelson,
1786–1835
m. F. E. Eyre

Horatio,
3rd Earl Nelson
b. 1823

Ellen Catherine
1817–1891
m. her cousin Horatio Girdlestone, d. 1864

issue

Mary-Anne
1813–1864

Emma Horatia
1804–1869
m. Henry Franklin
Foley

Twins — Susanna 1781–1864
Kitty 1781–1856
m. her cousin
Sir W. Bolton

MATCHAM FAMILY

Simon Matcham
Elizabeth Bidwell

GEORGE (1753–1833)
m. CATHERINE NELSON (1767–1842)

| George 1789–1877 m. Harriet Eyre of New House Wilts. | Catherine 1792–1831 m. Capt. J. Bendyshe, R.N. | Elizabeth 1795–1851 m. Lt. A. Davies, R.N. | Frank 1796–1808 | Harriet 1799–1838 m. Capt. Ed. Blanckley, R.N. | Horatia 1801– m. Capt. Mason, R.N. | Susanna 1802– m. Alex. M. Moore | Horace 1803–1821 | W. Alex 1805–05 | Charles 1806–1844 | Nelson 1811–1886 |

Eyre-Matchams

issue (Catherine)

issue (Elizabeth)

Catherine 'Toriana' 1835– m. William Ward 1864

issue (Horatia)

issue (Susanna)

| Ellen 1865– | Ethel | Caroline | Evelyn | Ada | Alice Lilian 1873– m. Dr. F. Styles of Brent S. Devon |

issue

WARD FAMILY

Marmaduke Ward 1711–72 (1) Anne Gogle (no issue)
of Derby, Rector of (2) Mary Buck
Trunch, Norfolk

Marmaduke Ward 1749–1813 Curate of Trunch — Eleanor Smyth, of Gimingham

| George 1783–98 d. at sea | Mary 1784 m. Rev. H. Green | Harriot 1786–1809 | Eleanor 1788–1862 m. Rev. W. Rees | William 1790–1811 Lt. Royal Marines lost at sea | Philip 1795–1859 Horatia NELSON 1801–1881 | James 1798–1862 Lt.-Col. 81st Reg. |

Rev. Charles Green

Children of Philip and Horatia Nelson:

- Horatia Nelson 1822–1888 Rector of Radstock m. Elizabeth Blandy — Issue
- Eleanor Philippa 1824–1872
- Marmaduke 1825–1886 Surgeon R.N.
- John James Stephens 1827–9
- Nelson 1828–1917 Registrar Chancery Ct. m. Jessie Bird of Pinner — Issue
- William 1830–78 Major Madras Staff Corps m. Catherine 'Toriana' Blanckley — Issue
- Horatia 1832–1890 m. William Johnson — Issue
- Philip 1834–1865 Lt. Bengal Native Infantry
- Caroline 1836–1859

BIBLIOGRAPHY

SOURCES OF EVIDENCE: ORIGINAL DOCUMENTS

1. *Greenwich Maritime Museum.*
   The Nelson-Ward Papers.
   The Trafalgar House Papers.
   The Girdlestone Papers.
   The Bridport Papers.
   The Eyre-Matcham Papers.
2. *The Victory Museum, H.M. Dockyard, Portsmouth.*
3. *Canterbury Cathedral Archives: Diocesan Records.*
4. *The British Museum.*
   Nelson Papers: Additional MSS 34,992, 34,989.
5. *Monmouth: Llangattock Museum.*
   The Nelson Collection.
6. *The Nelson-Ward family records,* by courtesy of the family.
7. *The Eyre-Matcham family papers,* by courtesy of the family.
8. *Parish Registers of the following Churches*
   Marylebone Parish Church.
   Slaugham, St. Mary's Church.
   St. Mary the Virgin, Merton.
   All Saints, Burnham Thorpe, Norfolk.
   St. Mary's Church, Burnham Westgate, Norfolk.
   St. Mary's Church, Brancaster, Norfolk.
   All Saints' Church, Stanhoe, Norfolk.
   St. Mary's Church, Bircham Newton, Norfolk.
   St. Botolph's Church, Trunch, Norfolk.
   Ss Peter and Paul, Swaffham, Norfolk.
   All Saints' Hilborough, Norfolk.
   St. Mary le Virgin, Cranwich, Norfolk.
   St. Andrew's Church, West Bradenham, Norfolk.
   St. Nicholas' Church, Wells-next-the-sea, Norfolk.
   St. Mildred's Church, Tenterden.
   St. John the Baptist, Pinner.
   St. Andrew's Church, Landford, Wilts.

ABBREVIATIONS

Greenwich Maritime Museum	NMM
The Nelson-Ward Documents	NWD
Trafalgar House Papers	TRA/NMM
Bridport Papers	BRI/NMM
Girdlestone Papers	GIR/NMM
British Museum	BM
Nelson's Letters to his Wife	Naish
The Morrison Collection of Hamilton & Nelson Letters	M
Sir N. H. Nicolas' Letters and Dispatches of Lord Nelson	Nicolas
Pettigrew's Memoirs of the Life of Lord Nelson	P
Jeaffreson's Lady Hamilton and Lord Nelson	J

BIBLIOGRAPHY OF PUBLISHED WORKS CONSULTED

HARRISON, JAMES, *Life of Lord Nelson*, 1806.

CLARKE, REVD. JAMES STANIER and MCARTHUR, JOHN, *The Life of Admiral Lord Nelson*, 1809.

SOUTHEY, ROBERT, *Life of Lord Nelson*, 1813.

Anon., *The Letters of Lord Nelson and Lady Hamilton*, 1814.

Anon., *The Memoirs of Lady Hamilton*, 1815.

GORDON, PRYSE LOCKHART: *Personal Memoirs*, 2 vols, 1830.

NICOLAS, SIR N. H.: *The Dispatches and Letters of Vice-Admiral Lord Nelson*, 7 vols, 1844–6.

PETTIGREW, THOMAS JOSEPH, *Memoirs of the Life of Lord Nelson*, 2 vols, 1849.

SHERWOOD, MRS. MARIA, *Life and Times*, ed. by her daughter Mrs. Kelly, 1854.

The Diaries and Correspondence of the Rt. Hon. George Rose, ed. by the Revd. Leveson Vernon Harcourt, 1860.

KNIGHT, MISS CORNELIA, *Autobiography*, 1861.

The Remains of the late Mrs. Richard (St. George) Trench, 1768–1827, 1862.

Life and Letters of Sir Gilbert Elliot, First Earl of Minto, 1751–1806, 3 vols, 1874.

PAGET, JOHN, *Paradoxes and Puzzles*, 1874.

—— *Lady Hamilton and Mr. John Cordy Jeaffreson*. (Blackwood's Magazine May), 1888.

JEAFFRESON, JOHN CORDY, *Lady Hamilton and Lord Nelson*, 2 vols, 1888.

BROWNE, G. LATHOM, *Nelson, the Public and Private Life*, 1891.

MORRISON, ALFRED, *The Hamilton and Nelson Papers*, privately printed, 2 vols, 1893.

The Jerningham Letters (1780–1843), ed. by Egerton Castle, 2 vols, 1896.

FOSTER, VERE, *The Two Duchesses*, 1898.

GAMLIN, HILDA, *Nelson's Friendships*, 2 vols, 1899.

Memoirs of Madame Vigée Le Brun, translated by Lional Strachey, 1904.

SICHEL, WALTER, *Emma, Lady Hamilton*, 1905.

HAYNES, E. S. P., *Lady Hamilton and Horatia* (Cornhill Magazine January–June), 1906.

EYRE-MATCHAM, M., *The Nelsons of Burnham Thorpe*, 1911.

MARIA-CAROLINE, REINE DE NAPLES, *Correspondence Inédite avec le Marquis de Gallo*, 1911.

MOORHOUSE, E. HALLAM, *Nelson in England : A Domestic Chronicle*, 1913.

SHERRARD, O. A., *A Life of Emma Hamilton*, 1927.

KEATE, E. M. *Nelson's Wife*, 1939.

EMDEN, PAUL H., 'The Brothers Goldsmid and the Financing of the Napoleonic Wars', *Transactions of the Jewish Historical Society*, Vol. XIV, 1940.

OMAN, CAROLA, *Nelson*, 1947.

KENNEDY, LUDOVIC, *Nelson's Band of Brothers*, 1951.

JOWETT, E. M., *A History of Merton and Morden*, 1951.

The Wynne Diaries, 1780–1820 : ed. by Anne Fremantle, 1952.

STUART, D. M., *Dearest Bess: The Life and Times of Lady Elizabeth Foster*, 1955.

NAISH, G. P. B., *Nelson's Letters to his Wife*, 1958.

WARNER, OLIVER, *Trafalgar*, 1959.

— — *Lady Hamilton and Sir William*, 1960.

TOURS, HUGH, *The Life and Letters of Emma Hamilton*, 1963.

FOTHERGILL, BRIAN, *Sir William Hamilton, Envoy Extraordinary*, 1969.

TOPOGRAPHICAL PUBLICATIONS

ACKERMANN, RUDOLPH, *Microcosm of London*, 1820.

LAUGHTON, PROF. J. K., 'Nelson's House at Merton', *The Wimbledon and Merton Annual*, 1903.

BARTLETT, REVD. W. G., *History of Wimbledon*, 1865.

CHAMBERLAIN, W. H., *Reminiscences of Old Merton.*

JAGGER, REVD. J. E., *Lord Nelson's Home and Life at Merton.*

HOARE, *History of Wiltshire*, 1837.

BRITTON, *The Beauties of Wiltshire*, 1825.

GILBERT, REVD. GEORGE, *Reminiscences.* Ed. Revd. John Shirley, Canon of Canterbury, 1938.

FURLEY, ROBERT, *History of the Weald of Kent*, 1874, 2 vols.

WARE, EDWIN, *Pinner in the Vale.* An Alphabetical History of Pinner, privately printed, 1955–7.

STREET, G., *Ghosts of Piccadilly*, 1960.

MACQUEEN POPE, E., *Goodbye Piccadilly*, 1960.

Newspapers of the Period, British Museum Newspaper Library, Colindale.

Somerset House, Registry of Births, Deaths, and Marriages.

INDEX

Allen, Bet, nurse-maid to Horatia's children, 253, 271, 318, 320, 329
Allen, Tom, Nelson's body-servant, 30, 253, 254
Ashfold Lodge, the Matchams' home: bought with gov. grant, 133, 134; description of, 142; Horatia's home, 218–25; let, 221; sold, 243; other refs., 169, 232, 233

Beckford, William, of Fonthill, 13, 15, 95
Beatty, Dr. William, Nelson's ship-surgeon, 279, 282
Beechey, Sir William, painter, 42
Bendysche, Lt. John, R.N.: marries Kitty Matcham in Paris, 240; wife's death, 281
Billington, Mrs., operatic singer, 174; career, 189; secretes Ly. H.'s property, 189, 201, 214
Biancchi, Signor and Signora, Neapolitan musicians, 70, 71, 87, 103, 142, 144, 169, 174, 189
Blackwood, Capt. R.N., 97, 104, 110, 111, 113
Blake, Rev. Robert Ferrier: engaged to Horatia, 229–30, 231, 234, 235
Blanckley, General and family, 231, 232, 240
Blanckley, Capt. Edward, 232, 234, 258
Blanckley, Catherine, Toriana: marries William Ward, 322, 324
Bolton, Anne (1791–1830), Ld. N.'s niece: schooldays, 43, 51, 56, 70, 79; Ly. H.'s protégée, 81, 129; letters to Ly. H., 81–2, 159, 170, 171, 179, 190; birthdays with Horatia, 84, 146, 147, 171; at Merton during Ld. N.'s last days, 89, 90, 91; delicacy, 81, 129, 174, 179, 226; courted by Henry Girdle-stone, 178–9; H'.s companion at Merton, 158–9, 269; letter to Horatia, 182; mother's illness and death, 190–1;

home at Burnham, 226; death, 269; other refs., 101, 142, 144–5, 226
Bolton, Eliza (Mrs. Girdlestone) (1789–1861); Ld. N.'s niece: schooldays, 43, 51, 56; holidays at Merton, 43, 56, 70, 79, 81, 87, 89, 90, 91; visits Ashfold, 154; marries Henry Girdlestone, 178–9, 180; numerous family of, 180, 325; death, 325; other refs., 131
Bolton, Ellen Catherine (1817–1891), d. of Sir William and Lady B., 227; married cousin Horatio Girdlestone, 337
Bolton, Emma Horatia, eld. d. of Sir William B., 62, 81, 82; fondness for Horatia, 128, 130, 171, 172, 179, 191 269, 275; marriage, 275; old and death, 275
Bolton, Mary Ann, 2nd d. of Sir William B., 191, 226, 275
Bolton, Susanna, Ld. N.'s elder sister (1755–1813), 27, 43, 50; visits to Merton, 50–1, 93–101; family of, 51, 64; character, 64; friendship for Ly. H., 81–3, 126–31, 156, 158, 159, 170–1, 173, 179, 182; illness and death, 190–1; receives gov. grant, 116
Bolton, Susanna, eld. d. of above (1781–1864), 82, 127, 128, 226, 275, 325
Bolton, Thomas, senior, Ld. N.'s brother-in-law (1752–1834): Ld. N.'s letter to, 50; career, 51–2, 93, 109, 284; other refs., see Cranwich; Horatia's guardian, 244, 256, 258, 259
Bolton, Thomas junior (1786–1835), 2nd Earl Nelson: boyhood visits to Merton, 43, 56–7; schooling, 51, 66; mother's fondness for, 129, 147, 179, 180; Ld. N.'s esquire, 61; at crammer's and Cambridge, 147–8, 156; character of, 56–7, 145, 147; letters to Ly. H., 144–5, 147, 179; heir to title, 153; acquires Bradenham Hall, 180; Earl N.'s late kindness to, 223, 241, fondness for

INDEX

and Horatia, 35, 119, 124; family life at, 39, 43–7, 50–1, 56–7, 89–101; Earl N. investigates affairs of, 118–19; visits of Royal Dukes at, 148–9; for sale, 155, 158; sold, 164; obliteration of, 164

Minto, Sir Gilbert Elliot, 1st Earl of: recollections of Merton, 45–6, 93, 94, 95, 97, 99

Moore, Alexander Montgomery: marries Susanna Matcham, 281

Nelson, Charlotte (1787–1873), d. of Rev. William N. Viscountess Bridport: schooldays, 22, 30, 35–6, 39, 43, 46; Ly. H.'s protégée, 56, 70–1, 74, 75, 78, 80, 87, 88; letters to her mother, 70, 71, 79, 80, 87, 88; kindness to Horatia, 75–6, 78, 88; Ld. N.'s letter to, 75; at Merton during uncles' last days, 89, 90; Cecilia Connor's letter to, 102; withdrawn from Ly. H.'s care, 108, 118; death of brother, 151–4; Ly. H.'s claims regarding, 200; marriage (footnote, p. 279); Duchess of Bronté, 279; help in editing Ld. N.'s letters, 284; death, 325

Nelson, Revd. Edmund (1722–1802), Rector of Burnham Thorpe, Norfolk, Ld. N.'s father: champions Ly. N.: 16, 27, 40, 41–2, 43, 44–5, 48; letters to his son, 26, 27, 41, 43, 44–5; portrait by Beechey, 42; visits Merton, 43; death, 49

Nelson, Frances Herbert (1758–1831), Viscountess N., Ld. N.'s wife ('Tom Tit'), 8, 9, 24; family attachment to, 16, 27; Ly. H.'s campaign against, 16, 19, 20, 21, 22, 23, 27, 40; Ld. N.'s decision to leave, 21, 24, 29; her letters to Ld. N., 26; devotion to Revd. Edmund, 41, 42, 43; circumstances of her parting from Ld. N., 138; strictures on Harrison's 'Life' of Ld. N., 138; reconciliation with Matchams, 257–8; other refs., 286

Nelson, Horace (1788–1808), Viscount Trafalgar, Ld. N.'s nephew: schooldays 22, 30, 43; Ly. H.'s protégée, 39, 43, 56, 71, 74, 79; at Eton, 88; Ld. N.'s wish he should marry Horatia, 67, 108, 124, 307; at Merton during Ld. N.'s last days, 90, 93, 94; created Viscount

Trafalgar, 107; parents' ambition for him, 108, 132, 148, 151; connections with Ly. H. severed, 108, 112, 132; at Cambridge, 132; his pets, 151–2; illness and death, 152–3, 154; Ly. H.'s claims respecting him, 200

Nelson, Vice-Admiral Horatio, Lord (1758–1805): hears of Horatia's birth, 5; intense paternal feelings of, 6, 11, 12, 18, 23, 24, 32, 34, 63, 72, 80, 84, 101; invents 'Thompson' couple to disguise correspondence with Ly. H., 6, 7, 11, 12, 17, 18, 23, 25, 30, 34, 39; makes financial provisions for H., 9, 10, 11, 12, 21, 67, 85, 104; jealousy of P. of Wales, 15, 17, 18, 20; buys Merton Place, 29, 30, 32, 33, 34; settles Merton on Ly. H. and Horatia, 35, 119, 124; at Merton, 36, 38, 39, 40, 90–101; his care for his father, 40, 42; fondness for sisters, 50–1, 52, 53; financial provisions for Ly. H. 60; text of Codicil benefiting H., 67, 68; his letters to Horatia, 68, 69, 73, 104; appoints Miss Connor governess to H., 69; letter to Charlotte N. re Horatia, 75; his account of her parentage, 78–9; urges H. be established at Merton, 67, 68, 69, 80, 83, 84, 85; farewell to H., 100; last letters to Ly. H., 101, 108; death at Trafalgar, 103; state funeral of, 124–5; 166, 148

Nelson, Mrs. Maurice, widow of Ld. N.'s brother: Ld. N.'s goodness towards her, 30, 47, 149

Nelson, Revd. Dr. William (1757–1835), 1st Earl Nelson, Ld. N.'s brother: countenances Ly. H., 16, 19, 31, 48; social ambitions of, 47, 48, 52, 53, 108; career of, 31, 47; at Merton during Ld. N.'s last days, 90–101; receives news of Trafalgar, 106–7; earldom conferred on him, 107; actions concerning Ld. N.'s last Codicil, 112, 113, 114, 116, 123; severs connections with Ly. H., 112, 132; executor of Ld. N.'s Will, 118, 119; receives gov. grant, 115–16; ambition for his son, 108, 132, 151, 148; illness and death of son, 151–4; Ly. H.'s accusations against him, 140, 154–7, 168, 200, 204; Ly. H.'s appeal for money, 199; promotes nephews' marriages, 223, 224, 234, 241, 242; receives Horatia at Trafalgar, 250–2; re-